Understanding Information & Communication Technology

Stephen Doyle

First published in 2000 by:
Stanley Thornes (Publishers) Ltd
Delta Place
27 Bath Road
Cheltenham
Glos.
GL53 7TH
United Kingdom

04 / 10 9 8 7 6 5 4

Acknowledgements

The authors and publishers are grateful to the NEAB for permission to reproduce material.
Every effort has been made to contact copyright holders and we apologise if anyone has been overlooked.

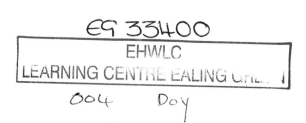

A catalogue record for this book is available from the British Library

ISBN 0 7487 3609 3

Typeset by GreenGate Publishing Services, Tonbridge, Kent
Printed in Great Britain by Scotprint

Contents

Introduction

Understanding IT is a new book that has been specifically written to cover the material needed for both the Advanced Subsidiary (AS) and the Advanced Level (A2) qualifications in Information Communication Technology (ICT). Although the book is mapped to the AQA syllabuses and follows their structure closely, it can also be used as a reference work in Information Technology for other AS/Advanced syllabuses as well as other level 3 ICT/IT qualifications such as BTEC, GNVQ Advanced or Access.

The structure of the book

The book is divided into two sections with the first section covering the material needed for the AS qualification or the first part of the Advanced qualification. The second section covers the material needed for the Advanced Level qualification. You will need to cover the second section only if you are taking the Advanced Level qualification.

If you are taking the AS qualification you will need to study Chapters 1 to 10 along with Chapter 20 on project work.

If you are taking the Advanced Level qualification then you will need to study *all* the chapters in the book.

The project chapter, Chapter 20, is the last chapter in the book and it explains what project work needs to be done for the two qualifications. It is worth looking at this chapter early on because it also explains about the requirements for the two courses.

How to use the book

If you look at the AQA syllabus you will see that this book follows its format very closely. Both the syllabus and the book follow a reasonably logical path through the material you need for the qualification. It would make most sense to follow through the chapters in the order they are presented, since each chapter may assume knowledge of material covered in a previous chapter.

Making the most of the features of the book

Here are some of the features of the book and the best way to use them.

Learning objectives

You will find a list of learning objectives at the beginning of each chapter which can be used to see what you should have learnt after completing the chapter. They can, of course, also be used to see which topics the chapter contains and also for cross-referencing to the appropriate section of the syllabus.

Questions

The questions are used to build up your knowledge of each topic so that you will be ready to try the past examination questions at the end of each chapter. They are mostly short questions, similar to those you might find in an examination, requiring a written answer in which you apply some of the principles you have learnt in the preceding section.

In addition to these short questions, there are exercises involving definitions of terms.

Definition of terms exercises
As you know, a lot of specialist terms are used in ICT and it is essential that you understand what they mean and that you can use them confidently when communicating your ideas. The definition of terms exercises are there to help reinforce your knowledge and understanding of these terms. You will find that the terms in each exercise are defined in the chapter. When explaining a specialist term, take care not to use another specialist term in your explanation.

Examination questions

This section, at the end of each chapter, contains actual past examination questions on the material contained in the chapter. It is important that you practise answering them so that you acquire the skills necessary for constructing answers in your examination.

Activities

These come at the ends of sections within each chapter. Activities are tasks you need to complete in order to build up and consolidate your knowledge of the subject. They require written answers, providing evidence for your key skills.

Tasks

Tasks are longer than activities and sometimes include a task 'debrief' to help you complete the task.

Case studies

Case studies are included in each chapter and these illustrate how *real* businesses and organisations apply the concepts developed in the chapter. You can use these as real examples when answering examination questions.

Key skills

Key skills opportunities are signposted throughout in the activities, questions, tasks and assignments. These will help you provide the portfolio evidence and test practice you need to claim your Key Skills qualification. The list below shows how the signposting in the text (C1.1, C1.2, etc) relates to the tasks you will undertake. It is worth noting that if you pass your AS Level IT you will be exempt from the external tests for IT Key Skills at levels 2 and 3. If you complete the full A Level (AS plus A2) you will have full exemption from IT Key Skills at levels 2 and 3 (i.e. portfolio and test).

C1.1
Take part in a one-to-one discussion and a group discussion about different, straightforward subjects.

C1.2
Read and obtain information from two different types of documents about straightforward subjects, including at least one image.

C1.3
Write two different types of documents about straightforward subjects. Include at least one image in one of the documents.

C2.1a
Contribute to a discussion about a straightforward subject.

C2.1b
Give a short talk about a straightforward subject, using an image.

C2.2
Read and summarise information from two extended documents about a straightforward subject. One of the documents should include at least one image.

C2.3
Write two different types of documents about straightforward subjects. One piece of writing should be an extended document and include at least one image.

C3.1a
Contribute to a group discussion about a complex subject.

C3.1b
Make a presentation about a complex subject, using at least one image to illustrate complex points.

C3.2
Read and synthesise information from two extended documents about a complex subject. One of these documents should include at least one image.

C3.3
Write two different types of documents about complex subjects. One piece of writing should be an extended document and include at least one image.

N1.1

Interpret straightforward information from two different sources. At least one source should be a table, chart, diagram or line graph.

N1.2

Carry out straightforward calculations to do with:
a) amounts and sizes;
b) scales and proportion;
c) handling statistics.

N1.3

Interpret the results of your calculations and present your findings. You must use one chart and one diagram.

N2.1

Interpret information from two different sources, including material containing a graph.

N2.2

Carry out calculations to do with:
a) amounts and sizes;
b) scales and proportion;
c) handling statistics;
d) using formulae.

N2.3

Interpret the results of your calculations and present your findings. You must use at least one graph, one chart and one diagram.

N3.1

Plan and interpret information from two different types of sources, including a large data set.

N3.2

Carry out multi-stage calculations to do with:
a) amounts and sizes;
b) scales and proportion;
c) handling statistics;
d) rearranging and using formulae.

You should work with a large data set on at least one occasion.

N3.3

Interpret results of your calculations, present your findings and justify your methods. You must use at least one graph, one chart and one diagram.

IT1.1

Find, explore and develop information for two different purposes.

IT1.2

Present information for two different purposes.

Your work must include at least one example of text, one example of images and one example of numbers.

IT2.1

Search for and select information for two different purposes.

IT2.2

Explore and develop information, and derive new information, for two different purposes.

IT2.3

Present combined information for two different purposes.

Your work must include at least one example of text, one example of images and one example of numbers.

IT3.1

Plan and use different sources to search for, and select, information required for two different purposes.

IT3.2

Explore, develop and exchange information, and derive new information, to meet two different purposes.

IT3.3

Present information from different sources for two different purposes and audiences.

Your work must include at least one example of text, one example of images and one example of numbers.

Knowledge, Information and Data

> ▶ To understand the differences between knowledge, information and data.
>
> ▶ To appreciate the value and importance of information.
>
> ▶ To investigate the control of information.

Introduction

All forms of human endeavour require some data or information. Take, for example, doing the weekly shopping, where the following information might be used:

- a list of the items that are required

- the amount of money the person has to spend

- the cost of each item.

When buying the goods, we need to process this information by working out the total price (assuming we are doing a check), then calculating the amount of change we need. Doing something with the information, such as performing calculations on it, is called **data processing**.

In an everyday sense, we use the words data and information to mean the same thing, but in computer usage these words differ slightly in their meaning and we need to be aware of this difference.

Data

Data consists of the raw facts and figures at the collecting stage, before they are processed. In many cases, data is apparently meaningless until it is processed in some way; this processing could be having a calculation performed on it, sorting it or even grouping the data in a certain way. Performing such operations on the data is referred to as data processing. Data processing results in information. In some cases this information may itself be processed further, by

what is called an **information processing system**, to yield higher quality, and often more valuable, information.

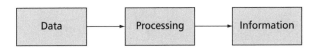

Figure 1.1 *The processing of 'raw' data results in information*

Information

Unlike raw data, information has a context and its meaning is dependent upon that context. This is best understood by looking at an example.

Take the following list of numbers:

$$19, \ 20, \ 19, \ 22, \ 26, \ 18, \ 18$$

These numbers may be considered as data, since they have no context and are just a list of values. They could mean anything: the ages of people in a group or the number of hours of television each person watches in a week. If we are told that they represent the highest daily temperatures in Southport during the first week in June 2000, they have now been placed in a context and are therefore information.

So information consists of data to which a meaning has been attached.

Knowledge

Knowledge is used to interpret and apply information. Once this is done, decisions can be made on the information received. For example, if you were driving a car towards a set of traffic lights and the traffic lights showed amber only, you would apply the brakes to stop. The amber light is the data, the information is 'to stop', and the knowledge you use to turn the data into information is from the Highway Code.

Data	Information	Knowledge
A green indicator light on a mobile phone is flashing	The phone is switched on and connected to the network and is ready to send and receive calls	The instruction manual which was supplied with the telephone
Core 01 IT01 AS Module 1	The first module in your A level IT exam for the AQA examination board	This is outlined in the syllabus supplied by the NEAB
The right-hand side indicators are flashing	The driver is intending to move to the right	The Highway Code
C3654Y	The code which needs to be input via the keypad to gain entry to the computer room	A code given verbally to you by the caretaker
1585	The VideoPlus number which you must enter to record the programme *Coronation Street* on a Monday night at 7.30 p.m.	The instructions from the manual supplied with the video recorder, and the programme number seen on the television page of a newspaper

Table 1.1 *The differences between data, information and knowledge*

Activity

Write down 30 pieces of information that might be attached (not in the literal sense!) to a telegraph pole. Here are a few to start you off and these may be added to your total.

- Who erected the pole?
- The location number of the pole.
- The diameter of the pole.

Information processing

Information processing is concerned with **input**, **processing**, **output** and **feedback**. Figure 1.2 illustrates these four steps.

At the input stage the raw data is captured from an organisation. This data may originate from within the organisation or outside it.

The processing stage converts the raw data into a form that is useful to the organisation. Just putting the data into some sort of structure, such as that imposed by a database, constitutes processing.

The output stage involves transferring the processed information to all the people who need it.

The feedback stage is not present in every system. It is where some of the output is transferred back to the appropriate members of the organisation to help them refine or correct the input phase.

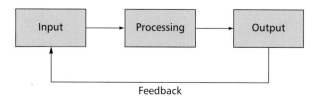

Figure 1.2 *A feedback loop*

TASKS

Data, information and knowledge

Look at the following table which shows the differences between data, information and knowledge using some familiar situations.

Data	Information	Knowledge
A set of traffic lights on red	You should stop	The Highway Code
A wagging tail on a dog	The dog wants to be friendly	Past experience
12.30	The time of the last train home	The train timetable
A red light on the television	The TV is in standby mode	The manual that came with the TV

As you can see from the above list, the data on its own may be meaningless without the context and it is only when the context is added that we can regard it as being information. Knowledge is needed to turn the data into information. In many cases, such as the dog wagging its tail, the knowledge is gained by experience.

The table is incomplete and your job is to add another five lines.

TASK DEBRIEF

- You will notice from the table that you can have visual, spoken and written data.
- Make sure that you have not confused the data and information columns.

Data is a value, or a set of values (e.g. all records at the collection stage), whereas information is derived data in the context of use (e.g. output of all records satisfying particular criteria.)

So, the data about employees in a personnel database would be raw data, but when we search the database (i.e. we do some information processing) to produce an ordered list of female employees who earn over £10,000 per year, we are now extracting information.

Data

Direct and indirect sources of data

Direct data originates from the source of the data while **indirect data** comes in a more roundabout way. Direct data is data that has been collected for a particular purpose, whereas indirect data is not collected specifically but is drawn from data collected for another purpose.

Suppose you are thinking of writing a textbook like this one for A and AS level IT. Before the publishers would think of committing a large amount of time and money to publishing it, they need to know the size of the market, because on this will depend the number of copies they are likely to sell. How do they obtain this information? One way would be to write to every person attending a secondary school, college, adult education centre, etc. in the country to ask them if they are taking a relevant course. The information collected in this way would be classed as direct data and obtaining it in this way would be very time-consuming and expensive.

It is much easier and quicker to use an indirect source, such as the examination board, and ask them how many candidates are registered to take this particular exam. There are only a couple of boards which examine the subject, so writing to them or ringing them up is relatively easy compared with using the direct source.

When a POS (point of sale) terminal is used, its primary aim is to record the transaction for the shop and the shopper. The itemised receipt is the thing the shopper takes most note of, but another important event happens behind the scenes. Each time an item is scanned, a laser beam reads the code in the bars and this code is used to obtain the details of the goods, such as the description, price, etc. The system is also used to help with stock control. Suppose we buy 20 tins of Heinz baked beans. When these are scanned at the POS terminal, the computer system automatically deducts this number from stock. In many stores this information is used further to re-order the goods once they fall below a certain level, called the **re-order quantity**. Historical sales data, such as how many loaves of bread have been sold on the same day going back several years, can be used by a bakery to gauge the likely demand for each product. Such data would have been collected primarily to record sales at the POS terminal, and so would be an indirect source of data for any other purposes.

Question

According to information obtained from a computer system, there should be 30 tins of Heinz baked beans on the shelf, but when a shop assistant checks, there are only 25. What could be the reason or reasons for this discrepancy?

Ambiguous data

Sometimes the same data can mean different things to different people.

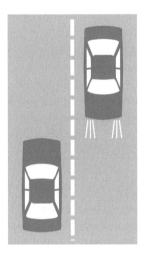

Figure 1.3 *Someone flashes their lights at you, but what do they mean?*

Look at Figure 1.3. Flashing one's lights can be classed as data but what does it mean? Possible interpretations of the data to give information may be:

- you may pass in front of me
- watch out since there is an obstacle in the road further on
- you are going along a one-way road the wrong way
- I am a friend and I am saying 'hello'
- there is a police radar trap further down the road
- one of your tyres is almost flat
- your lights are not on.

The data is ambiguous, so how do we decide which one is correct? We need to look at the context. We could, for instance, ask ourselves if we knew the person who was flashing their lights.

Question

What other questions might be asked in order to narrow the meaning of the data in Figure 1.3?

Ageing of data

Suppose the manager of a car parts shop wants a printout of the list of car parts currently in stock. As the list is being printed the shop doesn't stop selling parts, so by the time the manager receives the list, it no longer shows the true stock position. The more time that elapses before the list is printed, the more out of date the list becomes. In addition to more stock being sold, some new stock could be delivered. For this reason, all printouts should have a date on them, to prevent management decisions being based on very out-of-date information.

The role of date stamping

If you had a car loan and were given some money you might want to pay off the balance of the loan. You could ring up the finance company and ask for the amount of money needed to settle the loan (called the **settlement figure**). The information supplied by the computer will need to be date stamped, since in a couple of days you could have made another payment, and this would decrease the settlement figure. It is for this reason that any information extracted from a computer system must have a date on it and this process is called date stamping. Transactions, such as payments made, are also date stamped, since the company and other companies may need to know if all the repayments on a loan have been made on time. Customers quite often query transactions on accounts (bank statements, credit card statements, etc.) and the usual way to refer to them is by date. For this reason all transactions need to have a date stamp and this date is part of the search criteria used to extract information from the system.

The need to encode information as data

Information is often disorganised when just collected, and in an inappropriate form for storing and subsequent processing. To facilitate storage and processing, the information should be encoded as data. Often the information needs to be entered as data into a database, and databases require data stored in an organised and set format. The database designer must think about the structure that will be used to store data. S/he must be careful not to lose any of the fine detail, which may be important to the user.

Problems with the encoding of information

The main problem with encoding information as data is that it coarsens precision. This means that the information is rendered less accurate when it becomes data. This is best seen by taking an example. Descriptions of criminals on a police computer system might include 'eye colour' as one of the fields in the database. The person who designed the database might have decided to allow the user to choose from the following eye colours:

- blue

- brown

- green.

Suppose we are entering details of a criminal into this database from a form on which the person's eye colour is described as 'blue/green'. We now have a problem as to which category to use. The database only allows us to enter eye colour as blue, brown or green, so which one do we choose? We now realise that the eye colour data for other entries could be similarly inaccurate, so we may just settle for blue or green colour and not worry any more about it. It does, however, compromise the integrity of the database system and we may now have less faith in the results it produces. When we search the database for eye colour we now realise that blue eyes and green eyes could both include blue/green eyes as well. The coding system employed has made us unsure about the data, which is therefore not as precise as the original information.

Once data is encoded, the original data is often no longer available. In such a case, when the database is interrogated and information extracted, you may not realise that the data has been coded and therefore accept this information as the truth. For instance, if we search the database for people with blue eyes we might expect to get those with blue/green eyes as well, but these details could equally be within the category green eyes.

Here are the heights of ten people:

John	1.65 m
Chloe	1.50 m
James	1.98 m
Suzanne	1.75 m
Courtney	1.52 m
Jack	1.96 m
Stephen	1.78 m
Charles	1.47 m
Mary	2.08 m
Jane	1.88 m

Here are three height categories:

tall,   medium,   short.

1 Place each of the people in the list into the most appropriate category.

2 Compare your answers with other members of your class. How close were your answers to the majority?

3 Briefly explain why the method of categorising these heights into tall, medium and short is unsuitable.

4 Could you use a different method of coding which would make it easier for everyone to get the same answer? Briefly explain your method.

If there are such problems with coding, why code at all? Well, unless you want an unwieldy number of alternatives to select from you have to narrow the choice in some way, and this usually means coding the data. When setting up databases it is necessary to have a certain structure and to validate the data as it is entered into this structure. To enter the data we need to make it more structured.

Value judgements when entering data

The trouble with many forms of coding is that they rely to some extent on value judgements that may be different for different people. What one person describes as a particular colour may not agree with another person's opinion of the same colour. The colour being entered into the computer would depend on the person who entered it.

When you apply to university or a higher education institution, you fill out a UCAS form, on part of which your teacher/lecturer writes a character reference for you. Such a volume of text is difficult to store and interrogate, since to do this would involve breaking value judgements down into set answers. Instead of free text, your teacher may be asked to answer certain specific questions by choosing from a range of possible answers.

How would you describe the pupil's/student's punctuality? On a scale of 1 to 5:

1 never late

2 occasionally late but with a good excuse

3 lateness is occasional without any excuse given

4 regularly late

5 invariably late.

The database would need a corresponding field in which you enter one of the above numbers. To some extent this still depends on the person entering the data, but since there are many options to choose from, it is more accurate than some of the other coding methods that could be used. A balance always needs to be struck between keeping the coding possibilities to a minimum but including enough categories to make them an accurate reflection of the breadth of data. You need to bear this in mind when devising coding systems for fields in databases.

Activity

The following values are to be entered into a computer system; some of them depend on the value judgements of the person entering the data. For each one you are required to say whether a value judgement is needed.

1 a person's date of birth

2 the weight in pounds of a baby born in a hospital

3 a person's intelligence (low, medium or high)

4 a person's build (slight, medium or well-built)

5 road conditions (poor, average or good)

6 the total value in £s of an order

7 the number of days an employee has had off sick in a year

8 the current VAT rate (17.5%).

Information

One of the annoying features of telephones is that many of them let you know the number of the last caller, but do not give you any further details. It is then left up to you to recognise whose number it is or to ring the number and find out who has called you. Sometimes it may be someone trying to sell you something over the phone, so you may not want to phone them back. If you had a telephone number and wanted to know the person or organisation it belonged to without phoning back, how could you do this? One way would be to work from the front to the back of the telephone directory, looking out for the number. Clearly this would be painstaking and you could even miss the number. A better way would be to use a commercially available database where the phone numbers in the directory can be accessed in many different ways. All the information on such a database would be freely available from the phone directories (you can obtain phone directories for the whole country from a library). When you pay to access such a database you are paying for the time taken to key in all the records and to keep the file up to date. In other words, you are paying for the information held in the database.

Value and importance of information

All information can be classed as a commodity, and like all commodities it has a value; it may be bought and sold.

The monetary value placed on information depends on:

- the accuracy of the information

- the intended and potential uses of the information.

Information is never free, since a cost is always associated with collecting and storing data in the first place. It is important that the costs of obtaining information do not outweigh the financial benefits to be gained from the information. To make sure that this is the case, management usually perform a cost/benefits analysis before embarking on data collection. For example, if certain information results in a £200 increase in profit to an organisation, yet costs £250 to collect, it is not worth seeking the information. The information provided by a system will usually do some of the following:

- reduce costs

- eliminate losses

- reduce wastage

- use resources more effectively

- provide better management information to aid more accurate decision making.

It is important to remember that information that is collected and stored, but never used, has no actual value, since no decisions will be based upon it; it is superfluous and should never have been collected in the first place.

Financial markets (stock markets and money markets) are subject to rapid change and information systems are needed which react quickly to these changes and tell a broker whether s/he should buy or sell. Since large amounts of money are involved it is important that the information produced by the computer is accurate. The timeliness of this information is important: as, for instance, if the value of the pound were to fall rapidly the broker would need to sell pounds quickly and buy another currency whose value is rising. The speed with which the information is obtained and any resulting transactions made will be reflected in the profit.

Activity

Explain how each of the following has a value (but remember, something may have a value which is not necessarily financial):

- a list of current account customers whose accounts show a large credit balance

- a list of customers who have purchased new cars from a garage over the last three years

- an on-line database on CD-ROM of all the post-codes in the UK

- a list of credit card customers who have not kept their accounts in order.

Ensuring information is up to date

Since the processing of data does not stop when information is extracted, the data becomes progressively out of date as time goes on. Additionally, if changes are made which are not placed on the system, the data can no longer be relied upon and any information obtained from

it will be inaccurate. The task of keeping data up to date has a cost associated with it due to:

- frequent updating (e.g. typing in the changes)

- frequent collecting of data

- deleting out-of-date data or data which is no longer needed

- making sure that all copies of the data are updated so that everyone uses the same, amended data.

There needs to be a mechanism or system to ensure that changes are relayed to the right person, so that data used by the computer is updated. Many credit card companies have a section on the reverse side of their statements for customers to make changes to their name, address, etc. so that the company can then change their records. The main problem with this is that there is often more than one customer file, so any changes (such as change of address) need to be repeated on all the organisation's files for that customer. If you move house you will experience this problem: although you have notified the various organisations you will still have letters sent to your old address because one department in an organisation has failed to notify the other departments of the change.

Many companies keep just one pool of data in a large database called a data warehouse. All the different departments then use the same database, so when alterations are made they need be made only once for all the departments to use. This means data is consistent for anyone using data from the data warehouse. This idea is covered in more detail in Chapter 5, which looks at the organisation and storage of data.

Question

Customer details, such as name, address, telephone number, e-mail number, etc. are held in several different files by the same organisation.

What are the likely problems caused by this?

The overheads involved in ensuring that information is up to date

Keeping information up to date is expensive, since lots of time and resources need to be allocated to the task. A student's personal data might change during their time at a college. They might get married, divorced, change address, change telephone number, increase their qualifications and so on. Stored data will need to be amended. As well as actually making the alterations to the student records using the computer, there needs to be a system whereby the student lets the college know of these changes.

The costs involved in keeping information up to date are called the overheads and would include some or all of the following:

- **Collecting the data.** Forms have to be printed and staff have to collect this information.

- **Data conversion or direct input.** Data conversion involves converting the data into a computer-readable form. If special forms are used that contain data capable of being read directly by the computer, then these costs can be reduced.

- **Frequency of collecting.** The more often data is collected, the more likely it is to be up to date. But collecting data too frequently would be expensive, so a compromise needs to be reached.

- **Control mechanisms.** Control mechanisms prevent the information from being seen by anyone who shouldn't see it. Information is a marketable commodity and its protection costs money.

- **Validation.** Data being entered into a system is subjected to validation checks; some of the data will be rejected. In some systems, data which fails the validation checks will need to be investigated manually and this involves further costs.

- **Frequency of the processing cycle.** To keep information up to date it is necessary to perform some processing and this ties up computing time and other resources. It is therefore necessary to restrict the frequency of the processing.

- **Output.** Printing out stock lists prevents the printers from being used for other purposes, and the large volumes of paper used cost money. As well as the paper costs, there is also the cost of electricity and toner or ink-jet cartridges. The costs of all these may restrict the style or format of the output and its frequency.

Data mining

Data mining is a new technology which looks for meaningful patterns in data. It could be worth millions of pounds to companies who start to use it. In data mining we look at trends in data and analyse these trends for changes, knowledge of which enables companies to react quickly to the marketplace. Because of the amount of data involved and the complexity of the software used, it has not been feasible for companies to use this technique before now. Many of the companies which do use it have huge databases containing information about their customers, products, purchases the customers have made, etc. This huge, central pool of data is often referred to as a data warehouse and can be considered a corporate resource. Everyone who

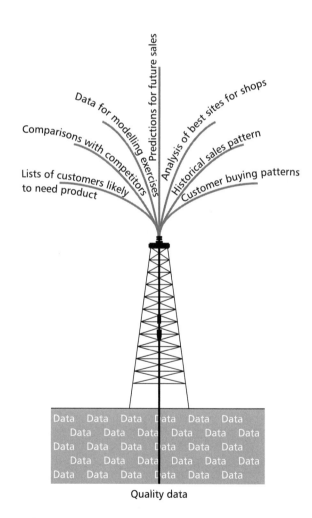

Figure 1.4 *By 'drilling down' into the mass of data, data mining extracts meaningful patterns in the data*

uses a computer can have access to the data provided no security restrictions apply. One of the large banks, for instance, uses a data warehouse to hold details on all its customer accounts; customer accounts total 45 million and for each account there are 220 fields. Multiplying these two figures together gives 9000 million, which is the total number of separate pieces of data captured (i.e. input into the system in the first place) and stored. Looking for meaningful patterns in such a huge mass of data is only now possible, with the introduction of data mining software which presents the results in the form of tables and graphs, and allows export of the results into popular office suites (software).

CASE STUDY

The Whitbread Group

The Whitbread Group has thousands of leisure and retail establishments and uses data mining to improve the quality of decisions made. The group uses this technique to look at its most successful outlets and then to look at the profile of the population which uses such outlets, obtained as part of a market research operation. The company then uses the data to look for those geographical areas with a similar population mix and possibly site new outlets in such areas. Using data mining has meant that siting decisions are more accurate and the company can be surer that a new outlet will be profitable.

Whitbread also carries out modelling exercises using the package. For example, the group can check what is likely to happen to the turnover of a store when factors such as size, location, store opening hours, etc., are altered.

The technique is called 'data mining' because important connections between groups of data may not be apparent at first; it is often necessary to 'drill down' through the data to find any connections. Whitbread uses this technique to analyse the data received from customer surveys and to look at the connections between groups of questions and the associations they have in customers' minds. For instance, Whitbread might ask a customer if the store is convenient, meaning is it near to where they live. However, the customer may say yes because it is next door to a video shop that he/she visits even though that shop is several miles from where he/she lives.

Control of information

When a large quantity of personal data is kept on a computer, certain legal obligations are placed automatically on the holder. The legal restrictions as to what may or may not be done with personal data are discussed in Chapter 4. It is also important to protect information against theft or damage because of its value as a commodity.

Legal rights and obligations when holding personal data

Much of the data stored on computers is about living individuals and is classed as personal data. Personal data is not just name, address and telephone number, since this data is readily available from other sources. It does, however, include school, college, medical and employment records, credit history and so on. This personal data is extremely important to many organisations and an Act of Parliament, called the Data Protection Act 1998, places certain rules and obligations on the holder of such personal data stored on a computer. They are no longer free to do what they please with such data. For instance, they are not free to disclose it to another organisation without the permission of the person to whom the personal data relates. They often get this permission by asking if the data subject would object to having their details passed to another organisation for marketing purposes. Because companies cannot simply pass personal data around freely, it has become very valuable. Companies who have collected data along with the permissions to allow its passage to other organisations, have a very valuable commercial resource which can be exploited.

As well as the right not to have their personal data disclosed without permission, the data subject (the person who the data is about) also has the right, in most cases, to see the data and have it corrected if it is wrong. Organisations must therefore have administrative procedures in place to allow this and must also make sure that such data is surrounded by adequate security measures. If personal data is not kept secure and is disclosed because the security is inadequate, data holders can be sued by the data subject, if he or she suffers any loss as a result of the disclosure.

The effect of ageing on information

Many items of information are only useful for a certain period of time. In other words, they have a limited lifespan. For example, a list of the items in stock at the start of a week becomes less reliable as the week progresses, until a new list is produced at the start of the next week. Last week's stock figures have no real use beyond the week they refer to, but sales figures for that week are more useful. They may be used to compare with this week's figures and make projections for the same week in future years. Supermarkets keep sales figures for all the items they sell each day over a number of years. This is particularly useful for an in-store bakery, where the manager has to decide how many of each item to bake that day. Bake too much and some will have to be reduced towards the end of the day, or even thrown away, thus lowering the profit. Bake too little and you have dissatisfied customers who may decide to shop elsewhere next time. Shops can examine sales figures for the same day in other years to predict what they might sell and this can be much more accurate than just guessing. So, if a bakery manager wants to know how many fresh white loaves they should bake on Christmas Eve, he could look back at previous Christmas Eves to see what was baked and what sold.

It is essential that all organisations keep records going back many years since there may be queries from outside organisations and other people regarding what has been done, or what has happened in the past. Sometimes it will be necessary to keep a record of all the transactions (bits of business) that have been performed over a certain period of time for the purpose of auditing. As mentioned before, any historical data needs date stamping to be of any use.

Information needs to be presented in a form which is appropriate to its use and should always be date stamped to make sure that out-of-date information is not being used for decision making.

Different access levels for on-line files

When terminals on a network are used to access a centrally held pool of data, some users only need access to certain directories, subdirectories or even individual files. You may further need to restrict the user in what they can and can't do when they access certain files. For example, some terminals in a parts department of a garage may simply be used to find out if a particular part is in stock. To do this the user need only see the contents of the car-parts file and need not be able to change the contents in any way. You can block one department's access to another's data. So, for instance, someone from the accounts department may be unable to access data held by the personnel department.

There are several levels of access rights available on a network which may be summarised as follows:

- **read** – the user can read all the files in a particular directory

- **write** – the user can change the data in a particular file or directory

- **create** – the user can create new files, directory structures and subdirectories

- **erase** – the user can erase certain directories and files

- **modify** – the user can rename directories and files and change their attributes

- **copy** – the user is allowed to copy work from one area to another and might be allowed to copy onto floppies (although this is rare because of the security implications).

Activity

Here is a list of sources of information which you might use in your everyday life. Your task is to choose which might be useful.

A copy of last year's timetable at school or college.

Last month's payslip for a part-time job.

Last year's diary.

Your bank statements for the last twelve months.

The receipts for items such as clothes, CDs, etc. which you bought last month.

The previous edition of the telephone directory.

For each one, explain whether it should be kept and why.

Reward Card

0123 4567 8901234

Loyalty / reward cards used by many large retailers are used to link you to your purchases, even if you pay cash.

QUESTIONNAIRE

WIN A FREE HOLIDAY!

Just answer a few questions

With a free chance of winning a holiday, many people will divulge information about themselves and their lifestyle.

VOUCHER
A Free bottle of wine with your next meal

Vouchers given by restaurants have parts to them where you fill in your name & address. This enables the restaurant to send you details about special events / offers.

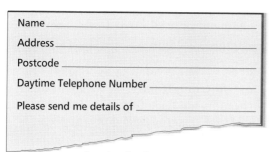

Name _____
Address _____
Postcode _____
Daytime Telephone Number _____
Please send me details of _____

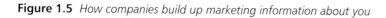

Enquiry slips in magazine articles.

http://www.business.com
Web sites you visit monitor your presence and you can be contacted via e-mail by the advertisers if necessary.

Figure 1.5 *How companies build up marketing information about you*

Use of information in marketing

How is marketing information built up about you?

If you look over a period of time at the post you and the other people in your house receive, a large amount will probably be unsolicited (i.e. information for which you have not asked). It is hard to think where many of the organisations could have got your address. If you look at Figure 1.5 you can see that data is often unknowingly supplied by you or through what you do, and companies are building up huge databases based on what goods or services you buy, when you buy them, how regularly you buy them, and so on. After processing this data they can often determine when you are most likely to make your next purchase. Such information is invaluable to companies who can then send you details of special promotions or offers for certain goods and services at exactly the time you are most likely to be considering them.

Marketing data

Huge amounts of data are collected, stored and processed to provide marketing information so that business opportunities can be identified and new products developed. Companies can also carry out market research to find out how satisfied customers are with products they have bought. Because of the huge increase in marketing data, particularly because of the use of customer loyalty cards, it is not surprising that IT is being constantly improved to make this data more accessible and easier to analyse.

Marketing data is now obtained faster and in more detail than ever before and it is being used to make important decisions, enabling organisations to react quickly to changes in the marketplace which in turn increases their effectiveness and profitability.

There are many questions that might be posed by a database set up for marketing, including:

- Who are our most important customers?

- What characteristics do they have?

- Are there any other customers who have similar characteristics?

- Can we produce a list of special sales promotions for certain customers?

- Can we produce a targeted mailing list to keep in regular contact with our customers?

- Can we predict when the customers are most likely to make a purchase?

Where does the data for a marketing database come from?

Companies need to hold information about their customers, such as name, address, contact name, goods bought, credit limit and so on. These details are used to perform the administration involved in ordering and paying for goods. Some companies go further than this and record details of people or companies who have simply made an enquiry but not yet ordered anything.

Suppose we work for a company making domestic appliances (fridges, freezers, washing machines, etc.) and are trying to create a marketing database. We may get the data about our customers from any of the following sources of existing data:

Purchase details – we can find out which of our products each customer has bought and even how long they have had them and the shop they were bought from.

Enquiries and orders – we can find out if customers who have made enquiries have actually gone on to place orders. We can look at the effectiveness of special offers such as interest-free credit, free insurance, etc. in influencing the customer to purchase.

Accounts details – we can look at how each customer has paid for the goods. This information can be useful if we want to investigate the use of store cards or special interest rates to attract new customers.

Service records – these are usually filled in as part of the guarantee or warranty. Sometimes manufacturers use this as an opportunity to extract further purchasing reasons from the customer. They may ask why they chose the product and what other products they looked at. Because of the need to analyse this kind of data using a computer, it is common to include the questions in multiple choice format. Manufacturers can also get important information about the reliability of their product from such records, since they will gather information such as the number of times the appliance is repaired and the nature of the repairs.

Data and information processing

To fulfil its aims and objectives an organisation will have to do some data and information processing. Data processing tends to be routine administrative tasks such as keeping track of business transactions (sales, purchases, stock, payroll, etc.). The data processing turns raw data into meaningful information, presented in its most useful form.

Information processing is less routine and is used to produce management information on which decisions can be based. It provides answers to questions such as 'Which is our best selling product?', 'Which customers settle their accounts promptly?' or 'Which customers have exceeded their credit limits?'.

Much of the information used by an organisation is internal, which means it comes from inside the company, although we have already seen that many organisations also need to know about their customers and competitors (external information). In a business, therefore, information is as much a resource as money and personnel, and is the key to its success. Any information system must produce high-quality information with the following features:

- **Completeness** – all the relevant information must be present so goods that are not in stock are not sold to customers etc.

- **Relevance** – no-one should have to wade through pages of computer printouts to search for the information they require. Instead they should specify what they require and the computer pick only those items of relevance to the user.

- **Clarity** – the information presented by the system should be clear to the user; any special coding system used should be explained.

- **User-specific** – sometimes reports (often the summary of information from a database) are passed on to people who have no real interest in their contents. More and more organisations only produce reports in response to user demands.

- **Cost effectiveness** – some reports are difficult to produce from a system and can involve lengthy periods of processing. Users should be made aware of the difficulties in producing such reports and also the cost of producing them. If the cost of producing the report outweighs the business advantages it confers, then they should be made aware that the information is probably not worth having.

- **Timeliness/up-to-dateness** – timeliness means that the information is delivered soon after it is requested. If the time between asking and receiving the information is too long the information becomes worthless.

Definition of terms exercises

A variety of terms are introduced in this chapter, many of which may be new to you. It is important that you build up vocabulary that can be used when writing essays or answering questions. Write a definition for each of the following terms used in Chapter 1:

> data, information,
> knowledge, data mining,
> data warehouse,
> Data Protection Act 1998,
> data processing,
> information processing.

Examination Questions

1 (a) What is meant by the term 'data'? *(1)*

(b) What is meant by the term 'information'? *(1)*

(c) Give an example which clearly shows the difference between 'data' and 'information'. *(2)*

(NEAB, Module ITO1, May 96, q1)

2 With the aid of an example, describe **one** problem which may occur when coding a value judgement. *(2)*

(NEAB, Module ITO1, May 96, q2)

3 Travelling sales representatives working in the UK can make extensive use of company credit cards to pay for goods and services. A company credit card is one that is issued by a company to its representative. All charges and information relating to each transaction are sent directly to the company.

(a) List **four** items of data which are captured each time the card is used. *(4)*

(b) Other than payment information, suggest **one** other potential use for information which can be derived from this data. *(2)*

(NEAB, Module IT01, May 97, q2)

4 Encoding information about value judgements as data can have the effect of reducing its accuracy or meaning. This becomes evident when the data is retrieved and used. Explain, with the use of **two** appropriate examples, why this may happen. *(4)*

(NEAB, Module IT01, Specimen Paper, q3)

5 A common way of permitting different levels of access to on-line files is the use of passwords. Once a password has been input, the user may be allowed to perform a number of different actions upon the data within the files, dependent on the level of access given to that password.

Describe **four** of these possible actions. *(4)*

(NEAB, Module IT01, May 97, q3)

6 Low quality information can be misleading, distorted or incomprehensible. This type of information is of little value to the decision maker. The output of good quality information is costly and dependent upon many factors.

(a) Identify **three** factors which affect the quality of the information. *(3)*

(b) State **two** factors which affect the cost of providing good quality information. *(2)*

(NEAB, Module IT01, May 98, q4)

7 (a) Information processing is concerned with:

Input

Processing

Output

Feedback

Briefly describe these four elements of information processing, using a diagram to illustrate your answer. *(6)*

(b) Explain the difference between 'knowledge' and 'information'. *(2)*

(NEAB, Module IT01, May 98,)

8 State **two** factors that affect the value of information and give an example of each one. *(4)*

(NEAB, Module IT01, May 99, q1)

What IT Can and Cannot Do

Capabilities and limitations of information systems

Why use an IT system?

We use IT systems for a variety of reasons, the main ones being:

1 **They offer fast repetitive processing.**
   Their use by the utilities companies (gas, electricity and water) shows this. Basically, the task the computers perform is simple: subtract the previous from current meter reading, then multiply this by the price, add on the standing charge and calculate and add the VAT. In addition, customer details must be added (name, address, method of payment, etc.). This is fairly simple for a computer but needs to be done millions of times in a short space of time.

2 **They offer vast storage capabilities.**
   The utility companies are amongst many organisations who hold details of their customers/clients. With the low cost of data storage, many people have a storage capacity on their PCs equivalent to that used by large companies ten years ago.

3 **They offer the facility to search quickly for stored data and combine it in a variety of ways.**
   The value of storing as much customer data as you can, is that if it is subsequently needed, it is already in the system. Storage capacity and cost are no longer issues in computing, but one still needs an efficient

and effective way of extracting required information in a meaningful form from all the data stored.

British Telecom maintains a huge database to record its customers and the telephone calls they make. BT can also tell when these calls are made (i.e. peak or off-peak), and can tailor their marketing campaigns to certain customers (e.g. people who make all their telephone calls during peak times, people who ring abroad frequently, people who ring only the same group of numbers, etc.). For example, with a scheme called 'Friends and Family', there is a 15 per cent discount on the ten numbers used most frequently by the customer. A search program is able to find these numbers.

The above factors mean that IT systems can be used to provide quality information.

The use of feedback for the maintenance of optimum stock levels

Most organisations hold some sort of stock. Such stock needs to be controlled for the following reasons:

● Keeping large quantities of stock is expensive. If the quantity kept can be reduced, the resources released (money, staff, space) can be put to better use in the organisation.

● If insufficient stock is kept, customers' orders or requirements may not be met and customers may therefore choose to go elsewhere for their goods.

Question

What are the costs associated with keeping large amounts of stock?

Feedback systems are used in some forms of stock control to reduce the difference between the stock kept and the stock required to satisfy customer orders. When there is constant feedback, comparisons are continually being made between the stock level required and the actual stock used. Figure 2.1 shows how the concept of feedback works.

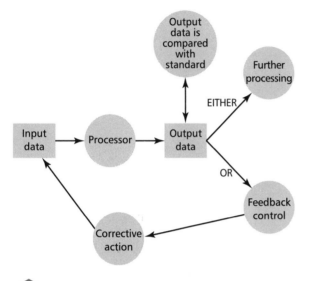

Figure 2.1 *The concept of feedback*

When looking at stock control systems we usually think of retailers and wholesalers, but nearly all organisations need to keep some form of stock. For example, car manufacturers have to make sure that stock is always available to supply the components for the production lines; the lack of just one of the key components can mean that the production line stops with an associated loss in production. Figure 2.2 shows the objectives of a typical stock control system.

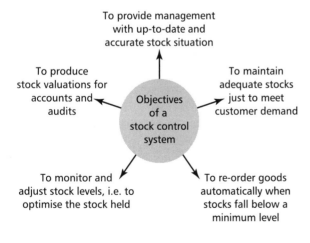

Figure 2.2 *The main objectives of a stock control system*

CASE STUDY

Tesco in pursuit of perfect stock management

Tesco has recently invested a huge amount in a new system which makes use of the 'just-in-time' concept, where goods are delivered to the stores as fast as they are being sold. This new system will cut the stocks of products in each store by about one-fifth and this will free some of the staff (who would normally be putting the extra goods on the shelves) to concentrate on giving a better service to the customers.

The new system replaces the old system of ordering fresh and packaged products, and it will allow individual stores to respond automatically to changing demand throughout the day. With the old system orders were placed depending on the average demand for the products over the previous five days, and this prevented the opportunity to respond to unexpected rushes on products. The new system will ensure that items like salads or ice-cream do not run out during hot weather or soup sell out during cold weather.

With the latest system, arriving goods are spread out over four or five deliveries per day rather than arriving as a single large delivery in the morning. Savings in manpower are also expected and this staff time can now be concentrated on some of the more customer-focused tasks.

IT solutions are being adopted to solve problems which would have been insoluble a few years ago and the advances brought by technology have meant that novel activities are being sought all the time. There are still some limitations, but even these are being pushed further and further back as the pace of advance in technology increases.

Some developments likely to increase the use of IT:

- Verbal communication with an operating system. For example, being able to simply say 'find me the letter I wrote to P Hughes on 1st December 2001' for it to appear on screen.

- A network computer in every home that can be used to order goods and services as well as provide information. France already has such a system, called Minitel, which is used to book travel tickets, order goods, look at the weather and send other people electronic messages. This is set to happen in the UK in the next couple of years.

- Combining the use of television, telephone and the Internet to provide access to huge quantities of video, data and information in every home.

- Video on demand, where you can simply select the film you want to view when you want to view it. You would no longer have to leave the house to rent a video as it would be sent direct to your house along a cable. At the moment this is not feasible because of the small bandwidth of the cable technology in use. Bandwidth is increasing all the time and compression techniques are being developed to reduce the huge volumes of digital data needed for pictures and sound.

Limitations on the use of IT

Hardware

Processor speed, memory size, disk capacity and data access speed have increased at an impressive rate over recent years. But with the increasing complexity of software and the tasks being performed, the technology of the hardware has been pushed to the limit. With developments in chip design, the speed of input into the computer and the speed with which the output is produced are often the limiting factors. Alternative methods of input that are faster and more accurate than the keyboard are being developed all the time, and this will speed up obtaining results.

Software

The ideal operating system would enable anyone to use the system with little or no training. Clearly we are a long way from this at the moment, but operating systems are becoming much easier to use, and the 'look and feel' common to application software that uses Windows, has enabled inexperienced users to learn unfamiliar packages quickly.

Communications

Communications now play an important part in IT, and technological developments enable more and more applications to be opened up, such as Internet telephony, voice mail, teleconferencing, etc.

Bandwidth

Bandwidth is a measure of the speed at which data can be transferred along a communication line. Bandwidth is limited at the moment and this has prevented real-time video and audio for videoconferencing, but with new technologies and new methods of data compression this limitation will eventually be overcome.

The role of communication systems

There is no doubt that the proliferation of cheap communication methods has made the world seem a much smaller place. Many youngsters in Britain now have the opportunity to converse with others of different cultures from all around the world, using the Internet. Many businesses operate on a global basis and their products, logos and offices can be seen all around the world. If everyone involved in an organisation is to keep in touch, communication systems need to be in place. Many of these communication systems are closed to outsiders to prevent them having access to company data, but many organisations are now seeing the advantages of allowing customers to interact with their databases, saving the company time and money on administration costs. This aspect of global communication systems will be examined in more detail later on.

Let us now look at the many devices and services that make up communication systems.

The telephone

The main advantage of the telephone is its availability and the immediacy of the response you get if the person you need to contact is available. All communication systems need to be widely available and easy to use to be of any real use. Yet there are also a number of problems with telephone communication and these include:

1 Only speech can be used. Documents cannot be passed from one person to another and this limits the use of the telephone, particularly for meetings.

2 You can waste a lot of time trying to contact someone who is often out of the office or always busy attending meetings, etc.

3 You can end up playing 'telephone tag' if both you and the person you are trying to contact are busy. They ring you up and since you are busy you arrive back to your desk to a message which tells you to ring them. You ring them and they are busy and someone leaves a note on their desk to ring you, and the process continues until you eventually get in touch.

4 If you are conducting global business, there are problems in using the telephone owing to the time differences around the world. Eastern USA is five hours behind Britain, so to reach someone going into the office at 9.00 a.m. in New York you need to ring them at 2.00 p.m. Countries in the Far East are particularly difficult to communicate with, since when we are leaving to go home for the day, workers there are just about to arrive for work.

Activity

Telephone systems in use 15 years ago had very few features compared with those of today. Your task is to evaluate the features of a telephone system for a business run from home. You can choose to look at an ordinary telephone or a mobile phone.

As part of your evaluation write a list of the features and for each one explain how the feature might be useful.

The Internet

The best way to describe the Internet is as a network of networks which enables people to exchange and share data. There is no one person or government supervising the administration of the Internet and to many people this is one of its attractions. There are security problems with viruses, pornography, etc., but for most people the advantages of being able to reach people all over the world to exchange ideas and information, far outweigh the disadvantages.

There are a variety of reasons for subscribing to services that enable connection to the Internet. Some people like to use the electronic mail service which is both quick and cheap compared with conventional mail. Others like to access the chat services and bulletin board services where they can communicate with others with similar interests. Others make use of the vast databases of information on every topic imaginable.

The main problem for all Internet users is finding the sources of information they require, and there are various pieces of software, called search engines, used to interrogate these vast databases.

What is needed to connect up to the Internet?

Several things are needed including:

- A PC (personal computer) or a network computer.

- A **modem** which converts the digital signals produced by the computer into analogue signals which can be passed along a telephone line. Alternatively, an ISDN terminal can be used which uses the digital signals produced by the computer but passes them along a digital line.

- Software from the Internet service provider (ISP). The ISP provides a permanent link to the Internet. When you log onto the ISP you are able to use the vast amount of data on their file server as well as using the server as a way of accessing the Internet. Some ISPs are free with the service being paid for by the adverts that appear on the screen; for others you have to pay a monthly subscription.

- A telephone line along which the data you send and receive can travel.

What are the costs involved?

The costs include:

- **Hardware costs** – the cost of the computer or terminal and the cost of the modem or ISDN adaptor.

- **Monthly subscription costs to the ISP (Internet service provider)** – unless one of the free services is chosen. Many ISPs charge a flat monthly fee regardless of how much time you spend on the Internet; others charge a lower fee which covers a certain number of hours use with an extra charge for each hour of use after that.

  Many ISPs provide free services where the only charge is the cost of a local call. Some ISPs offer 'unmetered' call access, so that the user pays no charges at all.

- **A quarterly rental charge** – if ISDN is used. Included in this rental is a set number of free hours' connection to the Internet.

- **The cost of the telephone calls made to your ISP** – normally at a local rate. It is important to note that although you could access a site in another country (such as the USA) you will still only be paying for a local telephone call to your ISP. Some ISPs have negotiated cheap telephone call rates with the telecommunications companies, so no matter what time of the day you call, it will only cost around 1p per minute. It is interesting to note that in the USA calls to local numbers, including the ISP, are free and this has really opened up the use of the Internet there.

What determines the speed of the Internet?

The speed when accessing and sending information over the net is determined by:

- **The type of material you are accessing.** Pictures and complex graphics take up larger files and these take longer to travel along communication lines. Simple pages of text are relatively quick.

- **The speed of your modem or the modem at the other end of the communication line.** Faster modems mean that files take less time to transmit from one point to another. Modem speeds are determined by their baud rate (the number of bits per second), but many of them now compress the data to make the file smaller before sending it, so you need to look at the baud rate and the compression factor when making comparisons.

- **The amount of other traffic on the Internet.** There are certain peak times that you need to avoid if you want quick access.

- **The bandwidth of the communication lines being used to make the connection.** The speed of data transmission will always be determined by that part of the connection with the smallest bandwidth. So where a path is made up of several links, the slowest link will determine the overall speed of data transfer.

What can the Internet be used for?

You can take part in chats
Chats on the Internet involve typing messages rather than talking, and the service enables you to take part in one-to-one discussions or group discussions. There are many 'chat rooms' where people talk to each other on all manner of subjects. Chat rooms are useful if you want specialist help. For instance, if you are interested in how to keep a certain kind of pet, you can enter a chat room for people who keep that pet. The nice thing about chat rooms is that you can talk to people from all around the world, although it is fair to say that you can also waste a lot of time (and money) doing this.

You can download files
If you have a problem with a printer driver or a virus, the Internet is the first place you should look for a solution. There are many free files on all manner of subjects that can be downloaded and stored on your hard disk. So, if you require some clip art to enhance your wordprocessed documents, you can look at the huge banks of clip art files.

However, whenever you download files from the Internet, you should check them with a virus checker, since the Internet is the easiest way for virus writers to distribute their wares.

You can use the Internet to look things up
Without leaving your home you can access the world's largest libraries for information. You can access dictionaries, encyclopaedias, atlases, thesauruses, research papers, timetables and so on. Generally speaking, if it is published, you will find it on the Internet.

You can send e-mail to your friends
One of the features provided by an Internet service provider (ISP) (Demon, CompuServe, AOL, Freeserve, etc.) is the ability to send e-mail to anyone connected to the Internet. The Internet has enabled anyone with a connection to send e-mail to anyone else in the world similarly connected. If you use a stand-alone machine, e-mail software is provided by the ISP and connection is provided via a modem or possibly an ISDN terminal adaptor. This system makes use of a dial-up connection and is called e-mail client. Sometimes, small local area networks (usually simple peer-to-peer networks) may be connected using simple operating systems such as Windows 2000 or Mac System 9.

For larger networks, a client–server model is used, where a larger, more powerful computer called the server is used to control the operation of the network. Another computer, not necessarily the server, is used to provide a link to the Internet.

Junk mail

One problem with e-mail is the amount of junk mail you receive mixed in with your important mail. Junk mail is those adverts that are sent in their thousands or even millions in the hope that there will be a few responses and hopefully some sales. Many such adverts are illegal and you have to be aware that many are simply ways of parting you from your money without giving you anything in return. The more you browse the Web, the more your e-mail address will be picked out (by the use of 'cookies') and the more of this junk mail you will likely receive. The term 'spamming' is used for when someone sends the same unsolicited message to lots of other people; 'spamcontrol' is the name given to the filters used to trap unwanted messages.

There are ways in which junk mail can be filtered out and most ISP software provides some way of doing this.

E-mail

There are many advantages and disadvantages in using e-mail and here are some of the main ones.

☑ Advantages

1 It is almost instantaneous. Mail is sent immediately and a reply can be received as soon as the recipient checks their e-mail box.

2 There is no need for the formality of a letter. E-mail is meant to be quick, direct and to the point. You do not need to worry about the odd typing or spelling mistake.

3 You can attach a copy of the sender's message with your reply, which means that they do not have to search for the original message.

4 If you discount the hardware and software which the user probably already has, then e-mail is cheaper than a letter. Even though you might be sending a message across the world, you will only be charged for a local telephone call and the time it takes to transmit the message.

☒ Disadvantages

1 Only a small percentage of people have the equipment to send and receive e-mail and this has hindered its universal use, but the percentage is rising and eventually the system will probably take over from the traditional mail service.

2 It may make users more casual about their approach to business; they may not realise that anything they e-mail is as legally binding as if it were written in a more formal document, such as a letter or contract.

3 Junk mail is a problem, although there are software solutions that filter out junk mail.

4 There are worries about security.

5 The system relies on people checking their e-mail boxes regularly.

E-mail snooping

Many organisations read their employees' e-mails. Although you may feel that this in an invasion of privacy, it is lawful. Usually the employer has to tell the employee via their contract of employment or company rules that it will be done.

E-mail without a computer

Many ISPs (such as CompuServe) provide a system whereby you can access your e-mail when you are away from your computer, using an ordinary telephone or mobile phone. All you have to do is ring up and dial a number, consisting of the telephone number of the system and a personal identification number. A computer-generated voice (which uses the latest text-to-speech technology) then gets to work, reading out who the message is from and then asking whether you want to listen to it. If you want, you can then have the message forwarded to any fax machine in the world. To tell the sender that you have received and read the message, you can send a standardised acknowledgement message in response. There are also new mobile telephones that can be used to directly access the Internet.

You can use it to keep up-to-date with events

There are many newspapers and magazines available on the Internet and you can even search for back issues.

You can play games

Years ago, if you wanted to play a game you had to find some friends who were of a like mind, which wasn't always easy. Now, using the Internet, it is much easier to find other like-minded people.

You can review software before you buy

There are many websites set up by the software manufacturers which enable you to download incomplete versions of their software for testing and evaluation before you make the decision to purchase. Some even sell their products over the Internet, which means you can order, pay and receive delivery in a few minutes, although only small files are distributed in this way because of the time it would take to transmit a large file.

Question

The Internet is a useful source of shareware and public domain software.

Explain the difference between shareware and public domain software.

You can order goods and services
Many companies are now reaping the benefits of advertising their products and services over the Internet and are finding it an excellent way of increasing business for a relatively small investment. An example of this was a drug company that was trying to promote a new product to treat headaches. It put an advertisement on the Internet and any surfers who came across the site and filled in their names and addresses were posted free samples. In one month alone around 30,000 people had registered to receive their free samples. Toyota, the car manufacturer, put banner advertisements on the Internet and in one year 152,000 web surfers had typed in their names and addresses and requested a brochure or video about one of Toyota's models. (Banner advertisements are those that appear when you are loading up material from the Internet.) Toyota used this information, along with information from dealers, to find out how many had actually gone on to purchase one of their cars, and they were amazed to find that around 7300 people had actually done so. This has now made the Internet the number one sales lead generator for Toyota.

Finding your way around the Internet
There are three main ways of finding your way around the Internet:

1 If you know the address of a site you can simply type it in. If you do not know the addresses of sites you can buy books (called directories) or buy one of the popular Internet magazines that contain them. Internet addresses are now as much a part of company

identity as phone or fax numbers and they nearly always feature in advertisements.

2 You can 'surf' the Internet; this means using hypertext links to move from one area of interest to another. These hypertext links are in the form of either underlined text or text in a different colour, on which you click to move to that site. If you are a website designer you need to make sure that there are plenty of links to your site so that you are likely to attract a greater number of 'surfers'.

3 You can use a special program, called a **search engine**, where you can enter certain key words or subject matter names, and the program searches for those sites with information containing those key words. Because of the huge amount of material placed on the Internet, it can be quite difficult to construct searches to narrow them down sufficiently.

There is a variety of search engines in use including:

Alta Vista	**http://www.altavista.com**
Yahoo!	**http://www.yahoo.com**
Lycos	**http://www.lycos.com**

Internet shopping: is it the end of the traditional shop?
For any shop the three most important things are location, location and location, but with Internet shopping location is immaterial and the store (usually just a warehouse to house the goods) can be in any part of the world. If the goods being supplied are of good quality and attractively priced, then people will find them and tell others about them. The costs of setting up an Internet shopping business are considerably lower than those of a traditional shop. With a traditional shop you need to find suitable premises and then pay to have the shop fitted out. In addition, there are sales staff costs, lighting, heating and rates. With an Internet shopping organisation, these costs are either non-existent or considerably reduced. The cost savings can be passed to the customer in the form of cheaper goods.

The large multiple retail stores are being threatened by Internet operators, which have enjoyed phenomenal growth in recent years. As an example, the largest bookstore in the world is no longer Foyles in London, as it was a few years ago, but Amazon Books, a relatively new arrival on the Internet. Amazon Books only has a website and a warehouse in America and holds around one million titles in stock which it can dispatch anywhere in the world.

There are now programs called 'intelligent agents' that are able to search out the cheapest goods. So, if you wanted a certain book you could type in the details and the system would respond with the outlet which sold it most cheaply.

Shopping using the Internet

☑ Advantages

- People who live in isolated rural areas now have access to products that were once only available in large cities.

- Disabled or elderly people can shop for goods without leaving their home.

- Delivery firms do well, owing to the increase in goods being sent direct to people's homes.

- People need to make fewer trips to the shops, thus reducing the congestion and pollution in towns and cities.

- Shopping will take less time and this will allow people more time to do other things.

☒ Disadvantages

- As more people work and shop from home, they could begin to feel isolated and 'cut off' from society. Less social interaction can be a factor contributing to the development of mental health problems.

- Not having to leave the house to do shopping means that you do less exercise and this could lead to health problems.

- Traditional forms of mail will decline as more and more correspondence is sent via e-mail.

- There are security implications when keying in your credit or debit card details for transmission over the Internet.

- It is easier to commit fraud, such as by creating websites for non-existent stores.

- You cannot inspect the goods you buy first, so it may be more difficult to get goods exchanged or your money back than with traditionally bought goods.

- People without access to the expensive computer equipment and services needed to access the Internet will be unable to shop in

this way and will probably end up paying more for their goods.

There are many new terms used when describing features and services provided by the Internet and it is important to understand exactly what they mean. You have been asked to define each of the following terms to someone who knows a little about computing but nothing much of the Internet. In defining these terms, try not to use another term in your explanation that also needs defining.

bandwidth	World Wide Web (WWW)
information/ superdata highway	ISP (Internet service provider)
HTML	search engine
browser	cookies
web page	intelligent agents
home page	

Fax

There are two main types of equipment: the dedicated fax machine and the fax machine which forms part of a computer system and makes use of special software and a modem. A dedicated fax machines scans a paper document and then sends it via a modem along the telephone line as a digital signal until it reaches the receiving fax, where a modem re-creates the image and the fax machine prints it out.

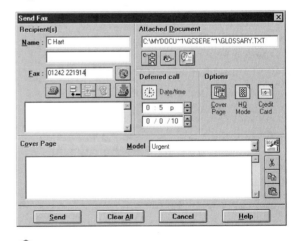

Figure 2.3 *Most modems allow you to send and receive faxes: this is handy if the receiver has a fax machine but no e-mail facility*

The other type of fax operation makes use of a fax modem and a small computer. The fax modem enables one computer to send a fax directly to another, eliminating the need to scan a hard copy (a printed copy) into a fax machine. If you are busy working on your computer when a fax arrives you need not break off and deal with it, since the fax modem automatically answers the telephone and stores the fax on your hard drive until you have a chance to deal with it. You are able to look at the fax on your screen by making use of special software and can print a hard copy out if you need it. The advantage of such a system is that the faxes may be stored for future reference and do not take up the amount of space that printouts would.

A fax is simply a picture of a page in graphics format, so it is not possible to transfer faxes directly to a wordprocessing package without using special software, called optical character recognition (OCR) software.

Teletext

Teletext is a service provided by the television companies; most televisions are able to receive the information. The pages of information are transmitted at the same time as the TV pictures and you are able to select the picture you want using a small remote control keypad. Teletext provides a limited number of pages and may be considered as little more than an electronic magazine/newspaper.

Viewdata

Viewdata is the name given to any system that provides data through a telephone network to a terminal or television screen. Viewdata is interactive, which means that the user can send information as well as receive it. In this way it is different from teletext where you can only select and view pages. Viewdata encompasses the Internet, since the Internet is provided over the telephone lines and charges are levied for its use (subscription to the service provider, the cost of the telephone call and occasionally a charge for some of the pages viewed).

Videoconferencing

Videoconferencing systems enable face-to-face meetings to be conducted without participants meeting in the same room. These systems make use of computers, small cameras, video

compression cards, sound cards, specialist software and communication lines. To hold a single frame of a picture at a reasonable quality requires a huge amount of data and when this picture is refreshed many times a second, then getting the data along a communication line at reasonable speed is quite a problem. Ordinary telephone lines, because of their small bandwidth, are not suitable because they would be too slow; much faster ISDN lines are used instead. In many cases, several ISDN lines are used to transmit the video (picture) and the audio (sound) signals, and although this does make the system relatively expensive, the cost needs to be compared with that of staff travelling large distances to meet in person. It is important that both the audio and video signals arrive together and without any undue delay, as this will make the system more acceptable and easier to use. Most videoconferencing systems make use of coders and decoders which compress and decompress signals, thus making it possible to send signals using a much smaller bandwidth. Use of coders has led to an improvement in the time delay and the quality of the sound and video pictures.

Figure 2.4 *The monitor for a videoconferencing system. Notice the camera on the top of the monitor*

In a real meeting, it is not just a question of watching and talking, since quite frequently presentations of information are made using handouts, slides, an overhead projector or a computer, and notes may be made on a whiteboard. Any videoconferencing system will need to have these extra facilities if it is to be of any use in business. Many of the cheaper systems available for home use lack these extra, more expensive facilities and are little more than video phone systems where you can see a picture of the person you are talking to.

Using videoconferencing equipment does take some getting used to and there is a tendency to look at the screen rather than at the camera, which means others just see the top of your head! Also, some of the simple versions which use a modem impose a time delay between you speaking and the person at the other end hearing you, so it is hard for two people to talk normally.

There is no doubt, however, that videoconferencing will make significant inroads into all areas of life when hardware prices and telecommunication charges start to decrease. One of the main manufacturers of videoconferencing equipment, Picturetel, have a website on www.picturetel.com.

Activity

Write down a list of the activities that are involved in a typical meeting.

What are the advantages and disadvantages of conducting a meeting using videoconferencing equipment rather than in the normal way?

Access to remote databases

Many organisations span international boundaries and they often have branches in many more countries, yet they still need to be controlled centrally. To do this they need a central pool of data which everyone can access remotely.

Many companies make use of the technology used when accessing the Internet for internal use; such a network is called an 'Intranet'. Intranets are a fairly new development and

their main advantage is that they are much cheaper to set up and run than a conventional network.

Using the Internet you can access many remote databases, for example research papers and books in libraries in many different parts of the world.

One useful on-line remote database used by many businesses is called Tel-Me, and this service is used to carry out credit checks on customers, keep up to date with the latest business news and look at share movements. Tel-Me also contains a national *Yellow Pages* which you can search for a variety of goods and services. Other services provided include booking travel tickets and accommodation, traffic reports, air and rail timetables. All these services mean that information can be obtained quickly compared with making telephone calls or visiting public libraries.

Internet telephony

Cheap 'global gossip' is now available using a service called Internet telephony. Using this system you can have an ordinary telephone conversation over the Internet for the cost of a local telephone call plus the monthly cost of the Internet service provider. Ordinary telephone calls use the whole circuit for the call whereas the Internet uses a system called packet switching which is based on a network of leased lines that are continually being used by other users. The cheapest system to use to make Internet telephone calls consists of a PC running special application software, an Internet handset, a voice card installed in the PC and a modem. For business users the hardware and software is more complex.

For domestic users the cost savings can be in the region of 65 per cent compared with those made using the conventional service, and the service is of particular use to anyone who is already on the Internet and who frequently calls friends and family abroad.

The main problem with the service at the moment is that the Internet was not designed for voice, and with the present amount of traffic it is likely to grind to a halt, so this form of telephony cannot be relied upon. If Internet telephony were to take off in a big way, the system would be unlikely to be able to cope with it.

CASE STUDY

Tesco Direct

Tesco Direct is a home shopping service provided over the Internet, where customers select goods, pay for them using credit or debit cards and then have them delivered to their homes. The advantages of the service are clear; no petrol needed to drive to the store, no parking problems or fees, no long queues and no complaining adults and children.

At present only a few areas of the country have been selected for the service, but it is set to increase and will certainly prove a boon to people who do not drive, who are disabled or who have such a busy schedule that they find it difficult to find the time to shop.

Each 'virtual' store has 20,000 products to choose from, which is about the same number as one of the larger 'ordinary' branches would stock. The user wheels a virtual shopping trolley around the departments, picking up goods along the way. The store is arranged just like an ordinary store and you can enter the various departments by clicking on the picture on the screen. The departments are as follows: bakery, deli and dairy, frozen foods, fruit and vegetables, general food, grocery provisions, health and beauty, meat and poultry, newsagent, off-licence and flowers and houseplants. The goods in each department are listed with their prices and to put them into your trolley you simply click on the goods and enter the quantity you require. There is also a calculator to keep track of the money you have spent. If you want, you can even specify the ripeness of the fruit to be selected.

Most people buy a very similar selection of goods each week so for these people there is a shopping list of the items they usually buy and they can either add or delete items to suit their needs. This has the advantage that they do not have to select all the items, so can save time.

There is a downside to the system. There is a £5 charge to cover the delivery service and you obviously need all the hardware and software and communication charges to gain access to the Internet. The software needed to order and the list of goods on offer are available free on CD-ROM from Tesco.

Putting the goods in your virtual shopping basket is done off-line using the data on the CD-ROM and this saves on the on-line costs, since it is this part of the service that takes the most time, but you can also do this on-line.

Activity　　　*KEY SKILLS　C2.2, C3.2*

You have been asked to evaluate the home shopping service, Tesco Direct, by the manager of a sheltered housing scheme who is in charge of a large group of accommodation for elderly residents who live independently in apartments. There are some communal areas, so the idea would be to site the equipment in these areas to enable the residents to order their shopping. The area the housing is in is covered by the Tesco Direct home shopping service.

The Tesco on-line site can be found at www.tesco.co.uk

On entering this site you will see a screen offering several options; click on the picture for Tesco Direct.

In your evaluation you will need to investigate:

- the costs associated with the system (assume they have no computer equipment at the moment)
- how easy the system is to use, bearing in mind that the system will need to be used by elderly people who will probably have little experience of computers
- how long it takes between ordering goods and getting them delivered.

CASE STUDY

Removing the administrative burden in schools

Read the following article:

> **Teacher's dream!**
>
> Take a register, write a letter, browse the Internet World Wide Web and use a radio signal to trigger an alarm ... options include grade recording and e-mail and two way paging ... all with the same electronic device, using radio to exchange data with the admin computer in the school office. A teacher's dream!

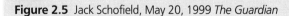

Figure 2.5 Jack Schofield, May 20, 1999 *The Guardian*

The article appeared in *The Guardian* newspaper. Here is a little more information about the system.

wNET (an abbreviation for wireless network) is widely used by over 12,000 teaching staff in schools and colleges. The hardware looks like a thin, notebook computer, only larger, and it may be used for the following purposes:

* to collect student grades in each subject (i.e. as a teacher's electronic mark book)
* to send and receive e-mail
* to act as a pager (useful for security)
* to access pocket Windows applications (Word, Excel and Internet Explorer)
* as a two-way link to the school's/college's information management system (called SIMS) which is used by the administration staff
* to tackle literacy and numeracy
* to access the vast educational resources on the Internet
* to assist with discipline, by allowing codes to be entered regarding pupils' action or behaviour.

Further information may be obtained from Bromcom computers, who manufacture the wNET system and who have a website: www.bromcom.com

Questions

1 What are the main advantages in using the above system for recording student/pupil attendance compared to the traditional paper-based register?

2 Explain what a pager is and how it might be useful in conjunction with the wNET system in a school or college situation.

3 The headteacher in a school is thinking of buying a wNET system and has come to you for advice. She would like to know how you think the e-mail and Internet access might be useful to teachers in the school. Write a short note to her, putting forward your ideas (you are in favour of the system).

Telematics (informatics)

Telematics is a term used by the European Commission for the exchange and processing of electronic data between networked computer systems. The data transferred need not be text; it can be multimedia, with sound, graphics, video footage, etc. The European Commission has put a large amount of money into research in this area via the Telematics Application Programme, whose brief is to use information and communication technologies to solve real problems identified by EC member states, and will therefore help these countries to grow economically and thereby boost employment.

At present, telematics is being used in applications such as distance learning, teleworking, telemedicine and remote management of air and road traffic.

Teleworking will be covered in greater detail in Chapter 3.

CASE STUDY

Telemedicine

The problem with many hospital systems is that they were created in the eighteenth century and are therefore paper-based, with staff moving the paperwork manually from one department to another. Since there are so many paper files, finding an individual's paperwork can be a lengthy process and unacceptably slow in an emergency situation. Couple this with the fact that files can be put back in the wrong place and never found again, or while they lie waiting on someone's desk are unavailable for use, and you can see that such a system has many weaknesses.

At the heart of any telemedicine system is a high speed communication link between all the devices involved (terminals, computers, imaging equipment, etc.). For instance, two large hospitals in London (Guy's and St Thomas's) recently merged to enable them to make better use of the resources associated with very expensive and sophisticated medical imaging systems. They installed a very high speed communication link between the two hospitals which enables X-ray images and images from body scanners to be sent from one hospital to the other – in the past staff and film used to move between the sites using the bus, which could take around 30 minutes in the busy London traffic.

The hospitals use a high speed ATM (asynchronous transfer mode) link that enables the pictures to be sent from one terminal to the other practically in real time. Using this link, the pictures can be sent to specialist medical staff for their immediate diagnosis and then on to a system that stores them for future reference.

X-ray images can be stored using a similar system and it is hoped that eventually all patient images and patient details, doctor's comments, etc. will be kept together as part of a complete patient record. This would then allow any doctor to see immediately all the information pertaining to a particular patient on any of the terminals situated throughout the hospital.

Malpractice and data theft

There is a spectrum of computer-related crimes ranging from petty offences, such as mischievously hacking into someone's e-mail box, to the more serious crime of fraudulently altering data. A hacker is a computer enthusiast who tries to break into a secure computer system and the process of doing this is called hacking.

Software and data misuse

There is a variety of ways in which data and software can be misused and this section looks at the main ones.

The problems

Alteration of data or software for fraudulent purposes

Software developers could, in theory, write a program code to divert sums of money into false accounts set up for their benefit. It is therefore prudent to have some way of preventing this. One way would be to select staff carefully and make these staff aware that security is taken very seriously by the organisation. If they think they are likely to get caught, they are less likely to contemplate fraud.

Most companies prevent such fraud by making sure that applications development staff (programmers, systems analysts, etc.) do not

have unsupervised access to any operational systems and data. This usually means that staff working on a new computer system use a different computer to the one being employed operationally to perform the day-to-day tasks which help run the company.

To avoid the alteration of data by operations staff (i.e. the staff involved in the day-to-day administration), companies use a technique called duplication of ability. What this means is that no one person sees any process through from start to finish. For example, the person who places an order should never be the same person who pays the resulting bill, since it would be possible to create a false company and place bogus orders that are subsequently paid for. Companies often rotate staff duties; this prevents this type of fraud because it is more likely to be discovered when the duty passes to another person.

Data theft

Data theft can occur for a variety of reasons. The first is where the data is of value to another organisation (industrial espionage). Such theft may involve a list of a company's best customers along with values of the sales made to these customers, or it might just be a pricing program.

Sometimes, data may be stolen by a disgruntled ex-employee who wants to damage the organisation or an individual within it. For this reason, when key employees such as computer programmers gives notice that they are going to leave, it is common practice that they leave right away without working their notice period (although they still get paid as if they had worked this period).

Software theft

Software theft usually means copying software without a licence to do so, and it is an offence under the Computer Misuse Act. The effect of copying software is to deprive the software producers of a return on the investment they have placed in the product, and in the end this makes the software more expensive. Software theft and its implications will be looked at in more detail in Chapter 4.

Compromising electronic emanations

Communication and IT equipment can emit unintended electronic signals when in use, and these can be picked up using special equipment, thus compromising the security of the system. This problem is called 'TEMPEST'. There are measures that can be taken to overcome this problem which, although expensive, are necessary if the data being used or transferred is of a very sensitive nature.

Hacking

Hacking has its roots in America when around twenty years ago youngsters, usually students, were able to gain access to the telephone system and make free phone calls to anyone in the world. They did this by using a tone generator to produce a signal at a certain frequency which switched off the charging equipment at the telephone exchange. Once they had done this they could make a free call.

When personal computers were developed and were connected to the phone system via modems a similar group of people then tried to crack codes and passwords to gain access to government and corporate databases. Most of these people were not malicious and once they gained access did little more than look at the data, but they did compromise the security of the system and obviously the authorities took a dim view of this. The motivation driving hackers is often to 'beat the system' and the more security hurdles are put in their way, the more of a challenge it becomes and the greater the hacker's determination to gain access.

To deter hackers, and make hacking a specific offence, the government brought in a law called the Computer Misuse Act 1990; this will be looked at in depth in Chapter 4.

The virus problem

A computer virus is simply defined as any program that replicates itself automatically. However, as well as doing this, most viruses carry a payload which makes them either display annoying messages or graphics on the screen or destroy your files (programs and data). There are many thousands of viruses around, but only about ten per cent are encountered frequently.

You may think that viruses are not a real problem since they are detected readily and removed, and if necessary all the software and data affected can be copied from backup copies. This is not as easy as it sounds in a business where the computer could be out of action for several days while the software and data are re-created. The computer affected could be a file server connected to tens or even hundreds of terminals. Another problem is that the virus could have gained access to the backup copies and destroyed some of these files too. Recent figures from the National Computing Centre suggest that the cost of an average virus attack on a business is around £4000!

What do most viruses do?

Some viruses, such as one called Friday 13th, are set to be triggered on a certain date. These viruses can be very destructive because you may not know that you have it until the day it does all the damage, by which time it could have also infected all the backup copies as well. Viruses which cause immediate damage are more readily spotted and therefore less dangerous.

Other viruses are more subtle in their approach and do nothing obvious, but instead destroy files one by one. Again these are hard to spot and can easily corrupt backup copies.

There is another type of program called a 'Trojan horse' that is not really a virus because it does not replicate itself automatically, but instead relies on humans to do the copying. Trojan horses consist of a useful program that also contains a damaging file. Because of the usefulness of the main program people copy them and pass them to friends and it is in this way that the damaging program is spread around.

Types of virus

Boot sector viruses

These are by far the commonest viruses and are transmitted by floppies being left in their drives when the computer is booted up. The computer looks at the boot sector on the floppy to see if it has any executable code and if it doesn't, it reports the message that a non-system disk has been inserted. The user will then usually remove the floppy and press a key to load the operating system from the hard drive. If a boot sector virus is present on the floppy it is loaded into the computer's memory where it stays and is then copied onto the boot sector of the hard drive when the operating system is loaded.

File viruses

File viruses attach themselves to executable files (i.e. those with a .COM or .EXE file extension) from where the viruses are copied to other executable files when these programs are executed.

Macro viruses

Macro viruses are a newer development and are able to infect data files. Most wordprocessors and spreadsheets now contain powerful macro languages which are able to automate some tasks and it is this macro language which is used to alter or destroy wordprocessed documents or worksheets. There are now macro viruses that are able to infect spreadsheet and database files.

Avoiding viruses

There are a number of actions that may be taken to prevent, or reduce the likelihood of, a virus attack and these are as follows:

- install the latest virus checking software
- do not place any disk in the machine without scanning it first
- scan all software and files that have been downloaded off the Internet
- most viruses have the facility to remain in the computer's memory while the power is on, so it is unwise to insert your disk after someone else without first switching the computer off and then on again
- never boot up from a floppy, as this is how the commonest type of virus (the boot sector virus) is transmitted
- do not allow the computer to be used for playing games since pirated games software frequently carries viruses
- public domain software and shareware can be copied freely, so it is quite common for them to contain viruses; if possible it is best to get these directly from a shareware library
- when computers are sent in for repair, the computer engineers frequently make use of special diagnostic software and this will have been placed in many other computers before yours, so you need to insist that all such software is scanned before being put into your machine
- transferring disks between machines is always dicey, so this should be avoided whenever possible
- many companies have a single PC connected to the Internet for downloading the latest releases of software, printer drivers, etc. rather than using their file server, which is crucial to the operation of the business
- keep daily backups of all your data.

Prevention is better than cure

It is much easier to try to prevent viruses from entering the computer in the first place than having to deal with the consequences afterwards. One of the main problems in trying to detect viruses is that they are constantly being created and are generally becoming more ingenious and therefore harder to detect. Because of this it is important to use the latest virus checking software and if possible to use virus detection software with monthly updates, to keep you protected against the latest viruses.

Security checks

In this section we look at which methods are available to ensure the security of data stored on a computer system. We also look at the ways in which deliberate alteration of the data can be prevented.

Data security protects against the accidental loss of data and it ensures that there is a means of restoring the data if such loss occurs. It also prevents the deliberate, unauthorised alteration of data once it has been accepted onto the computer system.

Data integrity procedures ensure that the data input to the system is correct and this is normally achieved by verification and validation checks. They also provide a means of tracing all the transactions and operations taking place on computer files, a process linked with the concept of an audit trail.

Saving your data

Regular file saving

There is a tendency when working with computers to save your material only just before printing. We are all apt to think, 'I'll just do a little more work and then I'll save it'. Regular saving at pre-determined intervals is an essential security measure and many people learn this lesson the hard way (usually after spending an afternoon typing, then losing everything when the power goes off just when they were going to save their work).

Many programs have an autosave facility that saves your work automatically, and you can alter the time period between the saves. Using this facility means that you no longer have to think about saving except at the end.

Why save regularly?

- Power surges cause spikes in the mains power that can result in work being corrupted.

- Power cuts cause work to be lost.

- Mistakes can be made that can't be easily rectified. Sometimes, particularly when using some new software, you may press a key accidentally which performs an action that you do not know how to reverse. It is sometimes easier to revert to your 'last saved' version than work out what you have done and correct it.

- Someone may unplug your computer by accident.

Write-protect mechanisms

Floppy disks (such as the 3.5 inch disks used to hold your projects) are read/write because data may be read off, as well as written to, the disk. If you need to make sure that data on a particular disk is not altered, you have to 'write-protect' it, and this is done by moving the plastic slide towards the edge of the disk as shown in Figure 2.6. When this is done you will notice that a hole is left and the disk is now write-protected. You will not be able to write to this disk without first moving the slide back down.

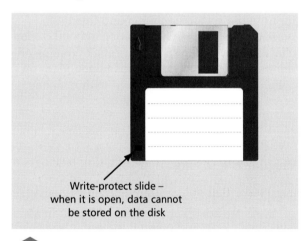

Write-protect slide –
when it is open, data cannot
be stored on the disk

Figure 2.6 *A 3.5 inch floppy disk and its write-protect slide*

Confidentiality

It is important that access to certain programs and data is restricted to certain personnel and there are a variety of security checks that can be put in place to achieve this. In addition to all these measures it is best to select staff carefully and make sure that they fully appreciate the consequences of any untoward activities. Usually staff have in their contracts of employment clear details of what they are not allowed to do.

Passwords

Most software, particularly spreadsheets and databases, allow users to specify passwords that have to be entered before the system can be entered and data accessed. Many users are put off using passwords because they are worried about forgetting them. If they have to write them down, this destroys the object of having passwords in the first place. Many users write them down on pieces of paper stuck to the back of the monitor and others use a piece of paper placed in the top drawer of their desk. Either way, they are the first places anyone will look. To keep passwords secure, they should be changed regularly to avoid people getting to know what they are.

Figure 2.7 Shows some tips to ensure your password remains confidential.

Non-disclosure

If staff are to use computers they must have access to data. It is therefore important to choose very carefully the staff who have access to private and confidential data. Often non-disclosure agreements are included in their contracts of employment to make sure that they do not disclose to any person or organisation, anything they may come across in the course of their job.

Access rights

Access rights are a facility offered by most local area network software which enables users to set rights to their directories, subdirectories and even individual files. This allows, for instance, a company's accounts to be accessed only by certain authorised people, like the company accountant. It is possible to allocate certain users 'read only status' meaning that although they can view the contents of a file, they are not allowed to make any alterations. Access rights for on-line files were covered in Chapter 1.

Recovery and restoration of data

Since data is so important to a company's operations, the loss of the data due to fire, flood, terrorist bomb attack or any other cause may mean serious disruption unless the data is restored to its original condition very quickly. All companies are sensible enough to keep backup

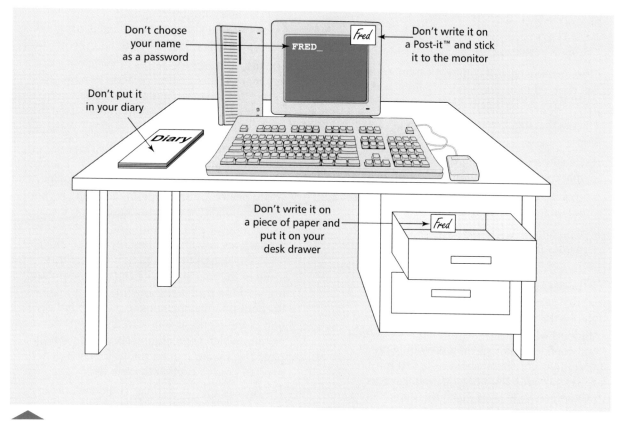

Figure 2.7 *Places not to hide your password and advice about passwords*

copies, but many of them still need to be sure that the backups can be used to re-create the original data, and the staff involved need to have regular practice at doing this. In some cases the hardware, software and data can be destroyed together. This actually happened to an insurance company's main computer centre in Manchester as a result of the bomb attack on the nearby Arndale Centre. During the attack, 600 pieces of computer equipment were destroyed, but the company had a contract with a data recovery organisation that held hardware from which the backup files from the insurance company could be recovered. By moving staff to another office, not far away, not a single day of trading was lost.

Answering an essay-style examination question

In A level Information Technology you will need to be able to write short, essay-style answers on a variety of IT-related issues and developments. The following section will give you some pointers as to how to answer essay questions.

Every word in the question is important, so you need to read it carefully, several times, and it is a good idea to underline the main words or terms.

The examiner will have a marking scheme that lists a series of points for which marks may be gained. You need to make sure that your answer covers as many of these points as possible. The facts are what you are marked on, not the flowery prose in-between, so bear this in mind when constructing your sentences and remember that you are being tested primarily on your knowledge of IT. Although the English used should be good, the facts are the important part. Use the mark scheme provided to help you divide your time between the parts of the question. If a two-part question has parts (a) and (b), and part (a) has five marks allocated to it while part (b) attracts up to ten marks, you need to spend twice as long (and write twice as much) on part (b).

Try to structure your answers. It is a good idea to write down a list of subheadings for each part of your essay and then write an equal amount under each.

Activity

'The development of communication systems has enabled individuals, organisations and society to operate on a global basis.'

Discuss this statement. Include in your discussion:

- specific examples of facilities and/or tasks that make use of communication systems
- specific examples of applications that make use of these facilities and/or tasks
- the communication technology and/or techniques that have enabled this development.

(20 marks)

(NEAB, Module IT01, Specimen Paper, q3)

Notice the word 'discuss' in the question. Many students when answering this type of question will confuse the word 'discuss' with 'write everything you know about ... '; you must avoid this error. Imagine you are talking to someone who has just made the statement. You are free to agree or disagree with them, but for this question you obviously need to agree with them, since the growth of communication systems has clearly enabled us to operate on a global basis. Having decided on this, you can now start looking at the rest of the question.

It is quite hard to provide a model answer for this type of question; it is a good idea to practice this sort of question and then pass each other's answers around to compare them. Although some of the content will be the same, you may have watched different TV programmes, read different newspapers and magazines and have had different experiences of communication systems, so what you are able to write will differ. Try to share each other's ideas. If you see anything relevant take a copy and pass it to your teacher/lecturer who can then photocopy it and distribute it to the rest of the group.

Basically, the question is divided into three parts, with each part probably carrying equal marks, so you will need to spend the same time and write about equal amounts on each part.

At a glance, the three parts of the question are fairly similar and there is a serious danger when answering one part of covering the answer to one of the other parts. It is therefore imperative

to look carefully at each word and it is a good idea to underline all key words.

The first part asks for details of facilities/tasks that make use of communication systems. This means that anything you mention here has to be to do with sending data from one place to another using cables, as in a small network, the telephone lines, ISDN lines, fibre optic lines, satellite or radio links.

It is a good idea to jot down a few key points to cover, before starting your answer. You can put these in pencil, next to the question on the examination paper. Because the marks offered for each section in the question are not indicated at the side of the question it is likely that some of the marks are allocated for presentation and the overall argument put forward. Because the marking scheme gives no indication of the marks, it is best to divide the 20 equally, which gives around six marks for each part. This means that six points for each part need to be discussed in the answer.

The answer for the first part could include any six of the following tasks/facilities:

Facilities

- electronic mail – internally over a LAN/WAN or externally on the Internet
- intranet – Internet technology used for an internal network
- teletext – (TV signal-transmitted information service)
- videoconferencing – using computers to transmit real-time audio/video/data
- telecommuting – using access to remote databases, electronic mail, videoconferencing to do work from home
- bulletin boards
- chat lines
- closed user groups (usually available to groups of people with a certain occupation or interest)
- electronic data interchange (EDI) – organisations exchanging data electronically rather than using paper documents

Tasks

- Research use – using company/organisation databases, on-line reference material (dictionaries, encyclopaedias, etc.), on-line libraries, etc.

- commercial use – to get latest software release information, for software support, for on-line user support

For the application areas, look at the answers you have put for the first part.

The answer to the second part could include any six of the following application areas:

- finance – insurance companies doing on-line quotes over the Internet, banks using ATMs (automated teller machines/cash dispensers), being able to perform on-line home banking
- environmental – remote weather stations sending data back to the weather centre computer, flood warning systems, pollution monitoring systems, computer controlled and co-ordinated traffic control systems, etc.
- marketing – conducting meetings using videoconferencing equipment for a new product launch, using the Internet for research to access government statistics
- retail – using the Internet to order goods on-line, shops exchanging data automatically with their suppliers (i.e. using EDI), retail customers using EFT (electronic fund transfer) such as Switch, using a terminal for credit card payment/authorisation
- manufacturing – producing goods directly according to customers' orders, process control in breweries, chemical plants, etc.

In part three, the communications technology and/or techniques that have enabled these developments would need to relate to the answers in the first and second parts of the question and could include some of the following:

- open systems integration (OSI) enables computers of different makes and technologies to communicate with each other
- the use of satellite links when sending data from one continent to another
- modems used to allow data to be passed along the ordinary telephone lines

- ISDN links which provide a faster and higher bandwidth than telephone lines
- private, leased lines to provide a secure link between systems
- LANs linking to WANs via a gateway
- the use of protocols which allow different computers to communicate with each other.

In your discussion of the above you could also mention some of the drawbacks with the technology as part of a counter argument, and these could include:

- problems of sending secure data over public lines when banking or shopping over the Internet
- incompatibility between machines
- the danger of a virus spreading throughout an organisation
- worries about computer hackers getting access to sensitive data.

Here is a recent, actual examination question which requires an essay-style answer, similar in format to the above question. Use the advice given to help you answer it.

'Networked computer systems (e.g. Internet) will revolutionise the way in which we shop.'

With the aid of specific examples, discuss this statement. Include in your discussion:

- the types of organisation likely to advertise on such systems
- the capabilities and limitation of such systems for this activity
- the potential security risks for the customers in using such systems
- the organisational impact of such systems
- the social impact of such systems.

(20)

(NEAB, Module IT01, May 1997, q9)

TASKS

KEY SKILLS IT2.1, IT3.1

Scenario 1: Proposed newspaper article on IT

Your local weekly paper is going to run a series of articles about new technology and how it might be useful to their readers. Since these articles will be published in the paper in the run up to Christmas, they will also help parents who may be in the process of buying computers for the first time for themselves or their children. The articles are to be made as interesting as possible and provide plenty of factual information. Since many of the readers of the article will have had little or no experience of the technology in the article, the editor has specified that the article must be written in such a way as to make it accessible to all the readers and not just those who already know about IT. This means that any technical terms will need to be explained, and it is no use explaining a technical term using another technical term that has not yet been explained.

The Internet: is it useful or all hype?

TASK 1

As a bright student of IT and in touch with all the latest developments in home computing, the newspaper editor has contacted you to write an article on the Internet entitled 'The Internet: is it useful or all hype?'. The main aims of the article are as follows:

- to explain what the Internet is
- to explain what equipment and software is needed to gain access to the Internet and typically what costs are involved
- to explain what interesting things can be done using the Internet.

Your task is to produce an interesting and informative article for inclusion in the paper in no more than 1000 words.

DEBRIEF

The bulleted points should have provided a framework. Did you remember to cover all the points mentioned? One thousand words is quite short for an article containing such a large amount of factual information. Did you manage to stick to this limit? In real life it is usual to have limits imposed on your work, either in terms of time taken or the amount of work involved.

TASK 2

The editor of the newspaper was very pleased with the feedback received from the paper's readers and she has now asked you to write a follow-up article covering the following:

- to suggest what a parent, worried about some of the material available (e.g. pornography), can do to prevent their child accessing it
- to suggest how the system can help children in their schooling

- to come up with a series of interesting websites which may help children with their education (you will need to include the web addresses of these sites and mention the type of material they hold).

DEBRIEF

Access to unsavoury material is a real deterrent when parents are thinking of arranging access to the Internet. Did you manage to research this using the Internet itself or did you use material from computer magazines? Many computer magazines are now on the Internet. Most of the access restrictors are software based, filtering out on the basis of certain words, but are there any other methods? For example, parents could sit with their children and access the Internet with them. They could remove the modem cable which would enable access only when they were there.

Did you mention that there are many on-line dictionaries, atlases, encyclopaedias, books, etc. which can be used for research into any projects they might have to do?

Did you also mention that there is a lot of educational software available that you can use to teach young children how to spell or to learn their multiplication tables? And that such software is free!

There are many educational sites. You may have taken a route which involved gathering the web addresses from a directory of Internet sites, but really, since your article is going into a newspaper to be read by large numbers of people, you need to make sure that such sites actually exist and that they have not been replaced by ones containing unsavoury material.

Useful Internet sites

- The British Telecommunication ISDN site is on:

  http:www.isdn.bt.com

- Information on the development of telematics and teleworking is available on the following sites:

  Telework, Telecottage and Telecentre Association website:

  www.tca.org.uk

  European Telework Online website:

  www.eto.org.uk

1 The illegal use of computer systems is sometimes known as computer-related crime.

(a) Give **three** distinct examples of computer-related crime. *(3)*

(b) Give **three** steps that can be taken to help prevent computer-related crime. *(3)*

(NEAB, Module IT01, Specimen Paper, q4)

2 A large company has introduced a communication system which includes electronic mail. This system will be used for internal use within the company and for external links to other organisations.

(a) Describe **two** features of an electronic mail system which may encourage its use for internal communication between colleagues. *(2)*

(b) Contrast the use of an electronic mail system with each of fax and the telephone. *(6)*

(c) Describe **two** functions the communication system might have, other than the creation and reception of messages. *(4)*

(NEAB, Module IT01, May 1997, q7)

3 A multi-national company is considering the use of 'teleconferencing'.

(a) What is meant by the term 'teleconferencing'? *(3)*

(b) List the minimum facilities required to enable 'teleconferencing' to take place. *(4)*

(c) Discuss **two** advantages and **two** disadvantages to the firm of using 'teleconferencing' as compared to traditional methods. *(4)*

(NEAB, Module IT01, May 1997, q5)

4 A company equips its sales staff with portable notebook computers. The IT department feels that a set of 'procedures' is required to ensure the integrity of the data and software held on the notebooks.

Suggest **four** different items that the company might include in its set of procedures. *(4)*

(NEAB, Module IT01, May 1997, q7)

5 A multi-national organisation maintains an information technology system which holds a large amount of vital and sensitive data.

(a) Describe **three** steps which should be taken to protect the data against deliberate theft or corruption. *(6)*

(b) Describe **three** steps which should be taken to protect the data against accidental loss. *(6)*

(NEAB, Module IT01, May 1996, q4)

6 Recent changes in communications technology have resulted in a blurring of the distinction between telecommunications and computing. Information services are starting to be provided on what is becoming known as the Information Super Highway (ISH).

(a) State the minimum facilities needed to gain access to these services. *(3)*

(b) Identify and briefly describe **three** types of information service you would expect to find when linked to the ISH. *(2)*

(NEAB, Module IT01, May 1998, q3)

7 Many market research firms use questionnaires as a means of gathering raw data for companies about the popularity of their products.

(a) Explain why information technology is widely used in market research. *(4)*

(b) Once the data has been collected, it can be used to give the clients information about their products. Explain the difference between information and data in this context. *(4)*

(NEAB, Module IT01, May 99, q4)

The Impact of IT

The role of information technology

Information technology has brought about many changes, which affect individuals, organisations and society, and in this section we investigate some of them.

The effect on the individual

There are many ways in which IT systems affect the individual, many of them by changing patterns and types of work. Most jobs now require some IT skills; employers expect potential employees to have them. It is for this reason that IT has become a compulsory subject within the National Curriculum, and is studied by all schoolchildren. As time goes on, these IT-literate people will filter through to the workforce and there will be fewer people without basic skills in wordprocessing, spreadsheets, etc.

Reduced numbers of manual jobs

Many traditional manual jobs, where few skills are needed, have now been replaced by computer-controlled machines. Assembly work on production lines, warehouse work where stock is moved from one place to another, and paint spraying are examples of tasks that have now been replaced by computer-controlled equipment such as robots and computer-controlled fork lift trucks.

De-skilling (or even elimination) of some office jobs

The number of people working in some areas of office work has been much reduced or even eliminated. Filing clerks, who kept files in a central registry and logged them in and out (rather like dealing with books in a library), have gone. Databases and data warehouses are now widely used instead, coupled with networks allowing terminals to access a common pool of data.

Another job which has changed is that of the typist. Before the introduction of wordprocessors, a typist's job was highly skilled because the words went straight onto the page and if a mistake were made (such as a word or line missed out) this could necessitate re-typing a whole document. With the use of a wordprocessor, a small amount of knowledge and a few keyboard skills, anyone can produce a letter that looks professional. This has certainly de-skilled the job of producing documents and has meant that many people prefer to produce their own. The same can be said of typesetting, since desktop publishing packages allow novice users to produce work closer to a professional standard.

The creation of new and more interesting jobs

The employment outlook is not all bleak. Many more interesting and highly skilled jobs are being created. These jobs within the computer industry include those involving developing new systems (systems analysts, programmers, software engineers), jobs for people who keep the systems working (network managers, computer operators, database administrators, engineers), those for people who design and build the hardware and those who provide a service (help desk staff, trainers, and people who contribute to the plethora of books and magazines to do with IT).

Many staff who would in the past have been involved in routine clerical tasks, can now do these tasks in much less time using IT methods. This leaves them more time for more interesting and profitable tasks, such as talking to customers, developing marketing campaigns, etc.

Reduced number of manual jobs

The opportunity of working from home

THE EFFECT ON THE INDIVIDUAL

De-skilling or even elimination of some office jobs

Increased unemployment

The creation of new and interesting jobs

The opportunity to work for yourself

The need to continually up-date skills

Figure 3.1 *The effect of IT on the individual*

The opportunity to work from home

People who work using computers need only a telephone and a personal computer, or a terminal, to gain access to their company's database. This has enabled more people to work from home and this 'teleworking' offers some people many advantages including:

- flexibility regarding the times they work

- the opportunity to live wherever they want

- such jobs are ideal for disabled people or people who have to look after young children

- there are no expenses involved in travelling, but household bills may rise.

Teleworking/telecommuting will be looked at in greater detail later in this chapter.

Increased unemployment

Although many new IT-related jobs replace less skilled jobs, there is no doubt that jobs created are fewer than those lost. This should cause a net rise in unemployment, with its associated social problems.

The need continually to up-date skills

Very few people starting work in a certain job will still be doing the same job in 20 years' time. Because of the pace of change in the technology, the nature of jobs changes and this necessitates staff re-training or updating their skills.

The opportunity to work for yourself

There are many opportunities for computer staff to work for themselves (i.e. to become self-employed). Many companies prefer to take on contract workers for a fixed period on a self-employed basis. Many people, particularly those whose skills are in demand, prefer this method of working and the salaries they can earn are particularly enticing. There are drawbacks in that they become responsible for the payment of their own tax and National Insurance contributions and there is always the possibility that when one contract ends, they may not have another one to go to.

The effect on organisations

Organisations are groups of people working towards a common purpose or goal; the term therefore includes businesses, factories, government departments, hospitals and schools. All of these organisations will be affected by the introduction of IT systems and some of the effects are listed below:

- Increased use of teleworking makes management of the workers more difficult, especially if they are working at home. Some managers see this as a threat to their position as more work becomes unsupervised.
- Companies have no control over the security of computer equipment in staff homes.
- Increased use of telecommunications means an organisation is more vulnerable to hacking.
- More staff are freed to work from home, so Health and Safety requirements are less of a problem (although legislation may change to take account of this).
- On-line costs associated with the increased communications traffic have to be met.
- Office costs are reduced (rental, heating, lighting, cleaning, office equipment, etc).
- Although teleworkers may become more productive they become less creative, as they are not able to bounce ideas off each other. Videoconferencing systems are one way around this.
- Staff working in an office may feel disgruntled when they see their colleagues being able to work from home and this could cause friction between the two groups.

The effect on society

The increased use of IT has a variety of effects on society as a whole and these include:

- Increased leisure time – in many countries the increased use of IT has meant that more work can be done in less time and this has led to a reduction in the length of the working week and an increase in leisure time. This time may be used by people to spend time with their families or to take part in the wide variety of leisure activities. Organisations involved in these leisure activities will grow as leisure time increases.
- Deserted city centres – many people may take part in home shopping over the Internet and this will lead to fewer shops in the city centres which could become isolated as more and more traditional shops close down.
- Never off the job – as teleworking becomes more popular, people will tend to sleep and work in the same place, free to work their own hours; they may feel that they are 'never off the job' and this could lead to stress.
- Increased stress at home – teleworking could lead to arguments and stress in families since the person who is teleworking may be expected to do household chores when they are at home all day.
- Equality for disadvantaged people – working from home will be a boon to handicapped people who can now compete on equal terms with the able bodied.
- Lack of privacy – as more IT systems are used, more data is collected about each of us, and whole profiles of our lifestyle are built up which could seriously erode our privacy.

There are many examples of everyday tasks that we do and take for granted but would not be possible without the use of IT. Many other tasks were performed before the use of IT was so common, but took much longer to do.

Activity

There are many tasks that use IT and would be impossible without it. Can you list twenty such tasks? Here are a few to start you off:

1 electronic mail

2 accurate weather forecasting

3 the use of debit cards such as SWITCH.

There are many ways in which IT or IT-related products have changed how we spend our leisure time. Many of these products incorporate chips (another name for microprocessors) in their construction.

From getting up in the morning to getting to school or college you will come across many things which depend on IT in some way. Write a list of them, and for each one, write down how IT has improved the operation of the device (if it existed before) or the use to which it is put if it is a new device.

The individual's dependence on IT systems

We all, to some extent, depend on IT systems in our everyday life. Here are some ways in which IT helps us or others.

- The time needed to do routine chores such as getting money out of your account, shopping, booking a holiday, making an insurance claim, etc. has been considerably reduced.

- Computer-controlled scanners and imaging systems used in hospitals have saved many lives.

- Cars are designed and made safer using the results of computerised modelling of accidents.

- Computer-controlled traffic and car parking systems reduce the time it takes to make journeys. In an emergency situation, the traffic lights along a certain route can all be set on green so emergency vehicles have a clear path through, thus saving valuable time.

- Computer-controlled motorway signs inform drivers of accidents, fog, ice, etc.

- Flood warning systems monitor the weather conditions and water level in rivers. These measurements are input to a computer model that then predicts the likelihood of low-lying areas being flooded.

- Computer-controlled braking systems, fitted on many cars, control braking in the event of an emergency stop, and stop the car going into a skid. This reduces the distance needed to stop the car and can therefore save lives.

- Many people store on computers all their personal data such as their letters, schedules, appointments, contacts and customers, personal friends' details, etc. Loss of any of these causes great annoyance and inconvenience.

- Many electric devices in the home use chips as part of their control mechanism and this makes them more 'intelligent', meaning they can operate with less human intervention. Modern toasters, washing machines, dishwashers, tumble dryers, central heating and hot water systems and burglar alarms all contain them. Take a tumble dryer, for instance. With the older tumble dryers you would simply decide how many minutes the damp washing should be spun for. This was very much a guess and necessitated having to go back to machine to see if the washing was still damp and needed to be put back for a bit longer. When the washing was dry, it may have been dry for some time, wasting energy in tumbling already dry washing. The latest dryers sense how much washing is in the drum and when it is dry. There are many other instances where life in the home has been made much easier by the use of IT.

- Advances in telecommunications have also made us more dependent. Loss of the telephone system, for even a short period, causes great inconvenience.

Organisational dependence on IT systems

Many organisations such as banks, building societies, the police, air traffic control, shops and so on, are very dependent on their IT resources, and the loss of their use, even for a couple of hours, can cost them millions of pounds. Worse still, in some situations it endangers lives.

Picture this situation. It is a Saturday morning in a large, out-of-town supermarket. All the tills (POS terminals) are in operation and there are a couple of customers at each one, each with a trolley full of shopping. Suddenly the network fails. Workmen digging up the road have cut one of the cables between the store and the main computer so they are unable to communicate with each other. What does the shop do? The manager of the store does not know whether the loss will last a couple of minutes or several hours. If they do not want to lose custom they need to act quickly. They cannot ask customers to wait, as many of the customers will have frozen food in their trolleys that will defrost. Their only option is to get each customer to give them a notional amount, say £20 for the goods in their trolley. This will please the customers but could cost the store tens of thousands of pounds if the network is out of action for a considerable period of time. You can see how dependent some organisations are on their IT system.

Consequences of the failure of IT systems

National Health Service IT systems are used not just for the administration of the hospital but also in equipment connected directly to patients. Such computer-controlled systems include equipment for monitoring the heart, dialysis machines and intensive care cots for babies born prematurely. Many hospitals have computer-controlled lifts including the ones used to carry patients to and from operating theatres. Lastly there is the hospital administration system, which although it will cause chaos if it fails, will not put patients lives directly in danger.

Society's dependence on IT

Many jobs, taken for granted and considered essential to modern living, would be impossible to perform without the use of IT. Here are just a few of them:

- Computer-controlled traffic light systems ensure that the traffic flow in towns and cities is smooth and our journey times are kept to a minimum. Fewer stationary and slow moving vehicles mean better use of fuel and less pollution.

- Accurate weather forecasting may mean that you know to cancel the barbecue which you planned for the weekend, but for deep sea fishermen, or people who work on oil rigs, the forecast can be a matter of life and death.

- When you make a 999 call you are put through to a 'command and control centre' where the emergency services co-ordinate all the activities. These systems enable the

maximum use of the resources available and ensure that a quick response is made to emergency calls.

- Credit cards, cash cards and debit cards enable us to be flexible and avoid us having to carry large sums of money around. Computers and communications systems are essential to these card services, which we depend on all the time.

- When you go into a supermarket you assume they will always have the goods you need, whatever the time of the day. This was not always the case; shops sometimes used to sell out of essential items such as bread early in the morning. The use of accurate sales-based ordering, and accurate forecasting using computers, has meant that shops now seldom sell out of goods.

- When you are travelling at 500 knots on a plane sharing the airspace with other planes travelling in different directions, you are dependent on computerised navigation systems on the aircraft and on the ground. Computerised air traffic control systems ensure that the aircraft are kept a safe distance apart. Computer controlled 'fly-by-wire' systems used in many modern aircraft help make flying safer, since they do not allow pilots to make manoeuvres that would place the aircraft in a dangerous situation.

- Computer-controlled patient monitoring systems in intensive care units ensure that medical staff are alerted should measurements of the patient's heartbeat, temperature and respiration stray outside certain limits.

The social impact of information technology

The advantages and disadvantages of information technology

When discussing the social implications of IT and communications technology it is necessary to look at both the benefits and the drawbacks in using IT.

☑ **Advantages**

1 Increased productivity means less wastage and more efficient use of resources.

2 Countries that make the most of IT usually have the highest standards of living in the world.

3 Many safety-critical systems make use of IT. Industrial processes, traffic control systems, control systems in aircraft all use IT to minimise the effect of human error on their operation.

4 Shorter working weeks free up more leisure time.

5 You can use the Internet to chat to people all around the world for the price of just a local telephone call.

6 Huge amounts of material on all subjects are available via the Internet which can be accessed from the comfort of your own home.

7 Use of IT enables some workers to telework.

8 There are many IT products available for disabled people. For example, there is a talking global positioning system which allows blind people to find out where they are.

9 Highly skilled jobs in computing are being created all the time, in areas such as programming, software engineering, network management, database administration, etc.

✗ Disadvantages

1 Total reliance on information technology has meant that when these systems are not available, another system needs to be in place until the IT system can be restored.

2 The use of IT widens the gap between richer and poorer countries. Many poorer countries do not have the expertise or money to invest, and these countries fall further behind.

3 Older people can feel isolated because they do not understand these new systems and feel they are too old to learn.

4 Because of the Internet, many people feel they are bombarded with too many items of information (called information overload).

5 The pace of technology moves forward so quickly that people do not have any period of stability: they are continually being asked to learn new systems.

6 Life without IT is slower and less stressful.

7 There are health problems (eyesight problems, repetitive strain injury, etc.) that can occur through working with computers.

8 Individual privacy is being eroded as more and more data about people is stored on databases.

9 Fewer less skilled jobs are available as many jobs are now performed using IT equipment.

10 Problems have arisen with young people being addicted to computer games or surfing the Internet.

11 It is much easier to access unsavoury material using the Internet.

12 Excessive use of computers can lead to a sedentary lifestyle with the associated health problems due to lack of exercise.

Activity

For the A level information examination, you are required to know about the potential impact of information technology in the following areas:

business	manufacturing
industry	commerce
medicine	home
education	crime

Your task is to research all of the above areas except for crime, which has been outlined in the next section to give you an idea of the sort of information required.

Crime

In this section we look at the impact of information technology systems in the fight against crime. The Police Information Technology Organisation (PITO) co-ordinates the information needs of all police forces in the UK. In particular, it deals with nationally held information.

At the heart of the PITO system are the following elements:

- The police national computer (PNC) provides 24-hour access to around 55 million records.

- The national automated fingerprint system provides 24-hour access to over 5 million records.

- The police secure radio communication project will eventually provide all the police forces with digital radios rather than the analogue ones currently used, which have the major disadvantage that they are very easy to hack into. This organisation is on the look out for any new technology likely to help the police.

Police IT systems can be divided into two groups: those used to prevent crime and those used to detect crime once it has been committed.

Crime prevention

1   Speed cameras and red light cameras are used to prevent accidents.

2   Surveillance is used to deter violent crime in cities.

3   Tagging of people on bail deters them from re-offending.

4   Tagging systems for goods, such as bikes, cars, etc., prevents them being stolen.

Crime detection

1   The police national computer is used to record the details of all crimes committed.

2   The national criminal intelligence is used to piece together information about individual criminals and illegal activities. The computer can interact with data supplied by Interpol, the PNC, Customs and Excise, the Inland Revenue and all the main banks. Using these sources together, information can be gathered on international organised crime, such as drug smuggling.

3   Computer systems for DNA profiling and fingerprinting enable conclusive evidence to be obtained.

4   Individual police headquarters' computers are used in the day-to-day administration involved when solving crimes.

Problems with the PNC and the other police IT systems

1   Illegal access to the PNC means that police officers or civilians can use the system for their own gain.

2   There are fears that the PNC will be privatised. The PNC stores criminal records, details of wanted or dangerous people, disqualified drivers, stolen cars and guns, and also the records of 30 million motorists. Some files indicate that people are HIV-positive. In addition details of 70,000 individuals of 'long-term interest' are also kept. The system also holds comments and information (amounting to little more than suspicion) about people who may have been involved in criminal activity.

The main concern is that the public might not give information to a private organisation since they may not think that the data is secure once the police are no longer looking after it. It could therefore be harder to gain vital prosecution evidence from witnesses.

The impact of technology on the location and patterns of work

For most people the only choice of workplace is either the office or the factory floor. Many people would prefer to live in a different part of the country, so it makes sense, if possible, for employers to satisfy this demand. If you talk to employees of a company you might find that many of them travel long distances to work each day, especially if they are commuting to the centre of a large city such as London. Clearly, it is wasteful for people to spend time getting to and from work. There is also the environmental aspect to consider. When cars are stationary in traffic they produce more exhaust fumes to pollute the atmosphere and valuable resources, such as petrol, are being consumed.

With the increased use of technology it is possible for many workers, especially those employed to do administrative tasks, to work from home and avoid travelling. Developments that have made this possible include the decrease in costs of communication and the increased use of networks that help share work.

IT developments that have enabled more people to work from home include:

- e-mail

- fax

- the Internet

- data warehouses (where an organisation's data is all kept in a huge, single database)

- videoconferencing

- high speed data links (e.g. fibre optic cables, satellite communication links, etc.).

Activity

There are many computer-related jobs in which working from home is possible. In some cases meetings might be needed from time to time, but this can be done using videoconferencing equipment.

For this activity you have to put an 'H' next to the following jobs where you think they are more suited to working from home:

- writing of software user guides
- help desk/user support
- programming
- systems analysis
- network management
- web page designing
- computer training; a tutor who travels around the country, training users at their premises.

Advantages and disadvantages of working from home

The advantages of working from home can be divided into three groups; advantages to the employer, advantages to the employee and those advantages which apply to both. There are also some disadvantages.

✔ Advantages to the employee

- no travel costs
- no time wasted travelling to work
- no time needed to get ready in the morning (you can work all day in your pyjamas if you really want to)
- more flexible working arrangements (you can work to fit around any commitments you might have, such as looking after children, elderly relatives, etc.)
- more opportunities for the disabled who find difficulty in travelling
- less stress (no late trains, traffic jams, etc.)

✔ Advantages to the employer

For teleworking/telecommuting to work, there must be clear advantages to the employer. The main advantages are as follows:

- smaller offices are needed, so fewer backup staff (cleaners, caretakers, etc.) are required and rates will be cheaper
- reduced overheads in maintaining an office; such overheads would normally include heating, lighting, canteen facilities, equipment (desks, chairs, filing cabinets)

- employers can employ people on the basis of productivity (i.e. by the number of orders processed, letters sent, etc.)
- working from home may make the staff more motivated; they might feel that the employer is fitting around their personal circumstances more or that it is a more entrepreneurial way of working
- there is no need to employ people just in the locality; if there is a skill shortage the employer is able to look further afield
- staff are less likely to spend time off sick
- it is possible to extend the working day, since some staff might prefer to work evenings at home
- bureaucracy can be minimised
- there is more flexibility in working hours; as long as the job is done it will not matter to the employer how long it has taken
- employers do not need to worry about Health and Safety issues as much
- homeworking enables firms to provide customer service at a lower cost.

✘ Disadvantages to the employer

There are a few disadvantages for employers in allowing workers to telecommute, including:

- a change to the employer's organisational structure might be needed in order to accommodate telework
- staff are given more freedom and it is more difficult to determine how hard they are working
- it is more difficult to organise emergency meetings
- the use of telecommunications might leave the firm more vulnerable to security breaches, such as the spread of computer viruses or hacking
- employers need to pay for office equipment and computer hardware and software for the employee's home
- telecommunications costs will be a lot higher.

✘ Disadvantages to the employee

Although working from home has its attractions, it may not suit everyone. Here are just some of the disadvantages:

- there may be a feeling of isolation

- if they are paid by the amount of work they do, employers may get the feeling that they are a slave to the computer

- many employers could use the opportunity to pay workers less, particularly since these workers are often not in unions

- some workers will be on short-term contracts with the associated lack of job security that this kind of works brings

- some employees may have the feeling that they never 'go home' since the boundary between home and the office does not exist

- the employee may find it difficult to create a quiet place in their home where they can work without being disturbed

- some senior staff may experience a loss of status; no smart offices, no secretaries, no company car, etc.

Effects on society of telecommuting

There are some effects on society as a whole in telecommuting and these include:

- reduced traffic congestion as fewer people travel to work

- air pollution is reduced as fewer car journeys are made

- prosperity is spread around the UK rather than concentrating in the commuter belts near large cities.

Read the following case study that looks at a person who has changed from being an office-based worker to a telecommuter.

CASE STUDY

Telecommuting

Paul Hughes works in software support for a software house which has clients all around the country and the world. The company specialises in stock control systems for the large DIY chains.

Paul used to spend two hours in the morning and evening commuting to and from the company's central London office. Now he is able to take up his love of animals by fitting the running of a small farm on a remote Scottish island around his computing job. Paul is able to provide users with help over the phone; he is able to sign onto his own company's computer system as well as the customer's. He still keeps in touch with his manager using a videoconferencing link and he also uses this to keep in touch with colleagues who do a similar job to his own. Paul agrees his milestones (dates certain parts of a long project have to be completed by) with his manager and finds the whole arrangement motivating. He has no problem in getting the work done. He particularly likes the idea of working on a job-by-job basis, and that as long as the work is done, if he works hard he can get it done quickly, leaving more time for him to spend running his farm or doing a variety of recreational activities.

Activity

Some jobs might be performed equally well from a home base or an office provided that the home contains the latest IT equipment. Answer the following questions.

1 A journalist writes primarily about football, works for a newspaper, but also writes material for some specialist football magazines. At the moment she works from the newspaper's headquarters in central London, but due to commuting problems has decided to work from home.

    She will need to buy a range of computer hardware and software to enable her to do this. Your task is to outline what she will need to buy.

2 Some jobs, such as journalism in part 1, are ideally suited to telecommuting while others are not. For this task you have to decide which of the following list are most suited. Once you have made your choice you need to explain why they are especially suited to telecommuting.

    - computer programmer
    - nurse
    - staff employed who deal with customer complaints for a washing machine manufacturer

- librarian
- chartered accountant working on his client's accounts
- software support staff on a help desk which deals with customer questions
- telesales person who cold calls potential customers and tries to get orders
- insurance salesman
- stock control clerk in a factory
- factory production worker.

Information and the professional: social, moral and ethical issues associated with the introduction of IT

Social issues

De-skilling of certain jobs

Take the example of a typist. Typing on an ordinary typewriter is a skilled job since mistakes are not easily rectified and the presence of too many can necessitate typing the whole document again. Using the wordprocessor means that many staff who were not competent typists can now correct their mistakes so easily that their documents can look as professional as those of a typist. The net effect is that typing work is now done by everyone at their desks rather than by a specialist typist.

Using a combination of hardware and software, many of the skills needed to do certain tasks are no longer needed and non-specialists can now master desk-top publishing, drawing packages, etc. after relatively little training.

More flexibility in the workforce

In the past there would have been clear distinctions about who did what in the workplace and each person had a clearly defined role. Employers now need a workforce with much more flexibility and it is common to find rotas where a person changes their duties many times in one day. For example, they might spend a few hours on reception dealing with visitors, then some time on the switchboard and then some time inputting customer's orders into the firm's database system. This adds to their job interest and from the company's point of view means that if a receptionist were off sick then there would be several staff who could cover for them.

Moral issues

People's morals might appear to change when they use computers; and sometimes they do not even seem to be aware of moral issues in this context.

For example, many people who would never dream of taking goods from a shop without paying for them, think nothing of copying an expensive software package costing thousands of pounds, thus depriving the developer of the revenue. If everyone did this there would be no incentive for people to invest their time and money in developing new products.

Hacking is another example. Many computer staff like to hear about how someone has managed to hack into a supposedly secure system and looked at the confidential information stored. They would not be so pleased if the same person broke into their home or office and starting rooting through their private papers, though. Even more interesting are stories of hackers breaking into bank computers and using the system to transfer large amounts of money to their own accounts. Some computer staff say that if a system is not secure then it deserves to be broken into. They say it is rather like leaving your front door open and then wondering why someone has stolen your possessions.

Read the following article.

Alleged super-hacker awaits trial

A Russian computer hacker has been extradited to the US following the largest ever theft over the Internet. The alleged theft from the American bank Citibank was for 6.25 million pounds. The accused hacker has pleaded not guilty to the charges of bank fraud, computer fraud and conspiracy. He was arrested in Britain and then extradited to the US where he is awaiting trial.

The hacker is accused of stealing money from Citibank branches around the world and then transferring the funds to bank accounts set up by accomplices in countries such as Germany, Switzerland, Finland, California, Israel and Holland. It is claimed that the hacker was able to put the money into these accounts using his home computer connected to the Internet, without once leaving his house in Russia.

This case is apparently the only known example of online bank robbery although experts believe that many such cases have occurred but have never been detected or reported. One of the problems the FBI face when dealing with bank thefts is that the banks are embarrassed by the thefts and prefer to conduct their own investigations using private security firms rather than go to the public law enforcement agencies.

The investigators in the case were concerned as to how the accused was able to obtain passwords and codes and how he was able to navigate his way through the sophisticated computer systems. They were concerned that there may have been some insider involvement although on further investigation this

was discovered not to be the case. The bank has also reported that all money stolen before it started monitoring the situation has been returned to the client accounts.

It is worrying that the accused may not have to face trial at all and could be offered a plea bargain instead in exchange for technical information as to how the alleged crime had been committed. Four of the people who are claimed to have helped him have been offered plea bargains by the US authorities.

This case is being followed by many financial institutions worried about computer crime and the security implications of using the Internet. They are particularly concerned that such cases raise the criminals to almost cult status in the eyes of some Internet users. These users are impressed by the technical knowledge needed to hack into very secure systems.

Activity

Read through the above article carefully and then answer the following question.

There are several moral issues in the above article. Can you say what they are and then explain each of them?

Ethical issues

Ethical issues surrounding the use of information technology generally focus on four

areas that we can refer to as PAPA for short. PAPA stands for:

- Privacy
- Accuracy
- Property
- Accessibility.

Privacy

How would you feel about the following:

- Corrupt police officers are ignoring security and confidentiality procedures and are selling details of car owners to private companies.

- A newsagent has its computer stolen, and from this thieves see when the papers for certain houses have been cancelled because the owners are away on holiday.

- Hospital staff, during a quiet period, decide to print out the medical records of all the people they know who have attended the hospital.

These are several of the many examples of organisations not being careful with your private information.

Accuracy

Mistakes are often made and can have far reaching consequences. For example, if you are allergic to certain medicines and the details are left out of your medical record, then if a doctor prescribes such a drug you could die as a result.

Other mistakes are not as serious. You could be refused credit because of a mistake on records held about you by credit referral agencies. It is imperative, therefore, that information held is accurate and that organisations takes appropriate steps to ensure the integrity of the data they hold.

Property

If you have developed a computer program during your time at work, who actually owns the copyright to the program? If your job is as a programmer and you have been paid as an employee for writing the program, then the company owns the program copyright. If you have developed the program in your own time at home, then you own it.

Accessibility

If information is kept about individuals, there needs to be proper security in place to ensure that only authorised personnel are allowed access to the system and this is normally done by the use of passwords.

The British Computer Society (BCS)

The British Computer Society is the professional body for people concerned with computing, which includes systems analysts, programmers, network managers, database designers, software engineers, etc. The society concerns itself with the developments in computing and the effective application of computing. It also promotes education and training, public awareness and sets standards of quality and professionalism for its members.

A summary of the activities of the British Computer Society is shown in Figure 3.2.

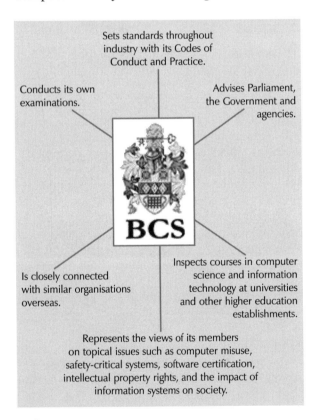

Sets standards throughout industry with its Codes of Conduct and Practice.

Conducts its own examinations.

Advises Parliament, the Government and agencies.

BCS

Is closely connected with similar organisations overseas.

Inspects courses in computer science and information technology at universities and other higher education establishments.

Represents the views of its members on topical issues such as computer misuse, safety-critical systems, software certification, intellectual property rights, and the impact of information systems on society.

Figure 3.2 *The main activities of the British Computer Society*

Code of Practice

The British Computer Society has a Code of Practice that is directed to all the members of the Society and concerns the minimum standards of practice to be observed by its members. Details of the code are shown below.

Personal requirements
The member should:

1.1 keep himself/herself, and subordinates, informed of such new technologies, practices, legal requirements and standards as are relevant to his/her duties

1.2 ensure subordinates are trained in order to be effective in their duties and to qualify for increased responsibilities

1.3 accept only such work as he/she believes he/she is competent to perform and not to hesitate to obtain additional expertise from appropriately qualified individuals where advisable

1.4 actively seek opportunities for increasing efficiency and effectiveness for the benefit of the user and of the ultimate recipient.

Organisation and management
The member should:

2.1 plan, establish and review objectives, tasks and organisational structures for himself/herself and subordinates, to help meet overall objectives

2.2 ensure that any specific tasks are assigned to identified individuals according to their known ability and competence

2.3 establish and maintain channels of communication from and to seniors, equals and subordinates

2.4 be accountable for the quality, timeliness and use of resources in the work for which he is responsible.

Contracting
The member should:

3.1 seek expert advice in the preparation of any formal contract

3.2 ensure that all requirements and the precise responsibility of all parties are adequately covered in any contract or tendering process.

Privacy, security and integrity
The member should:

4.1 ascertain and evaluate all potential risks in a particular project with regard to the cost, effectiveness and practicability of proposed levels of security

4.2 recommend appropriate levels of security, commensurate with the anticipated risks, and appropriate to the needs of the client

4.3 apply, monitor and report upon the effectiveness of the agreed level of security

4.4 ensure that all staff are trained to take effective action to protect life, data and equipment (in that order) in the event of disaster

4.5 take all reasonable measures to protect confidential information from inadvertent or deliberate improper access or use

4.6 ensure that competent people are assigned to be responsible for the accuracy and integrity of the data in the data file and each part of an organisation's database.

Codes of Practice and legal requirements

The British Computer Society is the professional body for computer professionals and there are many benefits and some status attached to being a member.

There is a variety of legal requirements when working with IT systems and these are enforceable by law; there are fines and even imprisonment for any deviations. The laws include the Computer Misuse Act and the Data Protection Act; the implications and penalties imposed are looked at in the next chapter.

There are several standards that any computer professional must maintain in order to be a member of the BCS and these are laid down in the BCS Code of Practice. The code is enforced by the BCS and any member who deviates from it can have their membership revoked. Because some employers know little about computing, it is difficult for them to know whether the person employed or contracted will be able to work to a professional standard. Membership of the BCS ensures that high standards of professionalism are maintained and this is why many employees prefer to take on BCS members and why it is advantageous to be a member.

Where Codes of Practice contain guidelines about the quality and standard of work a BCS member must maintain, they address some moral and ethical aspects of being a BCS member.

Code of Conduct

The British Computer Society issues a series of rules that members should observe during their professional careers. These rules make up the Code of Conduct which is divided under the headings:

- the public interest
- duty to employers and clients
- duty to the profession
- professional competence and integrity.

The public interest

1 Members shall in their professional practice safeguard public health and safety and have regard to protection of the environment.

2 Members shall have due regard to the legitimate rights of third parties.

3 Members shall ensure that within their chosen fields they have knowledge and understanding of relevant legislation, regulations and standards and that they comply with such requirements.

4 Members shall in their professional practice have regard to basic human rights and shall avoid any actions that adversely affect such rights.

Duty to employers and clients

5 Members shall carry out work with due care and diligence in accordance with the requirements of the employer or client and shall, if their professional judgement is overruled, indicate the likely consequences.

6 Members shall endeavour to complete work undertaken on time and to budget and shall advise their employer or client as soon as practicable if any overrun is foreseen.

7 Members shall not offer or provide, or receive in return, inducement for the introduction of business from a client unless their is full disclosure of the facts to the client.

8 Members shall not disclose, or authorise to be disclosed, or use for personal gain or to benefit a third part, confidential information acquired in the course of professional practice, except with prior permission of the employer or client, or at the direction of a court of law.

9 Members should seek to avoid being put in a position where they may become privy or party to activities which would conflict with their responsibilities in 1–4 above.

10 Members shall not misrepresent or withhold information on the capabilities of products, systems or services with which they are concerned or take advantage of the lack of knowledge or inexperience of others.

11 Members shall not, except where specifically so instructed, handle client's monies or place contracts or orders in connection for work on which they are engaged where acting as an independent consultant.

12 Members shall not purport to exercise independent judgement on behalf of a client on any product or service in which they knowingly have any interest, financial or otherwise.

Duty to the profession

13 Members shall uphold the reputation of the profession and shall seek to improve professional standards through participation in their development, use and enforcement, and shall avoid any action which will adversely affect the good standing of the Profession.

14 Members shall in their professional practice seek to advance public knowledge and understanding of computing and information systems and technology and to counter false or misleading statements which are detrimental to the profession.

15 Members shall encourage and support fellow members in their professional development and, where possible, provide opportunities for the professional development of new entrants to the Profession.

16 Members shall act with integrity towards fellow members and to members of other professions with whom they are concerned in a professional capacity and shall avoid engaging in any activity which is incompatible with professional status.

17 Members shall not make any public statements in their professional capacity unless properly qualified and, where appropriate, authorised to do so, and shall have due regard to the likely consequences of any statements on others.

Professional competence and integrity

18 Members shall seek to upgrade their professional knowledge and skill and shall maintain awareness of technological developments, procedures and standards which are relevant to their field, and shall encourage their subordinates to do likewise.

19 Members shall seek to conform to recognised good practice including quality standards which are in their judgement relevant, and shall encourage their subordinates to do likewise.

20 Members shall only offer to do work or to provide a service which is within their professional competence and shall not claim to any level of competence which they do not possess, and any professional opinion which they are asked to give shall be objective and reliable.

21 Members shall accept professional responsibility for their work and for the work of their subordinates and associates under their direction, and shall not terminate any assignment except for good reason and on reasonable notice.

22 Members shall avoid any situation that may give rise to a conflict of interest between themselves and their client and shall make full and immediate disclosure to the client if any conflict should occur.

Industry structure model

The British Computer Society's 'industry structure model' provides a set of performance standards for all staff working in information systems and in other related areas. The aim of this model is to aid in the recruitment, training and development of staff. The model was originally developed as a paper-based system, but it is now available to run on a PC or on a server over a network.

The industry structure model can be used for the following:

- to produce customised job descriptions from a series of standardised roles/tasks
- to assess the competence of information systems
- to establish individual and corporate training and development needs
- to provide training to recognised standards
- to plot career development paths.

The aim of the model is to provide an industry-wide standard and a career path for computer professionals. It consists of a framework showing the areas of work and levels of responsibility, and provides a way of mapping the level of a particular post to a job description and vice versa. The model does not depend on the particular staff structures or reporting structures of the

organisation employing the member of staff.

The British Computer Society website is at:

http://www.bcs.org.uk

TASKS

Investigation of the BCS website

The British Computer Society is the professional body set up for computer professionals and the Society seeks to set standards of professional, moral and ethical standards for its members. The idea is that people who employ a BCS member are safe in the knowledge of the competence of the member.

You are required to find out further details about the BCS from the BCS website at:

http://www.bcs.org.uk

In particular you will need to find out answers to the following:

- Why was the BCS set up?
- What levels of membership are there?
- Are they responsible for the setting of their own examinations and if so, what are they?

- In what ways can they help you get a job?
- What would happen to a member if they breached the Code of Conduct?

The BCS have produced a list of standards for the training and development of staff involved in IT, called the industry structure model. Outline what the industry structure model is and the reasons for its introduction.

It is important that computer professionals keep up to date with the latest developments in IT. What steps does the BCS take to help computer professionals keep up to date?

DEBRIEF

- Have you addressed all the issues in the above list?
- Make sure that you create a structure for your findings.

Contract work among computer professionals

Many computing facilities are now being outsourced, which means that the organisation contracts all its computing work to another company rather than using its own employees. This has had the effect of de-stabilising the jobs of many computer professionals who would have thought they had a job for life. Many of these now work on a self-employed basis, moving from one contract to the next. This often necessitates the contract worker moving around the country, so this discriminates against older workers who are more likely to have family commitments. It also discriminates against women who might have children to consider.

Although the rates for contract work are very high, these workers now have to make their provisions for training, pensions, tax, National Insurance and so on.

Why do computer departments use contract workers?

Some people involved in systems development are only usefully employed when new systems are being designed and implemented; if a system is not being installed or improved there is no work for them, although they remain on the payroll. Companies prefer to contract these workers on a job-by-job basis, as and when they are needed.

The benefit package to each employee on the payroll can be around 50 per cent of their salary, so someone who earns £20,000 a year could actually cost the company £30,000.

Contract workers are usually paid by the day, so if they do not work they do not get any money for that day. This means that contract workers usually have much better sickness records.

Disadvantages in using contract workers

Many contractors can earn very high salaries compared with their conventionally employed counterparts and resentment can build up when you get colleagues doing exactly the same job yet one is paid twice as much as the other.

Sometimes contract workers might not be as committed to the project as members of the permanent staff, since they might only work for the organisation for a short time.

Personal qualities and general characteristics for anyone working within the IT industry

It is hard to generalise about the types of people needed to do particular jobs in computing because some jobs are much more demanding than others, but a general list would include:

- an in-depth knowledge of the hardware and software necessary for them to perform their job

- a good listener and communicator with a calm, helpful demeanour

- the ability to work flexibly and prioritise work

- good at organising themselves so that they are able to use time and resources effectively

- a good team member since nearly all projects are too large for just one person to work on

- enthusiasm, energy and an innovative flair

- problem-solving skills

- the ability to learn and adapt to new technologies

- awareness of the business needs of an organisation so that they see IT as providing solutions to business problems

- good written communication skills enabling them to produce reports, technical specifications, user guides, training material, etc.

For any management responsibilities we could include these extra abilities:

- the ability to delegate work

- the ability to influence others

- the ability to manage internal and external resources

- the ability to prepare and deal with departmental budgets

- the ability to deliver projects within budget and on schedule.

Activity   KEY SKILLS IT 2.1, 3.1

For this activity you are going to research jobs within the computer industry using the following information sources, which should be available through your college library or lecturer. Most of these publications have accompanying websites addresses which are shown after the name of the magazine in the following list:

- ZDNET NEWS

> **www.zdnet.co.uk**

- Computer Weekly (£1.50)

> **www.computerweekly.co.uk**

There are also some websites for employment agencies who specialise in computer vacancies; here is a list of their web addresses:

- www.jncp.com
- www.freelanceinformer.co.uk
- www.coolwebjobs.co.uk
- www.abraxas.co.uk

You have been asked to investigate the job market in computing, and produce a report outlining your findings. In your report you will need to focus on the following:

- names of the jobs
- what the jobs entail
- what educational background they are looking for
- what experience is required
- what skills are in demand
- what personal qualities they find the most important.

Questions

A British Computer Society member has to obey the Code of Practice if he is to remain a member of the Society. In addition to this, members must obey all the laws that apply to anyone working in the IT industry.

1 Give the name of three laws that an IT professional should know about.

2 Explain the difference between a code of practice and a law that applies to IT.

Activity

A variety of terms are introduced in this chapter, many of which will be new to you. It is important that you build up vocabulary that can be used when writing essays or answering questions. Write a definition for each of the following terms used in the chapter:

- data warehouse
- the BCS
- telecommuting
- integrity
- privacy
- contract worker

Examination Questions

1 'The development of information technology has had significant effects on society, individuals and organisations.'

With the aid of specific examples discuss this statement. Include in your discussion:

the effects of information technology on society at large;

the effects of information technology on employment and work methods;

the effects of information technology on individuals.

(20)

(NEAB, Module IT01, May 1996, q8)

2 A professional organisation for information technology practitioners has developed what is referred to as the 'Industry Structure Model'. What is the purpose of this model and how does it work?

(6)

(NEAB, Module IT01, May 1996 q5)

3 'Codes of practice' exist for professionals within the information technology industry separate from any legal requirements.

Explain, with the aid of an example, the distinction between a legal requirement and a code of practice.

(3)

(NEAB, Module IT01, Specimen Paper, q7)

4 Professional progression within the IT industry requires more than just technical skills. Give **three** other necessary qualities and explain why they are important.

(NEAB, Module IT01, May 1997, q6)

Examination Questions

5 'The growth of communication systems may result in an increasing number of people working from home, often referred to as telecommuting.'

Discuss, with the aid of specific examples, the advantages and disadvantages to individuals, organisations and society of such methods of working.

(20)

(NEAB, Module IT01, Specimen Paper, q10)

6 'The development of communication systems has enabled individuals, organisations and society to operate on a global basis.'

Discuss this statement. Include your discussion:

specific examples of facilities and/or tasks that make use of communications systems,

specific examples of applications that make use of these facilities and/or tasks,

the communication technology and/or techniques that have enabled this development.

(NEAB, Module IT01, Specimen Paper, q10)

7 Individuals and organisations have become so dependent upon IT systems that the consequences of their failure could be catastrophic to the individual or the organisation.

Give **two** different examples of types of IT system for which failure would be catastrophic. In each case explain why the failure could prove to be catastrophic.

(4)

(NEAB, Module IT01, May 1997 q1)

8 Briefly describe **two** social impacts and **two** organisational impacts commonly identified as a result of introducing computerised information systems into business organisations.

(8)

(NEAB, Module IT01, May 1998, q2)

9 A software house is advertising for an analyst programmer to join one of their development teams. State **four** personal qualities that the company should be looking for in the applicants.

(4)

(NEAB, Module IT01, May 99, q2)

The Legal Framework

▶ To understand the implications of software and data misuse with special reference to the Computer Misuse Act and the principles of software copyright and licensing agreements.

▶ To consider the nature and purpose of data protection legislation.

▶ To look at health and safety legislation and its implications for all users of computer systems.

Introduction to the issues

Developments in information technology take place so quickly that it has always been difficult for the law to keep pace with the technology.

Since many organisations are completely dependent on their computing facilities, the lack of laws to deal with new situations encountered has left many organisations in a weak position. To overcome this problem, most organisations have had to put their own procedures in place, focused mainly on security, so that their computing facilities are not in danger.

There are some laws that deal with particular issues, but many lawyers and computer professionals see these laws as having been passed hastily, without being given sufficient thought, and as a result containing too many loopholes for them to be effective. Some computer professionals feel that the law 'lacks teeth' in many areas and it is possible to do serious damage to a computer system and escape prosecution, or, if a prosecution does go ahead, only get a short sentence compared with similar non-computer crimes.

As an illustration of the relative impunity with which some computer crime is carried out, some hackers or fraudsters are offered deals whereby they are not prosecuted but employed as experts to prevent other hackers from doing what they did!

CASE STUDY

Hackers at the Pentagon

In February 1998 computer staff at the Pentagon in the USA realised that their computer systems had been infiltrated by hackers who had systematically invaded their systems for a couple of weeks. Some people put forward the suggestion that the intruders might have done this to take part in a hacking competition in which they could show off their skills. These hacking attempts were so sophisticated that they circumvented all the complex security procedures and managed to access some of the Defence Department's unclassified networks.

What this attack showed is that if hackers can get into the most guarded of networks, such as the Pentagon's, then if they are determined enough, they can probably hack into any system.

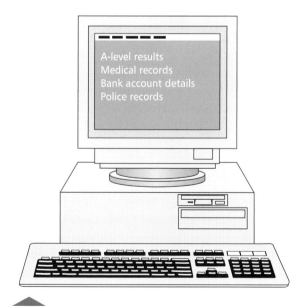

Figure 4.1 *Many ex-hackers are 'poachers turned gamekeepers', using their expertise as consultants who keep hackers out of other people's computer systems*

There are four main areas of the law that are relevant to the computer user and these are:

- copyright and patent law
- contract law
- criminal law
- data protection law.

Copyright law

Copyright law, as the name suggests, is the area of law that protects works produced by one person or organisation from being copied by another. Copyright is free: you do not have to register a copyright like a patent and once you have produced your original work, you are automatically covered. Copyright law protects software producers and the people who write manuals and books for them.

Patent law

Patent law protects against inventions being copied and would therefore, for example, protect the designers of a new, faster chip from having their design copied, produced and then sold. Unlike a copyright, a patent needs to be registered at the Patent Office in London and once this is done the invention is protected.

Both copyrights and patents are covered by a piece of legislation called the Copyright, Designs and Patents Act 1988.

Contract law

Contract law affects the computer user in a variety of ways. Many employees who work with computers have written contracts of employment and these set out clearly what they are and what they are not allowed to do. The contracts also set out what penalties there are for breaching the contract. There is a move towards system development staff working on short-term contracts, so contract law is particularly relevant to this group of people. Contracts also need to be drawn up for the supply of goods and services.

Data protection law

Data protection legislation is important legislation affecting all computer users, since failure to comply with the Data Protection Act 1998 can result in criminal penalties or other measures being taken against you. This Act will be looked at in detail later on in this chapter.

A large area of crime, dealing with hacking (e.g. gaining unauthorised access to a computer system), computer fraud and the damage or deletion of computer programs, is dealt with by the Computer Misuse Act 1990.

There is no doubt that the global use of computers, especially since the widespread use of the Internet, has led to some complex legal problems for the lawyers to chew over. In future society will have to address the problems of computer use spanning the legal systems across many different countries.

Software and data misuse

Software and data misuse covers the illegal copying of programs or data, damaging programs or data deliberately, hacking into systems or planting computer viruses on systems. In this section we look at all these activities, and at the legislation that is used to curb them.

Software copyright

The copying of software in breach of a licensing agreement of the software company is forbidden by the Copyright Designs and Patents Act and is a criminal offence under this Act. The police and the trading standards department of the local council uphold the law in this area and actively look for breaches of the law at computer fairs, car boot sales and in the classified advertisements of the computer press and local papers.

Although it is quite easy to pick up some types of misuse, it is difficult to check whether a particular person has illegally copied software on their hard drive. Instead, the software companies usually target businesses where they are tipped off by disgruntled employees.

An organisation called FAST (Federation Against Software Theft) has been set up jointly by the major software companies to guard against software theft and take action (usually by suing for damages through the courts) against anyone found stealing software. How does this work? Well, if FAST has very good reasons to suspect that illegal software is being used, then one morning a transit van full of police and FAST staff will wait outside the premises until the first employee arrives. This person will be shown a warrant, allowing the police and FAST staff to enter the building and remove any computer hardware or media that is suspected of containing illegal software. The entire computing facility of a company can be removed. Notice is not given, and the equipment that is removed will not be returned until after the court hearing if a prosecution takes place. This is clearly disastrous for the company since all the data needed for the day-to-day running of the business is removed in the process.

If illegal software is found (and it almost certainly will be if there has been a tip-off), then the directors of the company bear all responsibility, *even if they were completely ignorant of the illegal activities of their employees*; they could face unlimited fines or even imprisonment for up to two years.

Naturally, this is taken very seriously by anyone responsible for stand-alone computers or those on a network and special audit software is available for network managers who wish to check that all the software being used within an organisation is licensed and that the number of licences covers the number of machines using the software.

Licensing agreements

When you buy software you are not in fact buying it, rather you are buying the licence to use it subject to the conditions imposed by the software manufacturer. There is a variety of different licensing agreements but other than public domain, shareware and demonstration software, it will always be illegal to make a copy of software that has been licensed by somebody else, to use on your machine. This is clear-cut, but suppose you have a desktop machine and a laptop and want to use the same software. Can you legally do this? The answer varies from one software company to another, so it is necessary to read through your licensing agreement carefully to check. Also, it is very common to upgrade your computer, in which case you might need to copy the software from the old to the new machine. Again you would need to check the licensing agreement to see if this is allowed.

Most software manufacturers are quite reasonable and will allow both of the above. Many of them regard software like a book that may, once bought, be passed to someone else; but it would not be possible for two people to use the book at the same time. This, as you can see, solves the problems of the person with two computers, one at work, the other at home.

Copyright

Copyright ensures that creators of software and data are protected by law against other people copying the digital fruit of their endeavours.

Software piracy

Software piracy is the illegal copying of computer software, and is reckoned to cost software developers around £3000 million per year. In 1992 it was estimated that about 66 per cent of the software used in Europe was illegal.

If a company has developed its own software, rather than buying off-the-shelf software, it will have spent a lot of time and money on development. Large programs are usually written by a team of programmers, with each team member writing a particular section or module of the whole program. The number of 'man hours' taken to write the programs can be large.

Suppose five programmers work on a project and it takes each programmer 200 hours; the total number of man hours would be $5 \times 200 = 1000$ man hours. The programs for the police national computer are estimated to have taken around 2000 man *years* to write and test.

Copyright of data

Data paid for and collected by one organisation might be of value to another organisation and it is for this reason that data is also copyright. An example might be a database containing all the names, addresses and telephone numbers of all private and business premises in the country. It should be borne in mind that in many systems, the value of the data is far greater than the value of the hardware, which is much easier to replace.

The Copyright, Designs and Patents Act 1989

The Copyright, Designs and Patents Act 1989 makes it a criminal offence to copy or steal software.

Under the Act it is an offence to copy or distribute software, or any manuals that come with it, without permission or licence from the copyright owner (normally the software developer).

It is also an offence to run purchased software covered by copyright on two or more machines at the same time, unless the licence specifically allows it.

The Act makes it illegal for an organisation to encourage, allow, compel or pressure its employees to make or distribute copies of illegal software for use by the organisation.

The Computer Misuse Act 1990

With the widespread use of computer and communication systems, problems started to arise concerning their misuse. Concerns centred on a variety of uses that were not covered by existing laws. Several cases were tried where the court was unable to convict the people involved because older laws had been used, which had had to be interpreted to cover these misuses. One particular case involved a schoolboy using his computer and a modem at home to hack into the Duke of Edinburgh's electronic mailbox and read his correspondence. Other schoolboy hackers were able to get through to stockbrokers, hospitals, oil companies and even the Atomic Energy Authority's computer systems.

The courts were reluctant to use theft laws which weren't intended to cover these situations and advised Parliament that they would need to make new, more specific laws, and this gave rise to the Computer Misuse Act 1990.

The Act covers a variety of misuses that were not covered by existing laws. It deals with the following:

- Deliberately planting viruses in a computer system to cause damage to program files and data.

- Using computer time to carry out unauthorised work. For instance, a firm's computer could be used to run a friend's payroll.

- Copying computer programs illegally (i.e. software piracy).

- Hacking into someone's system with a view to seeing the information or altering it.

- Using the computer for various frauds; people have been known to put fictitious employees on the payroll program and steal money using false bank accounts opened in the name of these employees.

Offences under the Computer Misuse Act 1990

There are three sections that define the three types of offence under the Act.

Section 1

A person is guilty of an offence if:

(a) he/she causes a computer to perform any function with intent to secure access to any program or data held in any computer and

(b) the access he/she intends to secure is unauthorised and

(c) he/she knows at the time that it is unauthorised.

The maximum sentence for an offence under this section of the Act is six months imprisonment.

Section 2

A person will be guilty of an offence under section 2 of the Act if he/she commits an offence under section 1 of the Act with the intent of committing a further offence such as blackmail, theft or any other offence which has a penalty of at least five years imprisonment. They will also be guilty if they get someone else to do this further offence.

The maximum sentence for an offence under this section of the Act is five years imprisonment.

Section 3

A person is guilty of an offence under section 3 of the Act if he/she commits any act which causes an unauthorised modification of the contents of any computer, and at the time that he/she knows that the modification is unauthorised and he/she has the requisite intent.

The requisite intent is intent to cause a modification and by so doing:

(a) to impair the operation of any computer

(b) to prevent or hinder access to any program or data

(c) to impair the operation of any program or reliability of any data.

The maximum sentence for an offence under this section of the Act is five years imprisonment.

On looking at whether an offence under this Act has taken place, it is important to bear in mind that it is always be necessary to prove intent. The court would therefore have to show that the person who did the act knew they were doing it. In other words someone who just destroyed programs or data through their own incompetence or by accident, would not be guilty. The need to prove intent is a stumbling block for many attempted prosecutions and very few cases under the Act have ever come to court. This shows that either the scale of the problem is small (which is unlikely) or that the Act is ineffective.

Activity

Your task is to look carefully at the preceding section on the Computer Misuse Act 1990, then look at the following situations and say whether each person is guilty under the Act. If they are, you are required to state the section of the Act that applies to the situation. If you think an individual could not be prosecuted under the Act, you should state why not.

1 Miss Kendrick is using her home computer to access the Internet using her Internet service provider, and because she is a beginner, she starts to become lost in a series of websites. As she does not know what she is doing, she inadvertently ends up accessing the database of a large organisation. In trying to get out of the system she does some damage to the data before switching off her computer.

2 John Jackson is a mischievous computer hacker and wants to get his friend into trouble by getting him to hack into a bank's computer system and then change figures held in some of the bank's records. It is discovered subsequently that the alterations caused serious loss of money to the bank. Will he be guilty of any offence even though he himself did not do the hacking or make the alterations?

3 Susan Hughes is a personnel officer in a large company and as such is allowed to access the personnel database as part of her duties. Her friend asks her to obtain a printout and then she suggests that Susan makes some alterations to her file which will make it more likely that she would be accepted for a post, which would mean promotion in the company. Susan makes the alterations for her friend but a colleague discovers that the record has been altered and informs the manager.

4 Rachel Smith has been made redundant as a junior programmer and is naturally very annoyed with the firm; in the heat of the moment she erases all the program codes as well as all the backup copies of a program she has been working on for the last few months.

5 Paul is a bright A-level student who likes to show off his programming and technical abilities. To this end he has started to write viruses that he transfers to the hard drives of some of the computers in the college. Although these computers have virus scanners fitted, his new virus manages to evade these and before long all the computers and the floppy disks become infected, and now and again come up with Paul's name right across the screen. Although this particular virus does not do anything drastic, it involves technicians, lecturing staff and students in a large amount of work in trying to eradicate it.

6 Jane likes to play jokes on her colleagues, so when leaving, she decides to change the password for entry to the company's important database. She then goes on holiday where she is unable to be contacted. The company spends hours trying to find how to get access and in the end have to contact a computer consultant to help them gain access at great expense.

7 Stephen has just started a new job and is learning how to access the main database. He has had very little training from the company and is having to find out for himself. By mistake he issues a command that deletes a whole group of records. It is then found impossible to re-create them from the backup disks.

8 John works in the patient records department of a large hospital and as part of his job is allowed unlimited access to the records of all the patients, both past and present. When things are quiet, he looks up the records of people he knows, to see what they have wrong with them. On doing this he finds the record of someone he knows who is HIV-positive. He knows where they work so he attempts to blackmail them.

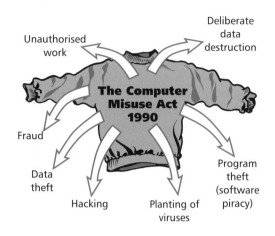

Figure 4.2 *The Computer Misuse Act 1990 has been compared by a leading lawyer to a badly knitted jumper containing many holes*

What data is held on individuals?

A wide variety of organisations, both private and public, hold personal information about each one of us. Personal information usually falls into one of the following categories:

Criminal information includes:

- details on all suspects, crimes and previously convicted criminals
- computerised records of all convicted criminals fingerprints
- DNA profiles of some criminals
- criminal details on suspects who may be involved in organised crime.

Educational information includes:

- medical details which could affect schooling
- examination boards hold details of exams passed
- schools information management systems (SIMS) hold personal details on all pupils in a school
- references for jobs, further education and higher education colleges
- reports give details of performance at the end of each term/year.

Medical information includes:

- GP records
- prescription details held by pharmacies
- hospital records (letters from GPs, appointments, treatment details, etc.)
- medical details held by life insurance companies
- medical details held by solicitors if compensation claims are made
- private health insurance details
- details of medical conditions of staff held by personnel departments.

Financial information includes:

- mortgage details held by a bank or building society
- loan details kept by a finance company
- bank account or building society details
- pension details
- credit and debit card details.

Employment information includes:

- personal details (name, address, illnesses, next of kin, etc.)
- references kept
- pension details
- payroll details
- tax details.

Marketing information includes:

- personal details (name, address, telephone number, etc.)
- income group
- details of family members
- purchasing frequency
- types of product bought
- interests and hobbies
- holidays taken in the last two years.

When mobile phones are switched on, their whereabouts can be located fairly accurately

Cameras at ports record the registration numbers of vehicles entering or leaving the country

Loyalty cards and credit cards link you to the purchases you make

ATMs (cash dispensers) record transaction details (date, time, location, amount withdrawn, etc). Some will secretly take your photograph

Internet 'cookies', without you knowing, record details of the web sites you have visited

Figure 4.3 *Your private life is becoming less and less private*

It may surprise you to know how much information about you is collected and stored without your realising it.

- Loyalty cards and credit cards link you to the purchases you make.

- Cameras at ports record the registration number of vehicles entering and leaving the country.

- When mobile phones are switched on their whereabouts can be located fairly accurately.

- ATMs (cash dispensers) record transaction details (date, time, location, amount withdrawn, etc.) and some even take your photograph!

- Internet cookies, without you knowing, record details of the websites you visit.

The Data Protection Act 1998

The widespread use of computers for the processing of personal data led the government to introduce the Data Protection Act 1984. With the increased use of computers, particularly those networked and the Internet, the 1984 Act has been replaced by the 1998 Data Protection Act.

The main purpose of the Act is to prevent the misuse of personal data and to give rights to individuals to whom the information relates. If they find that the information stored about themselves is wrong, they can have it altered or deleted, and in some cases might be able to claim damages through the courts for the distress or financial loss the wrong information has caused.

Another, less obvious reason for the Act was the fact that the other EC member states had data protection laws and it was necessary for the UK to have a similar act to allow the free passage of personal data from one member state to another, which was essential when conducting business.

Definitions of terms used in the Act

Before looking at the Act itself it is important to understand some of the terms used in it.

Personal data
Personal data concerns a living person who can be identified from the data.

Data subject
The data subject is the individual who is the subject of the personal data.

The Commissioner
The Commissioner is the person responsible for enforcing the Act. In addition the Commissioner is responsible for:

- promoting good practice by the people who are responsible for the processing of personal data

- making the general public aware of their rights under the Act.

The data controller
The data controller in a company or organisation is the person/persons given the responsibility of controlling the way in which personal data is processed.

CREDIT CARD COMPANIES
If you've ever been turned down for credit, when you know you're credit-worthy, do you wonder why?

DEPARTMENT OF SOCIAL SECURITY
You could receive the wrong benefits if the details held on computer about you are wrong.

COMPUTER DATING AGENCIES
Just because you describe yourself as tall, dark and handsome doesn't mean they always do.

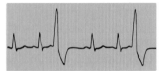

HOSPITALS AND DOCTORS
If you're allergic to penicillin and it doesn't show up on your computer records, it could show up in your health.

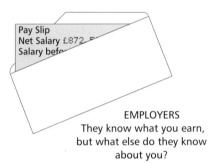

EMPLOYERS
They know what you earn, but what else do they know about you?

ELECTRICITY
Alongside the Gas Board and British Telecom, the Electricity Boards keep some of the longest lists of people's names and addresses in the country.

INLAND REVENUE
The amount of tax you pay is decided by the information they hold on their computer about you. Is it correct?

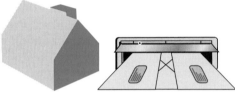

MAIL ORDER COMPANIES
You may not have given them your name and address in the first place, so what else do they know?

HIGH STREET RETAILERS
If you've moved into a property where the previous tenant was a bad credit risk, that's how retailers' computers might see you too.

Figure 4.4 *'There must be some mistake here.'*

The Act places obligations on those people who record and use personal data and these people are called data controllers in the Act. Data controllers must be open about the use of data by telling the Data Protection Commissioner (i.e. the person who enforces the Act) that they are collecting personal data, and how they intend to use it. They must also follow a set of eight principles, called the data protection principles.

First principle

This states that 'Personal data shall be processed fairly and lawfully and, in particular, shall not be processed unless:

- at least one of the conditions in Schedule 2 is met

- in the case of sensitive personal data, at least one of the conditions in Schedule 3 is also met.'

Schedule 2 (the conditions for processing)

Schedule 2 deals with conditions for processing and at least one of the following conditions must be met for all processing of personal data, unless there is a specific exemption. The conditions are as follows:

- The data subject (i.e. the person to whom the personal data refers) has given their consent to the processing.

- The processing is necessary:

  (a) for the performance of a contract to which the data subject is a party, or

(b) for the taking of steps at the request of the data subject with a view to entering into a contract.

- The processing is necessary to comply with any legal obligations to which the data controller is subject, other than an obligation imposed by contract.

- The processing is necessary in order to protect the vital interests of the data subject.

- The processing is necessary:

  (a) for the administration of justice
  (b) for the exercise of any function conferred by or under any enactment
  (c) for the exercise of any functions of the Crown, a minister of the Crown or government department
  (d) for the exercise of any other function of a public nature exercised in the public interest.

Schedule (the conditions for processing sensitive data)

The act gives a list of data regarded as being sensitive, personal data. Sensitive, personal data is information as to:

- the racial or ethnic origin of the data subject

- the political opinion of the data subject

- the religious beliefs (and other beliefs of a similar nature) of the data subject

- whether the data subject is a member of a trade union

- the physical or mental health or condition of the data subject

- the lifestyle of the data subject

- the commission or alleged commission by the data subject of any offence

- any proceedings for any offence committed or alleged to be committed by the data subject, the disposal of such proceedings or the sentence of the court in such proceedings.

At least one of the following (Schedule 3) conditions for processing in addition to at least one of the conditions for processing (mentioned in Schedule 2).

  For the processing of sensitive data to be lawful:

- the data subject must have given their explicit consent for the processing of the personal data

- the processing must be necessary to exercise or perform a job imposed by law on the data controller

- the processing must be necessary to protect the vital interests of the data subject, or where the data controller is unable to contact the data subject or to protect the vital interests of another person

- the processing is carried out by a body or association for trade union, political or religious purposes, not conducted for profit and where the data has been suitably protected from misuse

- the processing is necessary for the administration of justice or for a function of the Crown, a minister of the crown or a government department

- the processing must be necessary for medical purposes and be carried out by a health professional

- it must be sensitive data of a racial or ethnic nature and it must be necessary to have this information to ensure that these groups are treated fairly.

Second principle

This states that 'Personal data shall be obtained for only one or more specified purposes, and shall not be further processed in any manner incompatible with that purpose or purposes'.

Third principle

This states that 'Personal data shall be adequate, relevant and not excessive in relation to the purpose or purposes for which they are processed'.

Fourth principle

This states that 'Personal data shall be accurate and, where necessary, kept up to date'.

Fifth principle

This states that 'Personal data processed for any purpose or purposes shall not be kept for longer than is necessary for that purpose or those purposes'.

Sixth principle

This states that 'Personal data shall be processed in accordance with the rights of data subjects under this Act'.

Seventh principle

This states that 'Appropriate technical and organisational measures shall be taken against unauthorised or unlawful processing of personal data and against accidental loss or destruction of, or damage to, personal data'.

Eighth principle

This states that 'Personal data shall not be transferred to a country or territory outside the European Economic Area, unless that country or territory ensures an adequate level of protection for the rights and freedoms of data subjects in relation to the processing of personal data'.

The registration process

Anyone who holds personal information about any living individual must notify the Commissioner of their use unless they are covered by any of the exemptions to the Act. In order to notify the Commissioner, it is necessary to supply the office of the Data Protection Commissioner with the following information:

- the name and address of the data user

- a description of the purposes for which personal data will be used

- the type of personal data held

- where the personal data is obtained

- to whom the data will be disclosed

- a list of any countries outside the UK to which the data may be transferred.

There is also a fee payable at the time of registration. Not all data needs to be registered; the exemptions from the need to register are outlined below.

Exemptions from the need to register

There are several exemptions from registration under the Data Protection Act so any personal data falling under any of the following categories need not be registered. The significance of these exemptions to the data

subjects is that they no longer have the right to inspect the data and also have no rights to have such data altered or to be able to claim compensation if the incorrect data causes them any loss or distress.

Data is exempt where:

1 data is being held in connection with personal, family or household affairs or for recreational use

2 data is used for preparing the text of documents; this is often referred to as the 'wordprocessing exemption'

3 the data is used for the calculation of wages and pensions, or the keeping of accounts or the keeping records of purchases and sales for accounting purposes only

4 the data is being held in the interests of national security

5 data is being used for mailing lists, provided that only names and addresses are stored and individuals are asked if they object to personal data being held by the user.

What happens if an organisation fails to register?

If an organisation does not register its use of personal data, then provided it is not covered by one of the exemptions for the need to register, the organisation may be fined up to £5000 in the magistrate's court or an unlimited fine in the High Court.

The Data Protection Commissioner

The Data Protection Commissioner is not part of a government department but an independent officer appointed by the Queen; he/she reports directly to Parliament.

The role of the Data Protection Registrar is set down in the Data Protection Act 1998 and includes:

- the maintenance of a register of data users

- making information on the Act and how it works widely available

- encouraging organisations and individuals to comply with the data protection principles

- encouraging the development of codes of practice to help users comply with the principles

- acting as ombudsman when considering complaints about breaches of the Act

- prosecuting offenders or serving notices on anyone contravening the principles.

The rights of the individual under the legislation

Any individual (a data subject) is entitled to ask the person holding the data (the data controller) with a copy of the personal data held about them. They may either write directly to the organisation or to the Data Protection Commissioner for further information. Many data controllers will levy a small charge to cover the extra administrative costs they incur, but they have to supply the data subject with this information in a form that they can understand, within 21 days.

If the data is inaccurate, the data subject can challenge it and have it deleted or changed. If the inaccurate data has caused them damage in any way, they may be able to claim compensation through the courts.

As well as supplying the data itself, the data controller will also be required to tell the data subject about the purposes to which the data will be put and also to give details of anyone else to whom the data will be disclosed. If the data is unintelligible to the data subject, the data controller has to explain what it means.

You do not, however, have the right to see all the information held about you; certain data is covered in the exemptions from subject access outlined in the next section.

Exemptions from subject access

There are a number of circumstances in which data still needs to be registered under the Act, but where they are exempt from the subject being able to access the data held. The type of data that falls into this category is any which would be likely to prejudice:

- the prevention or detection of crime

- the apprehension or prosecution of offenders

- the assessment or collection of any tax or duty.

Is compensation payable?

If a person suffers damage or distress because of things the data controller does that contravene the Act, they may be able to claim compensation.

Figure 4.5

CASE STUDY

Data protection tribunal decisions

There have been several important cases involving credit reference agencies which, although they differ slightly in the facts of each case, the underlying reasoning behind the decisions was similar.

To understand this case study it is useful to look at what credit reference agencies do and how they work. When you apply for credit (a loan, store card, a credit card, etc.), a credit reference agency is contacted to determine your suitability for credit. There are four main credit reference agencies and they all use similar methods to extract information on which a credit decision can be based.

One area of concern to the Data Protection Commissioner was the fact that information was extracted from the databases via the address of the applicant rather than their name. The problem with this was that when a search was carried out, for instance, Mr Smith of Letsbe Avenue, Anytown, it would reveal information on anyone, regardless of their name, living at the same address. In many cases other people who might have had no association with the applicant for credit will have had their details looked at. If there was a person who was or had been living at the same address and who had a criminal record, or had defaulted in their payments in the past, then the person who was applying for credit could have their application refused. In such cases the applicant for credit could be refused credit simply due to the conduct of someone else, whom they may not have even known.

Another example which came to the notice of the Data Protection Commissioner was as follows:

An accountant, Mr Good, sold Mr Bad his house, but when Mr Good applied to a building society for a cheque guarantee card, he was refused. On being asked why he had been refused, he was referred to a credit referral agency. Under the Consumer Credit Act 1974 he was entitled to ask for a copy of the file they held about him, which he did. On Mr Good's file was a reference to Mr Bad saying that Mr Bad had a court judgment against him. The only thing they had in common, was that they had at different times, lived at the same address.

Mr Good was naturally annoyed at not getting his card and at seeing this reference to someone else not associated with him, on his file. Under the terms of the Consumer Credit Act he was entitled to have this entry amended or removed, but when he applied to have this done the credit referral agency would only add a note to say that the adverse judgment did not refer to Mr Good. They would not remove the entry about Mr Bad in Mr Good's file, so he made a complaint to the Data Protection Commissioner. Since there are many advantages to the credit referral agencies in using the address rather than a name (people can put in fraudulent applications in different names for credit using the same address, for example) they appealed against the enforcement notice issued by the Commissioner.

It is useful now to look at what sources of data are used by these credit reference agencies.

Electoral registration information

Anyone who is allowed to vote in an election has to fill in a form and this records all those eligible to vote, living at a certain address. The database therefore contains the names and addresses of people eligible to vote.

Court judgments

These are details of people who have had judgments against them and in many cases they will be people who have been dishonest or have not kept up the repayments for goods ordered using credit.

Credit industry fraud avoidance scheme details

Details of anyone who has been responsible for, or suspected of, fraud are included on this database.

Postal address file

This is a file which is obtained from the Post Office and contains all the postal addresses in the UK.

When the credit reference agency does a search, it first uses the postal address file and then seeks to match the address with all the entries matching it in the other files. It would therefore come up with the details of anyone living at a certain address, regardless of whether they had any links, financial or otherwise, with the applicant.

The Commissioner and her team carefully listened to the arguments put forward by the credit referral agencies and applied the first data protection principle that states:

'The information to be contained in personal data shall be obtained, and personal data shall be processed, fairly and lawfully'.

During the tribunals the Commissioner decided that the extraction of information about persons other than the applicant for credit, is capable of constituting unfair processing, in breach of the first data protection principle. The main argument put forward was that personal data about one individual which was not necessarily supplied by that individual, is being used to decide whether another unrelated person should be given credit or not. The Commissioner called this information 'third party information' and decided that the extraction of such information was unfair. The Commissioner therefore issued an enforcement notice which prohibited the extraction of data in this way. So credit agencies now cannot operate in this way.

Activity KEY SKILLS C2.2, C3.2

Before you attempt the following questions you will need to gain access to a copy of the detailed guidelines from your lecturer, or you can ask for your own free copy from the Data Protection Commissioner's office. You could also access the material on their website. See if you can work out answers to the following examples for yourself.

1 John fills in an application for a loan to buy a car. On the application form there is a box to tick if he does not wish details to be passed to another company who might send material about their goods and services. Subsequently, someone rings him up to try to make an appointment to sell him life assurance. He is very annoyed that his name and number have been passed on in this way. He writes a letter to the loan company. What will be the company's likely response?

2 A company purchases a list of names and addresses from another company so that they can send mailshots. Is this legal?

3 Betty is the membership secretary for the local branch of the Winemakers Society. Part of her role is to keep membership records and also to keep details of subscriptions. Will she need to register this use?

4 A company manufactures screw fittings which are supplied to other companies. A disgruntled employee goes to work for a competitor. and before he leaves, decides to copy the database of companies who make regular orders and the details of those orders. Is this an offence under the Data Protection Act?

5 A man applies for a mortgage. The building society will need to check that he is working full time and that he is earning the amount he claims. He signs a form permitting his employer to give the building society his salary details. Will his employer be allowed to pass these personal details on?

Questions

These questions all concern the Data Protection Act 1998.

1 A college keeps records about all its past and present students and these records contain details of their achievements, end of term reports, enrolment details, references and details pertaining to any disciplinary matters. They are currently kept on a database on the computer, but the college administration has learnt that they should be registered and there is concern that if they do so, the students could apply to see their personal records. The principal of the college suggests that to comply with the Act as quickly as possible, they should print out all the records and store them manually in filing cabinets. Afterwards they can delete all the student records from the computer.

Explain whether this would be a good idea.

2 Many people keep names, addresses, phone numbers, e-mail numbers and birthdays of their friends on a computer/personal organiser, for personal use only. Do they need to register this use? Explain why or why not.

3 Brian, a bright A level student, has just taken his examinations. He is told by his teacher, who is an examiner, that most of the marking is completed about three weeks after the examination. Rather than wait another three or four weeks he applies to the examination board to look at the details held about him which will no doubt include his results.

Do you think this application would be successful?

4 James is a hacker and has managed to steal a large amount of money from a high street bank and transfer it to a foreign bank account. He is conscious of the fact that he must not spend any of the money yet, until he knows he is in the clear. It is two years since the theft and he thinks he may have got away with it. He decides to use the Data Protection Act to request information held about him on the police national computer. Will his request be granted? Explain why or why not.

Current privacy concerns

There is no doubt that life now is not as private as it used to be, and there are many reasons to be concerned about some of the latest privacy issues. Business practices change as competitiveness between companies increases and also with the increased exploitation of the IT resources available. As a result of this, certain issues arise which really need laws to cover them. At present there are several practices which need scrutiny.

Caller line identification

It is possible to buy phones which automatically display the caller's number and although this is useful in preventing nuisance calls, many companies automatically make a note of the caller's number when an enquiry is made. They can then ring back or obtain the caller's name and address to send them advertising material. Although callers can withhold their numbers by dialling 141 before the number, many callers forget to do this. Most democratic countries, excluding the UK, have now passed laws outlawing this practice.

Data matching

Data matching involves using several databases to extract data referring to the same person. The result of trawling the data in such a way is to build up complete profiles of individuals that can then be used for marketing purposes. Many other countries have outlawed such practices.

Revealing criminal records to potential employers

Employers are not able to access criminal records directly, but data subjects are. Employers therefore make applicants exercise this right in order to reveal to the employer details of any possible record. The Data Protection Commissioner has suggested that enforcing subject access in this way should be made a criminal offence.

Other concerns

There are also concerns regarding DNA profiling, which identifies those people who are genetically more likely to suffer from certain illnesses, since these people could be discriminated against both at work and when they make an application for health insurance or life assurance.

European Union Data Protection Directive

The European Union Data Protection Directive was published in October 1995 when member states were given three years to pass national legislation to implement the Directive. This meant that in the UK the older 1984 Act needed replacing with the new 1998 Act.

The Directive aims to 'protect the fundamental rights and freedoms of natural persons, and in particular their right to privacy with respect to the processing of personal data'. The 1984 Data Protection Act did not refer to privacy but the 1998 act goes further and starts to address many of the privacy issues.

There are several elements in the Directive which are now incorporated in the 1998 Act:

- the inclusion of some manual records within the scope of data protection legislation

- rules about the legitimacy of processing

- special rules for the processing of particularly sensitive personal data (e.g. racial or ethnic origin, political opinions, religious or philosophical beliefs, trade union membership, and data about health or sex life, criminal offences or convictions)

- certain rules to protect freedom of expression and exemptions for personal data processed for journalistic, artistic or literary purposes

- a duty on all data users to comply with the data protection rules, whether or not they are registered under the new system

- some provisions designed to ensure that personal data being transferred to non-EU countries will be adequately protected.

The answer to hacking: encryption programs

There are special programs, called encryption programs, which code messages before they are sent along a communication channel; at the other end they are decoded. This type of program might seem the answer to many of the problems with hackers; however, there are other problems which are highlighted in the following article, taken from the *Daily Telegraph*, 13th June 1996.

TASKS

Read the article below carefully. It raises many important issues, the main one being that cryptography is now available to everyone who has access to the Internet. You have been asked to write a brief article explaining what exactly it is and why some people see it as a good thing while others see it as a threat. Once you have described the advantages and disadvantages in its use, you should say, with reasons, what your opinion is.

Authorities back down on secrecy code

Philip Zimmermann, a computer programmer, was told by the American authorities that he would not be prosecuted for sending around the world his program allowing secret messages to be transferred. This program allows messages to be encoded and to be sent in such a way that even the security services cannot crack them.

Philip's program, called the Pretty Good Privacy program, takes a message and jumbles it up into a series of numbers and letters that only the intended recipient can read. The worrying thing for the authorities is that even the FBI (Federal Bureau of Investigation) can not crack the code and

this means that completely secret messages can be transferred. Some computer experts reckon that the code is so secure from cracking that it would take a powerful computer running continuously for around ten years to crack it.

The Pretty Good Privacy program, called PGP for short, is useful to Internet users who feel that their Internet or e-mail messages can be intercepted by hackers, government and their employers. Using the PGP program allows them the privacy they see as a right.

Philip Zimmermann did not intend financial gain from the program and it was posted on the Internet

by some of his friends for people to download. This is where the problem started because the code is covered by the American Arms Export Act where it is classed as high-tech munitions (like missiles or other weapons), and this made its export without permission and a licence an offence.

Although the authorities found it acceptable to use the program in the US, once the authorities found it on the Internet they were worried that it could undermine national security and they started to investigate further. The view of the authorities in Britain is similar and a senior police officer at the head of the National

Criminal Intelligence Service said that the program could allow paedophiles to send pornographic pictures across the Internet without any fear of detection.

A leading American lawyer said that if the decision to prosecute Philip Zimmermann had been made, and he had been found guilty, he could have faced 51 months in prison.

On hearing the decision not to prosecute, Philip Zimmermann said 'This is not just for spies any more. It is for the rest of us. The information is here. The rest of us need cryptography to conduct our business'.

DEBRIEF

- Did you explain first what cryptography is and how it ensures that the information is kept hidden from everyone except the recipient?
- Did you give any examples of why cryptography is so important now that so much business is conducted over the Internet?
- You need to explain what type of data should be encrypted.

- Did you explain why many governments do not like information being sent over secure communication lines that even the security services are unable to intercept?
- Did you give the reader an idea of which side of the fence you are on and did you justify your opinion?

Health and safety

Other legislation that affects the computer user is the health and safety legislation that sets out guidelines for use of computers in the workplace. Before we look at the detail of the legislation, let us consider some health problems the computer user needs to be aware of.

There are several health problems that can occur when working with computers for long periods, but with awareness steps can be taken to prevent them. As more computers are used in the workplace, related health problems have increased. In this section we look at the main problems and how to prevent them.

Eyestrain

Most people who use computers have experienced this. Eyestrain is caused by several factors including reflections from lights on the screen, concentration on the screen for long periods and shifting focus onto paper. Both keeping focused on the screen and refocusing the eyes lead to eyestrain. The early symptoms of eyestrain are hazy vision which is usually followed by a headache. When this happens you need to rest and lie down if possible.

Preventing and relieving eyestrain

There are several ways of preventing eyestrain and these include:

Giving your eyes a break
This means taking a break from the computer screen every so often. Experts recommend that a fifteen-minute break should be taken every hour of intensive work on the computer. During this break you should try to relax if possible but if there is so much work to do that this is impossible, you should do some non-computer work in this period.

Refocusing your eyes every so often
This should be done every ten minutes; it means looking up from the computer and focusing your eyes on a distant object.

Use suitable lighting
You need to make sure that there are no concentrated sources of light, such as pendant lights that you have in your home, as these will produce reflections on the screen. Instead, fluorescent tubes should be used which have plastic covers (diffusers) that disperse the light and help provide even illumination of the work area.

Use a copyholder
Shifting your eyes from reading material to the screen can cause eyestrain, and if your neck also moves, this can also give rise to neck strain. It is best to use a copyholder which keeps the material you are working from at the same height as the computer screen as this means your eyes will not continually have to refocus.

Use adjustable blinds on the windows
A frequent problem is the glare from the sun on the screen; to get round this you can use adjustable blinds on the windows. Try to avoid the use of curtains since they cannot be easily adjusted and they also harbour dust since they are not as easy to clean as blinds.

Have frequent eye tests
Employees who work at computer screens are required by law to have their eyes tested, at the expense of their employer, every so often. If glasses need to be worn, the employer should also pay for these.

The effects of radiation

There have been many scare stories in the press about the dangers from electromagnetic radiation projected from computer screens. Many other devices also produce this radiation and most of the relevant research has been conducted near to radar installations and electricity power lines that emit quite strong radiation. There have been stories about pregnant women who have been using screens for long periods, having abnormal pregnancies, but there is little real evidence to support this. Nevertheless, many employers allow pregnant women to move to areas where there are not display screens. There are also many products advertised in computer equipment catalogues for devices that are placed over the screen to cut down this radiation.

Repetitive strain injury (RSI)

People who spend long hours at a keyboard can develop a condition called repetitive strain injury. Basically, this condition is caused by the constant pounding of joints in the fingers, hands and wrists during typing. When keying at high speed, the keys are pressed quite hard, so when the key reaches the end of its depression it stops, and a shock-wave travels up through the various bones in the hand causing damage to the muscles, tendons and nerves in the fingers, wrists, arms and neck.

Symptoms of RSI include soreness or tenderness of the fingers, wrist, elbow, arm or neck. If left untreated it can give rise to a painful condition similar to arthritis, that may cause long-term disability.

Good keyboard design, a well positioned keyboard, good typing technique and frequent breaks can help prevent RSI. Special keyboards and special wrist guards are available to ease fatigue and these are worth using.

Physical stress

Physical stress is a general condition brought about by the body working in the wrong environment or trying to do a task for which the body is not really designed. Physical stress causes direct damage to the body and a doctor can see the damage that has been done. Examples of physical stress include RSI, eyestrain, backache, etc.

Many employers are aware of these stresses and have tried to improve the situation by the use of ergonomically designed workplaces.

Psychological stress

Psychological stress can be caused by using inappropriately designed software. An example might be changing over to a new wordprocessing package and not being able to do a task that was quite simple with the previous system. You feel frustrated because you are wasting time and this gets worse if the job is urgent. Losing files or finding there is a virus on your machine which has caused data loss are some of the most stressful situations.

Because of the various health problems that can occur with incorrect computer use, the government have laid down certain laws that require employers to provide certain things. These are summarised in the sections that follow.

What are the regulations and what can be done about these problems?

Continual VDU use can cause a variety of problems to the users and there are regulations covering their use in the Health and Safety (Display Screen Equipment) Regulations 1992. Although these regulations do not contain detailed specifications relating to VDUs, they do set out some general objectives. Under these regulations, employers are required to:

- analyse workstations of employees covered by the Regulations and assess and reduce any risks

- ensure that workstations meet minimum standards

- plan work so that there are breaks or changes of activity

- on request, arrange eye and eyesight tests, and provide spectacles if special ones are needed

- provide health and safety training

- provide information.

We now look at the practical implementation of these regulations.

Inspections

Employers should periodically inspect the workplace environment and equipment being used to ensure that it complies with the law. Any shortcoming in the conditions, working practices or equipment should be reported and corrected. Inspection of desk, chairs, computers, etc. for risks to workers' eyesight and prevention of physical and mental stress should be carried out.

Training

All employees should be trained in the health and safety aspects of their job. They need to be told about the correct posture for the use of keyboards etc.

Job design

The job should be designed so that the worker has periodic breaks or changes of activity when using computers.

Eye tests

There should be regular free eye tests for computer users, with free glasses provided if necessary, at the employer's expense.

Systems and furniture

The law also lays down certain minimum requirements for computer systems and furniture. All new and existing equipment should now meet the following requirements.

Display screens

Screens must be easy to read and therefore have no flicker and be very stable. Brightness, contrast, tilt and swivel must all be adjustable and there must be no reflection off the screen.

Keyboards

Keyboards must be separate from the screen and tiltable. Their layout should be easy to use and the surface should be matt in order to avoid glare. There must be sufficient desk space to provide arm and hand support.

Desks

Desks must be large enough to accommodate the computer and any paperwork and must not reflect too much light. An adjustable document holder should be provided so as to avoid uncomfortable head movements.

Chairs

Chairs must be adjustable and comfortable, and allow easy freedom of movement. A foot rest must be available on request.

Lights

As we have mentioned, there should be suitable contrast between the computer screen and the background. There must be no glare or reflections on the computer screen, so point sources of light should be avoided and windows should have adjustable coverings such as blinds, to eliminate reflections caused by sunlight.

Noise

Noise should not be loud enough to distract attention or inhibit conversation.

Software

Software must be easy to use and should be appropriate to the user's needs and experience. Although it is allowable for software to be used to monitor an employee's performance, this is not allowed without the knowledge of the employee.

Other matters

Heat, humidity and radiation emissions must be suitably controlled.

Other hazards in the workplace

Besides the hazards related directly to the use of IT equipment there are some general hazards in the office.

Fire hazards

- **Overloaded power sockets** – never overload power sockets since this is frequently a source of fire. If there are not enough power sockets, the room should be rewired since the existing wires may not be able to cope with the level of power consumption.

- **Large quantities of paper lying around** – fires frequently start from cigarette ends disposed of in waste paper bins. A no smoking policy should be in force in office areas and bins should be emptied frequently. Paper stores should be kept away from the working area.

Obstructions

- **Trailing wires** – these are dangerous, so make sure that wires and cables are long enough to go around the walls of a room or are placed in plastic or rubber trunking.

- **Boxes of paper** – frequently, boxes of paper are left around the work area. As well as constituting a fire hazard, they are often the cause of tripping accidents.

Electrical hazards

- **The wrong size fuse** – fuses are designed so that if a fault occurs and the electrical current starts to rise, the thin piece of wire that makes up the fuse will melt. The melting fuse cuts off the electricity and prevents damage to computer equipment. Since computers, scanners, printers, etc. all use different amounts of electricity, you should always make sure that the correct size of fuse is used in each plug.

- **Bare wires showing** – there should be no bare wires showing from any plugs or sockets.

- **Tampering** – when taking the casing off any piece of equipment, make sure that the equipment is first unplugged.

Other safety considerations

- **Lifting** – any lifting of computers, printers, heavy boxes of printer paper, etc. should be performed with knees bent while keeping the back straight. There is a legal obligation on a company to show its employees how to lift properly, if lifting is part of that person's job.

- **First aid** – there must be a qualified first-aider available at all times if the organisation has over a certain number of employees.

- **Fire precautions and emergency evacuation procedures** – these should all be in place and should be practised at regular intervals. Employees must be told not to use lifts during emergencies.

Activity

There are many health and safety issues shown in the cartoon on the opposite page. Some of them are simply bad working practices, whereas others are more serious. How many of them can you spot? Write a list of those you identify and indicate what needs to be done to put them right.

All health and safety regulations in factories and offices are enforced in the UK by a government department called the Health and Safety Executive. Further details relating to all safety matters can be obtained from their website, the address of which is:

http://www.open.gov.uk/hse/hsehome.htm

Figure 4.6 *Is this office safe?*

Activity

Definition of terms

A variety of new terms is introduced in this chapter, many of which may be new to you. It is important that you build up vocabulary which can be used when writing essays or answering questions. Write a definition for each of the following terms used in the chapter:

hacker	patent
FAST	licensing agreement
public domain	shareware
software piracy	personal data
data user	data subject
encryption	privacy
RSI	Data Protection Commissioner

Match the Acts or Regulations

For the examination, you will need to understand which situations are covered by which of the Acts or Regulations mentioned in Chapter 4. The Acts and Regulations are lettered and you are required to match the letter with each of the situations below.

A Health and Safety Regulations

B Copyright, Designs and Patents Act 1988

C Computer Misuse Act 1990

D Data Protection Act 1998

1 Deliberate destruction of a computer program.

2 Laying down the minimum requirements of employers with regard to the physical working conditions of their employees.

3 Copying software packages and then selling the copies at a car boot sale.

4 Buying a single copy of software for a stand-alone machine and then installing it on a network to be used by twenty users, in breach of the licensing agreement.

5 Gaining unauthorised access to a computer system.

6 A company refusing a person access to the personal data held about them.

7 A personnel department not properly ensuring the security of its employees' personal data.

8 A student propagating a computer virus by attaching it to a program file and then transferring the two over the Internet to another person.

9 Making employers responsible for providing regular free eye tests for their employees.

10 Copying the design of a new, ergonomically designed keyboard without the original designer's permission.

Examination Questions

(The number in brackets is the number of marks allocated to that part of the question. Use these marks to gauge the extent of your answer.)

1 A national distribution company advertises its products by sending personalised letters to thousands of people across the country each year. This type of letter is often known as 'junk mail'.

The distribution company purchases the list of names and addresses from an agency.

(a) Describe **two** ways in which use of information technology has increased the use of 'junk mail'. (4)

(b) The company wishes to target letters to people who are likely to buy its products. How might this be done? (2)

(c) A person receiving this type of mail writes to the company to complain that it is acting illegally under the terms of the Data Protection Act. Give **three** statements the company may use in its reply to show that it is operating within the terms of the Act. (3)

(NEAB, Module IT01, May 1996, q6)

2 Describe **three** health hazards associated with computer use. (6)

(NEAB, Module IT01, Specimen Paper, q9)

3 A college maintains an extensive database of its full-time students. The database contains personal data, the courses the students attend, and higher education or employment applications.

(a) Describe how the college might keep the personal data of the students up to date. *(3)*

(b) The college wishes to sell the personal data to a local sports retailer. An agreement is to be written between the college and the retailer. Describe **three** issues, relating to the data, that should be included in this agreement. *(3)*

(NEAB, Module IT01, May 1997, q4)

4 The Computer Misuse Act defines three types of offence. With the aid of examples, describe each of these three types of offence. *(9)*

(NEAB, Module IT01, May 1997, q8)

5 The introduction of computer terminals and personal computers has been associated with a number of physical health hazards.

(a) State **three** health hazards which have been associated with prolonged use of computers. *(3)*

(b) Describe **five** preventative actions which may be taken to avoid computer related health hazards, explaining clearly how each action will assist in preventing one or more of the hazards you have described in part (a). *(10)*

(NEAB, Module IT01, May 1998, q6)

6 The term 'data protection' covers the maintenance of the integrity, quality and ownership of data handled by information technology systems. There are many ways to protect data, and there is also legislation to ensure that data is kept private and secure.

Discuss the Data Protection Act 1998, including reference to:

• objections to the Act;

• the information that should be recorded when registering with the Office of the Data Protection Commissioner.

(NEAB, May 1998, IT01, part q6)

7 (a) State **three** levels of offence under the Computer Misuse Act of 1990. Illustrate each answer with a relevant example. *(6)*

(b) Describe **four** separate measures that can be taken to prevent accidental or deliberate misuse of data on a stand-alone computer system. *(8)*

(NEAB, Module IT01, May 99, q5)

8 The use of Information Technology equipment has brought Health and Safety risks for employees.

Describe **four** such risks, and the measures that an employer should take to protect their staff from them. *(12)*

(NEAB, Module IT01, May 99, q6)

9 A company specialises in organising international conferences for doctors. The company has decided to make use of the Internet for advertising and organising the conferences.

(a) State, with reasons, the hardware that the company would need, in addition to their PC and printer, in order to connect to the Internet. *(4)*

(b) State the purpose of the following software when used for the Internet:

(i) Browser

(ii) Editor

(iii) E-mail software. *(3)*

(c) Explain **three** potential advantages for this company of using the Internet as opposed to conventional mail/telephone systems. *(6)*

(NEAB, Module IT01, May 99, q7)

5 *Relational Databases*

CHAPTER OBJECTIVES

▶ To understand the need for, the nature and purpose of a database.

▶ To understand the advantages of databases and other storage systems.

▶ To understand the need for data organisation.

▶ To select and justify appropriate file and database structures.

What is a database?

A database is an organised collection of data or information. From this definition, you can see that the data does not necessarily have to be stored on a computer. Most large collections of data are now computerised and the main advantages of using a computerised database is that is gives more flexibility in organising, displaying and printing, and it is much faster than any manual system.

Computerised databases can be divided into two types: the limited flat-file database suitable for only a few applications and the much more comprehensive and flexible relational database. We will now look at the two types of system and see what makes the relational database a much more effective tool.

The advantages of databases over other storage systems

The main advantages of a computerised database are as follows:

✔ Advantages

- You only have to enter the data once. All other applications make use of this centralised pool of data.

- Files/tables are linked; this means that if the data is changed in one application, the database is automatically updated in other applications.

- If you find, due to changes in the organisation, that it is necessary to change the structure of the database, then this is easily done. With a manual system it would be very difficult and involve a lot of work.

- Access to the information is very rapid.

- Complex search criteria can be constructed and these can be saved and used again or even modified.

- Everyone uses the same data so that data consistency is ensured.

- Validation checks can be performed on the data as it is entered, thus helping to protect the integrity of the database.

There are a few disadvantages:

✘ Disadvantages

- If the file server containing the database breaks down, none of the applications that use the data can be used.

- Security needs to be considered carefully as all the data is now held centrally.

- Users of the system will need careful training and this can be expensive.

Flat-file versus relational databases

Flat-file databases are little more than computerised card box files where a card (sometimes shown as a diagram of a card on the screen) can contain one record. A record is simply the complete information about a person or a thing such as a product, order, student, employee, etc. An item of information, such as surname, date of birth, product description, on a record is called a **field**. Flat-file databases are fine if you only want to store a list of names, addresses, phone numbers, etc. but they are unsuited to most business applications where more flexibility is needed.

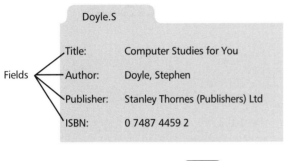

Fields — Title: Computer Studies for You
Author: Doyle, Stephen
Publisher: Stanley Thornes (Publishers) Ltd
ISBN: 0 7487 4459 2

Doyle.S

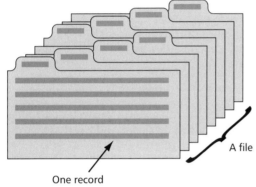

One record

A file

Figure 5.1 *The relationship between fields, records and files*

Disadvantages of a flat-file database

These can best be illustrated by considering an example. Suppose we created a flat-file database to hold the details about the orders made by customers to a company and a customer came along and wanted to order some goods. We would have to create a new record in the order file, and this would entail typing in details such as the customer's name and address and then all the details about the items being ordered. Clearly, there will be a lot of typing involved for each order.

Suppose a day later, another order for the same customer arrives. We would then have to create a new record for this order and fill it in again. Some of the information, such as name and address will be the same as for the first order, so re-typing all of this data would be a waste of time. Also, even if an order were identical we would still need a new record and have to go to the trouble of typing everything in.

This highlights one of the main problems with a flat-file database: data duplication.

The use of a more sophisticated database, called a relational database, would solve the above problems.

Relational databases

Relational databases sound complicated, but are in fact relatively simple. They do not store everything in a single file but instead use several files with relationships between them. The relationships between the files ensure that the data in one file can be combined and used with the data contained in one or more of the other, related files.

When talking about relational databases we tend to talk about tables rather than files although the tables are stored on the disk as files.

The main advantages in storing the data in this way lies in the fact that time is saved by not having to duplicate as much data, and this also means that less storage is needed and any subsequent processing or manipulation of the data is much quicker.

To understand the concept it is best to look at an example. Suppose we are setting up a database to process the orders made by customers. In a relational database, three main tables might be used with the following names:

- customer
- stock
- order.

With a relational database, instead of completing the customer details in the order file each time, we have a separate file, or table, for customers and get the customer's details from that. Each time we want the customer's details we simply get them from the customer file rather than having to type them out again. It is not possible to remove the data duplication completely since there will need to be a common piece of data in both of the files, such as a customer number, in order to form a relationship between the two tables. Once we have this piece of data, say the customer number, we just need to type it in and all the customer's details are obtained from the customer file.

Order table	Customer table
order number	customer number
customer number	customer name
order details	customer address

We now use two tables rather than one to store the data.

Also, instead of typing out each time the details of each item ordered, we can now put these in their own file or table, called 'stock'. This stock table contains a list of stock numbers, stock descriptions, prices and the number in stock. The main advantages in using the stock table are:

- we no longer need to type in the description and price for each item ordered

- we can tell if it is possible to satisfy the order from stock

- when there is a price change, we can change just the stock file.

All we now need to enter and store in the order file are the item number and the quantity, since all the other information can be obtained from the stock file.

So three tables can be used to store all the data: an order table, a customer table and a stock table. There are still some problems in storing the data in three tables and a further table is needed, called the 'order line' that stores the data in one particular order. The need for this extra, less obvious table, will be looked at later in this chapter.

By using a relational database you can see how it is possible to reduce the need to enter information over and over again with each customer order. Storing the data in tables and then establishing relationships between tables decreases the amount of disk space the data takes up and also makes for much quicker access and manipulation of the data. Additionally, since the data needs to be entered only once, the number of errors introduced will be smaller.

You can see why the relational database is such a powerful tool.

Search-query facilities

The whole point in storing data in a database is that it is easy to perform searches to extract data which satisfy certain criteria, such as people over the age of 65, women in the production department who have not had health and safety training, etc.

One way of searching for the data in a database is to use commands written in a certain language called structured query language (SQL). SQL consists of a small number of commands, and, like programming language commands, they must be carefully constructed, which can be frustrating for inexperienced users. In many ways SQL can be likened to a fourth generation programming language (4GL). A fourth generation language is a software tool that allows applications to be developed more quickly.

If we have a database containing employee records, we might want to obtain a list from the database of employees in the production department who earn over £25,000 per year. We could do this using the following series of SQL commands:

```
SELECT EMPLOYEE_NAME
WHERE DEPARTMENT = 'PRODUCTION'
AND SALARY >= 25000
```

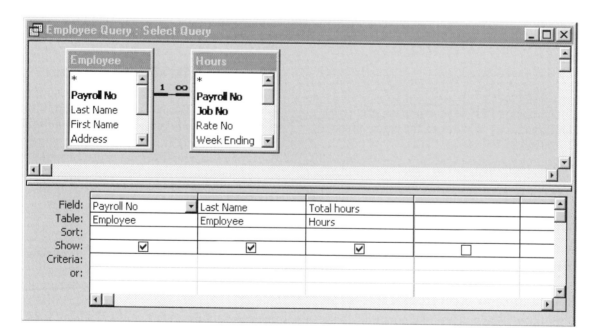

Figure 5.2 *A database query in Microsoft Access*

Query by example (QBE)

Query by example (QBE) provides a simple way of running queries without having to worry about the way the queries are constructed, as you have to when using SQL. QBE uses a simple way of selecting the columns you want to display; you can also specify simple search conditions and orders. QBE allows inexperienced users to access the power of a relational database without having to bother about the syntax of SQL.

In Microsoft Access, a relational database, you can display the relevant tables for the query, then select any fields you want to use. Once this is done you can then specify any fields you want to display, any that you need to sort into ascending or descending order, and finally specify any search criteria you wish to use. The computer then displays the results of the query or you can print them out as a report. In the example shown in Figures 5.2 and 5.3, we produce a list showing the payroll number, last name and hours worked, in ascending order, for all employees who have worked over 20 hours in total.

Payroll No	Last Name	Total Hours
132785	White	21
122122	Jones	21
132456	Wiggins	24
233247	Hughes	25
233478	Bryson	27

Figure 5.3 *The results of the database query in Figure 5.2*

To see how easy QBE is to use, compared with SQL, instructions to perform the same query by SQL are shown below.

```
SELECT DISTINCTROW Employee.[Payroll
    No], Employee.[Last Name], Hours.[Total
    hours]
FROM Employee INNER JOIN Hours ON
    Employee.[Payroll No] = Hours.[Payroll No]
WHERE ((Hours.[Total hours]>20))
ORDER BY Hours.[Total hours];
```

The structure of a relational database

The building blocks of any relational database are its tables and the relationships between these tables. Tables are collections of information arranged in rows and columns.

Field names are shown at the top of the columns and a record, which is more correctly called a **tuple**, is shown as a row. Figure 5.4 shows a table used to store the data about vehicles owned by a car hire firm.

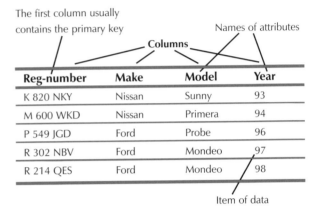

The first column usually contains the primary key

Columns

Names of attributes

Reg-number	Make	Model	Year
K 820 NKY	Nissan	Sunny	93
M 600 WKD	Nissan	Primera	94
P 549 JGD	Ford	Probe	96
R 302 NBV	Ford	Mondeo	97
R 214 QES	Ford	Mondeo	98

Item of data

Figure 5.4 *A table of data*

In Figure 5.4 the first column contains the primary key that has to be unique. In this case the registration number can be used for this, but in other tables it might be necessary to create a unique reference number if there isn't one already. It is important to note that each row in the table must be unique; there cannot be any duplicate lines for a given value of the primary key. To ensure that this does not happen, the database designer/analyst needs to be careful in designing the tables.

Record and file structure design

Since relational databases store the data in the form of a collection of related tables, the structure of the tables needs to be defined before data can be put into them. This is done using the database package more properly referred to as a relational database management system (RDMS). The structure for each of the tables needs to be defined and then saved separately. In Microsoft Access, the most popular RDMS for PCs, the table definition window shown in Figure 5.5 is used.

You can see in Figure 5.5 that the window is divided into two parts. The upper part is used to define the field name and the type of data allowed in that field, and to give a brief description, with examples, of the data that the field can hold. The bottom part of the screen is used to define the field properties for each field in turn and ensure that only allowable data is added.

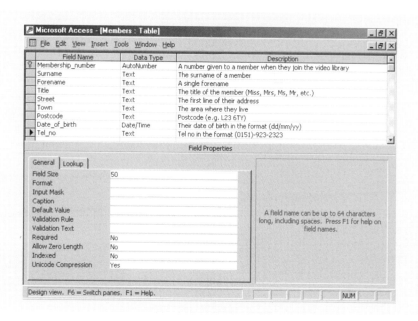

Figure 5.5 *The table definition window in Microsoft Access*

Primary keys

A primary key is a field that is used to uniquely define a particular record or line in a table. It is unlikely that any text field could be unique, so primary keys are nearly always numeric fields. If you make a field such as 'surname' a primary key, then if when typing in data you tried to enter a surname that had already been entered in a different record, the database would not accept it. It is necessary to make sure that a number uniquely defines the record. Such primary keys include membership number, product number, employee number, catalogue number, part number, account number, etc. If a primary key has not been defined, then most databases will create one automatically, (called an AutoNumber) which gives each record a number based on the order the records are entered. Thus the first record entered will be given the counter value one, the next two, and so on.

Secondary keys

Secondary keys are those keys that can identify more than one record. For example, a surname field in a student database would not necessarily be unique because several students could have the same surname. Surname is still a useful key to sort and search on, so it is termed a secondary key.

Foreign keys

A foreign key is a field in one table which is also the primary key of another. Foreign keys are used to establish relationships between the main table and the other, subsidiary tables.

Indexing and sorting

Suppose you wanted to find out about structured query language in this book. One way would be to look through the pages until you came across the heading. Rather than do this, a faster way would be to use the index at the back of the book. This is similar to the way a database produces an index.

When data is entered into records in a database, the order of the records is the same as the order in which the records were entered. The problem with this is that they will usually be in chronological order (i.e. ordered according to date entered) and we might want them in order of surname, product number, order number or employee number. We may even prefer a combination of orders; for example, by age and within each age, in alphabetical order. There are two options open to us. One is to sort on one or more fields. The main problem with sorting data in a database is that when the sort is performed, a new database is created with the data in its new order. You now have two databases, taking up twice the storage space. Each time the database is sorted into a different order, a new database is produced and this process rapidly eats up valuable storage space on disk.

To get around this problem we can use an index. Because of the importance of the primary key in defining a particular record, a primary key is always indexed. In addition to the primary key you can choose which other fields to index. Database software is able to process queries and searches much faster if a field has been indexed.

It is not possible to index all the fields in a database. The following fields can be indexed: text, numeric, currency or date. Although all the fields in the database, provided they are of the correct type, could be indexed, you should make sure that you only index those fields which are likely to be used for sorting or searching. The reason for this is that if all the fields have indexes, any subsequent editing or adding (called appending) of records would be slowed down considerably. The slowing down is because when records are added or changed an index table is created at the same time as the original table, so in any subsequent operations two tables are being manipulated.

To see how an index works we will look at producing and using one to place a list of names in alphabetical order.

The following table shows the record number, which is the order in which data was entered and the data, which is the surname. In reality surname would only be one of many fields in a student record, but we shall simplify by using surname as the only field.

Record number	Data
1	Davies
2	Adamson
3	Jackson
4	Rogers
5	Jones

In this case the data being indexed is the surnames of the students in a college.

Record number	Index
1	2
2	1
3	3
4	5
5	4

We now look in detail at how this is done. The computer takes the data (i.e. the surnames in record number order) and puts them into alphabetical order. A new table is then created which contains the record number of the first table as the index. For instance, the first piece of data would be Adamson which will be record 1 in the second table. We now put an index number in, which is the record number for Adamson in the first table (i.e. 2). This is done for all the surnames until they have all been ordered. We now have two tables: the one which is the original database table and a second which provides the index. Both of these tables need to be used when putting the data into alphabetical order.

Database structures

Database software allows the data to be held in a structured and organised way. Before data can be entered this structure needs to be set up. Consider the following before setting up the structure:

Choosing field names

Field names are normally chosen to match the attributes in the data model produced after the normalisation process, but they can be changed to make them more descriptive if you so wish. Field names should always describe the data the field is used to hold. Try to avoid using spaces in field names; instead use dashes or a combination of upper case and lower case letters.

Choosing data types

Careful choice of data types ensures that the person inputting the data into the database can only enter certain types into certain fields and this provides autovalidation.

In most databases, data can be of the following types:

- text (alphanumeric characters)
- memo (used for data in note form; a window will usually open where messages which do not conform to any particular format can be added)
- number (for numeric values such as integers, real numbers, etc.)
- date/time
- currency (monetary values to two decimal places)
- AutoNumber (a numeric integer which the computer automatically increments for each record added)
- yes/no (Boolean values)

- OLE (OLE objects, graphics and other binary data).

Choosing the field lengths

Date and currency fields have their field size pre-set, but others (such as numeric and text fields) need to have their field size specified, unless the default (i.e. the number the computer will set it to automatically) is acceptable. When choosing field size, think about the data being entered into the field and assess the likely maximum number of characters. If you choose a field size that is too small, then try to enter longer strings of characters, you will be unable to do so, which means you will have to go back to the structure of the table and alter the size. This is easily done and no data is lost in the process, so it does not matter too much if your estimates for field size are not spot-on.

Data types and validation checks

When data is being entered into the fields in a table, before you can move on to the next field, the database program checks to make sure that the data entered is allowable for that field. If it is not, the computer will display a message.

Single record retrieval

When data is stored in a flat-file database, the records are given a single key field that distinguishes them from other records, since no two records will have the same key field.

With relational databases the data is stored in several tables and relationships are established between the tables, so the tables are linked and their contents can be combined to produce reports. For each table there will be one or more keys that will uniquely identify a row in that table. For most tables a single field can be used as a primary key, but for others it might be necessary to use more than one. Because of the unique nature of the primary key or keys, they can be used to retrieve a single record in the case of a flat-file database, or a row in a table from a relational database.

Referential integrity

Suppose in a video hire database we used three tables: videos, members and rentals. In order to extract data from more than one of these tables, relationships would need to be established between the tables. When entering data into the rental table there would be nothing to stop someone entering a member number which did not already exist in the members table, which is undesirable if we want to protect the integrity of the database.

When enforcing referential integrity, the DBMS checks that the member number being entered into the rental table actually exists in the member table. When forming the relationships between the tables, most databases allow you to choose whether you want referential integrity enforced or not.

Questions

The manager of a tool hire company wishes to use a relational database management system to help keep track of the business. The database stores the data in three tables: tools, customers and rentals.

1 What are the main advantages to this manager in storing the data in a relational database rather than a flat-file database.

2 For each of the tables, identify the key fields and also list the other fields which would enable the manager to store the data with minimum redundancy.

Building a relational database

A considerable amount of analysis is needed to build a relational database successfully, and only when this is done does the developer know what fields are needed and which tables they should be in. When devising the fields, the developer should ask, 'what output is required from the database?' since you cannot output anything which has not been input or that can not be calculated from the input. To build a relational database successfully, you should follow these steps:

1 Thoroughly research the existing system and produce a clear statement of what the system is required to do.

2 List the entities (or tables) in the system you are looking at, and draw diagrams showing the relationships between the pairs of entities. Make sure that any many-to-many relationships are broken down by the creation of a new entity. Use the diagrams to draw a complete entity relationship diagram.

3 List all the attributes in the system. Remove any attributes that are unlikely to be used.

The attributes can be put in a list below the entity name.

4 Put the attributes in some sort of order in the list so that attributes describing the same sort of thing are kept together.

5 Normalise the data, converting it from the un-normalised form to 3NF (this is covered in Chapter 16). The normalisation process ensures that data is in a form that can be successfully and efficiently implemented. It places data in groups that can then be used as tables in a relational database.

6 Create the structure for each of the tables and decide on appropriate data types, validation checks, etc.

7 Determine the relationships between the tables and create them using the database software.

8 Refine your design. It is quite hard to get everything right first time, so you may have to make changes to the structure as you go along. Do not worry about this too much as most databases are flexible and it is easy to make changes to the structure even once data has been entered into the tables.

Database security

Many organisations keep a central pool of data using a DBMS, the security of which is critical to the organisation. Use of the system must therefore be within the framework of adequate security measures that will ensure that:

1 an item of data is only accessed by those persons who are authorised to do so

2 once the data has been stored inside the computer system, certain measures are taken to prevent it from being corrupted, lost or destroyed by any means.

Activity

Definition of terms

A variety of new terms is introduced in this chapter, many of which may be new to you. It is important that you build up vocabulary which can be used when writing essays or answering questions. Write a definition for each of the following terms used in the chapter:

database	flat-file database
relational database	file
record	field
SQL	QBE
table	primary key
secondary key	foreign key
DBMS	RDMS
referential integrity	

(Note: Most of the examination questions on relational databases will be covered in Chapter 16.)

1 The manager of a video hire shop uses a relational database management system to operate the business. Separate database files hold details of customers, video films and loans. Customers can hire as many films as they wish.

(a) For each of the files mentioned above, identify the key fields and list other appropriate fields that would be required to enable this system to be maintained with minimum redundancy. (6)

(b) Describe **three** advantages of using a relational database rather than a flat-file information storage system. (6)

(NEAB, Module IT02, May 1996, q7)

2 Database Management Systems provide facilities to extract data from a stored database.

(a) Name **two** common methods of setting up a query. (2)

(b) State **one** advantage and **one** disadvantage of the two query methods stated in part (a). (4)

(NEAB, Module IT02, May 99, q5)

6 Inputs and Outputs

Collecting data

Before data are processed, they need to be collected and then converted to a computer-readable form; this is called encoding the data. If the way that the data are collected in the first place is flawed in some way, then no amount of checking and processing can rectify this.

What is a sample?

Suppose you have a bottle of milk that has gone off and you take a small sip from it. Once you realise that the milk in your small sip is off, it is reasonable to assume that the rest of the milk in the bottle is off. In other words you have assumed that your small sample (the sip) mirrors the situation in the whole bottle (or 'population' as it is called in sampling terms).

This is the basis of sampling, which is used when it is not possible to look at all the data because its analysis would be too cumbersome and take too much.

There are two main factors to consider when planning a sampling strategy:

1 the sample taken should be representative of the whole population

2 the size of the sample should be large enough to enable sensible further analysis.

For example, we might need to know the average financial value of each order a company receives. If the orders we take as our sample just happen to be large ones compared with the rest, they would not be representative of the order values of the whole population. The data collected as a sample is correct, but it is the way we have taken the sample that is incorrect, and this means that any information gleaned from it will be misleading.

Examples of incorrect sampling strategies include:

● not taking into account the effect of seasonal factors in sales of items such as soft drinks, holiday bookings, fruit sales, car purchasing, etc.

● not taking into account the variations due to weather such as in sales of woollen clothes, gas, electricity, plants, etc.

● not taking into account geographical factors in circumstances such as when looking at average house prices, levels of unemployment, etc.

● obtaining the sample from a group of people that does not reflect the population as a whole.

Sampling rates

Sampling rates are a measure of the frequency at which the sample is taken. It is important when using these samples for further analysis, that the correct sampling rate has been used.

Suppose you are a sales manager and are looking at the sales performance of your team. You might decide to look at daily, weekly, monthly, quarterly and yearly sales. Which one would you use? Daily would be too frequent and result in too much data to analyse. Weekly might not give the correct picture, since sales sometimes take time to set up and all the orders could tend to come towards the end of the month. Take the table here, which shows the weekly sales figures for salesman, Mr A Forrest.

Week number	Sales made		Week number	Sales made
1	12		9	14
2	15		10	14
3	25		11	49
4	67		12	94
5	16		13	13
6	23		14	24
7	45		15	31
8	87		16	98

Weekly sales figures for Mr A Forrest

On looking at these figures it may seem that the salesman only gets sales towards the end of the month when the pressure is on to achieve the sales targets. The truth of the matter is that most customers order towards the end of the month for cash-flow reasons. So, although the data is correct, the information we draw from the figures might be incorrect.

If we turn these figures into monthly sales figures we have the following:

Month	Sales made
January	119
February	171
March	171
April	166

Monthly sales figures for Mr A Forrest

Notice that once the fine detail we see in the weekly figures has been removed, a clearer picture is seen from one month to the next. In this case monthly figures would be preferable since it is easier to compare with sales targets that would be set on a monthly basis.

It is important that the sampling rate is appropriate so that the data being collected yields the correct information.

Suppose you were an analyst for a car manufacturer and you had collected details about people who could possibly be interested in buying a new car in the near future. Not all of these people will be in the market at exactly the same time. Some may decide to buy a new car every two years, others might wait until their existing car comes up for its first MOT inspection and others might be in the market for a wide variety of different reasons.

If the company decides to stimulate their interest it may decide to send them brochures and details of special offers of finance, free insurance, etc., but rather than sending everyone the details, a better response might be achieved at less cost by targeting the people who are most likely to buy.

You could interrogate the database to extract a sample of people most likely to buy and just send these people letters. You could also follow these up a few months later, but if the frequency with which you took the data from the database were too great then the same customers could be sent details too regularly and this could put them off. In this case you would have got the sampling rate wrong if the customer becomes irritated.

If a company which makes ice cream wishes to investigate how much the sales of their products are influenced by the weather, then a daily sampling rate should be chosen, since weather in Britain tends to vary significantly from day to day. If an incorrect sampling rate (such as weekly) were chosen then the fine detail of changes in weather would be eliminated and although the sales *data* extracted would be correct, the *information* about the variation with sales would be incorrect.

Data capture methods

Data capture involves getting the data into a computer-readable form, and into the computer system in as short a time as possible and with as few mistakes as possible. The choice of data capture method depends mainly on the volume of data. Wherever possible, large amounts of data should be dealt with by a direct form of data capture, where the data is read directly from documents.

Human involvement in any data capture should be reduced to a minimum, since it is expensive (in terms of the wages), slow, and prone to errors. As technology advances, we are moving away from slow methods of data capture, such as the keyboard, towards new, faster methods, such as speech recognition.

Speech recognition

Speech recognition systems are gaining popularity as a method of entering data directly into the computer without using a keyboard. Unless you are a trained typist, you probably type at a speed of about 30 words per minute, but when this is compared with the speed you talk (typically 175 words per minute), you can see how any system that allows you to talk rather than type is going to save a lot of time and effort.

Although some systems allow you to speak directly into the computer to produce finished documents, they are far from perfect. With most of the cheaper speech recognition systems you have to take a short pause between each word, which takes a little getting used to, and the net effect is to slow the recognition down to a more leisurely 80 words per minute, around the speed of a typical touch-typist.

Most systems need the user to train the system to recognise the way they speak their words, and this training session typically takes from around 30 minutes to several hours. At first speech recognition systems make a lot of mistakes but they get better as they learn from their mistakes.

☑ Advantages

The main advantages of speech recognition systems are:

- they reduce the reliance on secretarial staff

- their use speeds up the flow of documents, since you no longer need to wait for someone to type the letter.

Although many organisations use speech recognition systems, lawyers seem to have taken to it more than most groups. Because of the nature of their work they have to send many individual letters. These were previously dictated into a dictation machine and then passed to an audio typist who typed the letter. The typist would then return it to the solicitor for checking and signing before it was sent in the post. All this took time, especially if a mistake was found in the letter and it needed altering. The use of speech recognition software has enabled solicitors to produce letters themselves, check them on screen and then print them.

Some people receive lots of e-mail messages each day; replying to them all becomes a problem if they are slow at typing, but speech recognition systems can be used to dictate replies. In addition to this, you can use macros so that if you say certain words such as 'senior management team', the e-mail is automatically distributed to a list of people.

Optical character recognition (OCR)

Optical character recognition is a method of inputting characters into the computer without

having to type them at the keyboard. The technique makes use of a scanner that senses the reflected light from the characters and effectively forms a 'picture' of each letter. Special recognition software then compares the shape of each character with shapes which have been previously stored, so it is able to distinguish each character individually.

Once the characters have been recognised and recorded it is possible to manipulate them on their own or use them in wordprocessed, DTP and spreadsheet documents. There are some difficulties with OCR; the main one is that the result is not entirely accurate, so spell checking and proof-reading are always needed. Also the copy to be scanned needs to be clear, so a photocopy of a photocopy will not be ideal!

OCR need not be used to capture the whole of a document; it could, for example, be used to capture a series of long numbers that would be too cumbersome to type. Optical character recognition is used in the turnaround document system, where a bill or statement is sent out and a tear-off slip is filled with the amount paid and sent back with the payment. It is then used by the original organisation as an input document. The customer account number, which is usually quite a long number, is usually input using OCR.

Figure 6.1 shows the use of a turnaround document to record payment of a gas bill.

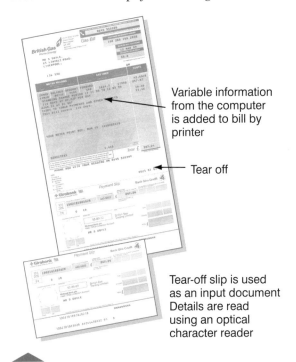

Variable information from the computer is added to bill by printer

Tear off

Tear-off slip is used as an input document Details are read using an optical character reader

Figure 6.1 *The use of a turnaround document to record payment of a gas bill*

Magnetic ink character recognition (MICR)

Magnetic ink characters are the rather strange looking figures seen at the bottom of a bank cheque. The characters are printed with special ink which contains a magnetic substance which when printed forms a pattern that can be read by the input device, called a magnetic ink character reader. These numbers have the advantage that they can be read by both a human and the machine. OCR could have been used instead, but with documents as sensitive as bank cheques a method was needed which would make it difficult for people to forge the numbers. MICR equipment is very expensive and complex and to date no one has managed to breach the security offered by this method.

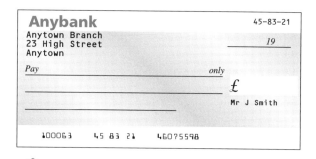

Figure 6.2 *A cheque makes use of MICR 6.6*

MICR is not widely used and its only large scale application is the reading of data on bank cheques, such as customer account number, branch code, and cheque number, which are all pre-printed on the cheque. The amount for which the cheque is written, is not known when the cheque is printed and has to be added by the bank when the cheque is paid in; it is typed in magnetic ink just below the amount box, before the cheque is sent by the bank to the clearing centre.

Optical mark recognition

Optical mark recognition is a quick and fairly accurate method of data capture. It involves using a form containing boxes which can be shaded in and a reading device, called an optical mark reader to read the responses. The main applications for this method of data capture include the responses on questionnaires, multiple choice answer sheet marking, checking football pools coupons and capturing lottery numbers.

Since optical mark readers work by sensing marks made in certain places on specially designed forms, if the marks are in the wrong place or the user places a tick near the box rather than shading the box in, the reader is unable to read the data and the form is rejected. The rejection rate using this method can be quite high (typically 30 per cent) although people are now more familiar with the technique owing to the National Lottery. There is an additional problem in that any folded forms might jam in the machine or be rejected. Figure 6.3 summarises the main uses of OMR.

Bar code reading

Bar coding provides an alternative to typing a code in. The number or letters are coded in a series of light and dark bars of varying widths. When the bar code is passed over the bar code reader, the code is automatically entered. There is usually a separate file containing the code and details such as product description and price, etc.

Bar codes can be found in many different applications apart from the obvious recording of goods in supermarkets. These application include using bar codes to track parcels by delivery firms, to organise luggage in airports and for recording details of borrowers and books in libraries.

Keyboard

The keyboard is the commonest input device in use, but it does have some severe limitations, mainly that it is slow, especially if the person using it is an untrained typist. There is also the problem of many errors being introduced during keyboarding. In computing we often refer to the 'keyboard bottleneck' where the computer can process almost immediately the data it receives, but input is slowed down to the speed of the typist entering the data.

Key to disk

This method of data capture involves the user typing in the data via a keyboard, directly into the computer, where it is captured and stored on disk or tape. This data is then run through a validation program, designed to pick out any errors in the input. Data is then processed along with the master file and a new updated master file is produced as a result of this processing.

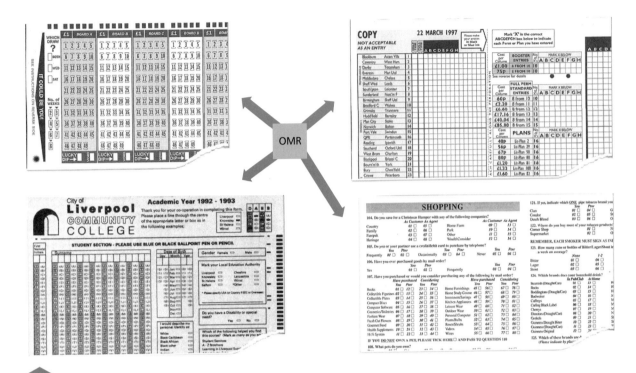

Figure 6.3 *The main applications making use of OMR*

Mouse

Most people who use computers know that a mouse is an input device, but it can also be used as a method of data capture. Commands can be entered using the mouse instead of the keyboard. Many database packages that use Windows enable the user to select fields from lists rather than having to make up the field names and type them in.

Magnetic strip readers

Magnetic strips can be found on most cash and credit cards and on customer loyalty cards. Data is encoded in the magnetic strip and each time it is used, the card is swiped through the reader which reads this data off the card. Information encoded in the strip can include credit limits, balances, points earned, etc.

Touch-tone telephones

Modern telephones work by having a different tone for each of the numbered keys, so for example, a number five has a slightly different tone to a number six. It is by using these different tones that the numbers dialled are recognised and routed to the correct telephone. Once connected, a touch-tone telephone can be used as a data entry device. In some home banking systems, the customer keys in their identification number using the phone keys. Once connected, the customer can select certain services, such as statements, using the same keypad. Many companies now use the touch-tone telephone to route calls made by customers from the switchboard to the correct department.

Using sensors to capture data directly

In some specialist applications, data from sensors might be captured directly and entered into the computer as a series of electronic signals, which can then be processed. Flood warning systems use sensors in rivers to detect the level of the water and if it reaches a certain maximum level, then flood warning alerts are given out so properties near the river can be evacuated.

There are many different types of sensor available, each responding to a certain physical property such as temperature, light, moisture, pressure, etc. If we wished to count the number of packets of soap powder passing along a production line we could use a beam of light which would be interrupted each time a packet passed between the beam and the sensor.

Other examples of using sensors include placing a pressure sensor across the road to count the number of vehicles passing as part of a traffic survey. This avoids the expense of using people to perform the task. Pressure sensors are also used to monitor the flow of traffic approaching traffic lights, so that the sequencing of the lights can be altered to minimise congestion.

Questions

1 (a) When discussing data capture we often talk about the 'keyboard bottleneck'. Explain what this means.

   (b) There are certain qualities that an ideal method of data capture would have. Give three such qualities.

2 State, with reasons, the most appropriate data capture method for each of the following situations:

   (a) monitoring the flow of traffic along a road

   (b) helping someone who is blind to use word processing software

   (c) marking multiple choice examination answer papers

   (d) entering a whole page of a document into your word processing package without the need to type it in

   (e) reading customer information on a new loyalty card used by a chain of restaurants

   (f) entering the details of bank and building society cheques at the central clearing centre

   (g) reading the details of the flight, etc. on the labels of luggage at an airport.

   (h) recording the membership number of a member who is borrowing a video from a video library

   (i) routing customer calls to the correct department in a large insurance company.

Error checking

There are serious implications in processing data that is incorrect, so techniques are put in place to minimise the number of errors. In this section the two main error detecting techniques called verification and validation will be looked at.

The differences between the accuracy of information and the validity of data

If a user types a person's surname into a database as 'Jones' rather than 'James' (the correct name) then the data in the database is no longer accurate although a valid piece of data has been entered. No amount of validation would be able to detect the error. A piece of data can be incorrect yet still be valid. Another example is where a number is entered into a field on which there is a range check which prevents any number greater than 1000 from being entered. If the keyboard operator misreads a customer as 700 instead of 100, then this will not be picked up by the range check since 700 is a valid item of data. So although validation checks can ensure that data is reasonable or sensible they cannot ensure that data are 'correct'.

Verification

The purpose of both verification and validation is to make sure that only accurate data is processed.

Verification is the process of checking data before it is accepted for processing. It is a pre-input check that does not need a special program. In most cases verification is performed by the person inputting the data and involves them checking what has been entered on the screen against the source documents (application forms, orders, invoices, etc). In other words, they are performing a visual check to make sure that exactly the same data appears on the screen and on the documents they are referring to. This should ensure that no error, particularly in typing, has been made by the person keying the data in.

There is another method of verification in which two people type in the same data and only if the data is identical is it accepted for processing. The serious disadvantage to this approach is that two people are performing the same task just to eliminate data entry errors. It is also possible that two operators could make an identical mistake so that it would still go unnoticed.

As more e-commerce is conducted over the Internet, companies use the customer to do the inputting. For example, with the on-line book store, Amazon, you type in your details and then select the books you want in your order by clicking on them and adding them to your shopping basket. You are a lot less likely to make a mistake in your own details than someone else, so this method of data capture is ideal from the company's point of view because it is free and more accurate. The customer is happy to do this, because the goods are cheaper over the Internet since administration costs are lower.

Validation

Validation is a check performed by a computer program as the data is being entered into the system. Its purpose is to trap any data that does not conform to certain rules. Validation is unable to stop all errors from occurring. For example, if someone enters the number of your house as 23 rather than 32, this will not be trapped by a validation check. Validation checks trap some of the likely and obvious errors, and help to ensure that the data accepted for processing are accurate.

Many relational database management systems allow the developer to construct specific validation checks when they are setting up the database. These allow only data conforming to certain rules to be entered into the fields.

The following range of validation checks can be employed.

Range checks

Range checks are used to ensure that the data being entered is neither too large nor too small, that is, it lies between certain pre-set limits. If the data entered does not obey these pre-set range rules, it is not accepted and the user is alerted by a message stating why the data is unacceptable.

Data type checks

Data type checks make sure that the correct type of data is being entered into each field. If you try to enter text into a numeric field it should be rejected. There is a variety of data types you can choose for each field, including numeric, character, logical, date and memo.

When specifying the data type for numeric fields, remember that some types of data with the word 'number' in their titles might not be proper numbers and should therefore be stored in a character field. Examples of this type include order numbers (e.g. D33003), telephone numbers (0151 987 9009) and membership numbers (000780). It is best to ask yourself, 'Am I likely to perform a calculation with this number?' and if the answer is 'no', use a character field.

Existence checks

It may be acceptable to leave some fields blank, whilst others need always to be filled in. For example, each employee in an organisation will be given an employee number when they join the organisation, so this field must be present in every employee record; if someone tries to enter a record without it, it should not be accepted. Other fields such as the employee's telephone number may be left blank, because they might not have a telephone.

Question

Which of the following fields in an employee database should always have data entered?

- date of birth
- employment start date
- National Insurance Number
- home e-mail number.

Types of error

There are many types of error that can be introduced when using an information system and different types of errors can be introduced at different stages. Most errors occur during the data capture stage and in this section we look at these errors.

Transcription errors

Transcription is the process of transferring data/information from either a document (an application form, order form, etc.) or from a conversation over the telephone, directly into a machine-readable form, by typing it in at a keyboard. More and more details are taken directly over the telephone, thus eliminating the need for paperwork. The operator who answers the phone also keys the details directly into the computer.

Transcribing information in this way is not without its problems, most of which centre around the care the operator has exercised. Errors resulting in incorrect data being entered are called transcription errors and these usually occur due to the following:

- not being able to read the writing on the source documents (confusing the letter S with the number five or zero with the letter O

- the person giving information over the telephone not speaking clearly

- the person taking the call misinterpreting what the caller has said

- typing mistakes made during the keying process.

Transposition errors

Transposition errors occur when two digits or letters are swapped, a situation which frequently occurs when typing at high speed. Examples include 'ot' for 'to' and '3423' instead of '3432'. The main thing is to notice that this kind of error has been made and to correct it, which should be done by careful proof-reading. With word processed documents, it might be possible to run the documents through a spellchecker, although these do not pick up all transposition errors. Using the results from an analysis of errors it has been shown that around 70 per cent of all errors are transpositional errors. Check digits, ensure that important numbers such as employee numbers, book numbers, product numbers, account numbers, etc. do not contain transposition errors.

The use of check digits

Check digits are usually added to long code numbers; they provide a way of trapping transcription and transposition errors. The check digit is an extra digit added to the end of the code and this number is calculated from all the other numbers. When a code number with a check digit is entered, the computer uses all the other numbers to calculate what the check digit should be. It then compares its calculated value with the actual check digit and if they are the same then the code is accepted for further processing. If there is a discrepancy, the computer alerts the user to re-input the number. Most check digit systems make use of the 'modulo 11' test, which is performed in the following way. The example we have chosen is that of an ISBN (international standard book number), which is a unique number present on all books (including this one) used by bookshops and libraries to identify a particular book.

Suppose a book with the ISBN 0 7487 2492 3 is input into a computer.

1 The computer removes the last digit (i.e. the check digit) and is then left with:
   0 7487 2492

2 The remaining nine numbers now have calculations performed on them. Working from the left hand side, the first number (i.e. 0), is multiplied by ten, the second number (7) is multiplied by nine, the third number (4) is multiplied by eight and so on.

The total is then found from the whole expression:

$$(0 \times 10) + (7 \times 9) + (4 \times 8) + (8 \times 7) + (7 \times 6) + (2 \times 5) + (4 \times 4) + (9 \times 3) + (2 \times 2) = 250$$

3 The total (250) is always then divided by 11 and the remainder noted (you will need to use long division to get the remainder). In this case 11 divides into 250, twenty-two times with a remainder of eight:

$$250 = (11 \times 22) + 8$$

4 The remainder (8) is then taken from 11 to give the check digit:

$$11 - 8 = 3$$

So 3 is the check digit.

5 Using this method the check digit will sometimes be 10, in which case X is used, as this avoids having to use two digits for the check digit.

Although it may seem a complicated calculation it needs to be so for transposition errors to be detected. The weighting given to the position of each number means that if two numbers are swapped around, this will give a different total and so a different check digit.
Also remember that the computer has no difficulty in performing this kind of calculation very quickly.

Questions

1 Here is a list of international standard book numbers for books which someone has asked you to order from a local bookstore. Because they were in a hurry when they copied the numbers down, some of the ISBNs are incorrect. Using the method shown in this chapter, check each one, show your working and say whether each is correct or not.

   (a) 0 7487 3029 X

   (b) 0 7487 2809 1

   (c) 0 7487 0381 0

2 Here is a correct ISBN:

ISBN 0 7487 2493 1

Here is the same ISBN but in this case there is a transposition error:

ISBN 0 7478 2493 1

(a) Explain what is meant by a 'transposition error'.

(b) By working out the check digits for the correct and incorrect ISBN numbers, explain how the incorrect number is detected.

3 Explain the difference between the verification and validation of data.

4 Describe two ways in which data to be entered into a database can be validated.

5 Data can be incorrect yet still be valid. By citing a suitable example, explain what this means.

Using validation expressions when designing databases

Databases allow the database designer to set validation rules for certain fields so that the data being entered must obey these rules to be accepted for storage and subsequent processing. To set a rule, you type in a validation expression which must be constructed with the correct syntax.

In the popular relational database Microsoft Access there are many different validation expressions and the following table shows just some of them.

Expression	Validation rule
>=Date()	The date entered must be either today's date or some date in the future.
Between 1 And 10	The number entered must be between one and ten inclusive.
Like "###[A-Z]"	The data entered must be in the format three numbers followed by one letter (e.g. 452B).
"2A" Or "2B"	The data entered must be either 2A or 2B.
<=100	The number entered must be less than or equal to 100.
=Date()	The date entered must be today's date.
"Male" Or "Female"	Only the words Male or Female can be entered.

In Microsoft Access, a text box containing a message can be made to appear when a user attempts to enter invalid data. For example, when paying for goods over the telephone by credit card you are normally asked for the expiry date for the card. A validation rule can be used to compare the expiry date with the date the order is made, to make sure that the expiry date is later; if this validation rule is not obeyed, then a text box appears to alert the user with a message such as 'This credit card has expired. Ask the customer to use a different card or cancel the order'.

Sources and types of error during processing

Input data can still be incorrect even though it has been verified (i.e. checked against the source documents) and validated. Incorrect data can arrive in a variety of ways and is usually due to human involvement, either at the data collection stage or the input stage. The only way to avoid errors is to keep human involvement to a minimum and therefore use direct methods of data capture such as MICR, OMR, OCR, bar coding, etc. whenever possible.

Mistakes that could occur during processing include:

1 A programming error that remains undiscovered during testing and only comes to light when a series of conditions apply. The year 2000 problem was an example of this; some application programs crashed when this date was reached owing to the programmer not having the foresight to realise that the date 00 in the year field will often be trapped by a validation check and cause the program to stop execution.

2 The computer operator uses the wrong transaction or master file or uses an old version of the data rather than the latest version.

3 When processing uses master files (files containing all the records) and transaction files (files containing all the changes which need to be made to the master file), the main problem which arises is if someone tries to alter a record using the transaction file when no such record exists in the master file.

In a batch processing system, a list of records that cannot be processed is given at the end of the processing run and these are dealt with manually or when the problem has been rectified they can be put through the system again.

Hash totals

Hash totals are meaningless totals that are used as a check. For example, we may have an invoice containing, amongst other things, the product numbers of the items being ordered. The item numbers could be added up and input separately. When the details on the invoice are keyed in, the meaningless total (called the hash total) is also keyed in. If the computer does not calculate this same total then it means that not all the items on the invoice have been keyed in or that a mistake has occurred.

Control totals

A control total is like a hash total, except that the total has some meaning. For example, the total of a batch of invoices has some meaning and could be used to check that all the invoices had been processed in a batch processing system.

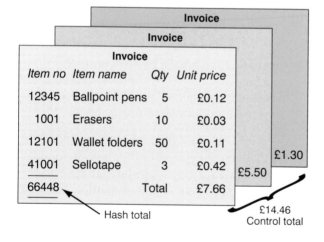

Figure 6.4 *Hash and control totals*

Lookup tables

Product codes, employee numbers, membership numbers, etc. are all unique and can be checked against a table by the computer each time they are used. This ensures that only valid codes are entered and subsequently processed by the computer.

Sources and types of error during transmission of data

When data is passed along a communication line it is important that the data is not corrupted in any way; if it is, it is equally important that this is detected and the data is re-transmitted.

The checking of data after it has passed along a communication line is performed using a parity check. Parity checking works in the following way. The computer adds up the number of bits in one byte and if the parity is different to the parity setting, the computer will report an error. It is possible to use either even parity or odd parity. Taking odd parity for instance, suppose we are sending the letter C along a communication line. The series of bits used to represent C in ASCII code is 1000011. Since there are three 1s in this code and odd parity is being used, then a 0 is added to the left-hand sided of the group of bits, so that the total for the byte is odd. If even parity were being used, a 1 would be needed so that total for the byte would then be an even number.

Modems have a chip inside them to deal with parity checks; the sending modem adds the parity bits and the receiving unit calculates what the parity bit should be. If an error has occurred, transmission parity will no longer be observed, and corruption is detected. The problem with parity checks is that if more than one error occurs and the errors compensate for each other, parity can still appear to be correct.

Methods of processing

Processing of data can be done on a transaction-by-transaction basis, or they can be stored up and processed in one go. In this section we look at the main methods of processing.

Batch processing

In batch processing groups of similar transactions, built up over a period of time, are collected and then processed during one processing run. Although you may think that batch processing is an old-fashioned method, it is an ideal method for a variety of applications and is still widely used.

The idea behind batch processing is that it is easier to allow similar tasks to build up over a period of time (daily, weekly, monthly, etc.) and then do all the processing together at the end of the period. This means that the existing data becomes progressively out of date as the time since the last processing run increases. This makes batch processing only really suitable for a fairly limited set of applications.

Batch processing is ideal where the data can be read from documents automatically and where the computer, once supplied with all the programs and data, can get on with the processing automatically. Applications for which batch processing is especially suited include:

- payroll
- month-end invoicing
- production of bank and credit card statements at the end of each month
- quarterly production of gas, electricity and telephone bills
- stock control
- the marking of multiple choice examination papers.

Batch processing runs are usually performed over a weekend or evening, when the computer is not being used interactively for dealing with customer enquiries.

The grandfather–father–son principle (ancestral file system)

There is always the chance that data contained on a master file could be accidentally or deliberately destroyed, for example by an inexperienced user, a power failure, a machine malfunction, etc. The loss of vital data could prove disastrous for any company so a backup method is needed to re-create the master file is necessary; the method most appropriate for batch processing systems is the grandfather–father–son principle.

The principle works like this. Basically, three generations of file are kept. The oldest master file is called the grandfather file and is kept with its transaction file. These two files are used to produce a new master file called the father file which, with its transaction file, is used to create the most up-to-date file called the son file. The process is repeated and the son becomes the father, the father the grandfather, and so on. Only three generations are needed so the other files can be re-used. Although the diagram shows tapes being used, the system is equally applicable to a disk-based operation.

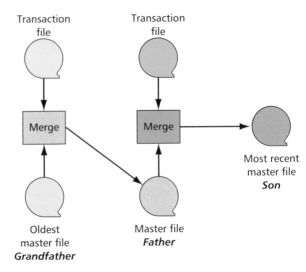

All these files are kept so that if one or more of the files are lost they can be recreated

Figure 6.5 *The grandfather–father–son principle, used for file security in batch processing systems*

☑ Advantages of real time systems

1 Batch processing can be performed during the evening when the computer is not being used interactively.

2 Once the inputs have been given to the machine and the correct software loaded, the computer system can be left to carry out the work with no human intervention.

3 Users do not have direct access to the system so there is a higher level of security.

4 Audit trails (checks performed by the auditors) are easily made since the processing of the data occurs at pre-determined intervals.

☒ Disadvantages of real time systems

1 Data is only up to date immediately after the processing run and goes progressively out of date until the next processing run. This limits its suitability to a small group of applications.

2 Staff workload is not spread throughout the period and tends to be concentrated around batch runs.

3 It is not usually possible to produce *ad hoc* reports.

Data flows in a typical batch processing system

In a batch processing system the input documents are batched together and this gives the main advantage of being able to control when a particular batch of input documents are processed. If there are any errors with any of the input documents then the batch containing the problems can be easily located. Normally a document, called a batch header slip, accompanies each batch and records details of the control totals and a number that relates to a register called the batch register in which all the details of the batches are logged. Control totals (such as the total of a whole batch of invoices) can be compared with a total similarly calculated by the computer, and this ensures that all the invoices have been processed.

Interactive processing

In interactive processing the processing system responds immediately whenever a change occurs. Interactive processing is also called on-line processing because the computer needs to have access to any files it needs immediately, so storage devices need to be on-line, necessitating disk rather than tape storage.

ABC Products has an on-line ordering system. Orders are taken over the phone. The main characteristics of ABC Product's on-line system are as follows:

- Customer data is acted upon immediately. The data obtained from customers over the phone is entered directly into the system.

- A check is made to confirm that the ordered items are in stock and they are taken off the stock list as they are ordered, to ensure that the stock file always shows the *true* stock position.

- The customer invoice is produced on the spot and sent to the warehouse so that staff can pick and pack the goods requested.

- The accounts receivable file, containing records of the amounts owed to ABC, is updated by the amount of the invoice.

When on-line processing occurs so rapidly that it affects the user's activities immediately, it is called real-time processing. This should really be called 'pseudo real-time' because with genuine real-time processing there must be no noticeable delay, which can only truly be achieved by a system using sensors such as in a process control system.

Some systems (such as those used for the selling of shares in the stock markets or the selling of foreign currencies in the foreign exchanges markets) react so quickly to the changes in the markets that they can be considered to be in almost real time.

Real-time systems typically include the following:

- airline seat reservation systems

- process control used to brew beer

- flying an aircraft using fly-by-wire or automatic pilot

- playing a fast-moving 'arcade' game on a home computer.

☑ Advantages

1 Since processing takes place immediately, the data held is always up to date.

2 Files are held on-line, which means they can be used to produce *ad hoc* reports.

3 The need for paperwork is avoided.

4 The workload on staff is spread evenly.

☒ Disadvantages

1 Audit trails are harder to perform because processing occurs continually as transactions arise.

2 There is very little paperwork associated with the system, so checking is made more difficult.

Many building societies now use on-line processing for their mortgage applications which means that the applicant sits down with one of the mortgage advisors and the computer guides the advisor through a series of questions. The advisor then fills in the electronic form with the applicants' details and if any problems crop up (such as them trying to borrow more than they can afford) the computer immediately informs the advisor. The advantage with this system is that the form can be filled in while the clients are present so that the advisor can help them with some of the questions. When all the questions have been answered the printer is used to provide the customer with a copy of the form to take away and also one to be signed and retained by the lender.

Pseudo real-time systems

A pseudo real-time system is one that takes a transaction from outside (such as a booking for a theatre or airline ticket) and then processes it before the next transaction is accepted. This means that two people who are in different travel agencies could not book the same holiday accommodation for the same period. The main advantage of pseudo real-time systems is that they prevent double bookings.

CASE STUDY

National Utilities: a typical batch processing system

National Utilities is a public company which supplies electricity and water to domestic users. Although the systems used for each side of the business are similar, in this case study we just look at the capture of electricity meter readings and their subsequent validation and processing to produce the electricity bills which are sent to customers.

Each meter reader is given a Psion organiser, which is a hand-held terminal used to store the addresses of the houses to be visited and the account numbers of these customers. The meter reader reads the meter and inputs the number into the organiser; so the data is captured remotely and off-line. As the terminal also holds estimated maximum and minimum readings (based on the electricity used over the same period for different years) the reading is compared with these when entered and any discrepancy brought to the attention of the meter reader. In many cases there will be a good reason why the reading is out of the range, but if the meter reader has made a mistake the reading can be re-input.

At the end of the day, the terminal is brought back to the office where the data is transferred via a cable to the main computer system on which the details are stored in a transaction file. The data obtained from all the meter readers is batched together and placed on the same transaction file. This transaction file will contain only the customer account number (which uniquely identifies the customer) and the new meter reading since all the other data is available on another file, the master file.

Because there are hundreds of meter readers, each batch of readings is input to the same transaction file and details are in no particular order.

The master file is arranged in order of customer account number and the processing run will take much less time if the transaction file is in the same order. So before processing, the transaction file is sorted so that it is in the same order as the master file. The transaction file is then processed alongside the master file which contains details such as customer account number, name, address, last meter reading, payment method and all the other details needed to calculate the amount of electricity used and produce an electricity bill. Batch processing is ideal for this since processing of millions of readings can take place overnight and once the high speed laser printers are filled with paper and the program started, the system can carry on with no human intervention.

Batch and control totals are used to ensure that all the records have been processed correctly. A new master file is produced containing the new details, and the transaction file along with the old version of the master file are kept safe as part of the ancestral file system used for backup purposes.

Questions

1 A couple of years ago, National Utilities used OMR forms to collect the meter readings. What are the main advantages in using the current data capture method compared to the old system?

2 In the above example, data capture is performed remotely, off-line, whilst the processing occurs on-line. Explain the meaning of the terms on-line and off-line in this context.

3 Explain how batch and control totals could be used in this batch processing system to ensure that all the data has been processed correctly.

The need for suitable output formats

When presenting material it is important to give some thought to the output format. Wads of computer printouts, which to a computer person might be interesting, are not likely to interest non-specialist staff involved in strategic decision making. In many cases graphics can be used to summarise statistical information and these can be presented as a series of slides. It is often said that a picture saves a thousand words and this is certainly true of information obtained from computer output.

Effective presentation also involves tailoring the output material to the audience. Output is used by different people for different purposes, so it is important to understand the use to which it is to be put and then to make sure that the output is in a suitable format and at a suitable level for that use. Information could be used by shareholders, directors, managers, staff or customers and each would require their own tailor-made output.

Activity *KEY SKILLS IT 2.3, IT 3.3*

Here is a table showing the monthly sales revenue in 2000 and 2001 obtained for a certain washing machine. The sales director needs to present this information to the board of directors and needs to make the figures look more interesting, so she has asked you to produce an appropriate graph.

Month	2000	2001
January	128900	145600
February	210780	240981
March	189000	210987
April	127900	146921
May	156987	230602
June	167322	170340
July	100782	110900
August	112800	132000
September	121567	143977
October	146980	178921
November	135320	187340
December	156855	198600

Your task is to present this information graphically, using suitable software, so that it can be presented to the directors.

Choosing the output format

As well as making sure that the output is tailored to the individual, it is equally important to make sure that the most suitable output format is used. The choice really depends on the subsequent use made of the output. A number of different possibilities are discussed below.

Text
Most output makes use of text, but word processors and desktop publishing packages are the main tools needed for this kind of output with presentation graphics and other packages using text to a lesser extent.

Numbers
Numbers are often presented in the form of tables which most word processors have facilities to construct. If calculations need to be performed on the numbers then a spreadsheet package will be found most appropriate.

Sound
Sound is the output from voice mail systems and part of the output from videoconferencing systems. It can also be used to accompany multimedia presentations.

Graphics
Computer generated graphics feature in many applications and clip art can be used to brighten up pages in word processed or desktop published material. Slide shows produced on the computer often make use of graphics.

Video
Video involves pictures and sound, just like the programmes shown on television. Until fairly recently video stretched the capabilities of the machines (as far as memory and processor speed were concerned) to the limit, but the technology has improved to the extent that such output is now feasible.

Animation
Still graphics included in presentations can seem boring when compared with the moving graphics many presentation graphics packages now allow you to create. These moving images bring presentations to life and make watching them a memorable experience. It is for this reason that many companies use animation as a way of helping sell their products. Microsoft PowerPoint and CorelDraw both have facilities for animation.

Output media
When people think of output from a computer they usually think of producing output on the screen or on paper, but there are other output media.

Output on disk

The owner of a small business might be asked by his accountant to send accounts for auditing on magnetic disk, thus avoiding the keying needed if they were simply printed out on paper. Such output also avoids the mistakes which might be introduced during the keying process. Even if the accountant uses a different spreadsheet package to the accountant, it will not matter because most packages allow you to import work into a different package.

Authors sending text to their publisher can do so using disk rather than posting a large manuscript (which they would need to photocopy first) and pay the cost of the postage. Once the publisher receives the disk, they are then able to import the work directly into their desktop publishing package without the need to key all the text, thus saving a large amount of time and money.

Output as electronic signals (on-line)

When e-mail is sent, the output is an electronic signal that is used as the input by the recipient's computer. You can also regard your web page or website on the Internet as an on-line form of output and this is now becoming an increasingly important form of output medium.

Projection screen

It is possible to produce output to a projection screen rather than output to a monitor, and this is the method used with videoconferencing equipment.

Dissemination/distribution

Many computer printouts contain too much information and managers/executives often spend lots of time wading through paper to find the information they need. With careful thought, the output can be designed to show exactly what the user is looking for. This is done by the careful use of search conditions.

When a database is interrogated it is important to think about how the results are best presented. You need to consider the fields that need to be included along with any orderings and groupings.

Activity

Definition of terms

A variety of new terms is introduced in this chapter, many of which may be new to you. It is important that you build up vocabulary which can be used when writing essays or answering questions. Write a definition for each of the following terms used in the chapter:

data capture	OCR
MICR	OMR
verification	validation
parity	batch totals

1 An international chain of department stores uses an information system to assist in marketing its produce by forecasting public demand for certain products.

(a) Suggest **two** factors which might be considered when planning a sampling strategy for forecasting public demand. *(2)*

(b) Describe a situation where an inappropriate sampling rate could lead to accurate data but inaccurate marketing information. *(2)*

(NEAB, Module IT02, June 1997, q3)

2 A well designed information system should be able to check that input data is valid, but it can never ensure that information is accurate.

(a) Explain the difference between accuracy of information and validity of data. Illustrate this distinction with a suitable example. *(4)*

(b) Describe **two** ways in which data capture errors may arise, together with techniques for preventing or reducing these errors. *(4)*

(NEAB, Module IT02, June 1997, q6)

3 A chain of estate agents has eighty branches. Daily transactions relating to house sales, purchases and enquiries are processed using a batch processing system on a mainframe computer at head-office.

(a) Outline the flow of data through such a batch processing system. *(4)*

(b) The company is considering changing from the batch system to an interactive system. Describe the advantages and disadvantages of moving to an interactive system. *(4)*

(NEAB, Module IT02, May 1996, q3)

4 A school uses an information system to store details of students' examination entries and results. As part of this system a program is used to check the validity of data such as candidate number, candidate names and subjects entered.

(a) Suggest **three** possible validation tests which might be carried out on this data. *(3)*

(b) Explain, with an example, why data which is found to be valid by this program may still need to be verified. *(2)*

(NEAB, Module IT02, May 1996, q5)

5 Describe **three** methods of data capture and give applications for which each would be appropriate. *(6)*

(NEAB, Module IT02, Specimen Paper)

6 A manufacturing company intends to use an information system to store details of its products and sales. The information system must be capable of presenting the stored information in a variety of different ways. Explain using **three** distinct examples, why this capability is needed. *(6)*

(NEAB, Module IT02, May 1996, q4)

7 A computer system can be described as being a "pseudo real-time system".

(a) State clearly what is meant by pseudo real-time. *(2)*

(b) Give a situation where pseudo real-time is essential, stating a reason why it is needed. *(2)*

(NEAB, Module IT02, May 1998, q4)

8 SupaGoods is a home sales company. Catalogues are left at people's homes. A local agent calls two days later to take orders and collect the catalogues. The agent sends the details of the goods ordered to the Head Office where they are processed. The completed order is returned to the agent who distributes the goods and collects payment.

(a) Describe **two** distinct methods of data capture for the agent. State **one** advantage and **one** disadvantage of each method *(6)*

(b) The orders are validated at Head Office.

(i) Explain what is meant by validation. *(2)*

(ii) Describe briefly **two** validation checks that might be carried out on an agent's order. *(4)*

(NEAB, May 1998, Module IT02, q5)

9 An office worker has created a macro which imports data from one spreadsheet file to another and then performs some calculations. However, the macro fails to work as expected when it is used.

(a) Explain the term 'macro' as used in the above description. *(2)*

(b) What could the office worker have done to reduce the chance of the macro failing when it was used. *(3)*

(NEAB, Module IT02, May 99, q3)

10 A nation-wide chain of retail clothing stores processes its daily transactions using a batch system based on a mainframe computer at a central location.

(a) Outline the flow of data through such a batch processing system.

(b) The company is considering a change from the batch processing system to an interactive system. Describe the advantages and disadvantages of moving to an interactive system. *(4)*

(NEAB, Module IT02, May 99, q9)

Hardware and Software

Hardware

Hardware is the term used for the physical components that make up a computer system. Generally speaking, if you can actually touch it, it is hardware. Hardware includes input devices, such as keyboards, the processor which is the brains behind the computer, and output devices, such a monitors and printers.

Input devices

Input devices are used to get data from the outside world into the computer. The ideal input device would be able to input the data automatically without any human intervention, accurately and quickly, and have a low cost.

Unfortunately, the ideal input device, which satisfies all these criteria, does not exist, so a compromise has to be found depending on the type of application. It is important to be able to match an input device to its application. In this section we look at the types of input device available, how they work and the applications to which they are best suited.

Scanners

Pictures can brighten up the dullest document and they are almost essential if you need to make up an interesting and attractive web page or website. Using a scanner, you can add previously printed diagrams and photographs using your wordprocessing, desktop publishing, web page/site design software. The most popular scanners are the flatbed scanners which look like rather thin photocopiers. There are also scanners into which the paper is fed and these have the main advantage of not taking up as much space on your desk. However, paper-feed scanners have the big disadvantage that you cannot copy from books without taking a photocopy of the page first, since they only allow a single sheet to be fed in.

Flatbed scanners work by passing a bright bar of light over the page to be scanned. The reflected or transmitted light is picked up by photosensitive

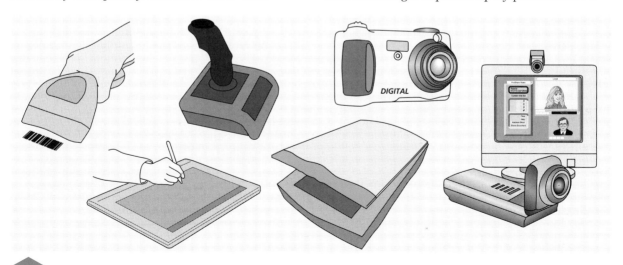

Figure 7.1 *Can you name the input devices illustrated?*

cells and assembled into a picture. Scanners are available which will scan to produce black and white or colour pictures, but you should always bear in mind that if you cannot print in colour there may not be a lot of point in scanning in colour unless you are using the picture for web page design or some other application where the output is not from your own printer.

Optical character recognition (OCR)

Optical character recognition uses a scanner in combination with special OCR software that can recognise individual characters in a scanned image. This enables a page of text to be scanned into wordprocessing or similar software as an alternative to keying text in from a source document (see Chapter 6).

There are two main situations in which OCR is used:

1   **For copying text into a wordprocessing or DTP package.**

    The hardware for this is usually a flatbed scanner where the page can be placed on the sheet of glass that forms the bed of the scanner. When the text is scanned, it is treated as a picture of the page and by using special optical character recognition software each letter is then analysed and recognised separately.

2   **For recognising accounts numbers etc.**

    Utility bills, such as gas, electricity and water, are scanned to input the amount number rather than the operator having to accurately type in such long numbers. If you look at copies of these bills these numbers are in very bold type.

Optical mark readers

Optical mark readers read marks made on specially designed and marked documents. They work by picking up the light reflected from the marks. Optical mark readers are ideal for reading the data from questionnaires, answers to multiple choice examination questions, menu choices in hospitals, football pools and lottery tickets. Once loaded the sheets can be read automatically and at high speed. The main problem with optical mark recognition as a technique is that the reject rate is high (people do not always obey the instructions on the sheet and answer sheets tend to get folded or trapped

in the machine) and a lot of marks are needed to capture quite a small amount of data.

Magnetic ink character reader (MICR)

These are expensive input devices that are used to read characters written in magnetic ink, usually on bank cheques. Account numbers, sort code numbers and cheque numbers are stored in the strange-looking characters in a magnetic pattern which enables them to be read automatically and at very high speed using a magnetic ink character reader. The main advantage of the system is the security it provides.

Digital cameras

Digital cameras have become very popular input devices because they are able to capture an image and store it digitally on a magnetic disk inside the camera. Their main advantage is that no film or development is needed which reduces the costs involved in taking photographs. In addition, with a normal film you can take around 24 to 36 pictures at a time, with the digital camera this can be in excess of 100. This means that more pictures can be taken without considering the cost and just the best ones selected for output.

Once pictures have been taken with a digital camera, the stored images can be loaded into the computer. Using special software they can be sized and the colour altered, after which the picture can be incorporated into a document. These cameras are very popular with those developing web pages or websites since the pictures need not be developed and then scanned in. Digital cameras are used by estate agents so that the pictures can be incorporated into the sales particulars for immediate display.

Bar code reader (laser scanner)

Bar code readers shine light onto a series of light and dark lines and the reflected light is analysed and converted to a code which is then used to identify the goods. Bar code readers are used in shops for reading the article number, but they may be useful in any system where a long identifying number needs to be entered accurately. Bar code reading systems are also popular in libraries for recording book and member numbers. They are also employed in luggage handling at airports, in stock control and in parcel/letter tracking systems. Barcode readers used to be quite expensive but cheap ones are now available with software, all for a couple of hundred pounds, which puts them within reach of most users.

Most bar-coding systems make use of an extra digit, called a check digit, that is added to the end of the number and used to check that all the other numbers have been entered correctly (see Chapter 6, page 93). You may notice this process taking place when you are out shopping and the POS terminal emits a beep when an item's bar code has not been read correctly. The operator then has to re-scan the bar code or enter it manually.

Figure 7.2 *Bar codes seem to spring up in all sorts of applications!*

The mouse

A mouse is an input device since it can be used to make selections and, depending on the selection made, the data chosen is then input into the system. Commands are often selected from pull-down menus in Windows-based software, an alternative to typing in commands using the keyboard or using the cursor keys. Other pointing devices similar to a mouse are looked at in Chapter 10.

The keyboard

The keyboard is the oldest input device and still the most popular. It is an appropriate input device for small quantities of data. For large quantities of data other alternative data capture methods need to be used which are quicker, and less prone to error.

Activity

In this section on input devices, only a few of the many input devices available were covered. Your task is to investigate the other input devices and write a small section about each one (how it works, what it is used for and the applications to which it is particularly suited). Here are a few to start you off:

- graphics tablet (digitiser)
- touch screen
- magnetic stripe reader
- tracker ball
- joystick
- light pen
- punched card reader.

Processing devices

The processor is the name given to the chip that performs all arithmetic and logic operations; it can be a whole computer or just one microprocessor. It may be thought of as the engine in any computer system and it is important that the right one for the job is chosen. Some of the more powerful computers have more than one processor and are capable of parallel processing, which means that they are able to run two or more parts of a program simultaneously.

With PCs, the main processor unit is usually taken to mean all the components inside the casing, excluding the power supply and storage devices (such as floppy disk drives and CD-ROM/DVD units). This typically includes the following components for a PC main processor:

- CPU (central processing unit)
- mother board (the board where all the built-in electronics are situated)
- controller boards (e.g. video and disk drive controllers which are attached to the motherboard)
- any additional special processors (e.g. maths co-processors)
- input and output ports (serial, parallel, etc.).

New processors, which have faster clock speeds (measured in MHz), are continually being developed.

Storage devices

There are many storage devices on the market and the computer user has a wide range to choose from. Most PCs contain hard disk drives with a storage capacity of around 12 GB (twelve gigabytes, which is 12,000 megabytes). Bearing in mind that the normal floppy disk drive only contains 1.44 MB, backing up a disk drive of this size would involve several thousand floppy disks and take hours. It is therefore no longer feasible to backup drives on to floppies, so many of the storage devices that follow in this section offer a way around this problem.

Floppy disks

Floppy disks are an important and popular storage device, but their low storage capacity (1.44 MB) has meant that they are really only suitable for transferring small files between computers or providing a backup for wordprocessing documents, spreadsheets and other undemanding packages.

Floppy disks, as the name suggests, are flexible plastic disks coated with a magnetic material and come encased in a plastic case. When the disk is placed in the drive, it rotates at 360 revolutions per second (which is a lot slower than hard disk drives) and this limits the speed at which the data can be read from, or written to, the disk; this is called the data transfer speed. Another limiting factor arises because the disks are not continually rotating like a hard drive, so the disk has to accelerate to operating speed before data can be read off or written to the disk. However, they are the most widely used backup medium and since nearly all computers have such a drive, there is no problem in transferring data from one machine to another via a floppy.

Hard drives

Hard disks are not usually a single disk rather a series of metal disks on a plinth. The top surface of the upper disk and the bottom surface of the lower disk are not used for storage, but all the other surfaces may be used, with each surface having its own read/write heads. Because the data for a particular file is stored not on a single disk surface but over several disk surfaces, the read/write heads can operate independently and this means that high data transfer speeds can be achieved. There is no time wasted waiting for disks to reach operating speed since the disks are rotating continuously.

Most hard drives are fixed inside the computer case but removable drives are available and these are useful for backing up an internal hard drive, since they may be locked in a fireproof safe.

Zip drives

These are cheap storage devices that plug into the parallel port of a PC. They consist of a single removable hard drive of the same diameter as a standard floppy disk (3.5 inches), and like the floppy are removable. The Zip disk looks like a standard floppy disk except it is much fatter. Typical storage capacities are around 100 to 250 MB, with transfer rates of around 1.4 MB per second.

Jaz drives

Jaz drives are similar to Zip drives but have a much larger storage capacity (around 2 GB on a single cartridge). The data can also be compressed using 2:1 compression and this means that 4 GB can be stored on a 2 GB cartridge. The cartridges on which the data is stored are removable and have a data transfer rate of around 7 MB per second, which makes them faster than most hard disk drives. Like Zip drives, they are light and are ideal for backing up personal computers.

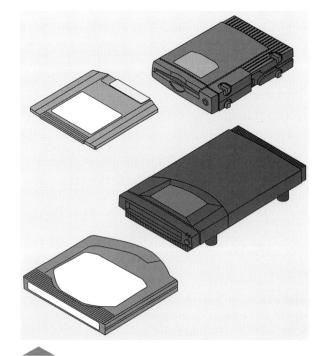

Figure 7.3 *Zip and Jaz drives are popular backup devices for PCs*

Ditto drives

These are tape drives which store the data on a tape contained in a removable cartridge. They can typically store 2 GB of data with data transfer rate of 10 MB per minute. They are easy to install and use and offer the facility to back up your data as you work.

Optical drives

Magneto-optical drives use a combination of magnetic and optical technologies. A laser is used to heat a recording layer on the disk before the data is written magnetically. Optical disks come in various formats and data written on these disks is very secure, so they are often used for long-term data storage.

RAID (redundant array of inexpensive disks)

Networked systems often make use of a RAID server which stores all the data on a series of high capacity, hard disk drives, linked together by a controller. RAID systems offer a high level of data security since the same data is stored on all the disks. This means that if one of the disks suffers a malfunction (such as a head crash), then the damaged disk may be removed without affecting the system, and the data can simply be used off one of the working disks. RAID disks offer the additional advantages of being easy to upgrade, but they are very expensive, costing several thousand pounds. RAID systems are examined in more detail in Chapter 8.

DAT (digital audio tape) drives

DAT drives can be internal or external and are able to run under most popular operating systems, such as Windows NT and Windows 2000. DAT drives are used mainly for backing up networks and make use of tapes that can typically store between 2 and 40 GB of data. They have the advantage that they are relatively cheap and can store large amounts of data on one tape. The main problem with DAT is that the heads on the tape drive need to be cleaned regularly and the tapes are easily corrupted or damaged. DAT is much cheaper than the digital linear tape covered in the next section and is an appropriate choice for backing up small to medium-sized networks.

DLT (digital linear tape) drives

DLT drives are used by larger systems and are compatible with all the major multi-user operating systems such as Windows NT, Windows 2000 and UNIX. They are supplied as external drives which are connected to the file server and use cartridges each capable of holding 70 GB of data. File transfer rate is extremely high (5–10 MB per second), so the time to access a particular file on a cartridge full of data is very low. DLT drives and their cartridges are not cheap, so this type of storage is limited to large-scale commercial stores of data. As with DAT drives, the heads need to be cleaned regularly. DLT drives are expensive but they are a reliable method for backing up large amounts of data quickly.

CD-ROM drives

CD-ROM disks are the best medium for the distribution of software because of their high storage capacity (typically 700 MB) and the uniformity of their use (most PCs come with a CD-ROM drive). Floppy disk drives with a storage capacity of 1.44 MB used to be adequate but many packages now need storage of tens or even hundreds of megabytes, so installing such packages using floppies is laborious.

There are many different CD-ROM drives available, each with a different multiplier (e.g. 40-speed, 48-speed or 50-speed). This multiplier refers to the speed at which the CD is able to transfer its data, called the transfer rate. When CD-ROMs first came out they had a speed of 150 KB of data per second; when a faster CD-ROM was developed with a transfer rate of 300 KB/s it was called a 2-speed CD-ROM. So a 40-speed CD-ROM has a data transfer rate of 40×150 kilobytes per second.

To write onto a recordable CD, a special and more expensive CD drive is needed and this type of drive is particularly useful if you are a software producer or are developing multimedia applications.

CD-R and CD-RW drives

CD drives are gradually going to be phased out with the introduction of DVD, but there are two sophisticated CD drives that are now becoming popular; CD-R drives use disks that can be written once and never overwritten. CD-R disks can be read by any CD-ROM drive. The CD-RW drives are read/write, which means the information written on them can be overwritten with new information, but they have the disadvantage that a special CD reader is needed to read them.

DVD (digital versatile disk) drives

DVD-ROM is set to replace CD-ROMs and soon all computers are likely to come with them supplied as standard. DVDs are high capacity optical disks, similar in many ways to standard CD-ROMs. At present the capacity of a DVD is about 24 times the storage capacity of a CD-ROM. Although a new reader is needed to read the DVD disks, this same reader can also read standard CD-ROM disks.

The main use to which DVD is put is to store high quality digitised video with up to eight hours' worth on a single disk. DVD will replace standard video recorder and videotapes providing higher quality digital video. In computing, they will probably be used for the storage of data and for the storage of video-based multimedia packages. Soon there will be a coming together of domestic television and the home PC to provide a wider audience with Internet access, videoconferencing, video on demand and digital video recording from a camcorder.

At present DVD-RAM is being developed so that it will be possible to record data to a disk by using a simple, inexpensive drive.

Activity

Using recent copies of computer magazines as your source, produce a document that compares and contrasts a range of the most popular backup devices that can be used with a stand-alone computer containing around 200 MB of very important and valuable data files. In your comparison you will need to include details such as typical storage capacities, prices, speed of data transfer and any other details you feel are important.

Output devices

Output devices are used to communicate the results of processing to the user as well as displaying the operating system and application software interfaces. As hard copy (printouts on paper) become less popular, due to environmental considerations, more information will be output electronically to another computer. You can start to see this happening with e-mail, where people read it once and then store in on their hard drive if they need to refer back to it. Few people bother printing their e-mail out.

Printers

Printers are used to produce hard copy output which can be taken away and studied or posted. There are several printer types and this section looks at the main ones.

Dot-matrix printers

Dot-matrix printers are impact printers that work by firing pins onto an inked ribbon which leaves a character on the paper. The main disadvantage with them is the low quality of the text and graphics produced and the amount of noise generated. They are very cheap to buy, reliable and cheap to run since the only consumable other than paper is the inked ribbon, which lasts a long time and is cheap. Dot-matrix printers are useful if you just want to see a draft result or if you need to use multi-part stationery, since an impact printer is needed for this. Dot-matrix printers have now been largely replaced by ink-jet and laser printers because of the higher quality of the printouts that the latter produce.

Ink-jet printers

Ink-jet printers work by spraying black or coloured ink onto the paper; and because there is no impact they are relatively quiet.

Although the initial cost of an ink-jet printer is set attractively low, the cost of the consumables (mainly the ink cartridges) can be high and many manufacturers make more money selling the consumables than from the sale of the actual printers! For perfect copies using an ink-jet printer, it is necessary to use special paper that has a whiter look and a glossy coating on the surface. This paper is expensive compared with normal photocopying paper and obviously adds to the running costs.

Many people buy ink-jet printers because most of them are capable of printing in colour, but the snag with this is that colour ink cartridges are needed which use three different coloured inks, and as soon as one of the colours is exhausted the cartridge is useless and needs replacing. One big disadvantage of ink-jet printers is that when the paper comes out of the printer the ink is often still wet and the image is easily smudged.

However, they do provide a low-cost alternative to a laser printer.

If you require colour printing on a limited budget then they will be your only choice since colour laser printers are very expensive to buy and run.

Laser printers

Laser printers make use of photocopier technology. They use a laser to mark out an image on the paper to which the toner sticks; this toner is then fused to the paper by heat. Since this process is quite fast, laser printers are ideal if you want quick, high quality printouts (typically ten pages per minute) and reliable hardware. They do have relatively high operating costs since toner cartridges need to be bought and the metal drum will need to be renewed periodically. Most laser printers are black and white; colour ones are available but they are very expensive.

Activity

You have been asked to suggest a type of printer from the choice of dot-matrix, laser or inkjet, to be used as a network printer by five terminals in a small business. Write a list of questions you would ask the business owner to make sure that you make the right choice for them. For each question, place in brackets after the question your reasons for asking it.

Graph plotters

These are used to produce accurate line diagrams such as maps, plans and three-dimensional drawings. They look more professional than those produced by a printer and are often the only choice if the drawing size is large. There are two types of plotter: the flat-bed plotter for small drawings and the drum plotter for large drawings.

Monitors (VDUs)

Monitors are the most popular output device and are used in nearly all applications. They are ideal for on-line enquiries where the results of a query can be displayed on the screen. Monitors come in many sizes, but with the introduction of Windows, there is a lot of information on the screen, which has meant that the standard sized screen has increased from 14 inch to 15 inch, although 17, 19 and 21 inch monitors have also become very popular. Monitor choice has previously been neglected when choosing computer systems and people have tended to spend the money on faster processors or larger hard drives rather than a better quality monitor. If, however, you were to compare monitors showing the same image, you would see that they vary widely and, as always, you get what you pay for. The monitor's screen resolution determines the maximum number of dots of light (called pixels) which can be drawn on the screen at any one time and is quoted using two numbers, the first being the number of horizontal dots, the second the number of vertical dots. A typical screen resolution is 1024×768 pixels.

Communication devices

Increasingly computers are linked together to share information and resources. There are many specialist pieces of hardware used in networking and many of these are discussed in Chapters 9 and 18. In this section we concentrate on those hardware devices you might use with your home PC.

Modems

A modem may be situated inside the casing of the computer (called an internal modem) or outside (called an external modem). It changes the digital signal from a computer to an analogue signal that can be passed along a telephone line. When the signal reaches a modem at the other end of the line, the analogue signal is converted back into a digital form, which can be read by the receiving computer. At one time, all the cable used for the telephone wires was made of copper and this type of line can only carry analogue signals, but now a mixture of copper wires and the more up-to-date fibre optic cable are in use. The fibre optic cable, unlike copper wire, can carry digital signals. The older, copper wires often transfer the data from the user's home or office to the telephone exchange where the data then takes a much faster path along high-speed digital fibre optic cables, until it reaches the other telephone exchange where it then transfers to the metal cables again.

As we mentioned before, there are two types of modem: internal and external. Internal modems are cheaper since they take the power supply from the computer so need no power supply of their own nor do they need a casing of their own.

At present there are two speeds for new modems: 33,600 bps and 56,000 bps (although many older modems run at slower speeds). Just as doubling the processor speed does not allow you to get a computing job done in half the time, increasing the modem speed from 33,600 bps to 56,000 bps will not halve the telephone bills, since the service you connect to may not be able to use the higher speed. As well as modem speed, the speed of data communication is also determined by the speed of the modem at the other end. The receiving modem is out of your control and there is nothing you can do about it. The speed of data transfer is also determined by the quality of the line, from the point where the data enters the telephone socket to the point where it enters the telephone exchange.

Having a modem attached to the computer opens up a whole world of communications and allows the computer to access millions of other computers all around the world, containing a huge amount of useful information. The most popular activities accessed via a modem are:

- surfing the web

- e-mailing friends, colleagues and business associates

- downloading free software (software upgrades, drivers for printers, scanners, etc., clip art, demo versions of new software and so on)

- sending and receiving faxes

- using voicemail to send and receive messages.

The type of modem determines the speed at which data is transferred along the line and many modems compress the data before sending so that it can be sent quicker. Since you have to pay for use of the line during transmission, often in the same way you would pay for the line if you were making an ordinary telephone call, any mechanism that cuts down transmission time is obviously welcomed.

ISDN adaptors

Fairly soon, all transmission cables will be digital and the modem will be an obsolete piece of equipment. You can get a digital line now, but it is more expensive. If you have a digital line, you no longer need a modem. Modems are not needed if you use ISDN.

With ISDN, digital signals are used throughout the system. You still need an extra piece of hardware, called a terminal adaptor, whose purpose is to buffer the data being sent by the PC. This prevents the computer from sending data along the ISDN line faster than the line can cope with it. The buffer is a bit like a 'waiting room' for the data. The ISDN terminal adaptor has another purpose. It converts the data according to the ISDN protocols (protocols are simply set of rules). Data transfer using ISDN is a lot faster even than using the fastest modems.

An even faster system of transmitting data is asymmetric digital subscriber line (ADSL), which is a new technology now being introduced. Using special equipment, ADSL allows conventional copper telephone wires to transmit digital data at up to 40 times the speed of the fastest modem.

Questions

1 A kitchen design company uses computers to help design kitchens. A member of the sales team goes out to see customers in their homes and takes measurements of the kitchen, takes into account the customer's preferences and then returns to the shop. All the measurements and preferences are transferred to a special kitchen design package that will draw the kitchen from various angles.

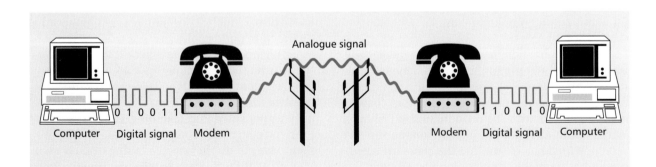

Figure 7.4 *Using a telephone line to carry data*

(a) What input devices might the designer use?

(b) For each of the input devices described in (a) say why each is particularly suited to its application.

2 A friend wants to gain access to the Internet. She has read in a computer magazine that either a modem or an ISDN terminal adaptor can be used.

(a) What is the purpose of a modem?

(b) How does the operation of a modem differ from the operation of an ISDN terminal adaptor?

(c) Bearing in mind that your friend has a limited budget and is going to be using the Internet for about four hours per week, which solution (modem or ISDN) do you suggest and why?

Nature and types of software

Software may be divided into two distinct types: systems software (sometimes called operating systems) and applications software.

Systems software

Systems software is the program used to control the hardware of the computer directly. Without such programs the hardware would be useless. Systems software is often said to form the bridge between the applications software and the hardware. The purpose of the system software is to take control of the inputs, outputs, interrupts and storage. In most cases it does this efficiently, without us being aware of it. Figure 7.5 shows how the operating system 'sits' between the hardware and the applications programs.

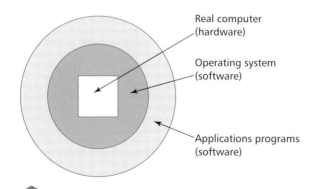

Figure 7.5 *The operating system 'sits' between the hardware and the applications programs*

Systems software performs two groups of functions:

1 The operating system ensures the efficient management of the computer's resources, such as internal memory, input and output devices and files. Operating systems are frequently multi-tasking, enabling the user to do one task while another is being performed. For instance, you can work on one document using your wordprocessing software while your previous document is being printed.

2 The operating system protects the user from the complexities of the hardware. This means that the user need only consider the operation of the application package being used. As an example, the user does not have to worry whether a file is being stored on a vacant part of the disk; the operating system does this automatically.

Here are some of the detailed tasks performed by an operating system:

- Performing certain diagnostic tests when the computer is first switched on (or 'booted up' as it is called). The operating system checks peripheral devices attached to the computer and also checks the memory by writing data to the memory locations and then reading it back to see if the data matches. If there are any problems, an error message appears on the screen.

- Scheduling and loading jobs that are to be executed, thereby maximising the computer's power and time.

- Selecting and controlling the operation of any peripheral devices.

- Dealing with any errors that arise and keeping the system running should any faults occur.

- Maintaining system security by checking passwords.

- Loading program files and data files into memory from the backing storage devices.

- Handling the interrupts that occur when there are problems with the applications software due to bugs or problems with the computer itself.

Systems software is taken to include the following groups of software:

- operating systems

- utility programs

- file management programs
- virus detection software.

Popular operating systems

In this section we look at the main operating systems on the market to get an insight into the main features of each, their strengths and weaknesses.

Windows 2000

To make computers as easy to use as possible, a very sophisticated and powerful operating system is needed which 'shields' the user from the intricacies of the hardware. Ideally the operating system should be compatible with all the existing software, be easy to use, fast and powerful.

Windows 2000, the latest operating system for PCs, has all the above features and will become the standard operating system for the latest PCs with their large memories (typically 128 MB), large hard disk capacity (12 GB) and the high speed processors (typically the Pentium with a clock speed of 1000 MHz).

Windows 2000 is not just a replacement for the popular operating systems Windows 95 and 98 but also a replacement for Windows NT which is Microsoft's preferred operating system for businesses who use networks. There are four versions of Windows 2000: Windows Professional 2000 is designed for the desktop user while the others are aimed at the corporate user.

In the Windows 2000 interface, everything hinges on the start button on the task bar and pressing this gives access to all the different utilities and applications on your system via a series of menus. When a new application is installed, it is automatically added to the menu list.

As with all good interfaces, the screens in Windows 2000 are not too cluttered and the design was based on thousands of hours of usability testing and a careful analysis of the kinds of tasks which users regularly perform.

The operating system Windows 2000 places many demands on the hardware and needs the following minimum specification to run successfully:

- at least a 133 MHz Intel Pentium processor or equivalent
- at least a 2 GB hard drive
- 650 MB of free disk space
- at least 32 MB of random access memory.

The main features of the Windows 2000 operating system include:

File encryption
File encryption is now provided as part of the operating system.

Plug and play
This part of the operating system allows you to connect any hardware (printers, scanners, graph-plotters, etc.) to the computer and the operating system will automatically allocate the hardware resources needed for the device.

32-bit architecture
The 32-bit architecture means that memory use is optimised.

Networking
Support is provided for multiple network servers and there are features which improve compatibility between devices attached to the computer.

The real advantages of Windows 2000 are found in the server versions which use an 'active directory' that makes managing files and applications easier for network operators. The network operator can select which groups of programs a person or group is allowed to use on the network. Programs such as games can be blocked.

If a program crashes, the user's files, programs and settings are stored in both the server and the desktop so the system can recover using the data on the server. If the server fails, the system is able to recover using the data held on the desktop. This makes Windows 2000 very stable for business users running networks.

Windows NT

The main strengths of Windows NT over the other Windows operating systems, such as Windows 98, are its stability and security. Both of these are of considerable interest to business users and this accounts for its current popularity in this sector of the market. Since many application programs contain bugs that can cause the computer to crash (for no apparent reason), an operating system which prevents the loss of data caused when a computer has to be switched off is of real value. Windows NT is a large operating system and needs much more storage space than other operating systems. The main drawback of Windows NT is its lack of 'plug and play' (the way the operating system automatically recognises the peripherals attached to it and configures them accordingly). If you convert from one of the other Microsoft operating systems, the device drivers will not work and you will have to select the new Windows NT device drivers from the lists provided. If you have very up-to-date peripherals to attach, or some obscure older ones, then you will need to track down device drivers from places like the Internet.

One very useful feature of Windows NT is the ability to select which operating system you will use, which is useful if you have packages which need to be run under a different operating system.

Windows NT runs faster than Windows 98 and also uses a better method for allocating files, which makes operating more stable and therefore reduces the risk of crashing.

Windows 2000 is a replacement for Windows NT rather than Windows 98.

OS/2 Warp

OS/2 Warp is an operating system produced by IBM which is used by most high street cash dispensers. It is also available for desktop machines. OS/2 is an extremely stable operating system and it is mainly for this reason that it is popular in commercial applications. One strength of this operating system is that it emphasises voice recognition as one of its main features. Speech recognition can be used to navigate around the operating system, although it has to be said that it takes some getting used to and using a mouse is probably quicker. However, the speech recognition system can be used for dictation, which is useful.

OS/2, like Windows 2000 and NT, has both multi-tasking abilities and facilities to enable connection to a network. The main difference between OS/2 and most other operating systems is that it uses the concept of objects. Objects are documents, folders, settings, etc., and when these are loaded, the application needed to run them is also loaded. This means that when you look at a list of documents and choose one, the system loads the wordprocessing software needed to run the document at the same time. One problem with OS/2 is that it does not have as many applications written for it as do other operating systems, such as Windows.

UNIX

UNIX is an operating system that is more widely associated with mainframe and minicomputers. There is a version called XENIX available for PCs. UNIX is written in the high level programming language C, and its main strength is that it is a multiprogramming, multi-tasking operating system that can run several hundred terminals if necessary.

Standardisation is one of the major problems with UNIX and this has hampered its widespread acceptance in the business world. There are three current UNIX standards and this means that a person who develops software may have to produce three different versions to run on all UNIX systems. Some software developers stick with a particular manufacturer and develop UNIX-based software that will only run on one type of machine (called a platform).

One of the main advantages of UNIX is its portability which means that it can run on many different types of computer. There is a powerful user interface, called the shell, and this is useful to experienced users, but getting used to it can be quite difficult for beginners. UNIX is quite hard for beginners to learn and many people describe it as 'an operating system designed by programmers for programmers to use'.

Linux

Linux is an operating system that is gaining popularity; its main advantage is that it is free. The Linux operating system is mainly aimed at the experienced computer user and because of its stability, security and remote management capabilities, it has gained popularity with corporate users. The main advantage of the operating system is that it is intuitive, meaning that it is able to work out what the user wants to do next. Users find it easy to use and quickly progress to using it at speed. Linux is used mainly as a network operating system and as more computers are networked together or connected to the Internet, its popularity is likely to rise. Some large software developers, such as Oracle and Informix, are developing applications to use Linux. At present there are not many applications available, such as wordprocessing, database and spreadsheets, and this has limited its popularity with home users.

TASKS

Scenario: an article on operating systems to be placed on a website

You have been asked to write a piece of text for an article aimed at new computer users. It is to be placed on a computer area by an Internet service provider. The article is intended to present the facts about operating systems to novice users to make them realise that there are many operating systems available.

TASK 1

The editor, for whom you are writing the article, has his own idea about what you need to include in your article and has suggested that you use the following format:

- a definition of what an operating system is and why computers need them
- the difference between applications software and systems software (also called an operating system)
- a brief introduction to four different operating systems in popular use

- a comparative study of each operating system saying what its strengths and weaknesses are
- a table providing a summary.

DEBRIEF

Make sure that in your descriptions of the operating systems you do not include any new terms unless these terms are thoroughly explained.

Use the Internet to do your research. You may find it helpful to use the websites of computer magazines, as these frequently have material to enable you to search for articles in back issues.

TASK 2

Produce a list of web addresses of sites where further information about each operating system can be found.

DEBRIEF

Make sure that you include after the web address a brief description of what can be found at each website.

Applications software

Applications software is the name given to software that allows the computer to be applied to a particular problem. Such software is therefore used for a specific purpose or application. Examples of applications software include:

- textual document processing (wordprocessing)
- text and graphic printed presentation (desktop publishing)
- numerical analysis processing (spreadsheets)
- record and transaction processing (databases)
- computer-aided design and graphic drawing (vector graphics)
- graphics/artwork processing (bitmap graphics)
- slide/picture presentation (bitmap graphics)
- accounts processing.

Applications software packages may be classified into three groups:

- generic software (sometimes called general purpose software) that may be used in any

kind of business or organisation and includes wordprocessing, database, spreadsheet, graphics and integrated software

- specific task software which is used for a particular task, such as stock control, payroll, CAD, modelling, etc.
- bespoke (tailor-made) software which is specifically written by the user for a specific application.

Bespoke (tailor-made) software

Bespoke software is software specially written for an application. The situation is a bit like buying a suit of clothes. You can buy one off the peg and put up with the fact that it does not fit perfectly, or you can get a tailor to take your measurements and make one for you. With the latter approach you get one that fits you perfectly and in the cloth you have chosen but it is relatively expensive.

Bespoke software is usually produced when there is no suitable package available and is an expensive and time-consuming approach, not to be undertaken by those without prior programming knowledge.

Many large organisations prefer to write their own software than have to fit their own procedures around an existing package. The final result is a solution that matches their needs perfectly.

Generic software (general purpose software)

Generic software, sometimes called general purpose software, is designed to be used for a huge range of applications; most organisations will have a range of such software.

Integrated packages

Many computer users now employ integrated packages such as Microsoft Office, Microsoft Works, Lotus SmartSuite, etc. Integrated packages are any group of applications which are together and embrace more than one area of functionality. Most integrated packages consist of wordprocessor, spreadsheet, database and graphics packages. Many people get their first integrated package 'free' with their computer when they buy it, although others buy a product which they know or which is widely used by others.

With some integrated packages, such as Microsoft Office, the individual components of the package such as Word, Excel, Access and PowerPoint are available separately, although it is usually much cheaper to buy them as a package.

Integrated packages vary widely in quality and you could find some parts of the package strong in some areas and weak in others. The whole reason behind integrated packages is that they should make it easier for users to move data between applications than it would be if individual packages had been used.

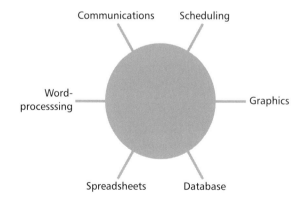

Figure 7.6 *The usual modules included as part of an integrated package*

Advantages of integrated packages

1 It is usually cheaper to buy an integrated package than to buy the equivalent modules separately.

2 The modules are designed to work well together so that it is easy to transfer data between applications (e.g. put a graph plotted using the results from a spreadsheet into a wordprocessed document).

3 There is consistency in the way the programs work, which means that they are easier to learn, especially if you compare them with separate packages from separate manufacturers.

4 They often encourage users to try a wider range of applications. For example, schedulers and communications software are sometimes supplied as part of the integrated package along with the usual wordprocessor, spreadsheet and database.

Disadvantages of integrated packages

1 Integrated packages, particularly the cheaper ones, may be weak in some of the modules. If you use separate programs you can choose the best possible package for each.

2 You may end up paying for modules you do not use or will never need.

3 Integrated packages take up large amounts of disk space and this is wasteful, particularly if you never use some of the packages included.

4 To facilitate the movement of data from one package to another it is often necessary for two or more applications to be open simultaneously and this places higher demands on the memory. It may be necessary therefore to upgrade the hardware by adding extra memory.

5 In some cases, where the applications can be bought separately or as part of an integrated package, some useful features are left out of the integrated versions.

Selecting appropriate software packages

A platform is the hardware used by an operating system, or the operating system used by an applications program. It is important when considering which particular application package to use, to take into account the intended platform.

In most cases application software is chosen first and the hardware capable of running that application selected second. It would be foolish to buy the hardware and then look to see if there was software available which did what you wanted. What frequently happens is that the computer is bought for a selection of applications, but other applications are then developed as needs arise.

Bear the following in mind when selecting appropriate applications software:

1 The software being considered should be capable of running on the existing platform, or if the platform needs to be changed the cost, time and expertise implications need to be considered.

2 The cost of the software may be a limitation since there is usually an overall budget for implementation that cannot be exceeded.

3 It is often a good idea to first obtain an evaluation version of the software; this may be a complete version without the print and save facilities. Sometimes such versions are available from the software producer's website and they can also be obtained on CDs or disks that frequently come with popular computer magazines.

4 Try to find out from existing users about any problems they have had with the software. Websites exist for users of most of the popular software.

5 Determine whether there are any bugs or other problems with the software. Articles in the computer press will often highlight any problems.

6 Is the software easy to install? How long will it take to install and can existing files from other packages be imported into the new package?

7 What technical support is offered? Do you have to pay for this support and if so, how much is it and how long does this support last? Do they leave you waiting on the phone for ages (i.e. in a call queuing system) until they answer your query?

8 Is the software producer reputable and have they been in business long and are they likely to be around in the next few years?

9 What are the details of the licensing agreement? Are you allowed to make a copy for your laptop computer?

10 What training is supplied by the software producer? If there is no training provided, are courses available in-house, at colleges or at private training centres?

11 What documentation is provided, how is it provided and is it easy to understand? If the documentation is weak, there may be books available which explain the software better.

Capabilities of software

Apart from the ability to do the job for which it is bought, there are other desirable features which a software package should have that will make life easier for the user. All of the following aspects of performance should be considered.

Links to other packages

Suppose you are using a database package to record details of school pupils. You may decide that it would be useful to keep a picture of each pupil as part of their record. In many packages it is possible to provide a link between one package and another, so the image of the pupil could be scanned in from a photograph or simply input from a digital camera. The image could then be adjusted in a package such as Photoshop so that each time a record is viewed using the database, the pupil's picture is obtained from the Photoshop package. When linked files are used, the object (the picture in this case) is stored in the same file that the image was obtained in. In other words, it is not stored in the database file. If you want to alter the picture you go to the Photoshop package, alter it and next time that pupil's record is displayed, the new version will be shown. Other examples of linking are:

- adding a company logo created in a graphics package to a report produced using data from a database

- using a graph produced from calculations made in a spreadsheet package in a report produced using a wordprocessing package.

Search facilities

Suppose you are working on a long document using your wordprocessing software and want to move to a particular section. Rather than read all the pages on the screen until you came across the right one, it would be easier to use a search or find facility with which you can move to the place where a certain word or combination of words occurs. With most wordprocessors you can also use the search facility for finding a particular document by examining the document description.

Macro capabilities

A macro is a high level programming tool which may be used within a program to automate a series of tasks or procedures. A macro consists of a series of individual instructions; to start the macro you have only to press a couple of keys on the keyboard or click the mouse a couple of times.

A macro is used with a particular application program. Macros will only run when the applications software has been loaded, so these programs cannot be run on their own.

You can create some macros without knowing anything about programming. The macro facility will automatically record your keystrokes or mouse movements and selections as you make them so that they may be automatically 'played back' when you need them.

Activity

Macros can be found as an advanced feature of most software. Using the software manuals or the on-line help menus to help you, find out how you could write a macro for a task that you find tedious when using either your spreadsheet or wordprocessing software.

Produce an easy-to-understand set of instructions that could be given to a friend who needs to perform the same set of tasks.

Applications generators

Applications generators are tools found with some applications software packages, particularly databases. With these tools, the user decides what needs to be done and which data and files are needed. Once this has been specified the applications generator will automatically turn these instructions into a program without the user having to write a single line of program code. The idea behind the

applications generator is that many functions, such as sorting, searching, updating, etc., are common to all applications even though the applications themselves may be completely different. Sections of the code will therefore be very similar. By using these sections of similar code, the applications generator can link files to produce a complete application.

Although applications generators can enable inexperienced people to produce simple programs, once the programs become more complex, the applications generators become less useful and the work of an experienced programmer is needed. Nevertheless, for simple programs linking several files together (such as a program to run a video rental shop), the applications generator is ideal.

Report generators

A report in this sense is a tabulated list of data compiled in a specific way. A report generator is an applications generator that produces a report made up from some of the contents of one or more files. Again, the non-specialist can produce these reports from carefully constructed statements. Nearly all database and accounting packages are able to produce such reports.

Editing capabilities

It goes without saying that any data which has been entered into a system will probably need to be altered at some stage so the ease with which editing can take place is an important factor when choosing software.

The ability to change or extend data and record structures

When designing a system around a relational database package, it is hard to get the design right first time and sometimes problems become apparent at a late stage when the structures for the tables have been designed and perhaps data has been entered. To correct flaws in the design it is necessary to make changes and these must be allowed by the software. If possible, the user should be able to adjust the existing data so that no data is lost in the process of modification.

Sometimes it may be several months before flaws are discovered. For example, in the table structure for members of a library, the surname field may have the number of characters limited to 25. If someone whose surname contains more than 25 characters joins, their surname cannot be input without first changing the length of the field in the structure. The package should allow this and still be able to put the existing data into the longer field.

Short access times

Time waiting for a computer to respond to instructions given to it by the user or the time taken when performing a search for specific information is annoying to the user, particularly if they have a customer waiting, so access time is an important factor when considering software.

Data portability

Can the data that has been created in one package be used with a completely different package, perhaps produced by a different software manufacturer? This is important because some software companies go out of business or get taken over by another company who no longer supports the product. It is therefore important to be able to transfer data between software packages. It is particularly important with databases and this is why the data in relational databases is stored in tables and not with the programs that manipulate the data. Since the data is kept separate it is much easier for different databases to read it.

There is a similar need with wordprocessor and desktop publishing packages, where documents produced by one wordprocessing package may be read by another when received. Portability is examined in more detail in Chapter 8.

Upgrade paths

It is in the software manufacturers' interest to create a demand for new, improved products and since many users prefer to stick with the software they know, most manufacturers produce upgrades to their existing package unless there are clear benefits in doing otherwise.

If you have thousands of documents created on one wordprocessing package, it is essential that any upgrade or new wordprocessor will read them. This applies to all software, not just wordprocessors, and the transfer from an older version of a package to an upgrade is a fundamental requirement. This ability is called the upwards compatibility of the software. If someone creates a document using the latest version of the software, in most cases it will not be possible to use the older version of the same software to read the file.

To get around this problem there are some utility programs available, called file conversion utilities, that convert files up and down and also allow files to be read by packages from different manufacturers. For example, you may have created a relational database using the relational database management system PARADOX and want now to change to a different RDMS, say, Microsoft Access. It there is a considerable amount of data stored in the database, typing it would be impractical, so it is essential that Access can read the data created in PARADOX.

Factors to be taken into account when changing or upgrading software

It is relatively easy for a home user to upgrade software and hardware at regular intervals. After all, they have only themselves to consider. A company may have hundreds, or even thousands, of computers and making changes to either hardware or software is a major undertaking which is not done without careful consideration of the consequences.

The training needs of users

Users cannot be expected simply to adapt to software changes without proper training. Training is quite expensive, and users need to be taken away from the job they are doing to be trained.

Increased use and cost of help desks

Help desks are used by large companies to sort out problems their staff have with software. New software means that this facility will be used more and this may involve an increase in the number of staff on the help desk with a corresponding increase in costs.

Possible hardware incompatibility

New or upgraded software usually contains more features which may mean that existing hardware will run too slowly with the software (or perhaps not at all) without an upgrade to memory processor. Printers and scanners frequently cause problems and it is worth checking first with the software manufacturer that the attached peripherals can be used with the intended software.

Time taken to install the software

Time must be allocated for installation of the software on each stand-alone machine or alternatively on the server. If there are large numbers of stand-alone machines, this installation can take quite a long time even though most software is now supplied on CD-ROM.

What are the costs involved?

There is always the choice between sticking with the existing software or purchasing new or upgraded software, and the costs need to be balanced with the benefits of using the new software. You can usually buy either individual copies of a package for each machine or a licence for a certain number of machines.

Reliability of software

Like any goods bought, software must be fit for the purpose it is sold for, and this means that it must do the job the manufacturers say it will. Some software does only what is expected within certain parameters; when these have been exceeded the software behaves unexpectedly. Unexpected behaviour could include crashing (when the cursor will not move and the only option is to switch off the computer) in which case any unsaved work may be lost in the process.

Problems when testing complex software

All software producers test their software thoroughly before bringing it to the marketplace, but due to the wide range of tasks to which it is put and the number of different peripherals and processor upgrades encountered, it is not always possible to take care of every eventuality. There are a variety of problems which may arise when testing software and some of these are described below:

- Users may install the software on a wide variety of platforms; software needs to be checked with all combinations of hardware and operating systems. There is also the possibility that the hardware or operating system being used may not have been around when the software was first written.

- There is often an economic requirement to bring a product to the marketplace at a certain time and if programming has taken longer than expected this may leave little time for testing.

- Because there are so many paths through a large program it is hard to be sure that every possibility has been thoroughly tested.

- The system may be used with greater volumes of data to those originally anticipated when the software was first written and this may cause problems.

- There may be a flaw in the test; the test data being used may not be appropriate for detecting the flaws.

Realising that software flaws are a reality, despite rigorous testing, software manufacturers are under an obligation to provide a way around any problems that arise. Software producers take a range of different approaches to satisfy the users in this respect, and these include:

- providing regular upgrades (new versions) of the software with the bugs fixed

- help lines so that users can get technical advice over the phone about problems they are having, such as conflicts with the hardware, software crashing for no apparent reason, etc.

- websites on the Internet where solutions to a variety of problems can be outlined; in many cases files or even entire new updates can be downloaded here

- providing newer, improved versions of software; they are sometimes offered at a discount or even for free

- many problems occur with printer drivers and other device drivers (sections of programming code that use the software to configure the hardware before use). Some items of hardware (such as scanners and digital cameras) may not have been in common use when the software was written, so extra software may be needed to cope with the new developments and this can often be obtained from the software manufacturer's website.

Configurability of hardware and software

When you first buy a system, it usually comes pre-configured, which means that it will have been set up to use whatever optional equipment (e.g. disk drives, memory, sound card, display adaptor, etc.) was originally installed.

However, if you plan to change any part of the system (for instance, you could put in some extra memory or add a peripheral device such as a scanner), you will probably need to re-configure the system. Luckily this is much easier than in the past, when you had to include some extra instructions and change some existing ones in a file called the CONFIG.SYS file. Most hardware devices come with special software, called installation programs, whose purpose is to re-configure the system automatically and most users are not even aware that this has been done.

Plug and play (PnP)

Plug and play is now used throughout the computer industry and applies to the ease with which peripherals can be attached to computers without the need to re-configure the system yourself. The operating systems Windows 2000 and Windows 98 use PnP, which means that if you want to add new peripherals such as graphics adaptors, DVD drives, sound cards or new hard drives, the operating system will automatically detect them and reconfigure the system so that they may be used immediately.

Installing new software

Installing new operating systems or applications software is a lot easier than it used to be. You used to have to create the directories in which the files were placed yourself and problems arose if your computer knowledge wasn't up to doing this. Although there were fairly clear instructions, a mistake could easily be made, since the instructions were usually typed in as a series of commands.

Things are now a lot simpler with the Windows operating systems. Most programs can be installed automatically, since most software comes with an installation program that creates directories and copies files. If you are doing the installation from floppies, your only task is usually to feed the correct disks into the disk drive when requested. Because of their large capacity (typically 650 MB), most software can now be installed from a CD-ROM, so you are no longer trusted even to perform the feeding in of floppies! The only problems you are likely to encounter are when the installation program tries to create a directory/folder or copy a file which already exists.

Peripheral drivers

Each peripheral device connected to a computer needs a driver to operate it. Some drivers for peripherals that normally come as part of the computer system (such as keyboards and hard

drives) are included as part of the operating system. Other peripherals need to have their device drivers installed separately when the device is attached to or installed in the computer. Drivers enable new peripherals to be developed that could never have been envisaged when the operating system was first introduced. Developing separate device drivers enables peripheral manufacturers to write drivers that will exploit the special capabilities of their devices. Drivers normally come on a disk with the actual device; they are installed as you would install any other software.

Printer drivers

There are many different types of printer, each with its own printing language (called a page description language or PDL) so special software is needed that enables applications software to communicate with the printer. This is the print driver which converts the print instructions from the applications software into a form that the printer can understand.

Problems with printers and screens

With some older applications software packages, you used to see special control codes on the screen. The code ^BThis is in bold^B, for example, meant that the text between the two control codes would be printed out in bold. It was very confusing to have these special control codes as well as your normal text on the screen. They were a frequent cause of error and you had to remember what all the codes meant.

It is much easier when the text shows as bold on the screen, avoiding the need for codes. When things are organised in this way the software is described as WYSIWYG (what you see is what you get) and whatever appears on the screen will be printed out by the printer. All modern software is WYSIWYG, but you may still see some older packages that do not have WYSIWYG interfaces.

Advantages of WYSIWYG

- There are no complicated control commands which appear on the screen and which need to be turned on and off to supply printing effects such as bold, italics, underscore, superscript and subscript.

- There is no need to have different colours on the screen to show printing effects (e.g. any text which appears in red would have been underlined when printed out).

- There will be fewer draft copies since mistakes in layout are easily spotted on the screen, thereby improving productivity.

- Objects that have been imported from other packages are much easier to format.

Activity

Definition of terms

A variety of new terms is introduced in this chapter, many of which may be new to you. It is important that you build up vocabulary which can be used when writing essays or answering questions. Write a definition for each of the following terms used in the chapter:

OCR	OMR
MICR	laser scanner
port	motherboard
MHz	MB
RAID	DAT
DVD	CD-R
CD-RW	ISDN
clock speed	multi-tasking
plug and play	Windows NT
UNIX	OS/2 Warp
generic software	bespoke software
integrated packages	macro
application generator	portability
WYSIWYG	drivers

Questions

1 'If software were tested thoroughly, it would never contain bugs.'

   A user makes the above comment after their computer had just crashed unexpectedly. Write a short paragraph explaining what problems there are in testing a complex piece of software such as a new operating system.

2 A home computer user wants to access the Internet and they have asked you about the pros and cons of using ISDN rather than an ordinary modem. Write a short paragraph explaining what each of these devices/services do and their relative merits and demerits.

3 When purchasing wordprocessing, spreadsheet and database software, many people choose to purchase an integrated package rather than buy each program separately.

   (a) Explain what is meant by the term 'integrated package'.

   (b) What are the main advantages in buying the integrated package rather than each piece of software separately?

   (c) Give two disadvantages of buying the integrated package over buying the separate components.

4 A large company is thinking of upgrading the hardware and operating system on the 100 computers it uses. What are the likely problems it might encounter during the upgrading of:

   (a) the hardware

   (b) the operating system?

1 When purchasing software, it is possible to buy either an 'integrated package' or separate applications packages that run under a common operating system environment.

(a) What is meant by the term 'integrated package'? (2)

(b) What applications would you normally expect an 'integrated package' to offer? (4)

(c) What are the relative advantages and disadvantages of an 'integrated package' over a collection of separate applications packages running under a common operating system environment? (4)

(NEAB, Module IT02, Specimen Paper, q4)

2 From the experienced user's viewpoint, give **three** functions of an operating system. (3)

(NEAB, Module IT02, Specimen Paper, q5)

3 A particular wordprocessing package is described as having a WYSIWYG (what you see is what you get) output capability. Give the advantages of using such a package rather than one which does not possess this capability. (3)

(NEAB, Module IT02, May 1996, q1)

4 Describe the difference between applications software and systems software, giving an example of each. (4)

(NEAB, Module IT02, May 1996, q2)

5 A spreadsheet package is described as having a macro facility. Describe what is meant by the term 'macro' and suggest a situation in which the use of a macro would be appropriate. (4)

(NEAB, Module IT02, May 1997, q1)

6 When installing or configuring a particular wordprocessing package, the documentation states that the correct printer driver must also be installed. What is a printer driver, and why is it necessary? (4)

(NEAB, Module IT02, May 1997, q2)

7 A company sells a range of health foods at five different shops. It also sells directly to the home from a number of vehicles. There are hundreds of different items of stock and many items are seasonal, so items of stock are constantly changing. Customers purchase goods and pay by cash, cheque or credit card.

The company is considering a computerised system to help manage sales and stock control.

Discuss the capabilities and limitations of current

communications devices,

input devices,

output devices and

storage devices

appropriate for establishing a computerised system for this company.

(NEAB, Module IT02, June 1997, q9)

8 When using any application package on a network, the user is often unaware that an operating system is working 'behind the scenes', managing system resources. Give **three** of these resources and in each case briefly explain the role of the operating system in its management.

(NEAB, Module IT02, June 1997, q4)

9 Given an existing hardware platform, selecting the most appropriate software package for a specific application can be a difficult process.

(a) Describe the criteria and methods you would use to select the most appropriate software package for a particular application. *(16)*

(b) Users may encounter problems when software manufacturers upgrade a software package. With reference to specific examples describe **two** such problems. *(4)*

(NEAB, Module IT02, Specimen Paper, q9)

10 You have installed a new piece of applications software onto a stand-alone PC. You then find that the printer attached to the PC fails to produce what can be seen on screen in that package.

Explain clearly why this might happen. *(2)*

(NEAB, Module IT02, May 1998, q2)

11 Why does commercially available software not always function correctly when installed onto a computer system? *(2)*

(NEAB, Module IT02, May 1998, q3)

12 There is now a wide range of software tools available to increase the productivity of the end-user. Two such software tools are Application Generators and Report Generators.

(a) Explain what is meant by an Application Generator. *(2)*

(b) Explain what is meant by a Report Generator. *(2)*

(c) Give an example of when it might be sensible to use each one. *(2)*

(NEAB, Module IT02, May 1998, q7)

8 *Moving Data Around*

CHAPTER OBJECTIVES

▶ To understand the importance of, and mechanisms for, maintaining data security.

▶ To understand the distinction between security and privacy.

Privacy and security – what is the difference?

Privacy of data means making sure that personal data is kept safe and not disclosed to anyone who is not entitled to see it. Privacy is covered by a law called the Data Protection Act. The Data Protection Act 1998 is dealt with in detail in Chapter 4.

Security means making sure that hardware, software and data are protected from any harm such as fire, theft, sabotage or virus attack etc.

Privacy

You probably consider it a fundamental right of any human being to be allowed to go about their lawful business without their activities being recorded or examined. Yet this right is rapidly being eroded and people are finding it very hard to do anything without others knowing about it. Privacy of data involves keeping personal data private.

Many of us unwittingly give out all sorts of details during normal day-to-day activities. When you visit a website and browse it is possible for the owner of the website to monitor your progress by seeing what part of the site you have looked at and how long you have spent there. This gives a website developer important information relevant to the success of the various parts of their site, but it could potentially be used for more sinister purposes.

Telephone companies keep records of all the numbers we have dialled and how long we were on the phone for, credit card companies record all the transactions we have made. Even cash dispensers record details of any transactions made including the date, the location of the cash machine and some may even take a secret photograph of you withdrawing your money.

Many of the large supermarkets now have so-called loyalty cards. Customers register by giving some details about themselves and then get points every time they buy goods from the store, which are added up and earn vouchers which can be used instead of cash. As well as ensuring the customer returns to a particular store chain, the cards also provide useful information about the customer and the items they purchase. The store can record how much you spend on food each week and which items you buy regularly. Here is a list of some of the things they might find out about you:

- the newspapers, magazines and paperback books you read
- whether you buy unusually large amounts of alcoholic drinks
- what method you use to pay for your purchases
- how much petrol you buy
- whether you have a diesel or petrol car
- if you are a vegetarian (i.e. by the lack of meat)
- whether you have any pets and what those pets are
- whether there are any young children in the family
- whether or not you eat beef
- whether or not you, or anyone in your family, is on a diet.

Let us look in a bit more detail at how organisations can obtain information about us.

Cellular phones

Cellular phones (mobile phones) use microwaves to transmit conversations and these may be intercepted. Your PIN (personal identification

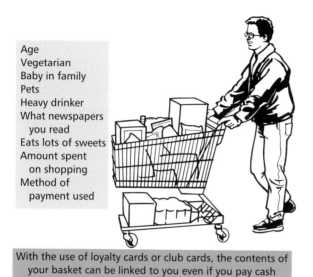

Age
Vegetarian
Baby in family
Pets
Heavy drinker
What newspapers
  you read
Eats lots of sweets
Amount spent
  on shopping
Method of
  payment used

With the use of loyalty cards or club cards, the contents of your basket can be linked to you even if you pay cash

Figure 8.1 *What your shopping may reveal about you*

number) may be detected and copied by people using sophisticated scanning equipment. It is also possible for the police and the security services to use equipment to determine the position of any mobile phone, provided it is switched on, and this can be used to monitor the whereabouts of criminals etc.

Credit/cash cards

When these are used the seller records what you have bought, where you have bought it and the time and date when the purchase was made.

Electoral roles

Everyone who is eligible to vote is placed on a register called the electoral roll, that records the names, addresses and dates of birth on a database. Unless you are on the electoral roll, you may find it difficult to get credit as this database is used when performing a credit check.

Telephone companies

Telephone companies keep records of all the calls made on a certain number and the times they are made. By coupling this with their database of phone numbers, names and addresses, they could, if they wished, get a detailed printout of all the names and addresses of the people contacted using your phone.

Cash dispensers

Every time cash is withdrawn from a cash machine, the date, time, location and the amount withdrawn is recorded. Some machines, for security reasons, even take a photograph of you as you withdraw the money and this is a particularly useful tool in combating fraud. People can no longer claim they did not use their cash or credit card if there is a photograph of them doing so.

Number plate reading systems at ports

All the major ports, from where car-ferries sail to other countries, have a number plate reading system, which means the plates of all cars arriving and leaving the port are automatically read and stored on a database. Using this system, the police and security services can monitor the movements of individuals and their cars, in and out of the country.

Surveillance cameras

Banks, building societies and any other premises where quantities of cash are kept, have cameras whose primary purpose is to act as a deterrent but which also provide evidence should a robbery occur. They are now a feature in many shops and town centres. Clearly, these cameras could be used for more sinister purposes if required.

Cookies

A cookie is the name given to the string of text that identifies you to certain websites that are able to catch your cookie. Cookie-catching websites are able to obtain information about you when you visit them and in many cases this information is used to send further information to you in the future, but it could be used for more sinister purposes.

Cookie catching websites work in the following way. When you visit certain sites they drop a piece of code, called a cookie, into the software used to access the Internet (called a web browser). As you enter the various sites, this cookie is used to build up a profile of your interests. If you access a lot of sites on programming, this will be picked up by the cookie and will give a good idea that you are a programmer. By tracking you through the various sites a detailed picture of you can be built up from a marketing point of view. This information is primarily used to send you details of products and services which might interest you.

The worrying feature of cookies is that they represent a way of watching consumers without their consent.

How to keep your life more private

If you are worried about the above infringements of your privacy there are a few things you can do, such as:

- do not fill in any questionnaires supplying market information

- do not buy any goods by mail order as they frequently sell lists of their customers to other companies

- do not give your National Insurance number to anyone who asks for it unless you are legally obliged to do so

- when filling in forms, remember to mark that you do not wish the information you have supplied to be passed on to anyone else

- pay by cash wherever possible

- do not enter free draws since they are often a ploy to get free marketing information about you.

Activity

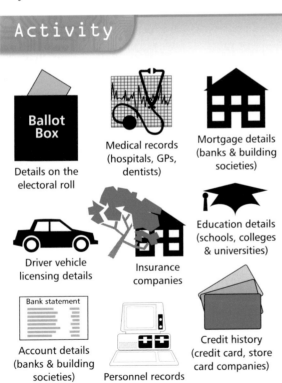

Figure 8.2 *Potential paths of data – when organisations acquire data about you, it may end up being shared, or even sold to other organisations*

Figure 8.2 shows just a few of the organisations that might hold personal details about you. There are many other organisations that hold personal data.

1 Add another ten organisations to this diagram and draw a small diagram to illustrate these in a similar way to the others. Finally write a short caption underneath.

2 Now add lines to your diagram, connecting organisations which would find it useful to exchange this personal data.

3 Mark four of the links which you have drawn in part 2 above, labelling them (a), (b), (c) and (d), then explain for each what sort of data might be exchanged and why this data would be useful to the receiving organisation.

Security

There are many aspects to security of computerised systems and it is worth looking at some of the threats before seeing how we prevent or minimise their occurrence.

Threats to security include:

- theft of hardware

- theft of software

- theft of data

- deliberate destruction of hardware or software by disgruntled staff

- destruction by natural disaster (floods, lightning, earthquakes)

- terrorist attacks

- alteration of data resulting in fraud

- destruction or hardware/software/data by fire

- espionage (company data is sold or given to competitors)

- malfunction of hardware resulting in data loss

- virus attacks

- industrial action (e.g. strikes by key computer personnel can cripple a company which relies heavily on IT)

- software bugs causing data loss

- mistakes caused by operators, such as processing the master file with the wrong transaction file

- errors when entering instructions to the operating system
- loss of electrical power
- hacking
- unauthorised access.

System security methods

To ensure the security of commercial and personal data, there are various security measures that can be used, including the following.

Control of access

Control of access may be divided into control of physical access and control of logical access.

Physical access controls

Physical access controls involve improving the security around the computer system. If the building is secure, then the computer system will be secure. To ensure the security of the buildings, some or all of the following need to be investigated.

Access to buildings

The following methods may be used to improve the physical security of the building:

- having fewer entrances to the building and using alarms on the emergency exits
- using security guards, in uniform, to patrol the buildings (these act as a deterrent)
- making all staff and visitors wear security badges.

Activity

Write a paragraph on each of the above to explain in more detail how each one improves the security of the building.

Automatic access control

Automatic access control means controlling the access to a room so that only authorised personnel are able to enter. Keys are unsuitable because they are easily copied and a lot of time can be spent getting security guards to unlock doors. Automatic access control is usually achieved by fitting a device on the door so that a

code has to be keyed in, or a card inserted, before the door can be opened. Sometimes the keypads are mechanical but in newer systems they are electronic and look like the keypad of a calculator. There are other systems that make use of small radio transmitters that look like those used with alarm systems or remote locking systems for cars.

The main advantage to having automatic devices to control access to the buildings or computer rooms, is that the security guards and receptionists are then able to deal with exceptional rather than routine access.

Activity

Look through computer equipment suppliers, and find out what devices are available to allow authorised entry to rooms but prevent unauthorised entry.

Access to computers

There are various factors to consider when preventing access, either to steal the equipment or data, or to gain unauthorised access to the computers.

1 **Location of computer equipment** – computer equipment should be kept away from visitor areas or areas where the equipment is visible from the street.

2 **Fixing of microcomputers and other peripherals to the desks** – this deters and prevents theft. Some systems include a lock, so the computer can be moved by authorised staff if needed.

3 **Hold sensitive data only on removable disks** – sensitive data should be held on removable disks so that they may be locked away when not in use.

4 **Lock the computer when not in use** – many computers have a lock on the front of the processor and a key is used to prevent it from being turned on by unauthorised personnel.

5 **Borrowing procedures** – this is not a practice to encourage. Staff get used to seeing other people carrying computer equipment out of the building and loading it into their cars. Security guards and staff should challenge anyone carrying equipment and there should be a set procedure for borrowing if necessary.

Logical access controls

Logical access controls are used to prevent unauthorised access to data files and software. There is a variety of logical access controls and these include the following:

1 **The use of passwords** – passwords are used to restrict access to certain files or data. The use of passwords involves entering a string of characters that have to match the password stored by the machine. If the password is too short, it is more likely to be guessed. The ideal length for a password has been found to be around six characters.

2 **Restricting the creation of user identities** – it should not be easy to obtain a user identity and so gain access to the computer system. User identities should be carefully monitored by the network manager or system administrator.

3 **The use of encryption techniques** – banks and other financial institutions make use of encryption techniques where data is coded before being sent via communication lines. The receiving machine then decodes the data. It is also possible to use these techniques to code data onto floppy or hard disks. Encryption is widely used when conducting e-commerce when customers have to enter their credit card numbers.

4 **Restriction of access to the operating system** – it is possible to restrict access to certain functions in the operating system. For instance, you could use a menu system so that the person never needs to access the operating system e.g. DOS, Windows, etc. This prevents them from copying disks or formatting the hard disk, for instance.

Security problems with networked computers

Many organisations are reaping the benefits of networking their computers together but in so doing they create a series of security risks that need to be addressed and minimised using a range of controls. For people to use network facilities, they must have easy access to the network that may be obtained from any of the terminals attached to the network. With proper security controls, it is possible to limit access to the data to only those authorised to use it, and

this minimises the threat to data, software and hardware. Although security measures need to be rigorous, they must not be too intrusive and put obstacles in the way of staff legitimately using the system.

Security controls that may be implemented include the following:

- Use passwords that have a minimum number of characters.

- Make sure that password use is taken seriously by all the staff and that passwords are changed regularly on a routine basis, despite protests from the users, who will sometimes forget them and have to be given new user accounts.

- Restrict the log-in time. The log-in time is the time the user has to log into the system once they have begun. The user usually has to type in their account name and their password. Some users will forget their passwords or mistype them, so a certain period is allowed. Once this period has elapsed, if the user has still not successfully logged into the system, they are locked out of the system and the network manager is alerted.

- Restrict the number of incorrect attempts at the password. This prevents unauthorised access to the system by someone inputting a series of guesses at the passwords.

- Use encryption programs to code data before it is sent along public communication channels; this prevents anyone making use of the intercepted signal.

- Use data redundancy on the file server. This means that more than one copy of the data is made and provides extra security in case a storage device fails.

Activity

A network manager is concerned about the casual approach to security that some of the users have. Before organising a meeting to try to make the users more aware of the importance of proper security, the network manager takes a trip around some of the departments to see what is going on. She visits several workstations in each department and makes a few points that she intends to raise at this meeting. On her trips she notices the following:

1 Many terminals lie idle, on-line while the user goes to the toilet or for a break.

2 Doors to offices are left unlocked even though they have keypads.

3 Passwords are written down on post-it notes stuck on the backs of monitors.

4 A quick look through diaries left on the desk-top reveals that not only have passwords been written down, but also the combinations of keypads to many of the rooms containing terminals.

5 On looking at the passwords chosen by the users many of them could reasonably be guessed, such as OPEN, ENTER, LETMEIN, etc. Others are the names of the person's spouse, children or their pets.

6 When users are away from their desks, confidential company data is left unattended on the desk. This data could easily be photocopied without their knowledge and sold to an outside organisation.

7 One user had left out their old and new diaries and in both diaries the same password appeared.

8 Many of the terminals were being used as stand-alone machines and when the network manager took a look at the file manager there were games and other unauthorised software loaded on the hard drives.

Write a short paragraph using the above notes as a framework to explain how each one of the above points compromises the security of the whole network.

Biometric testing

One of the problems we face today is the large number of personal identification numbers (PINs) and passwords we have to remember just to conduct our everyday business. These include PINs for cash dispensers, mobile phones, PINs for logging onto your network at work and onto the Internet. Another problem is that many of these numbers and passwords should be changed on a regular basis to maintain security. Many people forget their passwords or numbers and this causes lots of problems. It is not surprising, therefore, that other methods of checking identity when accessing a service are

being investigated and developed. Biometric testing is the one which shows the most promise.

Biometric testing makes use of any biological feature that is unique to an individual, such as the pattern on their retina or their fingerprint.

Fingerprint identification systems are now becoming cheap enough to be used widely for accessing banking services, network services, etc. The user places their finger into a scanner that scans the print and then matches it with a previously stored print; if they are the same then the person is allowed access. If the print does not match, then the operating system will not be loaded, preventing the person from accessing programs or data on the computer.

Eventually, when the price of such systems comes down, we will see them being incorporated into many everyday devices, such as monitors, keyboards and mice.

Iris scanning systems are being introduced which use a laser scanner to scan the pattern on this part of the eye.

Backup systems

Backing up means keeping copies of software and data to enable lost data to be recovered should there be partial or complete failure of the computer system. Backup copies are only useful if they are taken on an organised and regular basis. There are many causes of a total loss of data, including: fire, theft, flood, virus attack, operator error, sabotage, power failure and explosion.

Backup files are normally kept on a disk or tape and are removed from the computer or even from the building. The chances are that anyone who steals a PC will probably also look around for disks and tapes to steal and these could contain backup copies. So the computer and backup copies need to be kept away from each other. Many companies make use of waterproof and fireproof safes in which to store their backups; these have the advantage that it is no longer necessary to move the backups to another place. There are a variety of reasons why people do not make backups, and these include:

1 not having a blank spare disk on which to store the backup

2 the time taken to make the backup if there is a large amount of data stored and lots of disks are needed; it is best to include Zip or Jaz

drives which hold huge amounts of data and work quickly

3   backing up is generally done at the end of a day's work when people are in a hurry to get home, so they may decide to 'back them up next time'

4   users incorrectly think that hardware is now very reliable and that loss of their data very unlikely.

A backup strategy

All computers which contain valuable data should be backed up and have a backup strategy. For a stand-alone PC or a small file server running a local area network, probably the best form of backup medium is magnetic tape. There are many different types of backup tape drives and tapes; they may all be thought of as inexpensive and reliable ways of taking copies of important data.

All organisations should have a backup strategy. It is no use just keeping a tape in the backup drive and then remembering to take a copy every now and again. What is needed is a set time each day (or night) when the data from the hard drive is copied to the backup tape drive. After backing up, the tape is removed and safely stored away from the computer. The tape can be rotated on a weekly or monthly basis so that backups for a certain period are kept and the obsolete tapes re-used.

Every now and again, the backup tapes should be copied and the spare copy transferred off-site in case a serious fire, explosion, etc. occurs at the premises and destroys the computer systems and backup media.

Network backups

Backing up software and data is especially important on a network because if something goes wrong, all the users of the network are likely to suffer. Many networks making use of a server have an internal tape drive in the server which is used to back up all the hard disks in the server. Many tape drives use data compression when being used for backing up and this reduces the time taken to back up as well as the amount of tape needed. As well as hardware devices for backing up, some software is needed to support the backup, although in many cases this will simply be the operating system used, such as Windows NT or Windows 2000. It is possible to

have an automatic backup facility that takes backup copies at set intervals without the involvement of the network manager/administrator and many operating systems support this.

File servers holding all the data for a network are crucial to the running of the network; serious disruption can occur even if data is lost for a short period. In a supermarket the loss of the network means that the point-of-sale terminals (where customers pay for their goods) do not work. Although backups are kept so that any lost data can be recovered, this takes time and in some situations the time taken is unacceptable, so an alternative strategy has to be found.

RAID systems

Most networks are now being built using a RAID system. RAID stands for redundant array of inexpensive disks. RAID comes in six versions (0 to 5), each one slightly different. All the versions make use of a series of magnetic disks rather than just one. They are usually found within the casing of the server, although there are separate ones as well. RAID 0 does not offer any data redundancy, which means that the data is only stored once, so it is simply a method of increasing the performance of the disks by increasing the speed at which data is accessed. This is achieved by the use of **striping**, which means that when a file is stored, the data is written with a bit on each disk. Using this method, all the disks are read at once so data transfer is faster.

RAID 1 uses disk mirroring in which an exact copy of data on one hard drive is placed on another hard drive at the same time. The term mirroring is used because what one hard drive does, so does the other. If one of the hard drives in this system malfunctions, the other can take over and use its storage facilities. Transfer happens instantly, so there is a clear advantage over other backing up techniques where there is a delay while the data is re-created from backups.

RAIDs 2 and 3 use disk striping to improve performance and also use extra check disks to ensure that the data written to the other disks is reliable.

RAID 4 is almost the same as RAIDs 2 and 3 except the striping used is **block** or **sector striping**, which makes access to the data even faster than normal striping. RAID 5 is again similar, except this time it records checking data on not just one disk but over several disks.

If the network with RAID fails, then in RAID 2 the other mirrored disk is used to keep the network going, but in the other RAID systems, the information contained on the check disk (or disks) is used to re-create the data contained on the failed disks.

To improve network security further, a technique called **clustering** is used in which several files servers are networked together. This technique is looked at in Chapter 18 but the principles are described and shown here in Figure 8.3.

A single server and storage device

If either the server or the storage device fails, then the data is likely to be lost.

Server

Storage device

A single server with two storage devices

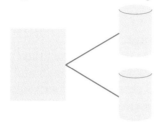

Here data is copied twice, i.e. it is 'mirrored' on the storage devices. Data integrity is improved but data can still be lost if the server fails.

A two server and two storage device cluster

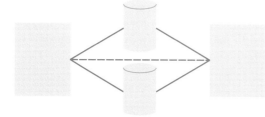

If either a storage device or a server fails the other server and storage device can in most cases recover a system. The dotted line is a high speed data link between the servers.

Figure 8.3 *Avoiding data loss by using clustering*

In most RAID systems disks may be removed in order to improve security.

Backup procedures

Backup is the creation of copies of programs and data so that should the original programs or data be lost, they may be re-created using the backup copies. Although there are many software utilities (e.g. Norton Utilities) available for the recovery of lost data, these are not able to recover data in every situation, so there is no substitute for a backup copy.

Backup copies should be kept on a separate disk or tape and should be stored away from the computer system. Some software keeps a backup copy on the same disk, but in such a case if the disk is stolen or destroyed by fire, then the backup copy is also destroyed.

Types of backup

There are two main types of backup:

Full backup – where all the data files are backed up. This would normally be done once a week but if there is a large amount of data that changes from day to day then it is best done every evening.

Incremental backups – where only the data which have changed since the last full backup, are backed up.

To make sure that the backup system operates correctly, managers sometimes copy some data and then deliberately 'lose' it to make sure that the relevant staff can re-create it from their backup files.

Rules for backing up

1   Never keep the backup disks near the computer. If the computer is stolen then unless the thieves are ignorant about computers, they will very likely take the disks as well. Never keep the disks in the drawer of your desk since this is the first place thieves will look.

2   If you hold a lot of data that would be very expensive to re-create you should invest in a fire-proof safe to protect your backups against theft and fire.

3   Keep at least one set of backup disks at a different site.

Disk failure

It is important to bear in mind that all microcomputers will suffer at least one serious fault during their lifetime. The hard disk unit has a mean time between failures of between 20,000 and 200,000 hours. This means that if a computer is used for 12 hours per day, five days per week, 52 weeks a year, you could expect its hard disk to break down once in about six years.

If the computer is being used as a file server (i.e. the computer used to control the network), it could be switched on 24 hours per day, 365 days per year, in which case the hard disk could be expected to fail on average every 27 months. Couple this with the chance of other components failing and you have a complete computer system likely to break down every 14 months.

Backup copies of the programs and data on the hard disk should be taken at regular intervals. A tape streamer should be used (which looks a bit like an ordinary tape recorder) or one of the many other suitable storage devices mentioned in Chapter 7. Transfer from the hard disk to the backup medium is fast and you do not have to supervise the operation. Should the hard disk become damaged, reverse transfer is also fast.

The grandfather, father and son system (the ancestral file system)
Data held on either a disk or tape master file could be destroyed by accident or by sabotage. For many companies, the loss of vital data can prove disastrous. However, using the grandfather–father–son principle, it is possible to recreate the master file if it is lost. This system is explained in detail in Chapter 6, page 96.

Forced recognition of security
Information technology is used extensively for a wide range of tasks including operating nuclear power stations, flying planes, keeping medical records, insurance records and keeping police records. With such information being held, it is very important that adequate security systems are in place to protect these systems against deliberate, natural or accidental harm.

Sometimes, rather than using gentle persuasion to make staff more security conscious, it is necessary to force them to recognise the security implications of their work. There are a variety of ways in which this may be achieved.

Non-disclosure agreements
These are terms that are placed in a contract of employment, which impose certain restrictions on employees, sometimes even after they no longer work for the organisation. They usually restrict passing valuable business information on to competitors. Sometimes they are used to prevent an ex-employee speaking about their previous employment. Such clauses have been used recently by the Royal Family to prevent their employees talking to the press. Although these are voluntary agreements, at the time of signing a contract of employment the employee is usually in a weak position and may feel forced to sign if they want the job.

The Official Secrets Act
This Act of Parliament is used to protect the privacy of information held by the Crown and thus to protect national security. Civil servants, military personnel, prison warders (in those prisons which have not been privatised) and policemen/policewomen all have to agree to abide by the Act as a condition of their employment. In taking such employment and signing the Act the employee is then legally bound to maintain a certain amount of security during the course of their employment.

TASKS

Research the following using computing dictionaries, books and the Internet

You are writing a corporate security strategy for a company and need to check on information about the following:

- write-protect mechanisms (used so that data cannot be accidentally erased)
- levels of permitted access to files contained by a network
- methods of re-creating data that has been accidentally erased or damaged (e.g. using Norton Utilities or other, similar packages).

Research each of the above using books, magazines and the Internet, and write a section on each to be included in the corporate computer strategy.

Include a list of the references you have used to produce your document.

DEBRIEF
Did you remember to include the web addresses of any interesting sites in your list of references?

CASE STUDY

These case studies are real and show some of the ways in which the security of a computer system can be compromised. They also look at what could be done in the future to prevent such problems re-occurring.

Case study 1
A food processing factory with a power problem

A food processing factory located high up in the Pennines suffered from regular thunder and lightning storms which could cause loss in electrical power for a couple of seconds, just long enough to cause the computer systems to fail. During these power cuts data was lost and had to be re-created from the backup copies. Sometimes as the data was being restored (using the backup copies), another power failure would occur. The net effect of all this was that the data had to be backed up four times a day and the data processing manager and his staff had worried looks on their faces every time a black cloud loomed overhead.

The problem was solved by making use of an uninterruptible power supply (UPS for short) that maintained power by using a series of batteries for a short time. In addition, the company decided to buy a generator, which meant if the power did not return fairly soon, then the battery power (which only lasted a short time) could be relieved by switching over to the generator.

Case study 2
A disgruntled employee causes havoc

A disgruntled ex-employee who had been dismissed returned to the computer room soon after and punched the code into the keypad to gain entry. He then went to one of the terminals, input his account name and password and gained access to the network. Because of his post as network administrator, he had administrator access to the file server and could therefore delete, change and copy files. He then wiped two of the disks containing all the company's data and then, realising that backup tapes were also kept, turned his attention to these. Using his key to open the fireproof safe where backups were kept, he then proceeded to move a small magnet across the surface of the backup copies thus destroying the magnetic pattern of the stored data on the disk.

All the company's data was lost since no backup copies were kept off-site, which is normal practice. The ex-employee was caught and convicted but this was little consolation to the company that nearly went bankrupt as a result, since details of all the people who owed them money were lost. Staff who have been dismissed should not work a notice period and should be asked to clear their belongings while someone watches them; they should then be escorted off the premises. All lock combinations and passwords should be immediately changed to prevent them gaining entry to the premises and the systems.

Case study 3
A virus attack

Miss Hughes was an advertising executive for a large advertising agency and often took one of the company's personal computers home at weekends to finish off work. Her son, who did not have a computer of his own, kept pestering her to let him use the computer. She eventually gave in. He loaded some games (his friend got them from a computer fair) from a CD onto the computer's hard drive. Arriving back at work after the weekend, Miss Hughes connected her PC to the company network and found that some of the files she had been working on at the weekend had been corrupted. Moreover, the network manager rushed in saying that a virus had been discovered on the file server.

Games and other unauthorised software should never be loaded onto machines containing company data since they frequently contain viruses. Allowing people to take computers home should not be encouraged particularly if the computers are subsequently reconnected to a network. Security and other staff will see people walking around with hardware and loading it into their cars until this is seen as quite normal and such activities will no longer be challenged. The company may be advised not to allow borrowing of computers or possibly to put into staff contracts that loading unauthorised software or data is a dismissible offence.

Case study 4
Chip and RAM theft

A college located all its administration departments on the ground floor of an office block. There was a reception area and from this members of the public could see the computers and other office equipment. Additionally, the computers could be seen through the window by people passing on the street. All the computers were bolted to the desks and it was thought that the risk of theft was slight. One night a window was forced and all the computers had their cases smashed and their processor chips and RAMS stolen. In the process some disk drives containing important college data relating to students were damaged.

There is always a danger in keeping valuable computer equipment on the ground floor of an office block, especially if it can be seen by members of the public. The college should consider moving this equipment to a higher floor or put metal bars on the windows to make the office more secure. Chip and RAM theft is quite common since they are quite easy to carry, conceal and sell.

Case study 5
System failure

A young, inexperienced computer operator was working in the computer room when he heard a loud grating noise coming from one of the hard disk drives of a minicomputer. He thought that the disk, containing all the company data, was faulty. He remembered that a backup copy of this removable disk was kept in the fire-proof safe, so he went to get it. He removed the master disk and replaced it with the backup copy. On trying to read data off the drive the same thing happened. An engineer was called who said that the problem was a faulty disk drive and that both of the disks that had been placed in this drive had had their data corrupted.

This was a case of inexperience and human error. There was always a chance that the fault was in the hardware, so inserting the only backup copy was a serious error. He should have instead used another disk with old data on it, so that it would not matter if it were destroyed. You should always step back from a situation and think of the best course of action to take rather than jump straight in with an ill-considered solution to the problem.

Questions

1 Distinguish between the terms 'security', 'privacy' and 'integrity' with reference to a file containing personal details.

2 A pharmaceutical company holds data about patients who are trying a drug. Since medical details about the patients are held on this database, the company wants to know what security procedures could be put in place to ensure the privacy of these data.

  (a) Give details of three logical and three physical methods that can be used.

  (b) It is suggested that the staff should be given a list of rules when working at a terminal. Write down eight rules that this list should contain.

Activity

Definition of terms

A variety of new terms is introduced in this chapter, many of which may be new to you. It is important that you build up vocabulary that can be used when writing essays or answering questions. Write a definition for each of the following terms used in the chapter:

privacy	encryption
security	biometric testing
website	RAID
cookie	

1 A computer system, that is normally in use 24 hours a day, holds large volumes of different types of data on disk packs. The main types of data stored are:

– applications software that changes only occasionally during maintenance;

– data master files that are updated regularly every week;

– transaction files which are created daily;

– database files which are changing constantly.

It is vital that these different types of file can be quickly recovered in the event of file corruption.

Outline a suitable backup strategy for each of these files explaining what data is backed up and when, the procedures to be followed, and the media and hardware needed. *(8)*

(NEAB, Module IT02, Specimen Paper, q8)

2 A publishing company administers its business by using a database system running on a network of PCs. The main uses are to process customer orders and to log payments. You have been asked about backup strategies and their importance.

(a) Give **two** reasons why it is essential that this company has a workable backup strategy. *(2)*

(b) State **five** factors that should be considered in a backup strategy, illustrating each factor with an example. *(10)*

(c) Despite all the precautions, some data might still be lost if there were a system failure. Give **two** reasons why this might be the case. *(2)*

(NEAB, Module IT02, May 1998, q6)

3 Explain, using examples, the distinction between security and privacy as applied to data held in a computerised information system. *(4)*

(NEAB, Module IT02, May 99, q1)

Network Environments

CHAPTER OBJECTIVES

▶ To describe the characteristics and relative advantages and disadvantages of networked and stand-alone environments.

▶ To look at the different network topologies.

▶ To describe the main features of local area networks and wide area networks.

▶ To describe the characteristics and relative advantages and disadvantages of client–server and peer-to-peer networks.

▶ To describe the factors which affect the rate and manner by which data can be transmitted.

▶ To look at the factors which affect compatibility between different systems.

▶ To understand the function of gateways.

Computer networks – what are they?

Computers are used as tools in many businesses. When a computer is used on its own without any connection to other computers it is said to be in a stand-alone environment. If data needs to be passed to another department in such an environment, it must be printed out on paper, or copied on to disk before being transferred to another person for entry into their computer. Information flow around organisations is continuous, so it makes sense to have a fast and easy method of information exchange. This can be achieved by connecting computers together by means of cables. A group of such computers is called a computer network.

Computer networks are everywhere. You can find them in organisations of all sizes, in schools, hospitals, government departments and now even in some homes. It is therefore important for everyone to know a little about

networks. In this chapter you will learn what networks are and how they have lots of advantages compared with using the same computers individually. Additionally, we will look at the different types and arrangements of networks and at some of the problems that need to be considered when computers are connected together. The information contained in this chapter is built on in Chapter 18, and it is important if you are studying for the A level examination (rather than the AS level) that you understand both of these chapters.

There are three parts to any network system:

1 **A sender of information:** this could be a person sitting at a workstation/terminal or data from an automatic measuring device, such as a traffic flow sensor used for sensing the traffic flow at a busy junction.

2 **A communications link:** in most cases this is a physical link where there is an actual wire or cable along which the data is sent. It may be a so-called logical link, in the case of sending the data as radio signals, where no physical link exists.

3 **A receiver of information:** this could be another workstation or remote computer.

Types of computer network

Computer networks may be classed as either LANs (local area networks) or WANs (wide area networks) and in this section we will look at the characteristics that determine which category a particular network falls into. Generally speaking, a LAN is confined to a single building whereas a WAN is the set of links between LANs making use of telecommunication lines that are either private or leased (i.e. rented).

Wide area networks (WANs)

Here is a list of the main features of a WAN:

● **Hardware is spread over a wide geographical area.**
A WAN consists of terminals and computing equipment connected over a large area, usually in excess of two kilometres.

- **Third party telecommunications equipment is used.**
  Because the hardware is spread out, telephone, radio or satellite communication links are used, which the organisation does not own. Telecommunications companies provide the links and each of these has its own rules, regulations and service charges.

Local area networks (LANs)

Figure 9.1 shows two typical LANs; one is used to share resources, such as a laser printer, the other is used to access centrally held data on a computer called a file server.

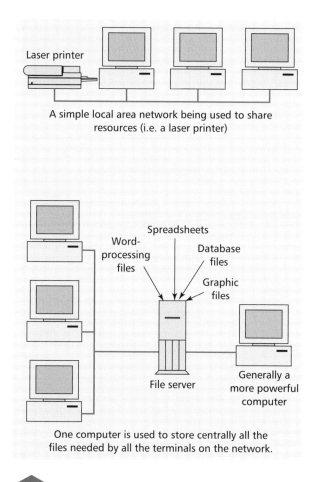

Figure 9.1 *Two diagrams of a local area network*

Here is a list of the main features of a LAN.

- **Linked hardware is confined to a single office or site.**
  Most LANs are in a single building or site although it is possible to use microwave links to connect to a nearby office or factory. We usually say that provided the distances involved are less than two kilometres, the network is a LAN.

- **All the wires and other devices needed for a LAN are owned by the organisation.**
  The backbone of a LAN in a single building is the wiring that links the terminals. All the equipment is owned by the organisation and it is up to the organisation to install and run the network as it sees fit.

Activity

Networks can be broadly classified into LANs and WANs. You have to decide which category each of the following networks is best classed as:

(a) A training room in a commercial organisation where the users can all access the same training files held on a computer in the same room. All 20 terminals use the same two printers.

(b) An oil company making use of videoconferencing equipment and a network to enable meetings to take place with branch managers of subsidiaries throughout the world.

(c) A large supermarket with a head office, several warehouses and hundreds of stores using EDI (electronic data interchange) to exchange data automatically with their suppliers and customers.

(d) A restaurant where the waiters take the orders using small hand-held terminals which then send the orders using radio waves to a main computer in the kitchen.

Private wide area networks

A private area network is a network which uses privately leased or owned lines and may be accessed only if you are a subscriber to the system. One such network is called JANet (standing for Joint Academic Network) and this is used to join together educational establishments in the UK.

Since the growth in the Internet, there are many more private wide area networks. Internet service providers (ISPs) enable anyone with a modem and suitable communications software to access their network and also allow access to the Internet if required.

In general ISPs are able to provide the following.

- **Instant messages:** you can hold a conversation interactively by typing messages at the keyboard and then receiving others back.

- **Electronic mail (e-mail):** electronic mail may be sent to other users of the system or anyone connected to the Internet by other service providers.

- **Message boards:** these enable people to have an open discussion on a wide variety of topics. This is particularly useful if you have a problem and need advice. You simply post your message on the message board and wait for any replies.

- **Directories of members:** this is a little bit like a phone book, but it can tell you more information than just e-mail addresses. Using this facility you can, for example, find people who share the same interests or hobbies as yourself.

- **Software downloads:** many people like to write programs for pleasure and are keen that others should use the results of their efforts. They do this by making their software freely available on the Internet from where it can be downloaded using the communications line. Some of this software is shareware which means that although you are free to download and evaluate it, if you find it useful you should pay a small fee to the developer, who will then usually send you documentation or a more complete version and register you for further upgrades, when improvements are made to the program.

- **Members' services:** these enable you to keep track of how much time you have spent on-line and more importantly, how much time you have to pay for. There are various help services on offer for beginners. There are services for controlling areas of the service which children can enter. Parental control can be exercised using software that restricts children using some facilities of the Internet. Parents can stop their children entering chat rooms or certain sites.

- **Hosted chats:** here you can chat away to someone famous. Usually there is a list of times when the person will be on-line.

- **A main menu:** here is the place where you can start looking for information under a wide variety of headings. Figure 9.2 shows the main menu from America On Line (AOL).

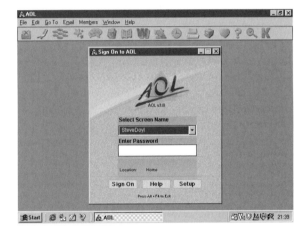

Figure 9.2 *The opening screen for AOL*

The advantages of a network environment

The main reasons for networking a group of computers together are as follows.

1 **A common pool of data may be shared amongst all the users without any need for duplication.**
Imagine there are two people working in an office using stand-alone machines and sharing the same client database. They will need identical copies of the same client database and any alterations they make to it will have to be notified to the other person and made twice over. This will involve the exchange of files on floppy disks or other storage media, from one machine to another. If you increase the number of people sharing the same database above two the problems multiply, with some users failing to update their database and different versions of the database developing. This is one of the main reasons why most companies use a network. Networking allows access to a shared client database and updating need only be done once, by anyone on the network.

2 **Hardware resources such as laser printers, plotters, scanners, fax machines, etc. may be shared by all the users.**

Many peripherals are quite expensive and spend much of their time idle, so if there are several users in an office, it makes sense to share facilities. It is possible to share them by having one computer connected to the peripheral; other people could then come along with their work on floppies when they needed to use the device. However, if this computer is being used, the person sitting at it will face constant interruptions. Another alternative is the use of manual switches which can be turned to make a connection between each computer and the peripheral, but a lot of cabling is needed and it is already half-way to being a network, so you may as well go further and have a proper network.

Using a network, all the resources attached to the network may be accessed by any user.

3 **Software may be shared.**
Network versions of popular software are available, making it cheaper than buying individual copies for stand-alone machines.

Since programs are downloaded from a central point (usually the file server), only one network version of the application software needs to be bought, and this is usually much cheaper. A licence is bought allowing a certain number of terminals to use the software.

4 **Security is likely to be improved.**
This is especially so if terminals with no processing power of their own and without disk drives are used. Many large organisations use diskless workstations which prevent users from stealing company data or software, as well as preventing the introduction of viruses via floppy disks.

If all the software is kept on a central computer, it is easier to make sure that no illegal software is being used by employees. The person in charge of the network (the network manager), can use special software to ensure that only software for which there are licences is being used on the network.

A network also provides a more secure environment for company data since with stand-alone computers, access to the computer usually means access to the data, whereas networks provide an additional layer of security with the use of passwords.

5 **Better backing up facilities.**
With a network, one person, usually the network manager, is responsible for the periodic backing up of data, rather than leaving it to individuals. The more closely controlled backup procedures mean that the users are less likely to lose data.

6 **Improved communication between users.**
All networks have a facility for electronic mail, which is quick and saves paper. If the network is connected to the Internet, this opens up a whole sphere of worldwide communication.

7 **Central maintenance and support.**
If new upgrades need to be added to software held centrally on a network, this need only be added to the file server instead of updating many stand-alone machines. Many organisations have different versions of the same applications programs in use which can all look slightly different. By having a single version all the settings for the users can be standardised so if someone moves to a different terminal the software will be identical.

Advantages of a stand-alone environment

A stand-alone environment is one where each computer is set up and used separately. Each computer needs its own copy of the operating system and the applications software used. In addition there will be an individual set of data and if data need to be passed from one computer to another it must be done manually.

There are some advantages in using stand-alone machines and these are outlined below.

1 **Cheaper hardware and software**
The wires, network cards and software needed to run a network are expensive so stand-alone machines provide a cheaper option.

2 **Less IT knowledge needed**
A greater degree of IT knowledge is needed to run a network successfully and this may mean employing a network manager/administrator.

3 **Fewer problems with viruses**
Virus infection will be less of a problem with stand-alone machines unless data and programs are frequently transferred from one computer to another.

4 **Not as hardware dependent**
In some cases, if a file server can not be used because of a technical problem, this affects the whole network. Such problems can not arise with stand-alone computers.

Network topologies

There are many different devices which can be connected to a network and these include servers, central processing units, backing storage devices, point of sale terminals, automated teller machines (i.e. cash dispensers) and so on. Many of these devices will be connected together by a wire or a fibre optic cable, but this is not always the case, since some could use a radio or satellite link, so there is no visible connection. Nevertheless, they are still 'logically linked.' There are many different ways or patterns in which the network of devices can be linked, physically and logically. In this section we look at some of them. The links in the following diagrams are shown as lines between the devices (or **nodes** as they are sometimes called). The ways in which they can be logically and physically connected are called topologies. There are many different topologies in use but the most popular ones are the ring, bus, mesh and star topologies.

Ring topology

In the ring topology, nodes are connected together to form a circle and no single terminal has overall control of the network. This type of network topology, used only for local area networks, is sometimes called a **peer-to-peer network** because none of the terminals is higher in status than others. Notice in Figure 9.3 that one computer uses its storage for the whole network and this one is called the file server. It is on this computer that all the programs and data for the entire network are stored. The main problem with a ring network is that for a node to communicate with a non-adjacent node, it is necessary for the data to pass through one or more other nodes. A break in connection between any of the nodes is hard to identify and will cause the whole network to fail. Another problem with ring networks is that as the data signal travels around the wires, it tends to degenerate and weaken, so special boosters, called **repeaters**, are used to increase the signal strength. Figure 9.3 shows the arrangement of the nodes (computers and other hardware connected to the network) in a ring network.

Data is controlled in a ring network by the use of **tokens**. These special messages are passed from node to node around the ring. When a node needs to send a message it waits for the token to arrive, captures it and transmits the message. Once the message arrives at the receiving terminal, the token is released by this terminal and continues on its travels around the ring until it is captured by another terminal waiting to send a message. Networks using physical or logical rings for the passing of tokens, are called **token-rings**.

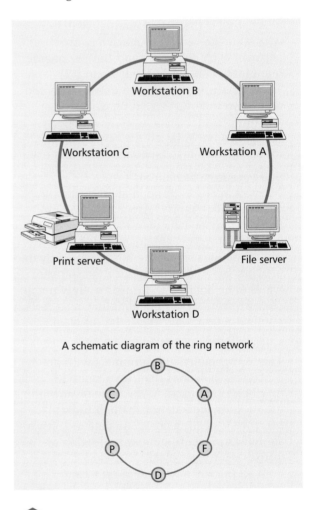

A schematic diagram of the ring network

Figure 9.3 *A ring network*

Advantages and disadvantages of ring networks

☑ Advantages

- All computers connected in the ring can access the token as it passes, so no terminal can 'hog' the network.

- Users may be added one by one (until the speed of access becomes unacceptably slow).

☒ Disadvantages

- If one computer fails, the whole network fails.

- It is hard to locate faults in a ring topology.

- Adding or removing computers will disrupt the network since there is only one path to follow.

Bus topology

In the bus topology, when data is sent from one node to another, it is sent simultaneously to all other nodes in the network. The main advantages of this is that it is not necessary for any node to pass the data onto the recipient. If one of the nodes is not functioning correctly, remaining nodes can still function without it. Bus topologies are of two main types: the **linear bus** and the **ring bus**. Neither of these has a central computer controlling the network so they may be considered further examples of peer-to-peer networks. The main disadvantage of a bus network is that since only one computer at a time can send a message, each time another computer is added to the network it seriously affects the speed of the network. Another disadvantage is that is quite hard to locate a fault such as a cable break or a malfunctioning computer.

The main advantages are that a bus topology is simple, reliable, does not need large runs of cable (so it is cheap), and it is very easy to extend with repeaters if the distance between the nodes needs to be increased.

Figure 9.4 shows the arrangement for a network using the bus topology.

Mesh topology

In the mesh topology not all the nodes are linked together, so may be regarded as a partially linked network.

The mesh topology is one of a group of topologies called **point-to-point topologies.** Here, messages can be sent from one node to another using a single link, or if there is no single link via a pathway consisting of several links. In Figure 9.5, if node A wishes to send a message to node E, there is no *direct* link, but it could send it to node B which could retransmit it to E. Using this method, node B stores the message, then examines it, to determine the address and network information contained in the package. When node B discovers that the package is not meant for it, it sends it on to the next node, which is E in this case. Figure 9.5 shows what is called a partially connected mesh network because each node is not connected to all the others. This is often used to reduce the amount of wiring between nodes, which in turn reduces the cost.

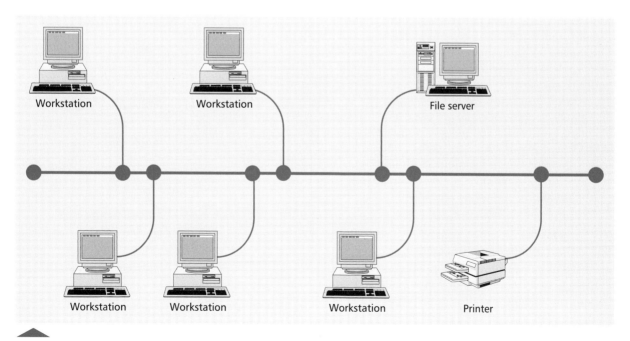

Figure 9.4 *A bus network*

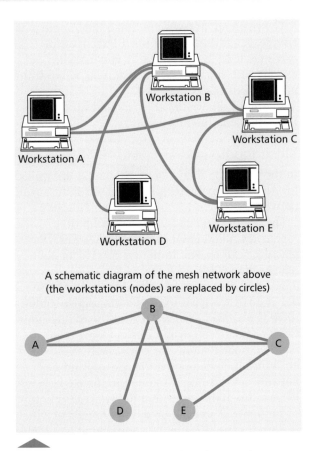

A schematic diagram of the mesh network above (the workstations (nodes) are replaced by circles)

Figure 9.5 *A partially connected mesh network*

nodes, it also manages the network file system. One main advantage of the star topology is that there is no contention for the pathways as all the nodes have their own line to the central node. This means that the volume of data passed can be higher than for bus topologies. Another advantage is that if one of the non-controller nodes (the ones not at the centre) fails, then the remaining links still work. If extra machines need to be added to the network, another hub with a greater number of ports can be used. Extra computers can also be added without disturbing the network. On the minus side we have seen that the operation of the central node is crucial and a large amount of cabling needs to be used to connect up a star and this can add substantially to the cost of the network.

The main advantage of the mesh topology is that if there is a problem with a link between nodes, there is usually another path that can be taken. The possibility of multiple paths is more likely to arise with larger mesh networks because of the greater number of possible paths between nodes. This makes mesh networks very **fault tolerant**. It is also relatively easy to locate the position of a fault on a mesh network.

The main disadvantages of mesh networks is that greater lengths of cable are used to maintain the extra links which are not always needed (apart from their adding extra paths), and this also makes them harder to maintain. Both of these features add substantially to the costs involved in setting up and running this type of network.

Star topology

The star topology shown in Figure 9.6 has one machine at its centre, whose operation controls the whole network. If this machine malfunctions the entire network becomes inoperative. The central machine is called the **hub node** or **central controller node** and as well as controlling the data passage between the other

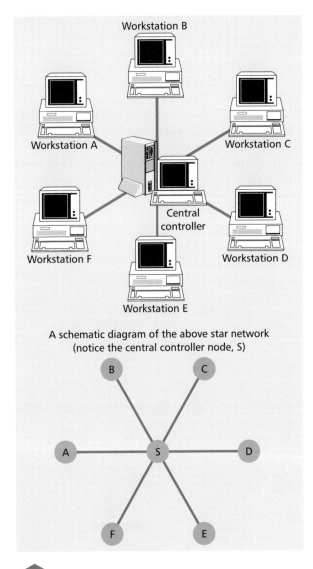

A schematic diagram of the above star network (notice the central controller node, S)

Figure 9.6 *Diagram showing a star network*

Activity

1 Each of the network topologies has its own particular strengths and weaknesses. In the explanation of the star topology, these were highlighted in a bulleted list under the headings of advantages and disadvantages. Your task is to identify the advantages and disadvantages of the bus, mesh and star topologies and produce bulleted lists for each.

2 A network consultant goes to visit a small business which has ten computers in a stand-alone environment. After conducting a fact-find and investigating the information flows within the business, the consultant tells them that they need a local area network. He also tells them that there are a variety of network topologies to choose from.

(a) Explain what a network topology is.

(b) The consultant has said that the following network topologies are available: star, bus, ring, mesh.

For the ten computers in the head office, produce a diagram showing how the computers should be connected together for each of the different topologies listed.

(c) By looking at the diagram you have drawn for the mesh network (assuming that it is not a partially connected mesh topology), work out how many wires would be needed.

Why can this be both an advantage and a disadvantage for this topology?

(d) The consultant says, 'it is important to get the bandwidth right'. What is meant by this statement? (See page 146.)

Popular networks

In this section we will look at some of the popular types of network and how they operate. For small LANs there are two main types of network: **peer-to-peer** and **client–server**.

Peer-to-peer

Your peers are people who are of equal status to you. In peer-to-peer networks, each computer is of equal status; in the other type of architecture, the client–server, the server is the 'king' of the network. Figure 9.7 shows the arrangement of the terminals in a typical peer-to-peer network.

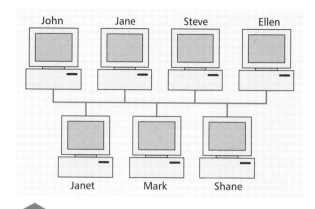

Figure 9.7 *Peer-to-peer networks are ideal for small networks (2–10 users)*

The important feature of peer-to-peer networks is that the file storage and printing facilities do not come from a single server, but instead from any of the computers connected to the network. Any of the workstations can use each other's resources such as CD drives, hard disks, tape streamers, fax, printers, plotters, etc. The main advantage of peer-to-peer networks is that they are quite easy to install and are economical to run, since you do not need a powerful server. However they have the disadvantage that they are difficult to manage on a large scale, and there is a noticeable decrease in speed if two people are trying to access the same hard disk at the same time.

To run a peer-to-peer network it is necessary to install a network interface card in each machine, cabling (usually thin coaxial cable known as thin Ethernet) to join up each machine, T-piece connectors to connect up each machine and a suitable network operating system.

Because of the disadvantages already mentioned, peer-to-peer networks are only really suitable for small networks with less than 20 terminals.

Advantages and disadvantages of peer-to-peer networks

☑ **Advantages**

- Only ordinary computers are needed; there is no need for a server or sophisticated network operating system as with client–server network.

- No network administrator/manager is needed as all the users manage their own part of the network.

- They are easy to set up and minimal technical knowledge is needed.

- Small peer-to-peer networks are less expensive to set up and run than their client–server counterparts.

- Each user is in control of their own resources and can decide who else on the network can access them.

- There is no reliance on one computer such as a server.

- The costs are much smaller than for a client–server network.

☒ Disadvantages

- The computers in this type of network have an additional load on them due to the resource sharing.

- There is no central organisation of data which makes data harder to locate since they could be on any one of the peers.

- Backups can not be performed centrally and it is hard to be sure that adequate backups are being made.

- The users need more specialist computer knowledge as they are now required to run their own computers.

- Security is not as good as with a client–server system.

- Because there is no central management, the peer-to-peer network is much harder to work with.

- There is no central point of storage for file archiving.

Client–server

With this type of architecture, a more powerful computer, called the client, is used to look after printing, file maintenance and any other peripherals connected to the network. The less powerful computers (called clients) are connected to the network and can use the services offered to them by the server. To understand the concept of client–server it is best to look an example involving a database.

Suppose we are using a database on a stand-alone machine for running a query such as producing a list of members whose membership has expired. When a query is run, the database program opens the file where the data is stored and then reads each record to see if it matches the criteria set in the query: if it does, it is stored in memory; if not, it is discarded. In this way the data for the query report is built up.

Figure 9.8 shows a single server client–server network that might be used in a local area network in a small office with between ten and 50 users.

If the same query had been processed using a network, then the file containing all the data would need to be stored on a central file server. This would enable everyone in the same organisation to access the same data. When the query is run on a PC connected to the network, every record will need to be passed from the server to the PC, which would create a huge amount of traffic on the network and slow down the network in the process. Many of the records passed to the PC will be discarded since they do not meet the criteria imposed by the query, so much of this network traffic is unnecessary.

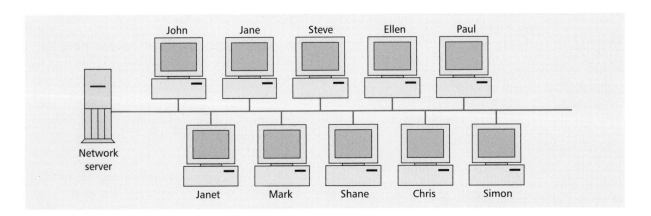

Figure 9.8 *A single server client–server network (10–50 users)*

With a client–server network, this problem is solved by running the server part of the application on the server; only the client part of the application is run on the terminal. It is now the client part that directs the server program to interrogate the database and extract data meeting the search criteria. Once found, the server only sends data matching the criteria back to the terminal (i.e. the client). Doing this reduces unnecessary data transmission through the network.

Client–server architecture is the preferred network option for most large companies because each terminal can access all network facilities without losing any of its own processing power.

The main disadvantage of client–server architecture is that the network is entirely dependent on the server for its operation and if it should break down this will affect every PC connected to the server. However, if the network is properly run and files are regularly backed up, there should be no serious problems with this type of architecture.

The server

To run a client–server network, you need a powerful computer to act as the server used for the storage and distribution of data around the network. A special electronic switching box called a **hub** is also needed to control the flow of data 'traffic' around the network. Another purpose of the hub is to allow machines on the network to operate without interfering with each other. If a fault occurs with one of the client machines, the other machines will still operate normally.

Many desktop PCs are now capable of acting as servers, but is better to use one specifically designed for the task. Most specially built servers include the required network cards as standard and they often contain an internal hub too, with the wires to connect up to workstations (i.e. terminals). Software is usually added and typically includes Internet gateway software and server management software, which helps improve the reliability and overall running of the network.

Many servers come with more than one central processing unit and it is now possible to buy PC servers with eight CPUs, which usually have more RAM than a standard PC would need. Because most applications are run using software stored on the storage devices connected to the server, the server needs a large amount of reliable backing storage for the system software,

applications software and the data needed by the applications. The backing storage devices could be high capacity, fast, hard drives or they could comprise a RAID system. Most servers have controllers that allow backing up devices such as external tape drives or optical disk drives to be connected.

Thin client computing

When computers were first developed, a large mainframe or mini-computer contained all the processing power of a system. Many dumb terminals would be attached to a mainframe system.

The PC was developed next and we now spread the processing power around or attach these 'intelligent' terminals to a central file server. There are many disadvantages to this approach, the main one being cost, because intelligent terminals need motherboards, processors, disk drives, etc. Using semi-dumb terminals reduces the cost of terminals and this means that networks can be considerably cheaper. The use of a server with dumb terminals is called a thin client system because the client terminals only contain the electronic components necessary for them to behave as a terminal. Typically they contain a small processor, graphics card, RAM and a network card. A computer which is used in this way is called a NetPC.

NetPCs contain no operating system as this is loaded from the network in which all the files for the system are stored. Because there are no disk drives, the network manager does not have to worry about the users loading their own, unauthorised software on the system or risk introducing viruses onto the system from infected disks. Another advantage is that users cannot make permanent changes to the appearance of the applications software since a standard version is loaded when the NetPC is booted up; this reduces the time needed for help desk staff to deal with altered software problems.

Advantages and disadvantages of client–server based networks
☑ **Advantages**
- There is strong centralised security.
- They allow all the users to access and work on the same central pool of data.

- Centralised backup is used which is usually the responsibility of the network manager/administrator and this means that data are less likely to be lost.

- Dedicated servers are likely to be much faster in sharing network resources than peers.

- Security is simplified since a single password can allow the user access to all the network facilities.

- Users are freed from the tasks associated with running and managing the network. The users of the network do not need to be as knowledgeable about computing since tasks such as taking backups, allocating user passwords, etc. are taken care of centrally by the network manager.

☒ Disadvantages

- Dedicated servers are expensive.

- The network operating system is expensive and applications software licenses are also expensive.

- The system requires a person who is in control of the central facilities, a manager or administrator.

Factors which affect the rate and means of data transmission

In this section we look at just the main factors that affect the means of data transmission and the rate at which it is transmitted.

Bandwidth

Bandwidth is a measure of how much data a network can carry at once. In some ways it is like a road carrying traffic; wider roads are able to carry a greater volume of traffic. A more technical definition of bandwidth is the difference between the highest and lowest frequencies that a signal occupies, which in turn determines the rate of transfer of data through a transmission medium. The transmission medium is simply the material through which the data signal passes.

Bandwidth is determined by two things: the transmission medium being used and the need to protect the data signal from any interference. Bandwidth is measured in the units of mega bits per second (Mbps).

On the Internet, the speed at which you can surf the web or download files depends on a couple of factors. First, the modem speed determines the rate at which the pulses are sent and received; as two modems are involved, communication will take place at the speed of the slower of the two modems. The type of cabling is also a factor, with fibre optic cable being the fastest. Together, the modem speed and cabling determine the bandwidth and hence the quantity of data that can be transmitted in a certain time period.

One way of reducing the transmission time of large files is to use file compression to make the files smaller. They therefore download faster, which in turn reduces costs. To use a compressed file, you need to be able to decompress it. On PCs the most common compressed file formats used are PKZIP and PKWARE. These files always have the file extension .ZIP. In many cases, when you sign off with the service provider, any compressed files which you have downloaded during your on-line session will then be decompressed. This therefore saves the cost of decompressing the files whilst still on-line.

Detecting errors

There is obviously no point in having high data transmission speeds unless the data received is identical to that sent. The objective of any data communication system is to get the data from one place to another in as small a time as possible, with no errors introduced in the process.

One method of error checking (parity checking) makes use of an extra bit added to the bits used to represent each character. Parity checking works likes this. The computer adds up the number of bits in one byte and if the parity bit is different to the parity setting the computer reports an error.

It is possible to use either even or odd parity. Taking odd parity for instance, suppose we send the letter C along a communication line. In ASCII code the series of bits used to represent the letter C is 1000011. Since there are three 1s in this code and odd parity is being used, then a 0 is added to left-hand side of the group of bits. If even parity were being used, a 1 would need to be added so that there were an even number of 1s.

Modems have a chip inside them whose purpose is to deal with parity checks. The modem at the sending side adds the parity bits and the receiving unit calculates what the parity bit should be, so if there is a discrepancy it knows that an error has occurred. The problem with parity checks is that more than one error can occur and the errors can then compensate for each other so the parity still appears to be correct.

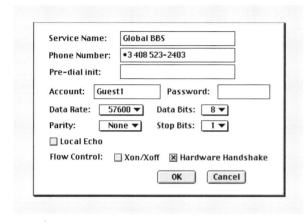

Figure 9.9 *The host mode settings menu*

Activity

1 If even parity is used to check a group of bits after they have travelled along a communication line, which of the following groups of data are correct (the parity bit used is the leftmost bit)?

   (a) 10000101

   (b) 01101010

   (c) 10001110

   (d) 01100101

   (e) 10101010

   (f) 01101100

2 Another system uses odd parity and once again the leftmost bit is the parity bit. Using the same bits as in 1(a)–(f), state which ones are now correct.

The transmission medium

The transmission medium is the material through which a data signal is transmitted. This medium can be nothing, as electromagnetic waves (radio waves, infra-red and microwaves) are able to travel through a complete vacuum.

Metal connecting wires

In the case of a LAN in a single building, the transmission medium can be simply metal cable connecting together the terminals and other hardware in one of the many topologies. Cabling can add substantially to the cost of a network, not just because of the expense of the cable itself but also the expense of installing the wires.

Different types of cable can be used and each one has its advantages and disadvantages.

Unshielded twisted pair

Smaller cables are twisted to help cancel out the interference produced from nearby pairs and also from any other electrical interference. The main advantage of this type of cable is its high transmission speed, cheapness and small size, which means that the cables are readily sunk into cabling ducts. The main disadvantage is that the cabling lengths have to be kept short. A section of unshielded twisted pair cable is shown in Figure 9.10.

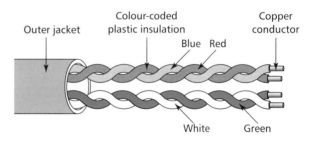

Figure 9.10 *Unshielded twisted pair (UTP) wire*

Shielded twisted pair

As the name suggests, this is similar to twisted pair cabling except that it contains shielding consisting of copper braiding which surrounds all the wires, and a foil layer around each pair of wires. The shielding protects the data signals from corruption due to outside interference. Such cabling is used in token-ring networks. Because of the high degree of shielding, this wire is suitable for high rates of data transmission. It does have disadvantages in that it is expensive, the cable is thick and takes up a lot of space, and it is only suitable for short cabling runs. Shielded twisted pair wire is shown in Figure 9.11.

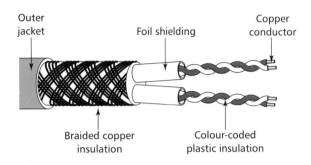

Figure 9.11 *Shielded twisted pair wire (STP)*

Coaxial cable

You will probably be familiar with coaxial cable as it is used to connect the aerial socket of a television to the aerial. This type of cable is used mainly with Ethernet and ARCnet systems and it has the advantage that very fast data transmission speeds can be achieved. It is in the mid-price range for cables. It has the disadvantage that the cable is quite rigid and hard to bend around sharp corners and that it is only suitable for medium distances (typically 0.5 km). Coaxial cable is shown in Figure 9.12.

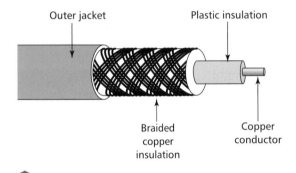

Figure 9.12 *Coaxial cable*

Non-metal cables

The speed of metal cables is limited by the speed of flow of electricity along a wire but fibre optic cables use light which travels much faster.

Fibre optic cable

Fibre optic cable works by transmitting the data signal as a series of pulses of light along a thin glass fibre with each fibre transmitting the signal in one direction. These fibres are then put into two bundles; one for forward pulses, the other for return pulses. Special devices are needed at the sending end, to change the electrical signals into pulses of light, and at the other end, to turn the pulses of light back into an electrical signal.

The main advantages are speed, the small size of the cables, the lack of electrical interference, increased security (because the fibre is harder to tap) and the length of the cables that can be used. The only disadvantage is that the method needs extra equipment to convert signals and the cables are expensive to make. This makes fibre optic cable more expensive than other media.

Figure 9.13 shows a section of fibre optic cable.

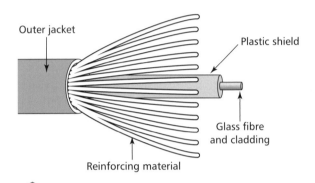

Figure 9.13 *Fibre optic cable*

Wireless media

We have looked above at all the types of cable used in networks, but there are many networks which use wireless media and in these cases the Earth's atmosphere is the path through which data passes. There are three types of wireless media: radiowaves, microwaves and infra-red waves.

Wireless communications can be useful in the following situations:

- Doctors, nurses and other medical staff may use them to enable access to a patient's medical details at their bedside. This saves the staff having to go back to their desks.

- Stock taking can be made easier by the stock takers inputting details into a hand-held terminal which has a radio link to the main computer. Many clerks in warehouses and stock takers in shops now use this system.

- Wireless systems can be used for the creation of temporary networks.

- Many offices are in listed buildings, which work under regulations forbidding wiring installation. Wireless systems are the only option in such cases.

Radiowaves

Radiowave transmissions are heavily regulated so that they do not interfere with the many other radio signals used for the emergency services, radar, etc. Because the power has to be kept so low so as not to interfere with more important radio transmissions, radiowave transmissions are usually limited to fairly restricted networks where wire-based systems would be too difficult to install, and to line-of-sight mobile communications. It is also possible to bounce radio signals off the Earth's atmosphere and this can be used to extend their range.

Infra-red waves

Infra-red signalling is limited to line of sight communication, which means that the transmitting device must be able to see the receiver.

Microwaves

Microwaves have a higher frequency than radiowaves and this makes them more suitable for sending data since transmission is faster. You often see microwave antennae or dishes on the tops of buildings and these provide a line-of-sight link between two systems. If the distance needs to be greater than this, relay towers are used.

Satellite systems can be used to transmit microwave signals from one side of the Earth to the other and for this, the satellite needs to remain in the same place above the Earth (called a geosynchronous orbit). Because the signal needs to travel the 50,000 kilometres from the Earth to the satellite, and the same distance back again, there is always a delay between sending the signal and receiving it, and this can cause problems, particularly if videoconferencing is being conducted.

Network adaptors

Network adaptors are sometimes called network interface cards (NIC). They are circuit boards that plug into the motherboard of the computer. Part of the network adaptor is a socket into which the network cable is attached. The purpose of the network adaptor is to convert the data from the form in which it is stored and used by the computer, into a form that can be transferred along the network cable. Because the network card determines flow control on the network, the precise type of NIC needed depends on the type of network used.

Figure 9.14 shows a network interface card. Notice how the data is sent in parallel from the computer motherboard into the card and then the card converts this to a serial flow along the network cable.

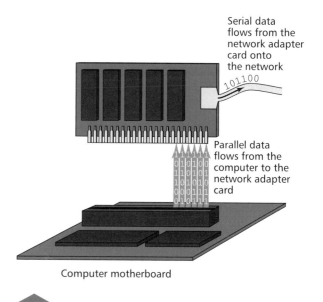

Computer motherboard

Figure 9.14 *A network interface adaptor/card*

Bridges

When two different local area networks, of the same type, need to be joined together, a hardware device called a bridge is needed to allow them to communicate with one another. The bridge works by receiving packets of data from one LAN and re-broadcasting the same data on the other network. Although the two LANs being bridged need to be of the same type, the networks can still run at different speeds since there is a buffer in the bridge where the data is stored until the other network is ready to receive.

Gateways

A gateway is the name given to the facility that enables connection to wide area networks and network facilities. Figure 9.15 shows gateways (indicated by the hexagons) being used to connect a series of star LANs together over a wide geographical area. Since each star cluster may be operating with different equipment and protocols, gateways are necessary to convert protocols and allow them to communicate with each other. Gateways therefore enable dissimilar LANs to communicate with each other.

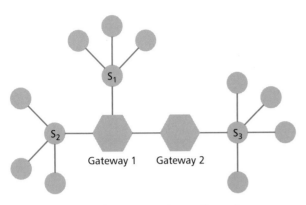

S_1, S_2 and S_3 are central controller nodes

Figure 9.15 *The connection between one gateway and another may be a phone line, a microwave link, a satellite link, etc.*

Multiplexers

Suppose we need to connect ten terminals to a single host computer. We could connect them using separate connections but this would involve a large amount of cabling and considerable expense. Instead we use a hardware device called a multiplexer that allows simultaneous transmissions of multiple messages using one communication channel. Two multiplexers are used, one at each end of the communication channel. The one at the host end is used to combine the multiple signals so that they may be sent along a single line; the one at the other end separates the signals so that they may be sent to their respective terminals. Figure 9.16 shows how each terminal needs its own pair of modems and a communications line. With a multiplexer (Figure 9.17), only one pair of modems and a single line is needed.

Routers

A router is a combination of hardware and software that makes a decision about the path that an individual packet of data should take, thus ensuring that the packet is sent along the backbone in the fastest way.

Hubs or concentrators

Hubs or concentrators are hardware devices which handle the cabling requirements of linking LANs together and linking these to WANs. In this way ring or bus topologies of the LAN can be connected to the backbone of a WAN.

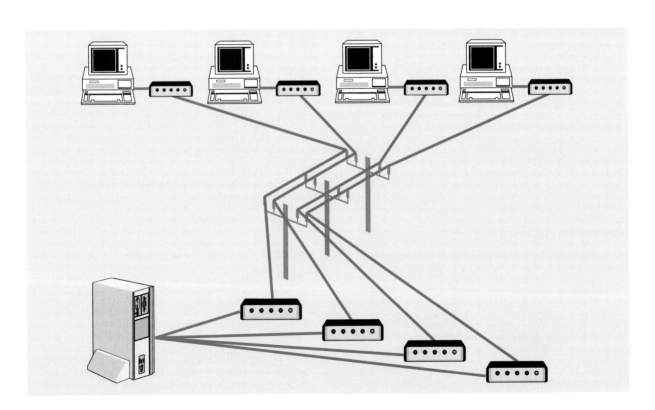

Figure 9.16 *Each terminal here needs its own pair of modems and a communications line*

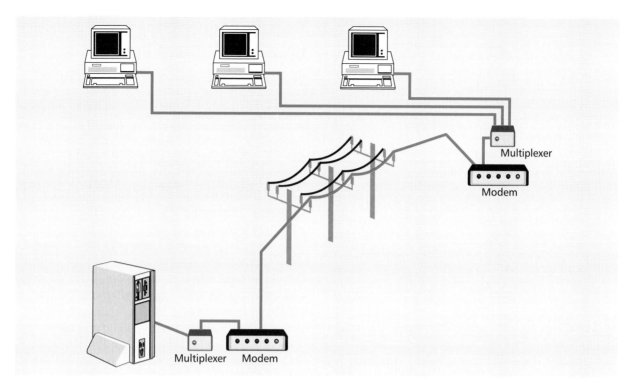

Network architectures

There are many different network architectures to choose from and the commonest ones are Ethernet and token-ring. The main difference between the two networks is in the way the terminals decide when to send data along the communication line. This process is called **line reservation**. Ethernet uses a system called 'carrier sense multiple access with collision detect' (CSMA/CD), whereas token-rings make use of electronic signals called tokens.

Ethernet

Ethernet is the most popular network architecture in use today. It uses the protocol CSMA/CD to control the flow of data through the transmission medium.

Figure 9.18 shows how CSMA/CD works.

Suppose terminal A wants to send data to another terminal B. First of all the terminal A network interface card puts data into packets; it then listens to the communication line to see if any of the other terminals are using it to send data. If the line is free it starts to send the packets of data across the network. If two terminals try to use the same line at the same time, the signals will collide and the combined signal will vary beyond that which is normal, so the system will know that a collision has occurred. A jam signal is then sent to all the network interface cards

Figure 9.17 *With a multiplexer only one pair of modems and a single communication line are needed*

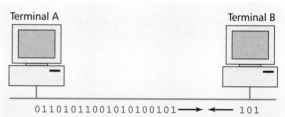

Terminal A, when the line is free, transmits its packet of data. Just before its arrival at terminal B, terminal B thinks the line is free and so starts to send its own packet to A.

Data signals collide and mix giving voltages outside the normal range; this signal is picked up by all network interface cards telling them to stop transmitting. After a random period they try again.

Figure 9.18 *How CSMA/CD works*

telling them to stop sending data, after which each waits a random time period before trying the line again. If collisions keep occurring, then after 16 attempts, the transmitting terminal gives up and reports back to the network operating system that it cannot deliver the message. Most Ethernet networks are able to transmit data at around 10Mbps.

Token-ring

Token-ring architecture is used for those networks that have a physical ring, or networks which can be managed as a ring (see page 140). In these cases each message can be sent from one terminal to another until all the terminals in the network have been traversed.

As mentioned earlier, a special message called a token is passed from one terminal to the next around the ring and if a particular terminal wishes to send a message it waits until the token arrives, captures the token and transmits the message. After the message has been received, the token is released by the terminal, and it carries on around the ring until it is captured by another terminal waiting to send a message. Networks able to use physical or logical rings for the passing of tokens in this way are called token-rings.

One of the main problems with this method is that occasionally the tokens are lost along the line. It is quite difficult to discover when this has occurred and also difficult to restart the token. Nevertheless, this method does tolerate broken links and terminals which are not responding properly, and so is useful where reliability, fault tolerance and a high rate of data transfer are needed.

Questions

1 Networks can be divided into two types: client–server networks and peer-to-peer networks. Describe the differences between these and discuss the relative advantages of each.

2 Explain how each of the following affect the compatibility between two computers trying to communicate with each other:
   (a) transmission rate
   (b) number of data bits
   (c) number of start bits
   (d) number of stop bits
   (e) parity.

Factors affecting the compatibility between different systems

Because networks can be so different, there needs to be some uniformity in the way they operate to enable them to exchange data. There are some agreed standards between the manufacturers of hardware and software, and in this section we look at these.

The standards for electronic communication

To ensure that they are able to communicate with each other, devices connected to communication lines must have certain characteristics in common so that they present electronic signals in a similar way. In other words, they need to be able to understand each others' signals. To achieve this, manufacturers need a common standard for electronic communication.

Unfortunately, a wide variety of organisations set standards for electronic communication. In this and all other chapters of the book where communications are mentioned, we use the terms defined by the CCITT (the International Committee for Data Communication).

Data representation

When a character (letter, number or symbol) is typed at the keyboard it is converted to a binary code which consists of a series of 1s and 0s.

Character	ASCII code	Character	ASCII code
A	0100 0001	N	0100 1110
B	0100 0010	O	0100 1111
C	0100 0011	P	0101 0000
D	0100 0100	Q	0101 0001
E	0100 0101	R	0101 0010
F	0100 0110	S	0101 0011
G	0100 0111	T	0101 0100
H	0100 1000	U	0101 0101
I	0100 1001	V	0101 0110
J	0100 1010	W	0101 0111
K	0100 1011	X	0101 1000
L	0100 1100	Y	0101 1001
M	0100 1101	Z	0101 1010

Figure 9.19 *Representing letters in ASCII*

These are transmitted along a wire until the character is received at the other end where it is decoded and converted back to the character again. Most computers represent characters using the ASCII code (American Standard Code for Information Interchange) and Figure 9.19 shows the 8-bit code for the 26 letters of the alphabet.

File transfer

In the early days of computing, normal communication channels were used to send data files from one place to another. For instance, if you needed to send data from London to Paris, then your computer and modem simply dialled the receiving computer and its modem and once connected, the data flowed. Once it had finished, the modem automatically disconnected. You only needed to pay for the telephone call for the duration of the data transfer.

Activity

The preceding paragraph details one way a data file can be sent using communications. Compare and contrast this method with other ways of sending data, such as by post or courier.

Although the above sounds simple enough, there are some serious problems that should be mentioned. If the data files are held on a mainframe computer there is a good chance that your computer may not be able to read them, since the formats used by the two computers are likely to be different. A key pressed on your PC may mean something completely different to an IBM mainframe that has its own character and control codes. Suppose the computer in Paris is an IBM mainframe computer and you are using a PC. One way around the problem is for your computer to behave in exactly the same way an IBM terminal would behave. When this happens we say that the PC is emulating an IBM terminal, and special software called a terminal emulation program is used for this purpose.

If when using a terminal you can make out what the characters say, but they are surrounded by strange symbols, it is likely that the wrong type of terminal emulation is being used. Two things can be done to rectify the situation: the emulation setting of either the PC or the host computer could be changed. In most cases, it will be the terminal's emulation settings that will be adjusted.

TASKS

Demon Wheels

Demon Wheels is a specialist company selling alloy wheels and high performance tyres to car enthusiasts. At present the company has five shops/fitting bays: Manchester, Liverpool, Chester, Birmingham and Newcastle. The whole operation is controlled from the head office at the Manchester shop.

The business is primarily a retail operation, selling the wheels and tyres to members of the public through advertisements placed in specialist car magazines. The company is also getting involved in selling through mail order to customers who do not necessarily live near to one of the shops. At present this is only a small part of the business but it is growing quickly and they do not have the administrative systems in place at present to cope with any increased demand in this area.

The head office is responsible for purchasing stock and it also deals with the mail order side of the business. The company owns vans that travel between the various shops and the head office at least once a day and these are used to transfer stock and paperwork.

The main problem the company faces is one of control and administration. The shops tend to run as separate businesses and the directors feel that a more consistent approach is needed. Each shop has two Pentium III 800 MHz computers, one of which they use for stock control and the printing of invoices, while the other is used for wordprocessing, spreadsheets and DTP.

The business has various problems as follows:

1 Each branch has a stock database that shows what stock it has and when stock arrives or is sold. The database is updated by the manager of the shop.

At the end of each day a stock list is faxed to the head office where one of the staff updates the main database held on a stand-alone machine. This database is then used to produce lists of stock that should be faxed to the manufacturers or importers.

2 If a customer comes in and requires a certain set of tyres or wheels and the shop has sold out of them, then the company may be able to get them from one of the other shops. But to find out whether another shop has them in stock, it is necessary to ring each shop to ask. They could use the stock database held at head office, but as this is only updated in the evening, a stock item could show as available but in reality have been sold earlier in the day.

Staff waste time ringing around the branches while the customer is left waiting. In addition, this practice pushes up the telephone bills considerably.

3 Because the ordering of new stock is performed centrally at head office, it is not possible for the staff in each shop to know when certain items will be available at the shop. This frequently loses business because customers may go elsewhere rather than wait, even though they might only have to wait a couple of hours.

4 When prices go up, it is necessary to make changes to all the databases in the shops and at head office, which is time-consuming and wasteful.

5 Many customers are introduced to the company by personal recommendations and the company keeps in touch with all customers by newsletter which shows details of special offers. As each branch keeps their own customer details, if a customer has shopped at more than one branch, they will get more than one copy of the newsletter sent to them.

6 The directors of the company are worried that unauthorised software is being placed on company machines and that they could be prosecuted.

7 Although all the staff involved in using the computers are instructed to take regular backup copies of their data, the head office is not sure whether this is done regularly.

8 The head office is all in one building. It has seven stand-alone machines and there are two laser printers attached to two of these machines. If other machines need printing facilities, it is necessary to transfer the data on floppy disk to one of the machines with a printer attached. This is very inconvenient, particularly if a person working at the machine has to be disturbed.

9 At present there are two fax machines that are both used heavily. It is necessary for the staff to move away from their desks to use them.

TASK 1

Demon Wheels have approached a computer consultant who has visited the head office and some of the branches and advised them that they need a computer network. They were also told that they needed a LAN with a gateway to a WAN.

You work at Demon Wheels and have been asked to explain what is meant by the following:

- a computer network
- a LAN
- a WAN
- a gateway.

DEBRIEF

When explaining any computer term to a novice you have to make sure that by giving your explanation to one term you do not introduce other specialist terms that have not been defined. Did you manage to do this? If you did not, then it might be an idea to look at the explanation again.

Notice also that only abbreviations are given for two of the terms. When this is done you need to say what the abbreviations stand for as well as giving a general description. If you are given a particular application, it will be clearer if your explanation relates to the particular context given.

TASK 2

By referring to the problems that Demon Wheels are experiencing listed in the scenario, explain how the network will benefit them.

Activity

Definition of terms exercises

A variety of new terms is introduced in this chapter, many of which may be new to you. It is important that you build up vocabulary which can be used when writing essays or answering questions. Write a definition for each of the following terms used in the chapter:

WAN	client–server	gateway
LAN	hub	multiplexer
EDI	net PC	router
ATM	bandwidth	CSMA/CD
peer-to-peer	NIC	
server	bridge	

Examination Questions

1 (a) Give **two** differences between a Local Area Network (LAN) and a Wide Area Network (WAN). *(2)*

(b) Discuss the relative merits of server-based networks and peer-to-peer networks. *(6)*

(NEAB, IT02, June 1997, q5)

2 A local surgery uses a number of stand-alone computer systems to manage patient records, appointments, staff pay and all financial accounts. The surgery manager is considering changing to a local area network.

(a) Compare the relative advantages of stand-alone and local area network systems. *(6)*

(b) Describe, with the aid of diagrams, two alternative network topologies. *(6)*

(NEAB, Module IT02, May 1996, q9)

3 Explain the function of a gateway when used with Local and Wide Area Networks. *(2)*

(NEAB, Module IT02, May 1998, q1)

4 At the central office of a landscape gardening company there are six employees. Each employee has a stand-alone computer system and printer. The company director has commissioned a business survey which indicated that it would be more efficient if the six PCs were formed into a peer-to-peer network.

(a) State **three** benefits that the company would gain from networking their computer systems as a peer-to-peer system rather than a server-based system. *(3)*

(b) What additional hardware would be needed to connect the six stand-alone computer systems as a peer-to-peer network system? State why each item is required. *(4)*

(NEAB, Module IT02, May 1998, q9)

5 Ring and star are two common network topologies.

(a) Explain what is meant by the term 'network topology'. *(2)*

(b) Give **two** advantages for each of the ring and star topologies that are not held by the other. *(4)*

(c) State **two** factors that affect the rate of data transfer between the computers in a network. *(2)*

(NEAB, Module IT02, May 99, q7)

10 The Human/Computer Interface

▶ To understand the purpose of the human/computer interface and the need for its careful design.

Human/computer interfaces (HCIs)

An interface is defined as the point where two objects meet. Human/computer interfaces provide the means by which the user tells the computer what to do and at the same time the computer can interact with the human user by producing a response. These interfaces are important because they determine the ease with which the computer can be used. When the manufacturer of systems software or applications software gets it wrong, then using the software can prove very frustrating and the user will be less likely to buy one of their products again.

The standard interface for inputting data into the computer is the keyboard with the computer giving its response on the screen. This is not the only type of human/computer interface, although it is the most common. There are many other systems that make use of IT and need a different type of interface. Process control screens, computer games, cockpit controls on fly-by-wire aircraft, information systems which can be used by members of the public, all make use of innovative user interfaces.

Improving productivity

Studying the human computer interface is important from the point of view of improving productivity and job satisfaction, and making sure that work practices are safe. In IT applications there is the need to facilitate an effective dialogue between the user and the computer.

Activity

Choose two of the interfaces listed below and write a short section about each one explaining how it is specifically designed for the task. Look out for any features of the interface which are specific to that use.

- a video recorder handset
- the interface for a games console
- the interface used in a cash dispenser
- the interface between the driver and the controls of a car.

The different capabilities of humans and machines

Humans receive information about the outside world using the senses of taste, touch, sight, smell and hearing. The ideal interface between humans and machines should incorporate as many of these as possible. Multimedia applications make use of our sense of touch via the keyboard, mouse, joystick and touch-screen monitors. By using speakers, the computer is able to issue instructions or even encouragement to the user. Sound may also be used to input instructions or data to the system by using voice recognition software.

Another interface, which makes use of as many of our senses as possible, is in the area of virtual reality. Virtual reality applications are programs that envelope the user within a simulated, three-dimensional world of sight, touch and movement. With such an interface, the user is able to interact in a virtual world. Figure 10.1 shows the main components of a virtual reality system: the glove, the head-mounted display, the speakers, the PC and monitor.

When user interfaces become sufficiently user-friendly, communicating with computers will be almost like communicating with another human being. We are clearly some way from this at the moment but successive versions of new operating systems and applications software are making interfaces easier to use.

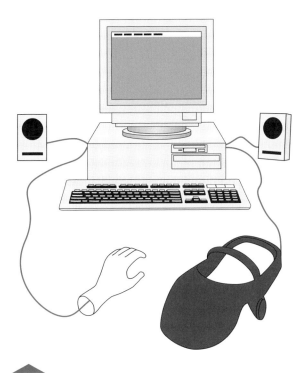

Figure 10.1 *The main components of a virtual reality system*

Choosing the right interface

Suppose you are playing a computer game, such as guiding a Formula One racing car around a track. The game's manufacturer and you will want to make the game as realistic as possible, as this will enhance your enjoyment. The graphics showing the track and the other vehicles can be made realistic, as can the actual performance of the car (cornering, braking, accelerating and so

on). This all adds to the realism of the game, but the thing that can let the game down is the human/computer interface. The worst interface would be the cursor keys and other keys to steer the car, change gear, accelerate and so on. A better interface would be a joystick, although this is not ideal as cars are normally fitted with steering wheels, gear sticks and foot pedals. You can actually buy such interfaces to make controlling the car as realistic as possible.

Figure 10.2 *Some of the peripherals available to make the user interface, when using simulation software for driving a car, more realistic*

Graphical user interfaces (GUI)

A graphical user interface (GUI) is used by many manufacturers with their operating systems. Microsoft Windows 98, Windows 2000 and the Apple Macintosh have GUIs. All the memory and file management activities are taken care of by these operating systems and it is possible for them to **multi-task**, with the user running more than one application at the same time. All these GUIs use a mouse to navigate around the screen; the mouse buttons are used to make selections from icons and buttons.

Dialogue boxes and pull-down menus are used as part of these interfaces. The work area is located in the centre of the screen and users are usually able to choose which toolbars, rulers and icons are displayed around this area. The user work area provides a moveable 'window' through which one can see the data being worked on; to move the data, the horizontal and vertical sliders at the side and the bottom of the screen are used. A typical window is shown in Figure 10.3.

What makes windows-based software particularly easy to use is that the interface is standardised across different applications

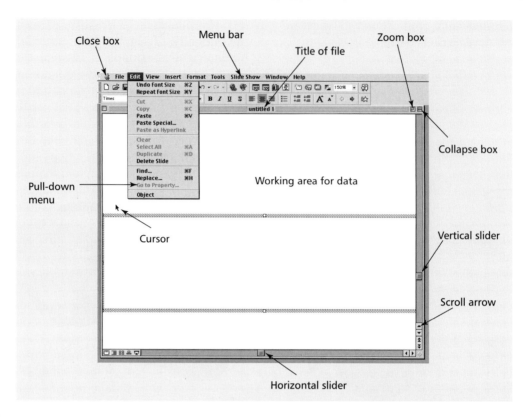

Close box · Menu bar · Title of file · Zoom box

Pull-down menu · Cursor · Working area for data · Collapse box · Vertical slider · Scroll arrow

Horizontal slider

Figure 10.3 *The components of a typical window. This window is from a Macintosh computer. A Windows computer will look slightly different, but the basic principles are the same*

packages. They all have similar icons, button bars, dialogue boxes and pull-down menus. This makes learning windows-based packages much easier.

A graphical user interface does more than simply control the hardware; it can be used by the programmer to influence how the user interacts with a program. In particular, it allows the programmer to standardise the way a program works. If a user knows how to open a document in a wordprocessing package, then if the interface is standardised, they will also know how to open a worksheet in a spreadsheet package. So standardising programs makes it easy for the user to transfer skills from one application to another.

The main features of a GUI

There are a number of features common to all GUIs and these are:

- **A mouse is used as the main input device.**
  By moving a mouse on a flat surface, the cursor can be made to move across the screen; the left mouse button is used to make selections.

- **Overlapping windows are used.**
  Many windows, even in different applications, can be opened simultaneously. You can therefore have a spreadsheet and a wordprocessed document on the screen at the same time and this makes it much easier if you are going to import data from one package into another.

- **They make use of many graphics features.**
  There are many graphical features incorporated into the design, such as icons, pull-down menus, toolbars, slide bars, selection boxes, dialogue boxes, etc.

Activity

Photocopy the figure on the next page and then mark on it the following:

the title bar
the vertical slide bar
the horizontal slide bar
the minimise button
the maximise button
the action bar
the system button.

Explain how each of the above is used.

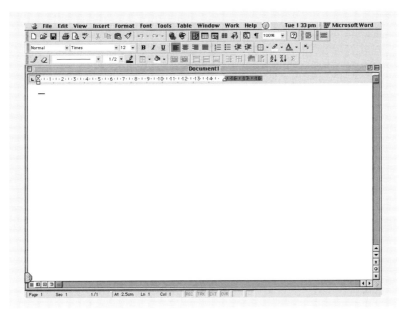

Figure 10.4 *An editing screen in Microsoft Word*

Questions

1 All systems software and applications software have user interfaces. Some systems software makes use of a command line interface while others use a graphical user interface (GUI). Explain the main differences between them.

2 Describe five features of a graphical user interface.

3 Give three advantages in using a GUI rather than a command line interface.

Clarity of structure and layout

If a graphical user interface is to be easy to learn and use, there are a few guidelines to bear in mind during its design and these include:

Reduce the mouse movements. Put items such as icons and menu selections close together if they are likely to be used together.

Use pull-down menus. The use of pull-down menus means that the screen is not cluttered with items to choose from, so the user has more of the screen available as their working area.

Design pull-down menus so that the selections used most frequently are situated at the top of the menu. This avoids the need to move down through the menu more than is necessary.

Include the facility to select which icons are displayed. There are usually many more possible functions that have icons than there are icons on the screen and it is possible with most user interfaces to choose a selection that the user is most likely to need. As well as specifying which are shown, the user can usually put the icons in any convenient position on the screen.

The advantages of having a common user interface for different generic application programs

The advantage of most users having the same operating system is that people can move between computers and still know how to operate them. The same can be said of different generic packages, such as wordprocessors, databases and spreadsheets.

Common commands

Where a number of commands can be issued using the keyboard, it makes sense to use the same combination of keys to perform the same task no matter which manufacturer has produced the software. This needs a certain amount of co-operation between rival companies and it can also mean that newer, improved user interfaces are harder to introduce. You have only to look at the standard layout of the typewriter keyboard to see how users like uniformity. Can you imagine what it would be like if every computer manufacturer decided they would have a different arrangement of keys on a keyboard?

The present arrangement was designed originally to cope with the mechanical properties of the typewriter, but ended up making it slow. Other shapes of keyboard have been developed over the years; they are more ergonomically designed but people's resistance to making the change has meant that there are very few of them in use, even though most users find they are an improvement.

Increased speed of learning

Once a user has been trained on, and has mastered, one package, other packages with similar user interfaces are much easier to understand. The user will understand how to pull down menus and make selections using the mouse and also know what each of the icons means. An icon for print or save will usually look the same no matter which package is being used.

Features of user interfaces that are common to all packages

The more packages you look at, the more you will notice the similarities between them. It is not that the software manufacturers are copying each other, but that they are satisfying user demand by incorporating features common to many packages.

TASKS

Common user interfaces

TASK 1

Spend some time looking at different user interfaces in different packages (some, if possible, from different manufacturers) and you will notice that there are many recurrent features.

For this activity you are required to investigate the common features of software packages.

Hint

You could approach this task in many ways; one might be to focus on one type of software (such as wordprocessors) and look at a variety of products in turn, making notes about features such as menu systems, loading and saving documents and so on. You may find it useful to make screen dumps so that you can compare the arrangement of features on the screen.

DEBRIEF

Interfaces from software created by the same manufacturer are usually quite similar, particularly if the individual software components form part of a software suite.

Did you look at the following?

- The arrangement of the overall screen.

- The use of pull-down menus and buttons.

- The design of the icons.

- The use of colours on the screen.

- The order of the menu selections in pull-down menus.

- The operations that need to be performed when files are imported from another package.

- The way in which you change the font size or font type.

- The way in which the printer settings are changed.

- How you can run another task at the same time (i.e. multi-tasking).

Designing systems and interfaces appropriate to disabled users

Interfaces for people with sensory impairments must be aimed at those senses which are unaffected by their disabilities.

A visually impaired person has two problems with most common interfaces. First they cannot look at the screen to see the menus, icons, etc. that enable them to make a particular selection, and secondly, they are not always aware when a mistake has occurred. The usual graphical interface is difficult to use and it is better if commands are issued using the keyboard. Before the introduction of the Windows operating system, an operating system called DOS (disk operating system) was used, which meant the user had to learn a series of commands to do certain things such as format a disk or copy a group of files. Many of these commands did not need to be typed in full, but could be issued using a single keystroke or a combination of keystrokes. The visually impaired user can issue DOS commands to the computer relatively easily. When hard copy output is needed, it is possible for an impact printer (such as a dot matrix printer) to produce the output on Braille which can be read by other visually impaired users.

Another approach is to use special software that converts the text or commands into speech. For example, wordprocessing software for visually impaired people enables the user to move through a document word by word, while the system reads them. By using this method, the user can detect any mistakes made. The user of this system also hears commands as they are issued, so mistakes can be detected and the command corrected.

Many users, particularly disabled users who have difficulty in pressing individual keys, may find speech recognition systems much easier to use. The main problem arises when what has been typed needs to be edited. There are, however, ways in which the user can direct the cursor for editing and then issue spoken instructions.

The importance to companies of adopting a common user interface

If you regulary work at a college or school, you will probably have to use lots of different computers in the course of a week. This means you are likely to experience some problems when using operating systems software or applications software. The problems usually involve the previous user having changed some of the settings on the interface. For example, they could have changed the screen or character colours. If you are using applications software, such as wordprocessing, there may be different margins set or toolbars showing on the screen. These are just some of the frustrations that occur when you have to share computers with other people.

Many commercial organisations do not have a desk for each of their employees; they consider it wasteful to do so because not all employees are working at their desks at the same time. This means that employees have to find a vacant desk with a computer if they want to do some work. So that changes to the user interface are not passed on to the next user of the system, companies make use of a network where the software is stored on the server. When a user logs on to the system they are presented with the same interface, and it is then up to them to change the settings for their own use during their log-in period, should they want to.

This avoids unnecessary calls to the helplines most large companies operate, to sort out problems caused by changed settings.

Summary of the benefits of providing a common user interface between packages

- The operational basics of one application can easily be applied to other applications.

- Key commands can be found in the same place for each application.

- There is consistency in toolbars and menus.

- Dialogue boxes, customisable features and operational features are similar.

- On-line help is provided in each application in a similar way.

Other types of user interface

Sometimes, users need only simple interfaces, when the variety of tasks to be performed is quite limited, for instance, entering customer order details using a terminal. In this section, we look at some of these other interfaces.

Forms dialogue

Forms on the screen are used in a similar way to paper forms. They enable data to be entered into the system in a pre-determined and structured way. The forms usually have the name of the data to be entered into each box at the side of the box and this tells the user exactly what they have to type in. If this is not sufficient, additional instructions can be added by way of an explanation. Forms can also have buttons added and pick lists that give the user a drop-down list of options to choose from. Check boxes can also be used, where the user can select one or more items by clicking on the appropriate boxes in a list. This arrangement is very popular when entering details into a database; if you do a database project you will probably have to design such a form for data input.

Forms dialogue can be classed as either formatted or free format. The difference between the two is in the flexibility offered to the user. With formatted dialogue interfaces there are fewer ways for the user to enter data into the computer and for this reason they are better suited to novices. With free format dialogue the interface is more complex and there are lots of ways of entering data. It is important that the designer of the interface matches it to the capabilities of the user, since a simple formatted dialogue design can annoy an experienced user with its lack of scope, while a novice could find overwhelming the choices in a free format dialogue system.

Command-driven interfaces

The main problem for users of command-driven interfaces is that to use them successfully, it is necessary to remember a large number of commands and also how to construct them. Although these interfaces often use help screens, in case you forget a command or need to look up the syntax, they are still very hard for inexperienced users to master. The users of command-driven interfaces have to learn a command language similar in many ways to a specialist programming language and which is almost as difficult to learn.

Users usually know what they want to do, but they do not know how to translate this into a series of commands. For this reason command-driven interfaces have become much less popular over recent years, and have been overtaken by graphical user interfaces.

Command-driven interfaces are also called command line interfaces because it is necessary for the user to type in a command next to the cursor on the line. Many operating systems such as MS-DOS (Microsoft disk operating system) and UNIX use a command line interface and in MS-DOS the user has to type 'C>DIR' to obtain a list of the files stored on the hard drive. Once all the commands are learnt, a command line interface can be quite fast, but you may waste time looking up commands and syntax details or making mistakes and then having to correct them.

Here is a summary outlining the advantages and disadvantages of using a command-driven interface.

Advantages

- They are very powerful and the user can achieve a lot with a single command.

- They are very quick provided you are an experienced user.

- They are very flexible and you can alter the parameters to do different things.

Disadvantages

- They are quite difficult to learn.

- They are less suitable for novice or intermittent users.

- They sometimes use obscure abbreviations or keywords and syntax is important.

- They are prone to typing mistakes.

Menus

There are several different types of menu that can be used:

- full screen menus

- pop-up menus

- pull-down menus.

Full screen menus

These are menus that take up the whole screen, which remain in view until the user makes a selection. Many opening menus for application packages are of this type.

Pop-up menus

These are usually brought up by clicking the right-hand button of the mouse; the user is then able to make a selection from a list.

Pull-down menus

To save space these menus are only shown if the user clicks on a particular item. To make a selection, the user clicks on one of the items in the menu. To cancel the operation, escape is pressed.

The potential for a natural language interface

It would be convenient if we had the same human/computer interface as the computers in science fiction such as *Star Trek* and *2001, A Space Odyssey*, in which people could simply talk to computers in the same way as we talk to another person. Since this is the most natural way of communicating, such an interface is called a 'natural language interface'.

'Natural' in this context means human-like and the idea is to get computers to behave more like humans so as to make it easier for us to communicate with them.

The most important aspect of a natural language interface is that the computer should be able to understand what the user wants it to do without requiring correctly structured commands and data names in a particular order. All you should need to do is to express yourself clearly, either by typing or speaking to the computer. Since people can say the same thing in a variety of ways, the computer would need to be able to interpret and understand what is being said accurately, and this is a major hurdle for developers of natural language interfaces. One person might say 'Can I have the sales of Mars bars for March?', and another might say 'Give me the revenue details for Mars bars sold in March'. In either case the computer should be able to give the same details. A natural language interface also needs to be able to cope with misspelled words, bad grammar and slang, either 'understanding' them or asking the user for clarification. If speech recognition is used, the interface will also need to cope with mispronounced words, different regional accents, etc.

The use of a natural language interface to access a knowledge base is the foundation of the area called **artificial intelligence**.

Pointer-based interfaces

There are other up-to-date interfaces besides GUIs and these are called pointer-based or gesture-based interfaces. They work by using a pen-like stylus or pointer to interact with the computer. With some systems, you can simply write in ordinary handwriting using the stylus on a special pad which represents the input device for the system. These systems need special software called handwriting recognition software. In some systems, particularly CAD (computer-aided design) systems, the user uses a graphics tablet or pad and the stylus is used to point to certain shapes or commands on the pad. The advantage with this system is that it allows the user to use freehand, using the stylus like a pencil. This is much easier to control than a mouse.

Some pointer-based interfaces do not even have a stylus and they instead make use of a touch-sensitive screen which can detect the pressure of a user's finger on the screen. You may have seen such devices being made use of in quiz machines. You can also see them in banks where they are used to present the user with a series of options and the user can make their selection by pressing the screen at a certain point.

For this activity you are required to produce screen dumps and import them into a word-processed document which represents a set of illustrated notes on the features of user interfaces.

CASE STUDY

Using a human/machine interface to unlock a person's potential

Stephen Hawking is probably the most famous physicist alive today. He has appeared in many television programs and has written best-selling books on popular science including the famous *A Brief History of Time*. What is remarkable is that he overcomes a tremendous physical disability to do this. Because of his disability he cannot communicate with the outside world without the use of special equipment. Had this specialist equipment not been available it seems unlikely he would have been able to communicate his scientific ideas in the hugely successful way he has.

Stephen makes use of a PC and a system called Equaliser. He can operate the system by wiggling one of his fingers on a switch. The screen shows a set of lines each containing several words over which a scanning system moves a highlighted bar. Stephen then waits until it passes over the word he wants, then he presses the switch with his finger to make the selection.

Pointing devices

Pointing devices enable the user to move the cursor to anywhere on the screen and point to a tool, icon, menu selection or button. The commonest pointing device is the mouse which seems to come with any new computer purchased. The mouse is the part of the computer system that wears out soonest because it is usually mechanical and has moving parts which wear. Mice usually come with either two or three selection buttons for making selections and some have a small wheel in the middle.

As well as traditional mice, there are also some other pointing devices which are better suited to some applications.

The trackball

If you turn an ordinary mouse upside down and rotate the ball using your hand, you have a simple trackball. Although it is quite difficult to use, after a while you get used to it. Trackballs are particularly useful if there is no flat surface on which a mouse can be moved and for this reason they are provided on laptop computers. Systems designed for members of the public or for children often make use of trackballs. One such trackball, called EasyBall, is designed specifically for very young children, so that they can learn to interact with the computer from an early age. It is also ideal for anyone who lacks the manual dexterity needed for using an ordinary mouse.

The touch-sensitive pad

There are two types of touch-sensitive pad; the mouse pad and the bit pad. The mouse pad consists of a touch-sensitive pad which works in a similar way to a mouse, in that it senses the

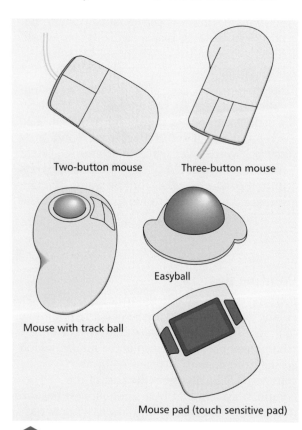

Two-button mouse   Three-button mouse

Easyball

Mouse with track ball

Mouse pad (touch sensitive pad)

Figure 10.5 *Some of the pointer devices that can be used with a pointer-based interface*

relative position of either your finger or a special stylus on the pad. By moving your finger (or the stylus) over the pad, the movement is transferred to the movement of the cursor on the screen. Mouse pads are useful when space is at a premium and for this reason they are popular with laptop computers.

The bit pad works in a slightly different way, by making use of absolute positioning. Unlike the mouse pad, if you move the pointer from one corner of the pad to the other, the cursor jumps from one corner to the other. This makes it quicker to use than the mouse pad since it is not necessary to move the stylus across the surface of the pad. The bit pad is ideal for drawing freehand on the screen since using the stylus on the pad is just like using a pencil or pen on paper. Full size bit pads are ideal for drawing or painting. The pad also has icons from which certain tools and functions may be selected by touching them.

Speech recognition

Using speech to supply both instructions and data to the computer moves us nearer to the natural language interface. It allows humans to communicate directly with the system and although it can be used in a wide variety of applications, it has only become popular as a method of communicating with the computer via the operating system OS/2, or when inputting text into a wordprocessing package. The main advantage with speech recognition as part of the user interface, is that there is no longer any need to learn commands or complex procedures. Speech recognition also avoids any need for difficult-to-use devices such as mice and keyboards.

Using speech recognition, the user has only to state what they want the computer to do. Of course, things are not that simple and there are a number of difficulties that need to be overcome. When speech recognition is used to issue commands, it is necessary for complex speech recognition software to understand what the user means, translate this into an actual machine command and then execute it. Problems include being able to understand different kinds of voices (e.g. male and female) and different accents. In addition to these problems the system also has to deal with background noise such as telephones ringing or people talking in the background.

You may have already used a speech recognition system in the shape of a telephone service where the computer asks you simple questions and then reacts to the responses given.

Using speech recognition and a natural language interface means that users will no longer need to interact physically with the computer using a keyboard or mouse. Instead, as long as the computer system can hear them, this will be enough. Just think, you could ask the computer to load the wordprocessing software and create a new document, then dictate your letter while hanging wallpaper! This would also open up lots of possibilities to disabled people who could then interact with the computer more effectively.

Speech recognition offers an improved interface for most people, who can generally talk faster than they can type. Also, if you tell the computer in general terms what you want, it takes a lot less time and explaining than it does typing the instruction.

Speech recognition will be particularly useful for the Internet since a user can simply describe what they want the computer to search for and an 'intelligent agent' will go away and look for the information.

There are some areas where speech recognition and the natural language interface may not be useful. For example, mathematical equations and programming steps are both difficult to describe using the spoken word. Handwriting recognition or a keyboard are more useful in these cases. There are occasions, such as when you are preparing a confidential document, when it would be inappropriate to speak aloud, so some silent form of HCI would be needed. Another example is the selection of options from a list, in which case the options would need to be read out. A keyboard or mouse is better suited to this type of application.

Keyboards

When you buy a computer it comes with a keyboard and mouse (or other pointing device in the case or portables and laptops). Coupled with a screen, these provide the most usual interface. However, this arrangement does present a problem for users who only type slowly and even more of a problem for users who have never used a computer before. It is for this reason that other interfaces have been developed for these situations. Even when software makes extensive use of a GUI, you can often still use the keyboard to work the computer, using a combination of keys. For an experienced typist, removing their hands from the keyboard to use the mouse will

slow them down considerably. Instead they can use a combination of keys (such as Ctrl and P at the same time).

Dedicated keys

A dedicated key is a key on the computer keyboard which is used for only one purpose. The purpose of the key cannot be altered using the applications software. The page up and page down keys are examples of dedicated keys.

Soft keys

A soft key is a key on the computer keyboard which may be used for different things by different packages. For example, the function keys F1–F12 all carry out different commands depending on which software is being used.

Activity

Compare and contrast the user interfaces provided by two similar pieces of software that make use of a graphical user interface. You can choose two applications packages or two system software packages. In your comparison, try to point out those features that are common to both and those which are not.

CASE STUDY

Interactive voice response at the South Western Electricity Board

This new type of user interface allows users to enter data such as account numbers and meter readings, using the keypad on an ordinary telephone. To do this, the user must have a touch-tone telephone and since many users do not, there needs to be another system in place. This backup system uses interactive voice response. Here the user hears instructions from the computer and then tells the computer what it needs to know (account number, meter reading, etc.).

One such interactive voice response system is used by the South Western Electricity Board (SWEB), in which meter readings are collected from customers over the telephone. Electricity meters are normally read each quarter but because of problems gaining access to the meter (people are often out when the meter reader calls), many quarterly bills have to be estimated from electricity use during the same period in previous years. The estimate is not always good and customers usually prefer to have an accurate reading taken. Using this procedure, the householder is able to read the meter and then telephone the reading to head office. The problem in doing this from the electricity board's point of view is the large number of staff needed to deal with these calls and hence the cost of providing the service. It is because of this that SWEB decided to make use of interactive voice response (IVR). Now the householder can make a free phone call to the centre and if they do not have a touch-tone telephone, the IVR system is used. Customers are first asked their account number, which they say clearly, and the system validates this to make sure that the account exists, after which the system links up to the mainframe computer. Customers then give their meter reading and the record on the mainframe is updated and a new revised bill produced and posted.

Questions

1 What are the major benefits to SWEB of using the above system compared with having staff with terminals answering the telephone?

2 What problems might this type of system have? Explain briefly.

3 The system described in the case study is particularly successful. SWEB can monitor its success by measuring the number of customers who hang up without completing the transaction. What makes this particular interface so successful? Explain.

4 Have you encountered another type of speech recognition system? If so, what was it used for and how did it work?

Activity

Definition of terms

A variety of new terms is introduced in this chapter, many of which may be new to you. It is important that you build up vocabulary which can be used when writing essays or answering questions. Write a definition for each of the following terms used in the chapter:

interface

HCI

graphical user interface (GUI)

icon

natural language interface

pointer-based interface

trackball

bit pad

Examination Questions

1 A different human/computer interface would be needed for each of the following users:

(i) a young child in a primary school,

(ii) a blind person,

(iii) a graphic artist.

For each user describe and justify an appropriate human/machine interface.

(NEAB, Module IT02, Specimen Paper, q7)

2 A travel agent uses an information system to help customers choose their holidays. The system is used by different types of user.

Justify different user–interface features which would be appropriate for each of the following:

(i) customers, who can interrogate a local off-line system to find details of all the holidays on offer;

(ii) travel agents, who use the system to make bookings;

(iii) staff who set up the system and maintain the accuracy of the database. *(10)*

(NEAB, Module IT02, May 1996, q6)

3 A college uses a range of software packages from different suppliers. Each package has a different user interface. The college is considering changing its software to one supplier and to a common user interface.

(a) Give **four** advantages of having a common user interface. *(4)*

(b) Describe **four** specific features of a user interface which would benefit from being common between packages. *(4)*

(c) Discuss the issues involved, apart from user interfaces, in the college changing of upgrading software packages. *(8)*

(NEAB, Module IT02, May 1997, q8)

4 Speech recognition systems for Personal Computers are now becoming more affordable and useable.

(a) State **two** advantages to a PC user of a speech recognition system. *(2)*

(b) Give **two** different tasks for which a PC user could take advantage of speech recognition. *(2)*

(c) Speech recognition systems sometime fail to be 100 per cent effective in practice. Give **three** reasons why this is so. *(3)*

(NEAB, Module IT02, May 99, q6)

Organisational Structure and Information Flows

CHAPTER OBJECTIVES

▶ To understand the basic concept of organisational structure.

▶ To understand the nature of a corporate information systems strategy.

▶ To look at the information flows, personnel and developments within MIS as part of the information systems in an organisation.

What is an organisation?

We often come across the word organisation when talking about IT so it is useful to have a clear idea of what it means. In general, an organisation consists of:

- a group of people,
- working together with a common purpose,
- to satisfy a series of objectives and carry out all those activities which contribute to those objectives.

The word 'organisation' covers a wide range of operations including banks, production companies, charities, government departments and professional practices.

Organisations can vary in size from a small business with a few employees to a large multinational company with offices throughout the world, employing tens of thousands of people.

Organisational structure

The type of structure adopted by an organisation depends on several factors including:

- the size and complexity of the organisation
- the diversity of the products and services produced or provided
- the geographical spread of the organisation
- the activities performed by the organisation

- the objectives and goals which are set out by the organisation.

Any organisation needs a structure, which shows the various departments within the organisation and the lines of communication between them. This means that the people within each department, or function, know whom they report to, and who reports to them. Organisational structures are of two main types, hierarchical and flat, and these are illustrated in Figure 11.1.

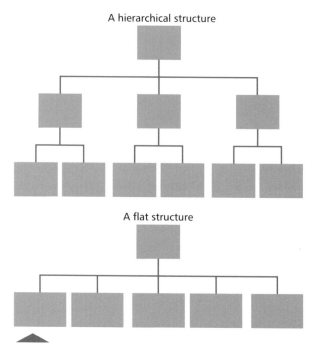

Figure 11.1 *The two types of organisational structure*

Hierarchical structure

Hierarchical structures are tree-like structures in nature, nearness to the 'trunk' indicating seniority; they are characterised by strong patterns of vertical communication. There are usually many different grades of staff between those at the bottom of the organisation and the person at the top. This type of structure can be represented by a triangle with the most senior executive at the top of the triangle and the other staff in layers, with increasing numbers of staff towards the bottom of the triangle. Large companies, with more traditional staff relations, tend to adopt this structure and it is also common in government departments. One problem with hierarchical organisations is that they are prone to bureaucracy since information has to be directed through the correct channels. Decision-making can be time-consuming, since problems must be referred up the structure.

The main features of a hierarchical structure are:

- At each level there are several staff members responsible to a person at the next level up. The process is repeated until the top of the organisation is reached.

- In a limited company the person at the top is the Managing Director who is ultimately responsible to the shareholders for the whole organisation.

- As the levels within the organisation are ascended, the number of people at each level decreases and this gives the organisation a pyramidal structure.

Flat structure

Flat structures are generally adopted by small organisations where people's roles and responsibilities are less rigidly defined. Most of the staff will know each other and there is usually less formality between the managers and their staff; staff work together as a team. With a flat structure there are fewer levels of seniority and staff have a wide variety of different roles. Small shops and family-run businesses frequently use a flat structure.

The main advantage of a flat structure is that members of staff are able to work more on their own initiative and this brings flexibility and creativity to their jobs.

CASE STUDY

A growing business

Two friends, Paul and Suzanne, set up an organisation called Future Proof Services. When they set up the business, both partners were on an equal footing and since they worked together, and could make decisions as they arose, things worked well. As the firm grew over the years they took on employees, and there needed to be a structure to the organisation so that employees were clear about to whom they reported. Since the founders were young and forward-looking, they did not want an organisation laden with bureaucracy, but preferred their employees to be able to approach them for help if need be, to work on their own initiative and make minor decisions for themselves.

Question

Which type of organisational structure, flat or hierarchical, would be most suited to Future Proof Services? Explain your answer.

Drawing organisation charts

An organisation chart is a diagram of an organisation's structure. Such charts show organisation functions, activities, posts, lines of responsibility, levels of authority, accountability, lines of communication and span of control. Sometimes organisation charts refer to particular people; others refer to particular functions or activities within the organisation. Some organisation charts do both, so you can put a name to a particular post. By looking at such a chart it is easy to determine a particular person's position within the organisation, to whom they are directly accountable (i.e. who their immediate boss is), and which staff are at the same level. Their responsibilities for more junior staff are also immediately obvious.

Organisation charts are useful aids when performing systems analysis, and like most diagrams they present the information more concisely than would a written description.

These are the steps taken when drawing up an organisation chart.

1 Write down all job titles, and to which job each one reports. In some organisation charts, you can attach a person's name to each of the jobs shown, but this has the disadvantage that if staff change the chart will require updating.

2 From the information gained in 1, complete a table similar to the one below.

Job title	Responsible to

----

3 The person who has no one to report to is the one in charge of the organisation. Place a box with the name of the post (and the name of the person if required) at the top of the page.

4 Find from the table in 2 the names of the posts that report to the person in charge and add them to the next layer down.

5 Continue by repeating the process for each post in the next layer, then move on to the next layer down.

6 Repeat until all the posts/staff are included.

Example

Look at the table to the right and the organisation chart in Figure 11.2, which was constructed using the information in the table.

Job title	Responsible to
Costing Supervisor	Chief Accountant
Managing Director	
Chief Accountant	Financial Director
Management Information Services Manager	Financial Director
Production Supervisor	Production Manager
Sales and Marketing Director	Managing Director
Transport Manager	Production Director
Office Manager	Chief Administrator
Senior Wages Clerk	Chief Accountant
Head of Planning	Production Director
Sales Engineer	Head of Marketing
Sales and Marketing Manager	Head of Marketing
Chief Administrator	Financial Director
Production Director	Managing Director
Production Manager	Production Director
Head of Marketing	Sales and marketing Director
Financial Director	Managing Director
Sales Administration Supervisor	Sales and Marketing Manager and Sales Engineer

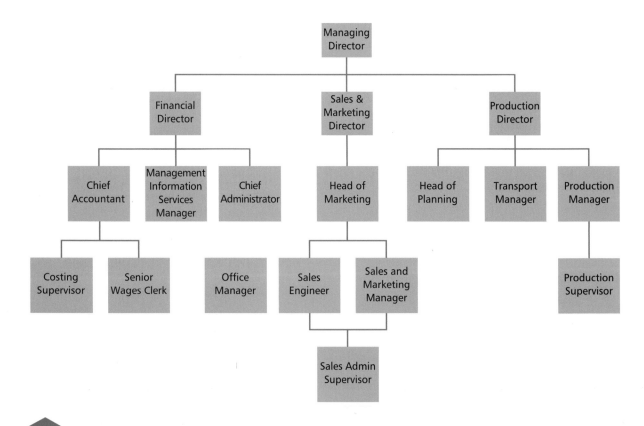

Figure 11.2 *Organisation chart from the information in the above table*

Activity

Here is a table produced for a certain organisation. It shows the names of the posts and to whom they are responsible. Your task is to use the information in the table to produce an organisation chart.

Name of post	Who they are responsible to
Promotions staff	Marketing Director
Marketing Director	Managing Director
Managing Director	
Sales staff	Sales Director
Development staff	Marketing Director
Sales Director	Managing Director
Personnel staff	Finance Director
Accounts staff	Finance Director
Delivery staff	Sales Director
Finance Director	Managing Director

Activity *KEY SKILLS IT2.1, IT3.1*

Organisation charts are subject to a great deal of change in large organisations and they have frequently to be re-drawn. Specialist chart-drawing software is available which includes a facility for drawing these charts, but they are usually drawn using generic software. Your task is to find software capable of drawing an organisation chart and then draw and print the organisation chart shown in Figure 11.2.

Functions within an organisation

A look at any organisation will probably reveal that it is organised according to certain job functions such as finance, marketing, personnel, operations, purchasing, design and sales. When considering organisations, 'functions' refers to these broad areas of activities, which have to be carried out in order to achieve the objectives of the organisation.

Functions may be classed as either **internal** or **external**.

Internal functions

Internal functions are distinct areas within the organisation into which the organisation may be divided. The functions obviously vary depending on the type of organisation, so some of the following functions will only appear in certain organisations.

Finance

The finance department (sometimes called the accounts department) is responsible for all financial record keeping. This involves keeping all manual or computer records about money coming into and going out of the business. The finance function also covers the payment of wages and the collection of tax and National Insurance contributions and making sure that the legal requirements for their collection are observed. The finance department also sets up department budgets and makes sure department managers do not overspend.

Marketing

The marketing function is the process of identifying, anticipating and satisfying customer requirements profitably. Marketing does not just apply to goods, it can also apply to services. For instance, your school or college will need to do a certain amount of advertising to convince pupils/students to enrol. Large companies generally have a separate marketing function, but in smaller businesses its role might be merged with the sales function.

Personnel

Only large organisations have separate personnel functions. Smaller companies tend to leave this function to individual managers rather than employ specially qualified personnel staff. The main tasks undertaken by the personnel function are the hiring and firing of staff, dealing with industrial relations, and staff training.

Operations

Some organisations do not make a product, but instead provide a service. In this case the day-to-day tasks of providing the service can be considered the 'production' part of the business, and it is often referred to as the operations function. Types of businesses which would have large operations departments include building societies and travel agents.

Purchasing

Companies that manufacture goods have to buy raw materials and components, which are then processed to produce finished goods or goods that are further processed by another manufacturer. For instance, a company could make switches out of metal, which it then sells to another company, which puts them in radios. The purchasing function is a crucial one in manufacturing companies since lack of a single type of component can hold up a whole production line.

To remain competitive, it is important for all organisations to buy components of an appropriate quality at the cheapest possible price and to make sure that the time scale for delivery is correct.

All organisations have a purchasing function, even if it is just services (gas, electricity, telephone, car rental) or office requirements (equipment, stationery, rental, etc.) that they are buying. It is necessary to have a system in place for purchasing. The purchasing function may be broken down into the following separate tasks:

- finding a suitable supplier

- establishing payment and discounts and negotiating delivery schedules/dates

- placing an order

- taking delivery of the order or chasing up delivery

- checking that the goods received are the same as those ordered

- paying the invoice.

Design

Not all organisations have this function. Product design, the production of plans and drawings and the preparation of scale models, are all tasks that can be performed by the design department. Often CAD (computer-aided design) software is used to help with design and it is possible using this software to view a two-dimensional plan in three dimensions without re-drawing.

Sales

The sales function of any business is its most important function since it drives the rest of the business. The sales function involves persuading customers to buy products or services. This may mean co-ordinating travelling representatives, telephone sales, preparing and sending mailshots, etc. It also involves interaction with the marketing function.

External functions

As well as internal functions there are external functions/entities which influence the administration systems and these are dealt with below.

Supplier/customer functions

Sometimes suppliers determine the administration procedure adopted. For instance, suppliers who provide parts for military aircraft may have to get staff to sign the Official Secrets Act before they can be given the contract.

Legal and statutory bodies

There are various legal and statutory bodies which can influence the way in which administration procedures are performed. Health and safety regulations influence the working environment and some working procedures. There are Inland Revenue, VAT and National Insurance requirements for ensuring that correct deductions are made from wages and passed on to the government. In addition to these there are certain obligations to be met under company law which applies to limited companies.

Figure 11.3 shows the external bodies who exchange information with an organisation.

Activity   KEY SKILLS C2.1, C3.1

There are many different external organisations that can affect the way that a business is run. Find out what the following organisations do, and state how they may influence the running of a business.

- Health and Safety Executive
- HM Customs and Excise Department
- Trading Standards Department
- the environmental control department of a local council

Information flow diagrams

Information flow diagrams show how information flows between the functions within an organisation; this can be between internal functions, or between the internal and the external functions. Figure 11.4 shows just some of the many information flows into an organisation.

Consider a mail order company selling goods that have been bought from a series of suppliers

Figure 11.3 *Some external bodies who may exchange information with an organisation*

and are then advertised and sold through a catalogue.

For the sake of simplicity we will assume the following list of functions: sales, customers, suppliers, purchasing, accounts, dispatch.

When constructing information flow diagrams, it is useful to remember the following steps:

1 Think about which functional areas you are going to look at. If you are investigating a large organisation, it may be easier to first limit the diagram to just a few functional areas, although it can be quite difficult to isolate certain areas. Look at the internal functions first and then see if any of them communicate with external functions in any way. In our example, both suppliers and customers are external functions, the rest representing internal functions.

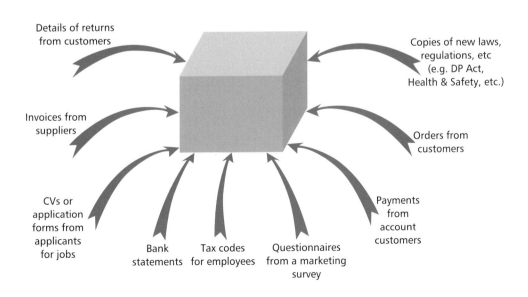

Figure 11.4 *Possible external information flows into an organisation*

2 Add lines showing the information flows. Write on each line the type of information that passes between the functions. You can also add the form that this information takes (e.g. documents, verbal or electronic).

3 Do not worry if you do not get the design right first time. One problem you may encounter after drawing several of these diagrams is that sometimes the flow lines start to cross each other; the diagram can end up looking like a plate of spaghetti. Try re-drawing the diagram, rearranging the boxes to prevent this.

4 Try not to include too much detail at first. Draw a simple diagram and then re-draw it, adding more detail.

Remember the whole point of an information flow diagram is to be able to identify all the functions and then be able to see the way information flows between them.

Figure 11.5 shows how a functional area, in this case order processing, can overlap with other functional areas. The overlap is another means of showing that there are systems in place to enable communication between them.

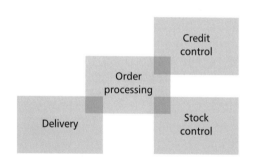

Figure 11.5 *The functional area of order processing overlaps with other functional areas*

Activity

Investigate the functions and information flows for two of the following types of organisation. Choose the two you are most familiar with. Some questions are included to get you to think about the system. You do not have to answer them but you will need to bear the answers in mind when explaining and illustrating each system.

Your college/school library

- How does a person join the library; what documentation is produced and how is it stored?
- What happens when the library buys a new book; what information about the book is needed and how is it stored?
- When a member of the library borrows a book, how are the details recorded?
- What needs to be done when a book is returned?
- What happens if the book is overdue by several weeks?

A college enrolment system

You should only attempt this one if you are at a college. Think about what happened when you first came to college.

- What forms did you fill in?
- Did you have an interview?
- Did you receive an acceptance letter?
- Did you have to turn up at a certain time on a certain day to enrol or was it done by your course tutor?
- What information did you need to supply to enrol?
- What forms were filled in during the enrolment process and what did the college do with them?

A video library

- What information needs to be recorded when a new video is bought and where is it held?
- What information (e.g. proof of identity, name, etc.) is needed when a person joins the library and in what form, and where are these details stored?
- What information needs to be recorded when a video is hired out; in what form are these details kept?
- What information is needed when letters are sent out to people who have not returned their videos?

A mail order company

- What forms of information (order forms, phone orders, Internet orders, etc.) are used when placing orders?
- Which payment methods are used?
- What information needs to be included with each order?

- By which methods can a customer pay for their goods?
- What information is needed so that goods can be picked from stock?
- What documents are sent with the goods if applicable?

Information flows

When an organisation is small, information flows are limited and most of the information flows to the manager who can then delegate tasks to the person most suited to them. This is usually the case for a small shop, for instance. As a business becomes larger, perhaps with the opening of more branches, it becomes clear that the owner of the business cannot be expected to deal with every piece of information. Some of the information has to be entrusted to others to deal with, and this usually means setting up different functional areas. Once the functional areas are in place, there must be a way of making sure that all data and information is directed to the relevant function.

When a business grows, it becomes much more complex; large corporations are often involved in many different types of business and this means that the information needs of the organisation also grow.

Information systems and organisations

Management information is the lifeblood of any business or organisation. The information can range from a single report outlining the profitability of a range of goods, to a large document outlining the profitability of all areas according to region. There are many ways in which the material for these reports can be obtained, but mostly it is from operational information supplied by the computer system. Most often management information is obtained by processing the data and information from day-to-day transactions. It is important that any management information requested is relevant, accurate, is in a form appropriate for the person who is to receive it and is presented at the correct time. Not all computer systems supply management information. For example, a payroll system that calculates all the necessary figures for paying the employees along with details of deductions such as tax, National Insurance, Pensions etc. is quite capable of operating without the need to supply management with information.

Data processing systems

Data processing systems are different from information systems, in that they automate many of the routine clerical and administrative procedures in an organisation. Order processing systems, stock control systems, routine billing systems (for gas, electricity, water, etc.) and payroll systems are all examples of data processing systems. Data processing systems are used to process the day-to-day data generated by an organisation during its normal operations. They are usually unable to supply management directly with information on which to make tactical or strategic decisions.

Information systems

The main aim of information systems is to supply information on which decisions can be based. For example, any booking system (holidays, concert tickets, etc.) needs to be able to tell the user about the availability of seats. If the cheaper seats have been sold, then the customer must decide whether they want to pay for more expensive ones. Information systems usually operate hand-in-hand with data processing systems (see above), and in the example of the booking system, once availability has been established, the tickets can be booked and printed via the data processing system.

The data processing system of a telephone company keeps track of all the calls made (date, time and number), and then processes these to produce a telephone bill. To this system could be added an information system which allows the company to find out which customers make frequent overseas calls, so that they can be targeted as part of a marketing campaign highlighting cheaper rates for overseas calls.

Many organisations are now using information systems to obtain greater value from the routine data held in their data processing systems.

Management information systems (MIS)

Systems that convert data from internal or external sources into information to be used by managers are called management information systems. This information needs to be in an appropriate form to enable managers at different levels to make effective decisions for planning, directing and controlling the activities for which they are responsible. Management information systems are a part of the systems used by all staff in an organisation, but designed primarily with the information needs of managers in mind.

For a manager, plenty of accurate information reduces uncertainty when making decisions. Decisions can be reached quickly and confidently because there is a high probability that the decision will be correct when based on sufficient information.

Most managers have specific jobs and responsibilities and any management information needs to be tailored to their individual needs. In the past when managers contacted the data processing department or database manager with a request for information, this was frequently met with the reply that the system could not produce the information in the form requested. Many large database systems, though well suited to the task of providing routine information gained during an organisation's data processing activities, were incapable of producing ad hoc reports.

Database systems are now much more flexible and many managers are trained to extract for themselves the information they need using a terminal and printer on their own desk.

Activity

A company manufactures barbecues which are sold through large DIY stores and garden centres throughout Britain. At present there are ten models ranging from the cheapest costing £35 to a top-of-the-range model costing around £400.

Your task is to look at the management information the production manager might need, and to compare and contrast his information needs with those of the managing director who is in overall charge of the business.

In order to understand the importance of management information let us look at an example based on the barbecue manufacturing company described in the last Activity box. This company employs eight area representatives. Their work is to visit, promote and sell to retail outlets. Suppose the sales manager responsible

for the representatives tells the managing director that salesman X, who is responsible for the north western region, has made £100,000 worth of sales in the last month. That sounds good to the MD, but is it? How can he decide? The obvious way would be to compare salesman X's sales with the sales the other representatives have made in the same period. He could also compare this value with the sales made for the same region going back several years. This might reveal a trend, for instance, that barbecues are becoming more popular. With management information systems it is easy to obtain such information and there is less need for specialist staff to extract the information from the computer system.

Executive information systems (EIS)

An executive information system is used to give personnel at the highest level of control (usually senior managers or directors) easy access to internal and external data. As these busy people do not have time to sift through huge amounts of data to find the information they require, executive information systems need to summarise the data from the main system. Most EISs allow the executive to 'drill down' from higher level information (showing less detail) to the more detailed information on which it is based. The EIS must also allow the manipulation of data so that comparisons can be made with previous weeks, months, years, etc.

Once data has been obtained from the system, the next stage is to present it in a way which makes it easy to understand. In most cases this will involve the use of graphics such as pie charts, histograms, line graphs and so on.

Many of the executives who use the EIS will have only limited experience of an information system, so the system needs to be user-friendly. The executives must also be provided with some analysis tools so that he or she can alter figures and see what happens (i.e. perform 'what-if' analyses). Although you may think this sounds very similar to the capabilities of a spreadsheet, spreadsheets do not offer the possibility of drilling down for data.

On-line analytical processing (OLAP)

On-line analytical processing (OLAP) is taking over from the older executive information systems. It is often used in preference to EIS because it is cheaper and more flexible. The definition of OLAP is that 'it is interactive, multidimensional analysis on an enterprise scale'. This means that you can explore data from the data processing system, moving directly between different queries and different levels of detail in the data. You will have already come across the concept of a 'query' when extracting information from a relational database, but relational databases do not allow 'drilling down' for more detailed data and do not include the complex analytical tools provided by OLAP. For example, if you want to extract details regarding the sales of a product X in store Y for the month of May, this can be done using the relational database management system by setting up a query. However, if OLAP is used, you can immediately ask how many of item X have been sold in all the stores last year compared with the year before and any previous years. From here you could use OLAP to drill down and get the breakdown for each product sold by each region for each week in a six-month period.

Decision support systems (DSS)

Decision support systems are used by management to help decision-making when the data used is unstructured. Unstructured data has much higher levels of uncertainty so it is more difficult to make the right decision. Decision support systems can determine the optimum choice from several possibilities and can also be used to extrapolate figures to provide forecasts (e.g. for future sales). Decision support systems do not actually make the decisions: they simply give the manager more information about the decisions they are proposing to make. Using a system should increase the probability of managers making the correct decision.

The main difference between a management information system and a decision support system is that the management information system plays a more passive role in the decision-making process, simply supplying the information in an easily assimilated form.

Questions

1 Explain the differences between a management information system, an executive information system and a decision support system.

2 What factors need to be taken into account when designing the user interface for an executive information system?

Information systems and personnel

There are many levels of staff in most organisations, which can be classified into the following three main types.

Strategic functions

This describes the work of the senior managers and directors who steer the company. These people are responsible for setting the overall objectives for the organisation and are concerned with such things as buying new businesses, selling unprofitable parts of the business, moving into new markets, moving to new sites, etc.

Implementation functions

Junior and middle management are involved in the implementation of the objectives identified by the strategic level of staff. This level of management makes minor decisions that enable the operations to be performed in an efficient manner. They are responsible for the day-to-day management of the business operations and much of their time is spent managing the many staff who report to them.

Operational functions

Operations are the day-to-day business activities the organisation is involved with; these activities occupy the majority of staff working in the organisation.

Activity

Your job is to allocate the tasks listed below to the level of staff best placed to deal with each, choosing from strategic, implementation or operational staff in each case.

- Looking at a company's market share to see what can be done to increase it.
- Allocating work to subordinates in an operations department.
- Dealing with staff rotas and staff sickness.
- Deciding on a buy-out of another similar organisation.

Corporate information systems strategy

All organisations should have a corporate information systems strategy. This is a statement of the long-term objectives and goals for its information systems.

Factors influencing organisational information systems

The success or failure of an information system within an organisation is influenced by:

- management organisation and functions
- planning and decision-making methods
- general organisational structure
- responsibility for information systems within an organisation
- hardware and software
- standards
- behavioural factors (personalities, motivation, ability to adapt to change)
- the efficiency of information flows.

Let's look at these in more detail.

Management organisation and functions

Managers do the following as part of their jobs:

- organise and implement
- plan (strategically and tactically depending on their level within the organisation)
- control and review.

'Organisation and implementation' is all about getting things done. This involves making sure that resources are available (materials, staff, equipment, etc.) to carry out the day-to-day operations of the organisation. As well as the operations side, managers have to implement decisions made higher up in the organisation.

Planning can be at different levels, with strategic planning setting broad objectives and formulating policy for the whole organisation, tactical planning setting medium- to short-term objectives, and operational planning dealing with jobs in hand.

Controlling and reviewing involves the individual manager looking at the overall performance of the department under his or her control. Targets are often set for departments (such as sales targets in a sales department) in this way.

Responsibility for information systems within an organisation

Responsibility for data processing is usually that of the data processing or IT department, but responsibility and ownership of the management information systems is usually less formal. Problems arise when individual managers of functional areas ensure that they get the management information they need by setting up their own systems from their budget allocation. In many cases, there is no consultation with the IT department about these acquisitions and they may not even know of their existence. This can cause problems for an IT manager who has overall control of the IT facilities, and it could compromise data security. Another problem is that individual managers may not be aware of the Data Protection Act and other relevant legislation. Finally, much of the data used for these systems may be duplicated by the various departments, which is a waste of time and other resources.

The best information systems are those that are developed formally after a careful analysis of the information needs of the organisation and consultation with all the end users of the system. It is now usual for information systems to be considered a corporate resource. All the data is kept together in a data warehouse and all managers have management workstations with software capable of extracting the information they require and in a format they can use. Using centrally held data means that data is not duplicated, and also that it is consistent across the whole organisation.

General organisational structure

With a hierarchical structure, there are many levels of staff, and information must be communicated up and down the various levels effectively to allow managers to make timely and effective decisions.

Hardware and software

Many organisations, when developing new systems, have a limited budget and so may have to make use of existing hardware and software. This means that often the optimum system cannot be developed and instead a compromise system is produced. Sometimes new developments may have to communicate with existing systems, as in the case of a management information system having to communicate with an existing data processing system.

Behavioural factors

The attitude of staff to change is an important factor to consider since for any successful system to be implemented, it needs the full co-operation of all the staff, especially senior managers. Senior managers are usually in charge of one particular functional area within an organisation and their attitudes to IT can differ. For example, a manager who is due to retire shortly could encourage rejection of a very good project so that they can have an easier life for themselves during their remaining time within the organisation.

During the development of the information systems, managers of the functional areas in the organisation should be consulted as it is important that they co-operate fully. Many of these managers will be given departmental budgets and the allocation of money and other resources can cause conflict between managers. This sometimes manifests itself when they have to work together as a team.

Motivation of staff is an important factor, and if staff members are poorly motivated, changes will be resisted and it will be much harder to gain the co-operation of more junior staff. Some staff may feel that the introduction of information systems somehow jeopardises their jobs and will naturally be concerned about this.

The efficiency of information flows

There are many factors that affect the flow of information and data in an organisation. Data and information originates within the organisation or from outside, and travels around the organisation to the different departments and up and down the various levels of staff. Without adequate flows of data and information to the various functions within the organisation, no management information system will be able to supply appropriate information at the right time and this will lead to bad decisions being made.

Organisation structure

The hierarchical nature of many organisations means they are more bureaucratic, since data has to be channelled through various levels of staff before reaching its target. An organisation with a flat structure has fewer levels and this makes it easier to route the information to the most appropriate person.

Geographical structure

Many organisations have a branch network with branches scattered throughout the country, or even the world, and this is only possible by using the latest communications methods. Distance need not be a hindrance, however, with wide area networks allowing data to be passed from one continent to another as easily as it can be between two terminals in the same building. Having more than one site allows an organisation to consider distributed processing, where all the processing does not take place on a single site. Distributed processing, although more complex to manage, has the advantage of enhanced security since both software and data can be transferred easily from one site to another. Videoconferencing means that face-to-face meetings can be held to discuss company strategy without anyone leaving their office.

The validity of the data

Only valid data should be processed and the validity of the data depends on the manner in which it was collected. Transactions should always be validated using appropriate and rigorous validation checks to ensure that only correct data is used subsequently. Because the data collected can be used by so many different systems, incorrect data can cause major problems. Many companies have systems that cannot collect data directly from transactions, in which case it is necessary to re-enter the details into a different system. Re-inputting data in this way can introduce errors, especially as validation checks are generally not a feature of such systems. If at all possible, data should only be input once. Most organisations are working towards this to reduce errors and also the costs of collecting data.

The volume of data to be collected and input

There are certain times in the year when an organisation is snowed under with work. This may occur when the end-of-year accounts are being prepared or during the preparation of monthly bills or invoices. Some organisations (e.g. firework manufacturers) may have seasonal variations.

Any huge increase in the workload without a corresponding increase in the number of staff, or hours that staff work, will delay the information flows to departments in the organisation. Routine operational tasks may then take priority, and staff may not be free to deal with requests for management information.

The processing cycle

The processing cycle determines when information can flow within or outside the organisation. For example, a payroll is processed every week for weekly paid staff and this creates the need for timesheet data to flow from the departments to the payroll department. Another example might be the monthly credit card statements sent by a credit card company to their customers; here the processing is performed on a monthly basis.

The specification of reports

Some information cannot be extracted readily from the system without writing certain programming code. Such reports will need to be sent to personnel with technical expertise and this can take time and cause delays.

The report timing cycle

Many reports are produced periodically (per week, per month, etc.). If a manager wants information in the interim period they may not be able to obtain it and may have to use the results from the previous report or wait for the next report. More and more routine management information can be obtained on an ad hoc basis, allowing managers access to the latest version of the information whenever they need it. This ideal situation can of course only be achieved if the manager has a terminal connected to a network able to access the data on which the report is based.

The report distribution cycle

Reports are sometimes generated and then passed from person to person with the most senior person getting their copy first. This introduces a time delay. With the widespread use of electronic mail in many organisations, such reports are easily distributed in their electronic form to everyone at the same time.

Compatibility of the software across the departments

If the software used by one department is incompatible with that used by another department it can cause problems, especially when trying to combine data from different departments. Sometimes such incompatibility can even necessitate re-inputting the data from one of the systems into the other, with a resulting delay and the possible introduction of keyboarding errors.

Data collection and the input of data

Data can be collected automatically from the processing of transactions generated in the day-to-day running of the organisation, or it may be collected and then input. Data input speed depends on the method of data capture and can affect the flow of data in an organisation.

Formal versus informal requests and responses

Many organisations process data centrally and any reports required by individual departmental managers are also produced centrally and distributed to managers via the internal mail. Many reports are generated automatically and distributed as a matter of routine; such reports include daily stock lists, monthly sales figures, lists of overdue accounts, etc. Other reports are asked for informally, such as the request after a sales meeting for the corresponding sales figures over the previous five years in order to make predictions concerning future sales. Such requests might be urgent and the normal, formal methods for requesting such information (e.g. by filling in a form and getting a senior manager to authorise the request) may take too long, so an informal request by a senior member of staff will prompt a more rapid response.

What can be done to review the current information flows?

To improve on the current information flows within an organisation it is necessary to perform a review of the current information systems. Such a review would use the following techniques:

- inspect the current input/output sub-systems

- track the documents used for input into the system

- track the documents used as output from the system

- interview the end users to see if they are getting the right information at the right time

- use questionnaires to find out how satisfied users are with the current information flows

- examine requests made for developments to improve the current system

- inspect the requests for reports and information from the current system.

Activity

Definition of terms

A variety of new terms is introduced in this chapter, many of which may be new to you. It is important that you build up vocabulary which can be used when writing essays or answering questions. Write a definition for each of the following terms used in the chapter:

hierarchical organisational structure

flat organisational structure

data processing system

management information system

Examination Questions

1 The manager of a company complains that the management information system (MIS) continually fails to produce the appropriate information at the right time. The person responsible for the MIS responds by blaming the 'inadequate data and information flow' within the company and requests a review of 'data and information flows'.

(a) State **six** factors which influence the flow of information and data within an organisation. (6)

(b) With the aid of examples, describe **three** techniques which could be used to review the current information flows. (6)

(NEAB, Module IT04, May 97, q8)

2 (a) What is the purpose of a management information system? (1)

(b) Why is such a system required by managers of an organisation? (1)

(c) Give **one** example of the use of a management information system within an organisation stating its purpose. (2)

(NEAB, Module IT04, May 97, q1)

3 With the aid of appropriate examples, explain the difference between formal and informal information flows. (6)

(NEAB, Module IT04, May 98, q)

12 Information Systems in Organisations

The difference between a data processing system and an information system

Data processing systems

Data processing systems are frequently called transaction processing systems since they record, process and report on the day-to-day business activities of an organisation. Such transactions might include processing customer orders, dealing with returns, arranging deliveries, processing payments made, dealing with queries, processing the payroll, dealing with stock and placing orders with suppliers. The main body of data processing concerns operational data. Operational data is essential for the running of the organisation or business. Data processing systems are mainly used by the operational level staff in an organisation.

Information systems and management information systems (MIS)

What do managers do?

Before looking at management information systems we need to remind ourselves of the role of a manager and the tasks involved in management. Managers are present in many layers of an organisation, from junior managers through to the senior managers and directors. What they do depends on their level within the organisation. Junior managers tend to deal with management at an operational level, that is, with the day-to-day issues. Senior managers deal with strategic matters and make major decisions.

All managers have to make decisions using information obtained from internal and external sources. The types of decision made fall under the following headings:

- planning
- directing
- controlling
- forecasting.

The lower layers of management are responsible for:

- day-to-day management of the operations staff
- allocating work to subordinates
- arrangement of staff rotas, dealing with staff sickness/absence
- motivating staff
- handling a departmental budget.

The higher levels of management are responsible for:

- strategic planning; this involves the setting of overall objectives and policies
- market share
- cash flow
- profits
- growth in profits.

It is important to remember that management information is really just a specialist part of information systems.

Figure 12.1 shows three levels of information for the three levels of management.

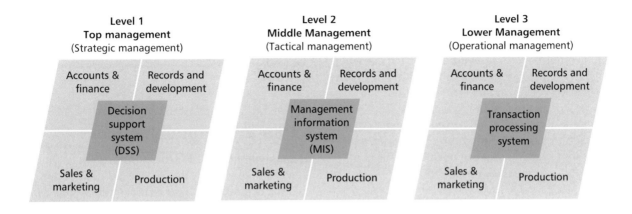

Figure 12.1 *The three levels of information for the three levels of management*

Figure 12.2 *The locations of supermarkets in a chain*

Look at the map in Figure 12.2 showing the location of shops for a large supermarket chain. These supermarkets have lorries that deliver goods from several large distribution centres situated for easy access to all the stores. At present, all the shops shown on the map are fed from a distribution centre in the Midlands but more shops have now opened in Northern England and a new distribution centre covering this area is to be built. The company now has to decide where to site the new distribution centre.

1 Explain the difference between internal and external information.

2 What are the main factors for choosing the location of the new distribution centre?

3 What information would be needed to make an informed decision?

4 Where would the information to base the decision on, come from?

Information systems are used to obtain information that enables users to make effective and timely decisions. An example of this is in an order processing system. When a customer rings up to place an order, the member of staff taking the order checks that the item is in stock and if not, how soon it can be obtained. The member of staff will then make the decision as to whether to place an order with the suppliers or not. Since management have the responsibility for making decisions, information systems used to supply information for managers on which they can base decisions are called management information systems (MISs). Management information systems go hand in hand with data processing systems, but are used for different purposes.

Activity

You need to be able to distinguish between a data processing system and a management information system. If the system processes raw data to produce routine information, it is likely to be a data processing system. However, if the data produced is communicated to managers at different levels, in an appropriate form, for them to make effective decisions for planning, directing and controlling the activities, the system is a management information system.

Here are some systems; your task is to say into which category they fall:

- a payroll system for processing time sheets and printing pay slips
- a system that compares the sales made of the same make of car over the same month for the last five years
- production of a list for a customer of all the main dealers in the country with a certain colour and model of car in stock
- production of a list of items to be ordered from the suppliers, produced from an EPOS system
- a sales analysis system to investigate trends in sales over a certain time period
- production of a list of debtors (customers who owe money) to be sent to the managers for their decision on what further action to take
- a system that produces sales figures for previous similar periods for the planning of production levels
- a system that analyses competitors' prices for similar products
- a system producing a report outlining the frequency of calls to a help-desk and the average time each problem took

- a system for producing a list of students who have paid their course fees, to be given to a course tutor.

The development and life cycle of an information system

The development of information systems should never be left to just the IT staff since it is the business managers who will use the system on a day-to-day basis. To ensure that the system supplies them with the correct information, in the way they require, they need to be involved in the design of the system.

For the system to meet everyone's needs, it must be carefully designed and there is a set order in which the system should be developed. The following is a list of the typical stages:

1 defining the objectives and scope of the MIS

2 a detailed systems analysis

3 the production of a detailed specification

4 choosing the software and then the hardware which will run it

5 implementation of the system

6 maintenance and review.

Figure 12.3 summarises the steps involved in an information system's development life cycle.

1 Defining the objectives and scope of the management information system

The objectives of the system are the things that we are trying to achieve when the system is implemented. The scope of the system defines how far the system will go.

2 A detailed systems analysis

This analysis examines what needs to be achieved, without being constrained by either the way of doing it or whether it is technically possible. Any current system is investigated and a fact-find is performed by asking all the users what they want from the new system. Once the analyst has collected information from all parties involved, he or she can sit down and start to design the system and finally produce a detailed system specification.

3 The production of a detailed specification

Once thorough analysis has taken place, the developer (or systems analyst) draws up a

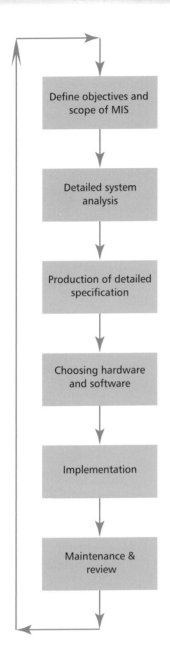

Figure 12.3 *The information systems development life cycle*

implementation of an information system, and these are as follows:

Clear time scales – projects tend to expand to fill any amount of time given to them, so it is important at the outset to agree on the time allocated to the parts, or tasks, that make up the whole project. Once these small tasks have a time scale, it is easy to work out (manually or by using project management software) how long the overall task should take.

Milestones can be used whereby parts of the project must be completed by certain dates. The project manager will review the project from time to time and if the time scales for some of the tasks are likely not to be met, then remedial action can be taken to put the project back on course.

Deliverables – are those smaller tasks that together make up the project. Before the project starts, the team needs to agree between themselves and with the users or project sponsor, what these deliverables are. When they are completed, the team meets with the users, or the project sponsor, to sign off these deliverables. This means that the particular task has been completed successfully.

Approval to proceed – most projects have a project sponsor, a senior manager or director of the organisation who will be in charge of the project. To get approval to proceed, the project team prepares a feasibility study examining the costs of the system and the benefits to be obtained from it. The feasibility report is a formal document outlining the results and conclusions of this study; it is presented to personnel who have the necessary authority to give the go-ahead for development of the system.

4 Choosing the software and then the hardware that will run it

In many cases specialist software can be bought and then modified. As the software bought will determine the type of processing, the number of terminals, the storage method, capacity and so on, it is essential that it is chosen first. Unless the system is very small (with only a single user) you cannot get away with buying the hardware and then wondering what you are going to do with it!

5 Implementation of the system

Implementation of the system means actually setting up the new system and transferring data from the old system to the new. If the other

systems specification in consultation with the managers and users. In this part the managers outline details of their management information requirements.

There may be a tendency to develop the information system informally, without using the various steps as outlined above, but this should be resisted as the use of a formal method always leads to a much better system.

There are other factors that contribute to the successful development and subsequent stages have been completed correctly, then implementation should proceed smoothly. As well as getting the system to run properly, the implementation stage also involves preparing user documentation and training the users.

6 Maintenance and review

Information systems need to be maintained so that they can cope with the many changes that occur in a business. At the time of development, users may not see all the potential uses of the information system, and as these become apparent, changes to the original information system will need to be made. There may even come a stage when the design of the information system is no longer compatible with the demands of the users. At this stage, the performance of the information system is reviewed with a view to possible replacement. If it is decided that the system should be replaced, the whole series of steps described above is repeated.

The success or failure of a management information system

Many information systems are not successful in either giving the end-user what they want or producing a working system at all. In some cases, the project goes out of control, with the costs escalating and the project falling behind schedule. Lack of project control can occur for a number of reasons: key personnel can leave, managers do not keep a grip on the schedules and costs, and so on. Some management information systems simply fail to live up to expectations. Some of the problems that users have when using poor management information systems are summarised in Figure 12.4.

Here are some reasons why the development of a new system might fail.

Lack of formal methods

There are many different ways in which a system can be developed, each called a methodology. Structured systems analysis and design methodology (SSADM for short) is the most widely used method, but there are others, and each method has its own strengths and weaknesses. What all these methods have in common is that the system is developed in a formal way. This avoids systems analysts taking short cuts and ending up developing a less than perfect system. Proper systems analysis does take

Figure 12.4 *Complaints users might make about their management information systems*

time and effort, but the result is usually much better than if less formal methods are made.

Inadequate analysis

If the system analysis is done by someone who is inexperienced, they might not fully analyse the information requirements of the organisation. Such an analysis will be based on incomplete information and will never produce a flexible and fully functional information system.

Inadequate analysis usually manifests itself when the system is unable to perform a key task or the system does not behave in a manner that is consistent with the original objectives.

Lack of management involvement in the design

IT specialists usually take charge of information system development since they know how to perform a rigorous systems analysis. However, their actual business knowledge about the areas they are looking at is much weaker than the managers who are in charge of these areas. It is therefore important that the managers are made part of the development team and that there is constant consultation between them and the developers of the system. The result of the collaboration will hopefully be a technically good system which meets actual business needs (i.e. meet both the data processing and the management information system requirements).

Over-emphasis on computer systems

Many systems analysts and development staff are very career conscious and often move from one company to another for a better job. Many are now self-employed consultants who go from one project to another. To ensure that they are experienced in the use of the latest hardware and software, they can end up recommending the latest technology in the interests of their own learning needs, without considering the needs of the organisation. Emphasis on the computer system can be a distraction from the more important information needs of the organisation. Some IT staff may be so impressed by capabilities such as processor speed, storage capacity, etc. of the hardware that they spend too little time on considering the complete system, or the interfaces between the system being developed and the other systems used by the organisation.

Concentration on low-level data processing

Data processing is the routine processing that is performed on data during the day-to-day running of the organisation. Although it is imperative that such tasks are performed, it is important to give equal consideration to information systems which give management the information for planning, directing and controlling the organisation.

Lack of management knowledge of IT systems and their capabilities

Management may not be aware of the latest developments in IT and usually place their trust in IT specialists who, they assume, will be aware of current technology. However, IT specialists cannot possibly be experts in all parts of the business, so it is up to managers to keep up-to-date with the latest developments in their particular area of management. For example, the personnel manager will probably subscribe to professional magazines and in these there will occasionally be articles on the latest developments in his or her area, many of which will involve IT. Without some IT knowledge, the organisation will be putting its trust entirely in the IT specialist, who may be an employee, work for a consultancy or be self-employed.

Inappropriate/excessive management demands

Many departmental managers within an organisation will be at the same grade as the person in charge of the IT systems. This means that they may have as much say in the design of any new system as the IT manager. This can cause problems since the system eventually developed may not be the one that the IT manager would have chosen. It might be technically complex, in an attempt to meet the demands of all the managers concerned, and as a result go over the time and budget allocated to it. Excessive management demands can cause problems when individual managers take too big a part in the development, continually wanting to change things. Non-IT staff need to be made aware that things cannot be continually changed as the project progresses.

Lack of teamwork

Since most information systems projects are large and cannot be undertaken by one person alone, information systems are usually developed by a project team. Each member of the team is allocated a part of the overall project. In many ways, working as a team member is harder than working individually since you may have to work closely with someone who you do not necessarily get on with. Another problem which can cause friction between team members is the unequal division of the work; some team members could feel that they are having to work much harder than others. If team members start to work as individuals, the whole project becomes very difficult to manage. Without careful monitoring, the project can go wildly out of control and end up being abandoned owing to spiralling costs and missed deadlines.

To work together harmoniously, a project team needs to reach a consensus on the overall aims and goals of the project. The team members should agree on a certain solution to the problem and stick to it. If the project involves a customer, then agreement should also be obtained from them, and the customer should be involved throughout the whole project. A customer who is kept informed in this way is much less likely to be disappointed, and have less cause for complaint if the new system does not match their expectations.

Lack of professional standards

The British Computer Society (BCS) sets minimum standards of practice to be observed by all its members. Many computer professionals are members of the society and membership shows the employer or the person paying for their services that the job will be performed in a professional manner. Not all computer professionals are members of the society; those that are not have no need to conform to the standards. As we saw earlier, some computer professionals are motivated by their own career progression and everything is done with this aim in mind. For example, if such a person needs experience in a certain new area of computing (say, the use of Intranets), they may try to persuade an organisation to get one regardless of whether it is needed, simply so that they can gain experience and add it to their CV. Some 'computer professionals', especially those engaged in contract work, may take on jobs for which they have little experience in the hope that they will 'get the hang of it' once they start work. BCS members are required not to take on any work that they feel they are not competent to perform. Because the financial rewards for computer contractors are so great, there are many contractors who are motivated by greed alone and these people often do a poor job.

CASE STUDY

A new air traffic control system

This true scenario, outlining the problems with a huge IT project, highlights many of the things which can go wrong. It also looks at what could have been done to put things right.

The project concerned is the new air traffic control system for the UK, which was due to become operational in 1999/2000. This system was already four years late when it should have replaced the ageing air traffic control system which was under a lot of pressure with the increased number of flights to and from the UK's airports. The system makes use of large mainframe and minicomputers that had been used for an air traffic control system in America. The software for the new system was developed from scratch and exceeded two million lines of programming code, even though the American system, which copes with a similar volume of air traffic, uses only one million lines of code. In 1995 the programs contained an estimated 21,000 bugs and there were also scalability problems, which meant that although the software worked for about 30 terminals, as the number was increased, the system failed. Most of the bugs were fixed by 2000 but it was not clear at that stage how long the remainder would take to fix.

At a late stage, the system was shown to the operational air traffic controllers who would eventually use the system on a day-to-day basis. These important end users should have been consulted at a much earlier stage and this would have meant fewer changes needing to be made to the system, all of which increased costs and delayed the project further.

At an early stage, the whole system showed signs of a project out of control. These signs included:

* Delays in the delivery of the system meant that the hardware and software would be at least seven years out of date; there is danger of replacing one out-of-date system with another.

* Consulting end users at such a late stage meant that software had to be changed to take account of their views.

* Original deadlines were not met and so revised deadlines were agreed; these revised deadlines were also missed.

* The people who were eventually going to use the system had no confidence in it.

* The project team strongly resisted an independent audit to determine whether the project was being properly and adequately controlled.

Activity   KEY SKILLS C2.3, C3.3, IT2.1, IT3.1

Projects that go drastically wrong are always of interest to computing professionals as they can learn by the mistakes of others. Occasionally, projects are so disastrous that they are newsworthy enough to reach the national newspapers.

Using CD-ROMs of the national newspapers, copies of newspapers such as *Computing* or *Computer Weekly* and the sites for these newspapers on the Internet, identify some interesting stories where projects have gone seriously out of control. Using at least three of these stories, produce an essay explaining the facts surrounding each case. You also need to identify why the projects went wrong. Explain where you got the information from in a bibliography at the end of the essay.

This essay is a substantial piece of work and should go through several revisions before the final version is produced. Your essay should be wordprocessed, spell checked and grammar checked. It should also contain headers and footers on each page containing your name, your group, the date, the title of the essay and the page numbers for each page.

Activity

Answer the following questions.

1 A management information system (MIS) converts the data from internal and external sources into information.

   (a) Explain what is meant by 'internal and external sources'.

   (b) Explain the difference between the terms 'data' and 'information'.

   (c) Describe briefly a MIS you have seen or read about; describe the data input into the system and how output is arranged to give the management information.

2 Many IT projects are started and never completed.

   (a) What are the main reasons for this happening?

   (b) Explain what is meant by the following:

      (i) deliverables

      (ii) milestones.

3 You are required to word a job description for the position of project manager in a large organisation. Using about one quarter of a page, write a job description for this post making sure that you include all of the following:

   - IT skills needed
   - IT knowledge needed
   - management skills needed
   - personal qualities needed.

CASE STUDY

HP Bulmer

HP Bulmer is a medium-sized British company based in Hereford and has been involved in cider making for over 100 years. Cider is an alcoholic drink made from apples; its consumption in the UK is growing at a rate of eight per cent per year. Currently, around 450 million litres per year are consumed. The brands produced by the company include Woodpecker, Max and Woodpecker Red (Figure 12.5).

Around 900 staff are employed, with about 500 using PCs and 50 using terminals. There are around 28 permanent IT staff and seven employed on a contract basis, with the majority of these involved in systems development.

The main activities of the company can be summarised as follows:

- **manufacturing** – making the cider by the fermentation of apples
- **trading and marketing** – dealing with customers who buy the cider and suppliers who supply bottles, labels, equipment, etc.
- **finance** – payment of wages, accounts, etc.
- **distribution** – stock control, dispatch, delivery, etc.

One of the problems that Bulmer had with its old systems was that a large number of appli-

Figure 12.5 *Three of the ciders produced by HP Bulmer*

cations had evolved separately in different areas of the business and this meant that the data from the different areas was not consistent. For instance, instead of a single customer file, there were three: one for order entry, one for invoicing and another for sales outlets (pubs, off-licences, etc.). This meant that the type of information obtained about customers depended on which of the customer files was being used. When the company wanted to produce sales analyses, conflicting results were obtained. It is for this reason that the company decided to rationalise and centralise its customer and product information.

The IT Director had to develop a new system to be controlled centrally but with clear ownership of each application by the department concerned. Steering groups and working parties were set up, consisting of members of staff from all the departments involved. Agreement was reached on all the definitions and concepts used so that everyone knew they were talking about the same thing. All the data for the system is kept in an Oracle data dictionary and the systems development and support teams all use computer-aided system engineer-

ing (CASE) design tools. CASE combines a variety of software tools to assist computer systems development staff in producing and maintaining high quality systems. Oracle, which should not be confused with the teletext service, is a relational database management system suitable for large, multi-user systems.

Within the IT department there are three systems development teams, with each team developing a group of associated applications. These teams cover between them the four core business areas mentioned above. Each team reports to the IT Director as well as to the head of the user department. Budgeting and delivery of the systems is the responsibility of the project sponsor, a senior director of the company.

The main objectives for the new systems include:

- efficient, auditable sales order processing

- accurate monitoring of revenue generation

- efficient distribution

- exploitation of opportunities in the marketplace.

The distribution management system

The distribution management system (DMS) covers sales order processing, warehouse management and distribution. Although the initial development costs were £2 million, the system is already making savings of £400,000 per year.

The distribution operation is large, with over 400 product lines being delivered to the main brewers, the 'big six' supermarkets and outlets such as the smaller off-licences. During heavy trading periods, the company organises the delivery of over 3000 pallets a day on 130 trucks.

Warehouse control

Facilities for controlling goods in the warehouses are available at the Hereford factory as well as the depots throughout the country. The system handles stock location and enables staff to order replacement stock and obtain accurate, up-to-date information on any item of stock in any of the warehouses. The system also helps plan the routes that the delivery lorries have to take and their stops along the way.

Customer service

Telesales staff are all located at the Hereford head office. Their job is to take orders, confirm the availability of goods and confirm delivery dates over the telephone.

At the busiest times, telesales staff take an average of over 1000 orders per day, ranging from a single line to several pages. On receipt of an order, the order details are automatically passed to the warehouse where a picking list is produced, along with the goods' location numbers in the warehouse. A place in the warehouse is also assigned to the pallet on which the goods are placed. Once goods have been placed ready for dispatch, a dispatch note is produced.

The new system has resulted in many benefits besides the obvious financial ones. It is now possible to track all stock movements, and an accurate dispatch note can be produced. Under the old system, the dispatch note was printed before the stock was picked, so it

Figure 12.6 *Inputting telesales orders*

sometimes needed to be amended by hand if part of the order was unavailable. Management information about orders is now vastly improved, and customers are more satisfied with the service they receive.

Profitability management system

An account manager is responsible for the sales and servicing of a group of major customers. To assess its sales success under the old system, Bulmer looked only at the volume of cider sold. However, this was misleading since it did not take into account the profitability of the sales. In the past, sales figures had been easily increased by negotiating a price at which the company was making very little profit. Now the system assesses the account managers on their sales, taking into account how much they have spent on marketing, advertising, special promotions and discounts.

Weekly sales report

A sales report lands on the desk of each director and senior manager every week, and is the most important piece of management information they receive. It presents the sales of each product and expresses them as a percentage of the budget figure.

Electronic data interchange (EDI)

There is now a move away from using paper to transfer information between Bulmer and its main customers. Instead, data is transferred electronically. This is how Bulmer and one of the large supermarket chains use EDI to cut out the use of paper (see Figure 12.7):

- prices for the goods are agreed between Bulmer and the supermarket chain
- Bulmer enters the agreed price on the system
- this price file is sent electronically to the supermarket head office
- there is confirmation that the retailer has received this file

- the retailer can then place an EDI order
- Bulmer loads the vehicles with the pallets containing the order, and as each pallet is loaded, a barcode on the side of the pallet is scanned and the information used to build up a delivery note
- the delivery note is then sent electronically to the retailer
- goods are delivered to the retailer
- the retailer confirms delivery and confirmation is sent using EDI to Bulmer
- when this confirmation is received, Bulmer automatically issues an invoice
- the invoice is automatically paid and money transferred from the retailer's bank account to the Bulmer bank account.

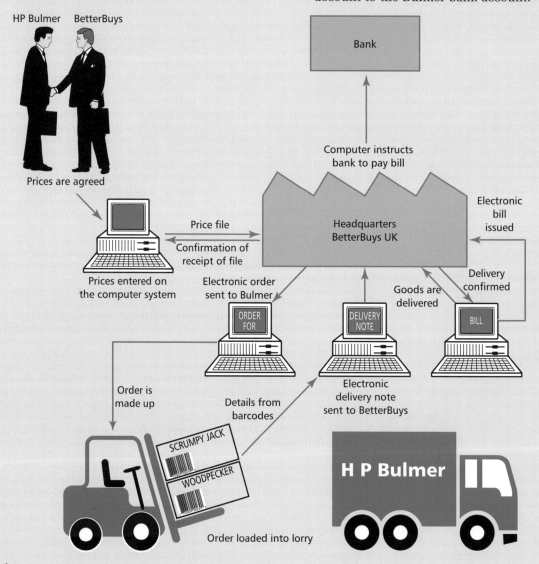

Figure 12.7 *How Bulmer and its main customers use EDI*

The keg information system

Bulmer sells draught cider through tens of thousands of pubs, wine bars and restaurants throughout the UK. The keg technicians are responsible for installing and repairing the equipment needed to dispense the draught cider at the bar. This equipment includes the pump you see on the top of the bar, the cooler unit and all the pipework which goes to the aluminium barrel (keg).

When something goes wrong with the equipment or a new customer needs the equipment installing, a telephone call is made to head office where the scheduling is organised. The schedules for each of the 19 technicians scattered throughout the UK are transferred overnight to the technicians' hand-held terminals.

During the day the technicians record what they have done that day using their hand-held terminals, and this information is relayed back over the telephone lines to Bulmer's head office where the central computer files are updated. Using this system, the technicians are able to deal with more calls each day than under previous systems, and the staff involved in co-ordinating this activity can be engaged in another task. A future development might be to give technicians portable modems in their cars so that the files can be updated in real time. If any problems arise in the course of a day, then the technicians can be alerted and the one closest to the location of the problem can deal with it as soon as their schedule permits.

Process control

The cider-making process at Bulmer's Hereford cider mill was previously carried out by the traditional methods which had changed little since Percy Bulmer founded the business in 1887. Today, the old equipment has been replaced by the latest computer-controlled technology. Cider maker Jonathan Blair now has a computer terminal to assist him in the art of cider-making (see Figure 12.8).

In 1994 the company invested £20 million in a brand new cider-making plant, the most modern of such plants in the world. All the processes such as fermentation, microfiltration (to remove the yeast and make the cider clear) and the movement of the cider around the plant, are controlled by computer. Figure 12.9 shows a production worker checking on the computer the flow of cider, and Figures 12.10 and 12.11 show the inside of the fermentation hall and a view of the 15-metre tall fermentation vessels from the outside. Overlooking the hall is a control room where one person can run several processes from a computer screen.

So that the changeover to the new equipment went as smoothly as possible, staff took part in hands-on simulation courses. Here they could use computers to simulate control of the new system. This meant that any mistakes could be learned from without risking a 230,000-litre batch of cider. Use of the new equipment allows Bulmer to produce a consistent, high quality product at a lower cost.

Figure 12.8 *Cider maker, Jonathan Blair*

Figure 12.9 *A production worker checks the flow of cider on the computer*

Figure 12.10 *Inside the fermentation hall*

Figure 12.11 *Fermentation vessels from the outside*

Activity

1 Bulmer has listed the four main areas of its business as:
   (a) manufacturing
   (b) trading and marketing
   (c) finance
   (d) distribution.

   Using business studies textbooks and information contained in the case study to help you, write a series of short paragraphs outlining which tasks would be performed in each of the above areas.

2 Bulmer identified certain problems with the old systems. Identify which systems they were and how the new system is an improvement.

3 There are several systems identified in the case study. Here are the names of some of them. For each one, decide, with reasons, whether they are data processing systems or management information systems.
   • the sales order processing system
   • the keg information system
   • the distribution management system
   • the profitability management system.

4 Bulmer hopes to use electronic data interchange (EDI) with all its major customers. EDI was mentioned in the case study. Using suitable software, produce a diagram on computer to explain how this works.

Activity

Definition of terms

A variety of terms is introduced in this chapter, many of which may be new to you. It is important that you build up vocabulary that can be used when writing essays or answering questions. Write a definition for each of the following terms used in the chapter:

   data processing system

   information system

   management information system

   EDI

   Oracle

Examination Questions

1 (a) What is the purpose of a Management Information System? (1)

(b) Why is such a system required by managers of an organisation? (1)

(c) Give one example of the use of a Management Information System within an organisation, clearly stating its purpose. (2)

(NEAB, Module IT04, May 97, q1)

2 The management of a company wishes to introduce a computerised diary/scheduling package which is known to be compatible with the existing software base. With the aid of examples, give **three** factors which could influence the success or failure of this exercise.

(NEAB, Module IT04, May 97, q2)

3 (a) What is meant by a Management Information System? (4)

(b) State **four** factors which could contribute to the success or failure of a Management Information System. (4)

(NEAB, Module IT04, May 98, q3)

4 The manager of a local company complains that the company's information system continually fails to provide the correct level of information. State **four** possible reasons, why the system is failing. (4)

(NEAB, Module IT04, May 99, q1)

Information and Data

In Chapter 1 we looked at knowledge, information and data; in this chapter we examine how data is turned into valuable information that is subsequently used by management to help make decisions. For information to be of value to managers it needs to be relevant and it also needs to be correctly interpreted by these managers.

Data

Retailers and banks frequently study their customers to understand how they behave when on their premises. For example, a customer may be followed around the store to see what catches their eye or to investigate any goods they might pick up and then put down again. This observation is carried out alongside interviews with customers to find out about their buying habits etc. Since retailers and banks may have hundreds of branches and the investigation could be performed at any one of them, the study could prove very costly and time consuming.

Real-time image understanding technology

There is a new technology, called 'real-time image understanding technology', that can be used to monitor the activities of customers when on the premises of a retailer or bank. Motion-detecting and tracking technology combined with camera sensors placed throughout the site can watch customers and their buying habits. The data produced is called 'customer activity analysis data' and the following types of information can be collected:

● the numbers of customers entering and leaving during the day

● the accurate location of high traffic areas so that these can be chosen for special offers, notices, etc.

● the number of customers looking at display material or special promotional offers

● the continuous, automatic monitoring of shoppers in each queue so that the manager can be informed immediately if queues are building up and more checkouts should be opened.

Customer interaction mining

All the large multiple retailers collect and analyse transaction data so that they can understand their current stock position and so improve on their stock system. Many retailers now collect data about product returns, customer inquiries, price checks and customer complaints. Even those customers who do not buy anything may have their browsing behaviour examined by the system mentioned above. Customer interaction data is sales data plus all the other data to do with a customer's relationship with a retailer. The term 'customer interaction mining' means the analysis of the customer interaction data to gain insight into retail customers' behaviour.

Characteristics and classifications of information

There are many ways in which information can be classified; it can be classified according to:

● the source of the information

● the level of the information

● the time the information relates to

- the nature of the information
- the frequency with which the information is supplied
- the use to which the information will be put
- the form of the information
- the type of information.

Let us look at these in greater detail.

The source of the information

Information can be categorised according to whether it comes from within the organisation (internal information) or from outside (external information).

Internal or external information

Examples of internal information include:

- staff rotas
- customer credit limits
- details of overdue accounts
- forecast of next year's profit.

Examples of external information include:

- marketing information from a questionnaire sent to all customers
- budget information on changes to the tax system
- details of the Data Protection Act.

When you are deciding whether information is internal or external, you need to know from whose point of view the information is being considered. So an electricity bill is internal information from the point of view of the electricity board, but external information from the point of view of the customer to whom the bill is sent.

Activity

Here are some sources of information. You have to decide whether they are internal or external sources. The context of the information is shown in the table. Copy the table and complete the final column to show whether the information is internal or external. The first row of the table has been completed for you.

Type of information	Context	Internal or external?
Telephone bill	A school	External
A list of all the estate agents in an area, obtained from the Yellow Pages	A company who sell specialist legal software	
A copy of the 1998 Data Protection Act	The IT department of a hospital	
A list of a companies ten best customers	Obtained from the sales processing system	
A purchase order placed with a supplier	The purchasing department	
A purchase order placed with a supplier	The supplier's order processing department	
A product price list	Given to the sales staff	
Notices of employees' tax codes	Given to the payroll department	
Completed questionnaires about the quality of the service	Handed out by an airline	

The level of information

There are three main levels of information, categorising it according to the purpose to which the information is put. Although the levels depend on an organisation's structure, it is often the case that one person's data is another person's information at a different level. The three levels of information are strategic, tactical and operational.

Strategic information

Strategic information is used by senior managers and the board of directors for making strategic decisions, such as the development of new products or services, the acquisition and sale of new premises, the numbers of staff employed, and so on. Senior staff members are responsible for steering the business and they determine the overall direction the organisation takes in the future. To do this they have to be provided with strategic information.

Tactical information

Tactical information combines information and instructions from the strategic level of management with operational information.

Tactical information is more detailed than strategic information, but is still summarised.

It is mainly the middle managers of a business who use the tactical information. Many of them, as well as being responsible for their particular functional areas, are also involved in some short- to medium-term planning.

Operational information

Operational information is passed down from the tactical level above and this is used mainly for the day-to-day management of the operations side of the business, such as the planning of resources and organisation of manpower. Information at the operational level must be detailed and precise. Much of the information dealt with at this level is fairly routine and deals mainly with problems occurring with particular transactions.

Activity   KEY SKILLS IT2.1, IT3.1

Here is a list of some information; you have to decide whether it comes under the category strategic, tactical or operational.

1 Marketing information concerning whether an Internet Bookstore should start selling cars

2 An individual's sales figures used to review their performance

3 Information regarding the acquisition of another company

4 Planning a staff rota to cover the Christmas holiday period

5 Information concerning the launch of a new product

6 Information for the directors concerning the proposed dividend payments to shareholders

7 Job allocation to production workers in a factory

8 Sales figures about a new product, used to assess its market share

9 Details of employees' pay at the end of the month's payroll run

10 Details of the number of phone calls made to a computer help desk

11 Stock lists used to identify those products that need re-ordering

12 The new National Insurance scales following a budget.

The time the information relates to

Information can be classified according to the time period to which it belongs. We can put information into the following classifications: historical, current and future.

Historical information

Historical information is past information; all companies and organisations need to keep this to sort out queries that may not have been spotted at the time. Apart from this, many organisations use historical information for planning or for making comparisons. For example, a manufacturing company might wish to compare the sales of one product in a certain period with similar periods in other years.

There is a legal requirement under the Companies Act for companies to keep proper records of past transactions for accounting purposes. Increasingly, companies are keeping information about the people they deal with and this is added to the huge amount of information already kept.

Current information

Information comes to us in many different forms. It may be written, visual, aural (spoken) or in other sensory forms. In business written communication is very important because there is evidence on what has been agreed. As more business is done over the telephone, aural information is more direct and quicker. In e-commerce, the information is transmitted electronically and more transactions are set to be conducted in such a way.

Future information

Future information is about what is likely to happen in the future. We can never be sure about this, so it is a forecast. This is the least accurate of the types of information and is usually used for making planning decisions, such as how many staff are needed to cope with the increase in business, or the change in production required to accommodate a predicted change in demand.

The nature of the information

Primary or secondary information

Another way of categorising the source of the information is to divide it into primary and secondary information. Primary information is collected directly from an information source. The value of sales in a certain month, obtained from department invoices, would be classed as primary information.

Secondary information is collected indirectly; for example, collecting marketing information from customers who are ordering goods. If a company wants to know whether it is paying its IT staff the market rate, it could contact IT departments in other companies directly to see how much they are paying. This would then be primary information. It is difficult to do this however, so instead the company might contact an organisation that collects information about salaries and obtain the information indirectly from them.

Quantitative or qualitative information

Information can be classified according to whether it is quantitative or qualitative. Quantitative information can be measured in numerical terms. The total value of sales in a year, a person's age, the exchange rate from pounds to dollars, are all classed as quantitative information. Qualitative information is usually difficult or even impossible to measure numerically, so other ways of describing it need to be used. For example, the morale of a project team, customer satisfaction, customer loyalty would all be classed as qualitative information. Qualitative information tends to be concerned with opinions, so it usually depends on the experience and judgement of the person supplying the information.

Computer systems are better suited to dealing with quantitative information, since it may be built into mathematical models and used in mathematical formulae.

Formal or informal information

Information can also be classified according to whether it is formal or informal. Formal information is usually generated in companies from their management information system in the form of reports. Such reports are circulated to the relevant members of staff and the results influence decisions which affect the planning and strategy of the organisation. Other methods of communicating information in a formal manner include memos, newsletters, agendas and minutes of meetings.

Sometimes, in order to reduce bureaucracy, information is communicated by face-to-face meetings or over the telephone. Such information is classed as informal information.

The frequency with which the information is supplied

Some information, such as printouts of current stock items, can be printed out on a daily basis, whereas other information, such as sales figures, are produced on a weekly or even monthly basis. Other information, such as the company accounts, are generated on a quarterly and annual basis. More and more systems operate in real time (i.e. the information is automatically updated according to the transactions taking place), and the information supplied using such systems is always up to date. Although this sounds simple, in practice few organisations are able to supply information immediately because not all the systems on which the information depends are able to interact with each other.

The use to which the information will be put

Information may be used for planning, control or decision making.

The form of the information

Information we receive comes in many different forms. It can be written, visual, oral (spoken), or in other sensory forms such as smell and taste. In business, written communication is very important because it provides physical evidence of the information it contains. However, oral communication, especially via the telephone, is more direct and quicker. E-commerce combines the advantages of both these modes of communication, and an increasing number of transactions are set to be conducted in this way.

The type of information

Information needs to be detailed if it is to be dealt with at an operational level. It may also be aggregated if the information needs to be collected from several sources. Sometimes a sample of information is collected which is used to represent the population as a whole.

The characteristics of good information and delivery

All successful information systems are able to supply good information. Information should have the following characteristics if it is to be useful.

Information must be relevant

Only information relevant to the required purpose should be supplied, as this saves the user spending time extracting what they want from reams of reports or printouts. When supplying information, it is important that it is not 'padded out' with unnecessary material to make it look more substantial. Management often only needs an overview of the situation, in which case too much detail is superfluous.

Information must be accurate

Information has to be accurate because in most cases it will be used for decision making. Often decisions have to be made using incomplete information, and this may be sufficient provided the limited information is accurate. It is also possible for the information to be too precise. For example, invoices have to be accurate and precise to the penny, but when quoting monthly sales figures these can be rounded off to the nearest one hundred or one thousand pounds (in some large companies even to the nearest one hundred thousand pounds). The main reason for this is that these figures need to be discussed at meetings and used in simple arithmetic calculations. As well as actually being correct, information supplied should be authoritative, which means that the people using the information have faith in its correctness and are happy to base decisions on it.

Information must be complete

It is hard in any organisation to base decisions on incomplete information. For example, a customer may ring up and order some goods, which a salesperson says will be delivered the next day. If the salesperson does not have a stock list, they have incomplete information regarding the stock position. It is important that the salesperson has all the relevant facts when taking orders.

Information must have the user's confidence

If the user spots that some of the information they are using is obviously wrong, they will probably lose confidence in the system that produced it. For the user to have confidence, all the facts and figures must be correct.

Information must be presented to the right person

Information from any information system should be provided only to those people who are in the most appropriate position to use it. Giving such information to everyone wastes time and effort and may even cause problems, because some of the people who did not need the information may feel compelled to do something with it.

Information must be presented at the right time

Sales figures should be circulated before a sales meeting so that they can be studied, referred to and used for decision making. Without information at the right time, wrong decisions can be made. Many decisions must be made quickly and management information systems should be able to accommodate this.

Information should be presented in the right detail

Senior management frequently receives reports containing detailed figures and diagrams when all that is really needed is an overview of the situation. The lower the level of management, the more detailed the information needs to be. The lowest level of management only needs details of daily operations to make decisions about scheduling, stock control, payroll, staff rotas, etc. Top managers and directors should not have to wade through mountains of detail when summary reports and exception reports are all that is needed.

Information should be supplied via the correct channel of communication

All the best organisations have one thing in common. They all have well-managed channels of communication through which all information passes quickly between the people who need it. Communication channels include formal reports, memos, telephone calls, face-to-face conversations, meetings, e-mail, fax and videoconferencing. Companies are increasingly using EDI (electronic data interchange) where the computer controls the flow of both internal and external information between a customer and a supplier.

Information must be understandable

The meaning of any information should be clear to the user. Any abbreviations or codes should be explained. Information cannot be used properly unless it is fully understood and it is important that information is unambiguous otherwise it could lead to members at a meeting talking at crossed purposes.

CASE STUDY

British Telecom digging deep: a data mining case study

British Telecom has 1.5 million business customers making 87 million calls per day and using around 4500 products. Keeping track of this huge amount of data for marketing purposes is an immense task. BT wanted to examine the requirements of individual customers, but to do this, it was necessary to hold large amounts of data about each customer, and to find a way of searching through this data for patterns.

Initially BT set up an ordinary database and a management information system, but sales and marketing personnel found they could not submit *ad hoc* queries to the system and obtain replies in a reasonable timescale. BT eventually decided that a data mining facility was needed. It also decided to outsource the data warehouse (the huge central collection of data) to a company with experience in the field. The hardware to run the data mining application uses multiple processing technology which allowed BT to fit all its data into one very large memory.

After a period of outsourcing, BT eventually went back to developing its own in-house data warehouse because it had a better understanding of the data. The hardware which BT eventually bought consisted of: 170 parallel processors providing 2.5 GB of RAM. The power of this hardware reduced the time needed to obtain query results from hours or minutes to just seconds.

The data mining system, with its speed of reply, gave the sales and marketing department the ability to conduct well-targeted customer campaigns which paid for the cost of the data warehouses between 20 and 50 times over in its first year.

One of the senior BT managers said 'We are able to identify purchasing profiles for individual products as well as those customers who could be at risk to competitors such as cable companies'.

Before the system was introduced, the sales team did not have much faith in the data obtained from the marketing department, since it was little different from the impression they could form for themselves. Now, both sales and marketing can employ the user-friendly GUI to build and navigate queries and to drill down through the data to discover additional sales and marketing opportunities which were previously hidden.

Information flows

In a manufacturing company there are typically the following functional areas:

- sales and marketing
- purchasing
- production, stores and distribution
- accounts and finance
- research and development
- personnel.

Information needs to flow within and between functional areas and the efficiency with which these flows take place is a measure of the efficiency of the whole organisation.

The main concern of the sales and marketing department is to sell the products to customers. To do this, the company has to make sure that the goods they are making satisfy a market need and that they are priced competitively compared with similar products.

In most cases the customer places an order, but before it is accepted, the person taking the order checks with the stores that the order can be satisfied. Once the order is accepted, a confirmation is sent to the customer and the accounts department is sent a copy of the order, so that an invoice can be raised and sent to the customer. At the same time, the accounts department might check on the credit-worthiness of the customer if they require credit or, if they are an existing customer, determine whether they have satisfactorily settled their previous account. The system in place for dealing with sales generates management information as the transactions are made, and this is used by management for such things as comparing actual sales with targeted sales. Any problems that arise can also be dealt with on an *ad hoc* basis. For example, a customer's purchasing department might place a large order before paying a previous invoice; a decision then needs to be taken whether to extend the customer's credit.

To make sure that the production department always has components in stock, ready to be assembled into the finished article, the purchasing department needs information about outstanding orders and the current stock situation so that goods and materials can be replenished. When stocks fall below the minimum stock level, an order is made to the suppliers and a copy is sent to the accounts department so that it can anticipate payment to the suppliers when an invoice is received and falls due. Again, management is kept informed of any problems that arise.

The production, stores, and distribution functions have the task of making sure that components are always available in stock to keep the production department going. Once the goods are made they need to be stored until they are picked according to a customer's order, packed and then despatched.

Balancing the speed of producing information with its accuracy

Management at all levels needs information on which to base decisions. These decisions might be concerned with controlling, organising or planning but they all need to be based on information that can be relied on to be up to date and correct. As well as the timeliness of obtaining information and its reliability, the completeness and relevance of the information are equally important.

Sometimes historical information is needed, such as the numbers of students who started a course, the number who left and the number who passed their exams, along with their attendance records. This information might be needed by the senior managers in a college to assess the quality of various courses. Such information would have to be collected by members of staff, then passed to senior managers. Time would normally be needed to collate all the information, but if there were insufficient time for this, the people involved would have to guess at the figures. This illustrates how in some situations you can have a conflict between speed and accuracy. At other times there is no such conflict because the organisation knows well in advance that the information will be needed so accurate results can be available at the right time. An example of

this would be producing the end-of-year accounts for a business.

In situations where information is needed for control purposes (such as in production or quality control) then speed and accuracy are important to avoid costly delays or poor quality.

Information is also needed for planning purposes and in some cases this information may be collected over a very long period (in some cases years).

Accuracy of information costs money and this cost has to be justified in terms of benefits obtained from the higher degree of accuracy. If the benefits of having more accurate information do not outweigh the costs of producing it, there is no justification for having that degree of accuracy.

Causes of delays in information flows

There are many causes of delays in information systems. The following are the commonest.

The structure of the organisation

Hierarchical structures within an organisation can cause delays in information flow since information has to move up and down through the many levels of management. As more people deal with the information and decisions permeate through more levels to reach the staff lower in the organisation, the whole process takes longer. Flat structures have fewer layers of management so the information flows are simpler and quicker.

The production of reports

Reports are printouts obtained by applying search criteria to a database or other information system. Some reports are complex and demand a lot of processing time. Once a report is produced, it must be checked and then copied before being distributed. This takes time, and problems with the printer, photocopier and distribution (i.e. the internal or external mail) often delay flow of this important information.

The data processing cycle

Data capture is the first stage in the data processing cycle. Breakdown in data capture hardware such as optical character readers, bar code readers, etc. causes delay in the capture of the data and hence in the production of summary information at the end of a processing run.

The volume of data being processed

Certain times of the year (such as Christmas) can result in unusually high volumes of transactions. Processing of these transactions has to be given priority at these times and the time devoted to this can cause disruptions to other information flows.

The software

Software can be pushed to the limit by users' demands for more information. Sometimes these demands cannot be satisfied unless a programmer uses 'fancy programming tricks' to enable the software to do something it was not really designed to do.

Methods of data capture

Data capture involves getting information into a form that can be processed by a computer. There are various methods of data capture, each with their own advantages and disadvantages. The choice of method depends on many factors. Before looking at the methods available, we will consider what properties the ideal method of data capture would have. The ideal method would:

- be accurate to ensure the integrity of the data stored

- be fast

- not involve high labour costs – this usually means that the method needs to be automatic

- need only cheap equipment.

Unfortunately there is no single method of data capture that satisfies all the above conditions, so the choice of method is usually a compromise.

By far the commonest way of capturing data is by inputting it via the keyboard but this is slow and inaccurate and also expensive because of the wage costs. If a large quantity of data has to be input quickly, the keyboard could be too slow so other methods of data capture must be investigated. Data can be collected more accurately and cheaply with computer-readable documents using such techniques as MICR (magnetic ink character recognition), OCR (optical character recognition), OMR (optical mark recognition) or by using voice recognition.

Sometimes data from one system is stored on magnetic media and then transferred to another system using the magnetic storage as the input to the other system. This method eliminates the need to re-enter data and means that extra errors are not introduced in the process.

If a large amount of data needs to be collected, it is essential that this is done on a document that can be input directly into the information system. Completed questionnaires should fall into this category. Provided the questions are worded properly, questionnaires are a very good way of assessing customers' opinions; large quantities of such questionnaires can be very useful from a marketing point of view. The quality of the information obtained from such processing is very high.

Accuracy checks

To make sure that computer output is accurate, it is necessary to check that the input data is correct. There are various ways of ensuring the integrity of the data and these can be divided into verification checks and validation checks. These have been covered in Chapter 6, but let us look at these again.

Verification of input data

Verification means checking the input data before it is accepted by the computer for processing. In many cases, verification consists of comparing the input with the original document to ensure that the data matches. In other words, the input is proof-read. It is important to note that this does not necessarily mean that the input is correct, since all that is being checked is that what is on the source document matches exactly what has been entered. The information on the source document could have been incorrect; for example, a customer might have filled in an order form using an out-of-date catalogue. The verification check only ensures that no typing errors have been introduced at the keyboard entry stage.

Another method of verification involves two people typing in the same data; if the two sets of data are identical they will be accepted for further processing. The problem with this is that two people need to be paid for doing the same job, and, although unlikely, it is possible they might make identical errors which therefore go unnoticed.

Validation of input data

Validation is a check to ensure that data being entered meets certain criteria. It is impossible to be completely sure that the data is correct; a name could be misspelt each time and no amount of validation checks would detect this. However, validation checks can trap some of the likely errors and go some way to making sure that the data is accurate. Validation checks are sometimes performed as part of a separate program, although many databases such as Microsoft Access enable the user to specify certain characteristics of the data to be entered into each field.

There is a variety of validation checks, including:

- **Range checks** – the input data is compared with pre-determined upper and lower values to make sure that it lies somewhere between the two. If an item of data falls outside the range the user is alerted so that it can be checked.

- **Data type checks** – these make sure that the correct type of data is entered into certain fields. You can specify fields as numeric, character, date or logical. If you try to enter a letter into a field which has been specified as numeric, the program will not accept it. It is important that numeric fields are only specified if they are to contain the sorts of numbers that could have calculations performed on them. So order numbers (like 004564) and telephone numbers should be placed in character fields.

- **Existence checks** – some fields must always be filled in whereas others are optional. All people have a date of birth but not everyone has a telephone number.

- **Consistency checks** – these check one data item against another to ensure consistency. When a customer orders goods from a catalogue, for instance, and the order details are entered into a processing system, the computer could check that the price and catalogue number entered are consistent with those already stored.

Audit mechanisms used to manage the data capture

All computer systems which process transactions involving money need to be audited. An audit is a check to make sure that the results from the computer are correct and that they haven't been interfered with in any way. Auditing prevents fraud and often acts as a deterrent against crime.

Auditing with a paper-based system is relatively easy, since it is possible to trace individual transactions through their various stages of processing. An auditor (the person who performs the audit) can trace an order through the different stages to the point at which payment is made to the supplier.

Many financial transactions which take place using computers do so with little or no paperwork, so the traditional method cannot be used. Instead, the computer provides what is known as an audit trail. An audit trail is a record of the file updating that takes place during a specific transaction. It enables all operations that have taken place to be checked from the records on file.

An audit trail allows the auditor to pick a transaction at random, and check that the transaction has gone through the correct processes, that any money has gone into the correct accounts and that any output or reports produced by the system are correct. It is also possible to pick a balance or total, and identify all the transactions that have been used to calculate it.

Effective presentation of information

All information should be conveyed in such a way that the intended audience is able to understand it. The presentation of the information must be appropriate to the level of those who are to use it.

Presentation of database reports

Database reports no longer consist of the contents of entire databases printed on poor quality paper by a dot-matrix printer. Today, successful information systems need to present information in the most effective manner. Only selected information should be supplied, and this should be grouped logically (in alphabetical order, numerical order, date order, etc.). The report should be printed using an easy-to-read font and be of high quality, which usually means using a laser printer.

Printed information from a computer is usually presented in the form of reports. There are various types of report, and some reports combine more than one type. The main types are described below.

Operational reports

Operational reports are needed on a day-to-day basis; they are essential for the successful running of the organisation. They are usually provided at regular intervals and include daily work in progress, weekly sales figures, daily stock reports, lists of debtors, etc.

Summary reports

Summary reports provide a summary of the data held in a database. Nearly all management reports are summary reports because managers do not want to waste time searching through huge volumes of data for the items which interest them. Examples of summary reports include the sales figures for a certain product and a list of customers who owe money after a certain date.

Exception reports

To be able to make forecasts, senior managers of organisations need to know about current trends. Managers tend to be more interested in the unusual than the usual. So, for example, they would be more interested in customers whose payments are overdue than those who have paid. Successful information systems should be able to differentiate between normal and exceptional situations, and exception reports are usually required by management to help with decision making.

Other examples of exception reports include a list of customers who have exceeded their credit limits, sales which are beyond those forecast and lists of goods which have been in stock for more than one year.

Data grouping in reports

A data grouping report takes data from a variety of sources and groups it together into a single report. For instance, one of the directors of a company may wish to visit their ten best customers in the north of England. This information could require consulting the customer file (their names and addresses) and the sales file (the sales figures).

Presentational graphics

Presentational graphics packages are used to create artwork and pictures, perhaps for use in a slide presentation or, increasingly, to be presented in an electronic format. Such material is mainly created and stored as bitmap images.

Text charts

When concepts can be better conveyed in words than pictures, text charts make useful handouts or slides for a presentation. Text charts are ideal for making comparisons or presenting the benefits and drawbacks of a particular issue. When text is used in this way it is often a good idea to present information as a bulleted list.

Graph charts

These are used mainly for numerical information. Rather than simply listing numbers, it is better to make them visually appealing by presenting the information as bar charts, pie charts, etc. You can more easily make comparisons by placing charts alongside each other; you might, for example, compare the monthly sales figures over one year with those for the next year.

Many spreadsheet packages have a graphics facility. The user simply enters the numbers and selects the appropriate type of chart; the graph is then produced automatically.

Figure 13.1 shows pie charts that illustrate turnover profile over two years.

Slide shows

Using presentation graphics, it is possible to develop a slide show that consists of a series of slides presented on a computer screen. The software also enables you to print charts onto transparencies or slide film (the latter needs special equipment) for presentation using an overhead or slide projector. You can, of course, also print the slides onto paper for use in handouts. With a colour printer you can make the slides very eye-catching.

Pictures

Slides produced using presentation graphics packages often utilise images such as photographs that have been scanned in, clip art, company logos, graphs, charts, etc.

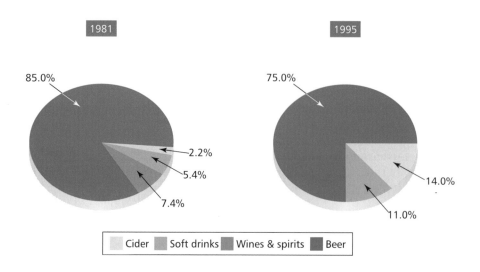

Figure 13.1 *Pie charts illustrating UK drinks turnover profile 1981–1995*

CASE STUDY

HP Bulmer sells itself

HP Bulmer is the UK's largest cider producer. Company presentations are regularly given to the City, potential and existing customers and to the company's own staff. To meet the wide range of presentation demands, Bulmer has developed a system for producing presentations. Because of the high costs involved in sending presentation material to outside agencies, the company is now able to produce the material itself. The reputation of a company rests on how others see it, so good presentations are vital.

Bulmer now has a presentation graphics unit with equipment for scanning in photographs, usually of the company's products but sometimes of the various processes and equipment used in cider-making. A high specification PC is used to prepare material on a 37-inch screen and this is then printed on a colour laser printer. Staff in other departments are also able to produce work on their own PCs using a package called Freelance and then use the network to transfer their work to the presentation graphics department for colour laser printing. As well as providing colour output on paper, the unit also produces acetates for overhead projectors and 35 mm slides. The unit can produce slides for use on liquid crystal display (LCD) projector which is used in larger presentations to project a computer screen onto a large white screen.

The department is staffed by two graphics analysts who work on their own projects as well as checking on the material from other departments to ensure that it is of a high standard.

The cost of sending the material to an outside agency used to be around £200,000 per year; doing the task within the company has reduced this to about £70,000 per year.

TASKS

Graphic presentations

HP Bulmer, the cider manufacturer in the Case Study, has its own presentation graphics department. You have just started working in this department as a trainee analyst and have been given the following task.

The task is to produce presentation graphics to illustrate the information shown in the table below, which describes how the cider market has grown over eight years. As well as showing the growth of cider sales overall, it also shows the market share between draught cider (cider from pumps on the bar top) and packaged cider (bottles, cans, flagons, etc.). The title of your graph/graphs should be 'Cider market growth'.

Year	Draught (million gallons)	Packaged (million gallons)	Total cider (million gallons)
1988	28.7	36.3	65.0
1989	26.6	34.6	61.2
1990	30.4	39.2	69.6
1991	31.9	44.6	76.4
1992	30.8	45.0	75.8
1993	32.9	52.3	85.2
1994	33.9	58.0	92.0
1995	36.2	63.4	99.6
1996	38.6	76.1	114.8

TASK 1

Using the information in the table, plot the three sets of data using a single set of axes. The 'time' axis (the one for the years) should be horizontal while the vertical axis should be used for 'volume of cider'. You may use either spreadsheet or presentation graphics software. If you are unable to plot the three sets of data on the same set of axes, you should draw three separate graphs with suitable labels. Remember to label the axes and add a legend to distinguish between the lines. Save your graphs and print them out.

TASK 2

You have now been asked to draw some conclusions about the graphs you produced, in particular to comment on the following:

- What are the long-term trends in each of the three graphs and what fine detail do they show?

- Are there any differences between the growth in popularity of packaged and draught ciders?
- Are there any two consecutive years between which the growth has been more substantial than between others?

You have been asked to present your findings on an overhead projector acetate. You should use a bulleted list and the guidelines that follow, given to you by the analyst.

The analyst has also suggested that you use some bitmap images of the company logo and/or some scanned images of the company's products, such as labels from their main brands. She has included some of the images for you to scan. You can, if you like, get some labels off bottles and try to scan your own in; remember that the cider must be a Bulmer product. (When you have finished, be careful disposing of the bottle contents!) You may need to alter the size and positions of the images.

Guidelines for overhead projector presentation

Simplicity

Keep the information on the slide simple. Research has shown that there should be no more than six words per line and six lines per slide. The tendency is to put too much detail on the slides and use them as notes rather than as a presentation of the main points.

Brevity

In a presentation most listeners can retain only between three and five brief points. Any more could bore or confuse your audience.

Language

Keep the language simple and avoid the use of any specialist jargon which might be known only to a few of the audience.

Notes

Do not use the graphics for notes. People do not want to see reams of text and if they do need notes, it is best if you give them copies after the presentation so that they can refer back to them.

Graphics charts

Try to present numerical information in a more interesting way than just a list. Use bar, pie, line and other charts to help get the figures across to your audience.

Fonts

Don't mix too many fonts on the same diagram and do not over-use upper case (capital letters). Use both upper and lower case letters.

When you are happy with your slide, save and print it. If you worked for Bulmer you would have the luxury of outputting your acetate using a colour laser printer; however, you should simply show your tutor the graphic on screen to demonstrate how you have used colour.

Activity

Definition of terms

A variety of terms is introduced in this chapter, many of which may be new to you. It is important that you build up vocabulary that can be used when writing essays or answering questions. Write a definition for each of the following terms used in the chapter:

external information

internal information

primary information

secondary information.

1 A manager uses a bespoke application which cannot produce reports in the exact format required but does allow the export of information to a spreadsheet. The manager uses this facility to export the information, improves the layout of the information and produces several graphs. This takes her several days. On presenting the reports to colleagues she is questioned over the accuracy of the information as many figures appear to be out of date. Describe how this problem may be overcome.

(NEAB, Module IT04, Specimen paper, q4)

2 'The quality of management information is directly related to its timing.'

(a) Discuss this statement paying particular reference to:

- the different purposes for which the information may be required;

- the relative merits of speed versus accuracy. *(6)*

(b) In planning the information flow within a system, where are the delays likely to occur and why? *(6)*

(NEAB, Module IT04, Specimen paper, q9)

3 A sales manager claims that he is always provided with 'quality' management information from his Management Information System.

With the aid of examples where appropriate, describe **five** characteristics of good information. *(10)*

(NEAB, Module IT04, May 98, q8)

4 Information systems are capable of producing strategic and operational level information. With the aid of examples, explain the difference between these two levels of information, clearly stating the level of personnel involved in using each one. *(6)*

(NEAB, Module IT04, May 99, q3)

14 Legal and Security Aspects

▸ To understand the legal aspects of IT within an organisation

▸ To understand the need for a corporate information technology security policy

▸ To appreciate the importance of subjecting IT applications to an audit

▸ To understand the need for disaster recovery management

▸ To look at the way that the current legislation is enforced within organisations

Introduction

There are many legal considerations which regulate the use, by companies, of IT equipment, programs and data. In this chapter we look at the way legislation influences how organisations operate. We also look at security problems raised by these legal obligations along with what companies can do to make staff aware of the need for security, and what action organisations can take to minimise any loss which occurs.

Question

Some laws are specially aimed at the use of IT. Name all the laws that an IT professional should know about.

Corporate IT security policy

All good companies maintain strict security to protect their competitive advantage, ensure that the company's quality image is upheld and protect from unauthorised disclosure any personal information kept about their customers and staff.

As organisations become more IT-dependent in their day-to-day operations, the availability,

integrity, and confidentiality of the information stored is of paramount importance. It is therefore necessary to protect these systems, in a cost-effective manner, with appropriate levels of security.

Information systems are vulnerable to two threats, **accidental** and **deliberate damage**. Accidental threats include human error, fire, failure of equipment, and natural disasters (floods, earthquakes, etc.); deliberate threats include fraud, sabotage, vandalism, arson and espionage. These threats can come from within the organisation or from outside.

To deal with these threats, all organisations should have a corporate information technology security policy. This policy should be produced by, and have the backing of, the senior management and directors. The corporate IT security policy is a document covering all aspects of security within an organisation. It also contains conditions and rules that need to be obeyed by all staff.

Misunderstandings about what employees are required to do will occur unless the communication between the management and other staff are of the highest standard. It is therefore desirable for organisations to spell out to employees what is acceptable and unacceptable behaviour with respect to computers and IT systems. Many organisations have a document called an 'information technology policy statement' that covers all aspects of computer operations, and which all users are expected to read and then sign to say that they have understood and agree to abide by it. Some organisations go further than this and have training courses covering the corporate IT security policy. Such courses tell employees what they can and cannot do and also give some insight into the reasoning behind the rules. Courses often explore the Computer Misuse Act and the Data Protection Act, and generally raise awareness of the threats to the information held by the organisation.

There are many things a corporate IT security policy should address, a few of which are covered next.

Human error

What happens if I press this button?

Equipment error

Natural disasters (floods, fire, earthquakes, etc)

Deliberate acts (fraud, vandalism, arson, espionage, etc)

Figure 14.1 *Accidental and deliberate threats*

Prevention of misuse

There are many things an IT manager can do to prevent misuse. For example, not letting users gain access to the operating system can prevent almost everyone from deleting (deliberately or accidentally) certain key files. The use of **firewalls** can prevent users accessing undesirable parts of the Internet and these are particularly useful in separating legitimate from unauthorised Internet usage.

There are many physical security methods that prevent unauthorised access to the machines as well as logical security methods, such as the use of passwords that limit a user's access to certain programs and files only.

Detection

It is one thing to talk about misuse of computers, but quite hard to detect such abuse, since staff will try to hide it.

As we will see later, management has to make sure that there are adequate provisions for audit trails that can be used to detect fraud. Some systems make use of sophisticated computer audit fraud detection models that look for abnormal activities in business transactions. They are then able to take action quickly to minimise any further damage.

With networks, the network operating systems usually provide an access log to show the network administrator who is using which files. Some systems allow the network manager to see exactly what any user is doing on his screen. In this way they can see if staff are playing computer games or loading unsavoury material from the Internet.

Investigation

When IT resources are scattered around a building, or even over a wider areas, it is hard for the person in charge of IT security to ensure that all hardware and software is being used in accordance with the corporate IT security policy.

Once a security breach has been detected, it is necessary to make sure action is taken. In many cases the action taken will have the force of the contract of employment or security policy that all employees have signed. Any punishment will act as a deterrent to others, but it is extremely important to make sure that the whole matter is dealt with fairly. If one person is punished for loading and using unauthorised software on their machine, the organisation needs to be fairly sure that this person has not been singled out when such activities are commonplace across the whole organisation. When members of staff are disciplined in this way, industrial relations can become strained but if staff are treated fairly, other employees usually see the need for the organisation to take appropriate action.

Before taking any disciplinary action the organisation needs to be certain that the right person has been accused. Sometimes the police have to be involved and on occasions the organisation will know that the money is going missing but not know who is committing the fraud. In examples such as this, the police can work undercover within the organisation by pretending to be ordinary employees. Most network operating systems can identify who has altered files and many employees will not be aware of this or that it can be used to investigate any suspicions.

Procedures used to prevent security problems

A variety of operating procedures are available to help prevent security problems. For example, each user can be given a code of practice that outlines things that they must do when accessing information.

Procedures such as preventing access to operational data and programs by development staff (programmers and systems analysts) are desirable to prevent the opportunity for fraud.

Procedures such as rotation of staff duties are also used to prevent fraud, since it is less likely for two people to conspire at fraud, so one may discover any previous fraud.

Staff responsibilities

When staff use IT facilities, they incur a variety of computing and legal responsibilities. An organisation is responsible for the acts of its employees when they are at work, so it is important that all staff are aware of what these responsibilities are. Even if an organisation does not know about the acts of some of its employees in breaking the law, it can still be held liable. This happens if it can be proved that the organisation has not taken sufficient steps to prevent the illegal activity.

Disciplinary procedures

Disciplinary procedures should be put in place by the managers and put into effect should all else fail. It is obviously much better if staff members voluntarily comply with all aspects of the corporate IT security policy, but if not staff need to understand what the likely consequences of their action will be.

Examples of disciplinary regulations are as follows:

- Using the organisation's computers for the playing of games is not permissible, and the penalty for non-compliance is first a written warning followed by dismissal if the first warning is not heeded.

- Computer disks containing data or programs are not allowed to be taken out of, or brought into, the organisation without the written permission of the IT manager. The penalty for non-compliance is first a written warning and if this is not heeded, dismissal.

Many organisations operate a series of sanctions that they apply. These sanctions differ in their severity and are usually applied in the following order:

1 a spoken warning given by a manager
2 a written warning
3 the suspension or termination of a person's contract
4 police involvement.

Activity

You have been asked to draw up a list of things which are not allowed in the school's or college's computer room or when using the computer equipment. You should state specifically what is not allowed and state the penalty for not obeying the rules.

The contents of a typical corporate information technology security policy

A typical policy would include the following:

1 **The need for security**
   This section explains to the readers (i.e. usually all members of staff) why good security is necessary. It also identifies some threats to the organisation's information systems. If staff realise the need for security measures, they will take them more seriously.

2 **Policy objectives**
   Here an organisation lists the objectives, such as:

   - to ensure that company officials and employees are aware of, and fully comply with, all the relevant UK legislation
   - to provide a means of identifying unauthorised access, actual or attempted, to data and resources and a framework for taking appropriate action.

3 **The scope of the policy**
   This states how far the policy goes and mentions some of the areas covered. It could include such material as, 'It is the policy of the organisation to ensure that contingency plans for security emergencies are drawn up, kept under review and periodically tested'.

4 **The responsibilities for security**
   Outlined here are the responsibilities of members of staff employed by the organisation, and contractors who provide services to the organisation.

5 **Implementation**
   In this (usually large) section, an organisation outlines how it will implement its security policies. As well as protecting the company assets, an organisation has to make sure that all members of staff comply with any current legislation applicable.

   In most cases implementation can be classed under three headings:

   - organisational and procedural security
   - physical security
   - logical security.

Organisational and procedural security

Organisational and procedural security covers such things as:

- the classification of information – this describes how sensitive or confidential information is and also the restrictions for access

- how systems should be developed – it is best that they are not developed by a single person. Should that person leave or fall sick, a major problem could arise

- procedures for the recovery of data files lost – and any contingency procedures for the loss of communications lines or equipment

- a disaster recovery plan – which ensures the continued availability of IT resources should a loss of computing services occur

- changing the controls – the controls are the procedures that must be adopted so that any changes to hardware or software cause minimum inconvenience to the day-to-day operations of the organisation

- legal procedures – covering the implications of the Data Protection Act, the Computer Misuse Act and other legislation

- procedures that outline the acquisition of computer equipment

- personnel security controls – covering such things as making sure there is more than one member of staff covering any key position, such as network manager.

Physical security

Physical security controls make sure that premises, personnel, computers, telecommunications and data are protected from unauthorised access, accidental and deliberate damage, man-made and natural hazards.

In this part of the policy document the following sections are usually present:

- access – to buildings, computers and stored data

- use of equipment – for instance, it must be used entirely for company purposes

- security of data, information and documentation

- maintenance of equipment

- fire prevention and detection

- disposal of printouts, media and equipment

- unattended computer access.

Logical security

Logical security access controls ensure that access through computers and terminals to an organisation's data, programs and information is controlled in some way, so that only authorised access is allowed.

Logical access controls include not only the use of passwords, but also cover the monitoring of terminals that have tried to gain unauthorised access but have failed. Related to logical security are two specific issues: network security and data and program integrity.

Network security

Most organisations (except very small ones) make use of computer networks. This raises many additional security problems such as **hacking** and **tapping**.

Data and program integrity

This part of the report looks at the business controls that exist to maintain the accuracy and completeness of the data held by information systems. An organisation also needs to mention the controls it has in place to prevent unauthorised copying of programs and data, and outline the rules about putting non-work-related software onto its computers.

Activity

Using the above framework as your guide, produce an information security policy for a school or college. This policy should cover the use of the IT systems by the administrative staff as well as by teachers/lecturers and also students/pupils.

When producing the document you should bear the following in mind:

- Colleges and schools hold a lot of personal data (student records, personnel records, medical details, examinations results, references, etc.)
- All schools and colleges are connected to the Internet and this brings a variety of security problems that you will need to deal with.
- You will need to decide who will enforce the rules you make regarding the use of IT equipment.

- Many students like to play games on the school's/college's systems when they should be working.
- Because so many students bring disks into the school/college, there are serious problems with viruses.
- Remember the intended audience of your document. Not everyone will understand the technical terms used and they might not be as familiar as you think with computers.

Disaster recovery management

Disaster recovery management consists of looking at the threats to information systems, the likelihood of their occurrence, and the costs and measures that need to be taken to avoid them altogether, or to minimise the damage they do if they occur.

Potential threats to information systems

Threats to the security of an information system come from all directions, both internally and externally. It is usually up to the data processing manager to assess what damage could occur and the likelihood of such an occurrence.

Disaster planning and recovery is a bit like commercial insurance; those in charge of any organisation need to ask 'what if such and such were to happen'?

Below is a list of just some of the many threats to information systems:

- viruses
- fire
- damage associated with floods, earthquakes, lightning, volcanoes, etc.
- hacking (tapping into communication lines)
- systems failure owing to machine malfunction
- fraud
- power failure
- sabotage
- theft (hardware, software and data)
- blackmail
- espionage
- terrorist bomb attacks
- chemical spillage
- gas leaks
- vandalism
- spilling a drink over the computer equipment
- failure of the telecommunication links

hardware, software, documentation, people, communications channels and data.

2 Identify risks to the above and the likelihood of their occurrence.

Some things are almost certain to happen sooner or later (such as a power cut), whereas others (such as an explosion) are much less likely, but all threats need to be taken into account. Senior management has to decide what level of risk is acceptable to the organisation. Most organisations have a corporate IT security review which looks at the computer processed information to identify the risks of unavailability, errors and omissions, abuse and unauthorised disclosure and to determine their potential implications. Each risk needs to be examined from a security point of view and the effect and likelihood of its loss assessed. The aim is to identify those systems crucial to the organisation and to look at the possible short- or long-term loss of these systems.

Here are just some of the many consequences of system loss:

- cash flow problems as invoices are sent out late

- bad business decisions through lack of management information

- loss of goodwill of customers and suppliers

- production delays caused by not having the correct stock available

- late delivery of orders causing customers to go elsewhere

- stock shortage, or overstocking, caused by lack of adequate stock control.

Physical security

Physical security involves protecting hardware and software using physical rather than software methods. The two main purposes of providing physical security are to restrict access to the computer equipment, and to restrict access to the storage medium.

As a first step in restricting access it is often advisable to control access to the building or room containing the computer system. If unauthorised access is gained despite access restrictions, there need to be other physical factors to prevent computers and equipment from being stolen.

Physical restrictions include:

- controlling access to the building by the use of uniformed security guards and special locks operated by security badges

- controlling access to the room by using keypads on doors; a code is then needed to open the door. Special magnetic cards can also be used to the same effect

- using locks on computers to prevent them from being switched on

- locking computers away at night or securing them under steel covers.

Restricting access to terminals is more difficult using physical methods; since rooms can contain large numbers of terminals, it may be impractical to secure them all or lock them away. Instead you have to use software security.

Software security (also called logical security)

If people do gain unauthorised access to a room containing computers or computer terminals, there needs to be a second line in the defence mechanism to prevent them gaining access to the software or data. This is achieved using software security. Software security usually consists of passwords to restrict access to certain programs, files and data. This means that anyone seeing the terminal or computer switched on cannot just go up and access whatever data they want.

Questions

1 (a) Explain the difference between physical security and logical security.

(b) A stand-alone computer is being used. Give three methods which can be used to provide physical security, and three methods that can be used to provide logical security.

2 An organisation wishes to review its policy on passwords. Produce a short document (a single A4 sheet) explaining why passwords are needed and how staff should choose them.

3 Explain the difference between integrity of data and the security of data.

4 An IT manager is worried about the misuse of IT facilities by certain members of staff.

(a) Describe briefly three types of misuse of data.

(b) Explain how the misuses you have identified in (a) can be detected.

(c) Most organisations make use of a 'computer information security policy'. Describe the advantages in having such a policy.

Document security

It is really no good having excellent IT security if the results of processing, in the form of hardcopy printouts, are left on top of someone's desk for everyone to see and possibly photocopy. As well as physical and logical security, we need to consider document security.

It is important that any printouts or reports are locked away when not being used and that they are shredded before being put in the wastepaper basket. Any unwanted documents on microfilm or microfiche should be incinerated to destroy them.

Communication security

When communication channels are used to transmit data, the data can be intercepted, read and possibly altered. The chance of this happening increases if the ordinary telephone network is used. There are many techniques that can be used to ensure communication security, but the main method is encryption. Banks were the first commercial users of encryption to send secure electronic transfers of money from one branch to another, or between branches and ATMs (cash points). Most commercial companies now send confidential information to their branches or use the system to trade electronically. Obviously, too, many private users want to send their e-mails without risking interception. With the huge increase in e-commerce, encryption has become a very important issue.

How does encryption work?

Encryption works in the following way. Suppose Jayne in London wants to send a secure e-mail to Jack in Paris. When Jayne has typed in her e-mail she presses the 'encrypt' option on her mailer software. The software verifies with her whom she wants to send the e-mail to. She chooses Jack's name from the list presented of all the people for whom Jayne has a public key and to whom she can send encrypted messages. The encryption software then automatically mixes and re-mixes every binary bit of her message

with every bit in Jack's public key. The result is a mix of binary data that can only be unscrambled using the same software and Jack's private key. When Jack receives the e-mail in Paris, he selects the 'decrypt' option and the software then asks him for a password. He types in the password and this decrypts his private key. The private key is a very long number and the computer uses this to perform calculations which unscramble the encrypted message from Jayne. If the message were intercepted, it could not be read without the private key used to perform the calculations needed to unscramble the message.

A 'digital signature' can also be added to the message by Jayne, which is checked by Jack's software to ensure that the message really came from Jayne. This prevents other users sending Jack a message claiming to come from Jayne.

There is more about encryption on page 305.

Legislation

In many cases, the procedures adopted in an organisation are determined by a variety of legal requirements imposed on them by government agencies. Many of these legal requirements apply to the company as a whole, whilst some of them, such as the Computer Misuse Act 1990 are specifically aimed at the use of technology. Current legislation covering the legal responsibilities of staff in the workplace, using IT equipment, are as follows:

- The Copyright, Designs and Patents Act 1988

- The Data Protection Act 1998

- The Computer Misuse Act 1990.

If you need to know more about these Acts, you should refer back to Chapter 4, where they are covered in detail.

Many staff, particularly those who work outside a specialist IT department, may not be aware of the many pieces of legislation applicable to them, which set out what they can legally do with computer equipment, software and data. It is therefore necessary for the management to educate the users as to what they can and cannot do and what the consequences, for both them and the organisation, could be if they fall foul of the law.

As mentioned previously, an organisation is responsible for the acts of its employees whilst they are at work and the company is legally liable for certain illegal acts an employee might commit. For example, where there are lots of PCs scattered throughout a company, employees may be tempted to copy software onto their machines without a proper licence. If this happens, even if the company knows nothing about it, it can still be prosecuted and fined. There need to be clear guidelines spelling out what employees are not allowed to do and these are usually incorporated into their contracts of employment. To disobey any of these rules may result in disciplinary action being taken.

Any rules will need to cover the following:

1 copying company data

2 copying unauthorised software to machines for which it is not licensed

3 making copies of company software without permission

4 tampering illegally with software or data

5 removing computers from the office for use at home

6 accessing personal data.

The Data Protection Act 1998

The Data Protection Act 1998 gives individuals certain rights to protect them from misuse of the personal data held about them. In the Act 'personal data' means information relating to a living individual who can be identified from that information (or from that and other information in the possession of the data user). This definition includes any expression of opinion about the *data subject*, but not any opinion of *the data* made by the individual.

The implications for organisations of The Data Protection Act 1998

The Data Protection Act 1998 lays down eight data protection principles, ascribes certain responsibilities to the users of personal data and affirms certain rights to individuals who are the subject of that data. Most organisations hold personal data and will therefore have to register their data use with the Data Protection Commissioner.

Each use of personal data has to be registered and it is important that everyone in the organisation understands this so that they do not set up their own database holding personal data about which the security manager knows

nothing. If any members of staff need to keep personal data on computer, this use will also need to be registered.

There must be operating procedures in place so that personal data is not disclosed via a telephone call or to anyone attending in person, unless steps have been taken to establish whether disclosure is allowed under the Register entry.

Trading in personal data

Personal data is a very valuable commodity and when one company collects personal data, it can be sold to various other companies and organisations. Some catalogue companies make as much money through the selling of the personal data they collect about their customers as they do selling goods to them! Although you might think that under the Data Protection Act companies are not allowed to trade personal data in this way, it *is* allowed provided that the data subject (i.e. the person who the personal data is about) has given permission. If you look at order forms or application forms for insurance or loans, there is usually a box to tick if you do *not* wish your details to be passed to other organisations who may send you details of goods or services. Most people do not think too much about this and do not tick this box; they then wonder why other organisations send them junk mail or seem to know so much about them.

Why is this personal data so valuable?
Mailshot targeting
Suppose you ran a company making and installing swimming pools and wanted to do a mailshot for a very special offer. Since only a small number of households would want, have the space for, or the money to pay for, a swimming pool, it would waste both time and money to mailshot everyone. Instead you could mailshot only those in a certain socio-economic group (i.e. the people who have the money to buy). To do this data is needed, usually bought from other sources. Having lists of people who match certain criteria lies at the heart of a successful mailshot.

Customer purchasing profile
By looking at the recent purchases made by an individual, it is possible to predict their likely future purchases and this information can be passed or sold to other retailers or companies. When you are asked to fill in questionnaires, they often ask you how many holidays abroad

you have taken in the last year and also how many you have booked for the present year. From this information, a shrewd guess can be made as to when you will be likely to decide on your next holiday, so that new brochures can be sent to you. Another example is that of a person who moves into a new house. Shortly after moving, he or she is likely to purchase new carpets, curtains, light fittings and general DIY goods. Companies involved in these areas then notify the individuals of any special offers.

Customer purchasing analysis
By examining when customers are likely to buy a product, such as a new car, manufacturers are able to use this information along with the data from previous sales periods to more accurately predict demand and set their manufacturing quotas accordingly.

Are there any advantages to the customers in this profiling?
Easier availability of credit
To get a loan approved used to take around a week, but now so much personal information is kept on computer and it is easier for credit companies to make a decision. Credit checking takes only minutes and this has speeded up obtaining credit to buy goods.

Goods are more likely to be in stock
By predicting the demand for goods more accurately, companies can have a more accurate purchasing model. This means they are less likely to disappoint customers by having goods go out of stock, and likely to meet demand quicker when goods run out.

Customers are targeted for goods and services directly
Details of goods and services, with special offers, can be sent to potential customers at the times they are most likely to want to see them, which could save the customer time looking.

Methods of enforcing data protection legislation in an organisation

Various problems relating to the Data Protection Act that may crop up in an organisation and these include the following:

1 As noted above, users may set up their own databases on desktop PCs. These could contain personal data and therefore put the organisation in breach of the Data Protection Act since these uses will not be known about by the company and therefore will not be registered.

2 People may create approved databases but not know about the Data Protection Act and how it applies to what they do.

3 Users may be unaware of the importance of security relating to personal data. It is no use having effective security methods surrounding the computer, if printouts of personal data are left lying on a desk for anyone to see.

What can be done about the above problem?

● Each department should have a designated data protection controller/officer to give advice within the department and inform of possible breaches of the Act. There should also be a data protection co-ordinator for the whole organisation.

● Every employee should be given a detailed job description outlining what they are allowed and not allowed to do.

● Anything which gives the slightest cause for concern should be followed up.

● Passwords should be remembered and not written down and left in an obvious place. Users should not use names of their husbands, wives, children, pets, etc. as these are the first things tried by anyone who wants to gain illegal access to the system.

● Machines should be surrounded by proper physical security so that it is impossible to steal the computers easily.

● Users should be forbidden from creating their own databases without authorisation.

● All users should be educated about the implications of the Data Protection Act. Each member of staff needs to be aware of the organisation's obligations under the Act and the terms of their registration.

● Passwords should be changed regularly in case they become common knowledge.

● Users should not be allowed to bring disks onto, or take disks off, the premises.

● The network management system should provide a log which records which person has used or seen which record.

- Access levels should be set up for each member of staff on the network, allowing them to see only things that are necessary for the performance of their jobs.

1 What steps can an organisation take to make sure that its staff comply with the current data protection legislation?

2 Most terminals automatically log off the network if there has been no user activity at the terminal for a specified time. This time can be set by the network operating system. Explain why this is desirable.

Software misuse

To comply with the Computer Misuse Act 1990, all users should be trained to understand how the Act affects their behaviour when working with company data and software. The level of training a particular person needs will depend on the role of the individual concerned. When designing systems, it is a good idea to make the initial screens, or signing-on screens, show warnings concerning the Computer Misuse Act and the consequences of unauthorised access.

Methods of enforcing software misuse legislation in an organisation

There are a number of things that may be done to prevent users falling foul of the software misuse legislation, such as:

- Users should be banned from adding unauthorised software to their machines.

- To prevent breaches of the Act, hardware and software should only be bought from reliable and approved sources.

- No data disks that have be used outside the organisation should be placed in any machine without first being scanned for viruses.

- Separation of duties should be applied to users. This means, for example, that no person should be responsible for any function from commencement to completion, thus making fraud more difficult to commit.

- A clear, unambiguous job description should outline what employees are allowed and not allowed to do.

- Staff should be forbidden in their job description from doing other work on the company's computer.

- Managers should perform regular audits of the software on every machine to check for any unauthorised software.

Methods of enforcing health and safety legislation in an organisation

Regular inspections should be made of the working environment and a report given to the senior management on all the computer equipment and office furniture, outlining anything that does not conform to the current health and safety regulations.

All staff should be trained to use good practice when working with computer equipment (adjusting seats, VDUs, desks, etc) and they should also understand that health and safety issues are the responsibility of *everyone* in the organisation.

Staff should be sent for free eye tests once a year if they are working with VDUs and if they need glasses or contact lenses these should be supplied by the organisation, free of charge.

Management should make sure that all faulty equipment is removed from the workplace immediately.

Audit requirements

You may be familiar with the idea of an audit from accounting. In IT, an audit is a systematic assessment of a computer system, covering both hardware and software. Many information technology applications are subjected to auditing and to do an audit it is usually necessary for the software to generate an audit trail. Using the audit trail from a sales order processing system, for instance, it is possible to trace an order from the point where it is made by the customer, to the payment for the goods by the customer. It is therefore possible to check that all payments for goods had corresponding orders from customers and even that the orders were actually despatched.

An important purpose of an audit is to look for evidence of fraud. Audits look at the evidence and follow up any irregularities. Although only a few records can be checked when performing an audit, it is nevertheless a deterrent, since staff realise that there is someone checking things and they are more likely to get caught. Many organisations are funded from central government and taxpayers need to feel sure that this money is being used properly. Take a college, for example. Colleges are funded from central government and part of the money a college receives is based on the number of students it has enrolled. One way of increasing funding would be to add a couple of bogus students to the register for each course. The names and addresses could be invented and if anyone wanted to know where they were, the college could simply say that they were off sick that day. Auditors from the funding council who audit the colleges have to make sure that this is not being done. To do this, they make sure that the college has introduced a student tracking system in which there is a series of documents or computer records relating to each student. The auditor can pick a particular student and ask to see all the documentation and records relating to them or even to see the student. In other words, the college needs to provide an audit trail that can be followed through for checking purposes.

Activity

You have been given the job of auditing the units (sums of money) claimed by a college for the students it has enrolled on courses. You have been given a list of students on each course but when you enter one of the classes and ask to see the register (called an *auditable document*), only half the students are actually there. The lecturer says that half the class are sick. What enquiries might you make to determine that these students actually exist?

When transactions (bits of business) are performed on the computer, there may not be corresponding paperwork, as a major benefit in using the computer is to avoid the inefficiencies of a paper-based system. So that the system can be audited, the software produced will have a function built in which provides an audit trail. The audit trail

provides evidence of what has happened in the system. For example, if a record has been deleted, the audit function will provide evidence of the record before deletion along with the date and time it was deleted and the name of the member of staff who performed the deletion; it may even include the reason the record was deleted.

In summary, the purposes of an audit are to:

- prevent fraud; audit trails make it harder to commit fraud and act as a deterrent, since this checking process increases the likelihood that thieves will be caught

- make the senior management more certain that figures produced (such as sales totals) are accurate

- enable shareholders, owners, etc. to feel sure that the accounts produced by an organisation are accurate and a true reflection of the financial state of the organisation.

Audit programs

Audit programs are special, usually stand-alone, programs. This means they are separate to the package being audited. They are designed to supply test data which is then processed according to the applications software being run. This tests the effectiveness of the applications software and internal controls can be assessed in this way.

Using audit trails, it is possible, for instance, to track an order from the point it is made through the system. One can check that goods have been actually produced, picked and sent to customers. One can also check that customers actually receive them (usually evidenced by a signature on a delivery note), by looking to see that payment has been made and that there is an entry in the company's bank account for the amount.

Audits are not used simply to prevent and detect fraud; they may also be used to detect and prevent abuse of a system's facilities. Take for example the police national computer (PNC) which contains a smaller version of the Driver Vehicle and Licensing Authority database, containing all the registered details of vehicles and drivers. Since the registration number of a vehicle is unique, it can be used as the primary key for performing searches to identify the owners of vehicles.

CASE STUDY

Abuse of the police national computer

One oil company ran a promotion a few years ago to encourage drivers to buy their brand of petrol in preference to others. To this end, the company placed a list of car registration numbers at each petrol station and if you were the owner of one of these numbers, you won a prize of one thousand pounds. Some police officers noticed this promotion and realised that they could type the winning numbers into the police national computer to obtain the addresses of their owners. They did this and then rang the lucky owners, saying that if the owner gave them a sum of money, they would tell them where they could get £1000. Naturally, many people agreed. Eventually the officers involved were found out and severely reprimanded. An investigation showed that abuses of the PNC were widespread and that many private companies had paid to receive information that it contained. Clearly these abuses had to stop and now in order to interrogate the database, police officers have to identify themselves and the reason why they require the information. In addition to this, an audit can be performed where a particular search on the PNC is investigated to make sure that it was necessary and that it was a legitimate use of the system.

CASE STUDY

A terrorist attack

On a Saturday in June 1996 the police received a coded warning that a bomb had been planted at the Arndale Centre, Manchester's premier shopping area. Just over an hour after a speedy evacuation of the Centre and the surrounding area, the bomb exploded, injuring over two hundred people and destroying a large part of the Centre and ripping apart many of the business premises surrounding it. The bomb, which was the largest bomb explosion in peacetime Britain, caused extensive damage to the offices of the Royal and Sun Alliance insurance company where some staff were injured.

As these offices housed the company's mainframe computer, it was initially feared that the day-to-day operations of the company would be severely affected. The staff in the Liverpool office, which contained terminals that were networked to the mainframe, found that there was still some life in the system, even though there was extensive damage to the building the computer was housed in. There was some optimism that the system could be recovered, but to prevent the likelihood of gas explosions from the ruptured gas mains, the fire brigade cut off the electrical power. Most of the hardware had been irreparably damaged during the explosion. However, like most sensible companies, the Royal and Sun Alliance had a contingency plan which involved a contract with a specialist data recovery company who had similar hardware and copies of software being used by Royal and Sun Alliance. Because they needed staff to operate the computer who understood the insurance business, the Royal's staff were transported to the offices of the recovery company and they set to work recovering data from backup media which were kept off-site. By Monday morning, all the data had been recovered and a temporary switchboard had been set up. Not a single day's trading had been lost.

Question

What can organisations do in order to minimise the damage caused by:

(a) a power cut

(b) a virus attack

(c) an inexperienced operator wiping the magnetic media by mistake

(d) the deliberate alteration of important data by hackers

(e) the key members of staff leaving with all the organisation's IT expertise and knowledge

(f) a loss in the communication lines in a WAN

(g) loss of access to their premises owing to fire in a nearby building

(h) the deliberate destruction of company programs by a disgruntled employee.

Activity

Definition of terms

A variety of terms is introduced in this chapter, many of which may be new to you. It is important that you build up vocabulary that can be used when writing essays or answering questions.

Write a definition for each of the following terms used in the chapter:

misuse	contingency plan
security policy	risk analysis
logical security	audit
physical security	

Examination Questions

1 Many retail organisations have developed large databases of customer information by buying data from each other.

(a) Describe **two** possible uses these organisations could make of the data they purchase. *(4)*

(b) Some customers may object to data held on them by one organisation being sold to another organisation. Describe some of the arguments which either of these retail organisations may use to justify this practice. *(4)*

(NEAB, Module IT04, Specimen paper, q2)

2 A particular college uses a computer network for storing details of its staff and students and for managing its finances. Network stations are provided for the Principal, Vice-Principal, Finance Officer, clerical staff and teaching staff. Only certain designated staff have authority to change data or to authorise payments.

(a) What are the legal implications of storing personal data on the computer system? *(4)*

(b) What measures should be taken to ensure that the staff understand the legal implications? *(4)*

(NEAB, Module IT04, Specimen paper, q3)

3 Many accounts packages have an audit trail facility. Explain why such a facility is necessary, what data is logged and how this information can be used. *(6)*

(NEAB, Module IT04, Specimen paper, q6)

4 A company uses a computer network for storing details of its staff and for managing its finances. The network manager is concerned that some members of staff may install unauthorised software onto the network.

(a) Give reasons why it is necessary for some software to be designated as unauthorised. *(2)*

(b) What guidelines should the network manager issue to prevent the installation of unauthorised software onto the network? *(2)*

(c) What procedures are available to the company to enforce the guidelines? *(2)*

(NEAB, Module IT04, May 97, q6)

Examination Questions

5 Some IT applications use software which maintains an audit trail.

Name one such application and state why this facility is necessary. *(3)*

(NEAB, Module IT04, May 98, q1)

6 'Information Systems are mission critical, the consequences of failure could prove disastrous.'

Discuss this statement, including in your discussion:

– the potential threats to the system

– the concept of risk analysis

– the corporate consequences of systems failure

– the factors which should be considered when designing the 'contingency plan' to enable a recovery from disaster *(20)*

Quality of language will be assessed in this question.

(NEAB, Module IT04, May 98, q9)

7 List **five** distinctly different potential threats to an information system. Give **one** way of countering each potential threat. *(10)*

(NEAB, Module IT04, May 99, q4)

8 A particular organisation is upgrading its computer-based stock control system. The previous data collection system was OMR based.

(a) State **three** other alternative methods of collecting stock control data. *(3)*

(b) What factors, other than cost, will determine the method of data capture. *(4)*

(c) The software used to control the system must support and audit trail. Explain what is meant by the term 'audit trail', and state why this functionality is necessary. *(6)*

(NEAB, Module IT04, May 99, q5)

9 'Legislation will have an impact on the procedures used within any organisation.'

Discuss this statement. Particular attention should be given to:

– the different aspects of IT related legislation which affect organisations;

– the types of formal procedures which are used to enforce legislation;

– the potential differences between legislation and company policy.

Illustrate your answer with specific examples.

The quality of your language will be assessed in this answer.

(NEAB, Module IT04, May 99, q9)

Implementing IT Systems

User support

Problems will always occur when people use computers and these problems can often leave the user unable to use the facility. Appropriate training increases the number of problems that can be solved by the user and this leaves only the occasional, more technical problems to be resolved. During the introduction of new hardware, applications software or operating systems, the number of problems encountered by the users increases, and for this reason many companies do not respond to every slight update in hardware or software the way some home users might. There are many ways in which an organisation can deal with the problems encountered by users, and organisations use either one or a combination of the methods outlined here.

Existing user base

If you are working in an office with other more experienced users and you encounter a problem with a particular piece of software, it may be useful to ask someone you work with for their help before approaching anyone else. It is reckoned that about 80 per cent of IT problems in organisations are solved by non-IT staff. If the problem cannot be solved in this way then you can make a telephone call to a help-desk that may be in-house (i.e. within the company) or provided externally by the company who supplied the hardware or software.

Help desks

In most large organisations, user support is provided by the use of help desks. Help desks are usually manned by someone from the IT department, although with the growth of outsourcing, the help desk may be outside the organisation. The purpose of a help desk is to give expert advice to users regarding any software and hardware problems they might have.

With dumb terminals, which have no processing power of their own, user support is easy because if all the computing power and storage facilities are in one place and if a terminal is not working, then it may simply be replaced by one that is. With stand-alone PCs and PC networks, the situation is more difficult since the user will usually have the processing power and storage on their desks. The problem is exacerbated when users start unofficially adding to their systems bits of hardware such as scanners, printers, more memory, etc. or start installing software without any regard to the organisation's information technology policy. The addition of some peripheral devices to a network has been known to cause the failure of the whole network.

By logging each call to the help desk it is possible, first, to assess the performance of the help desk, and secondly, to look at the frequency of the users' problems. For example, one particular problem might crop up time and time again, and rather than just deal with these calls as they arise, it might be better to resolve them by changes to the operating procedures or by specific training for the users. Such training should in the long run reduce the numbers of calls made, which will in turn reduce the costs of running the help desk.

Some companies have made use of intranets to enable users to trawl through a knowledge base and therefore seek the answers to simple problems themselves, without the need to consult a member of staff on the help desk. Other companies use the web to send messages from users requesting help to the help desk rather than use the telephone. Replies to the user's requests for help can be sent back over the web and this saves time trying the help desk number only to find it continually engaged.

Logging the calls to the help desk

A computerised call-logging system is used to record the calls made to the help desk and this log will generally record the following information:

- The user's registration number. All users of the network or stand-alone computers have a user registration number. By using this number the help desk personnel can identify the name, department, software they are authorised to use, etc. by interrogating a data file stored on the system.

- The date and time of the call.

- The duration of the call.

- Whether the problem could be sorted out immediately or whether one or more return calls were needed.

To provide an efficient service to the users, the help desk must be carefully managed and users' problems resolved in the minimum amount of time. It should be borne in mind that time spent talking to the help desk is time away from the task in hand, so the sooner the problem is resolved, the sooner the user can return to productive work.

It is often necessary for calls to the help desk to be routed to people with expertise in a particular area, so a hardware problem would be directed to the person who knows most about hardware, for instance. Large help desks are normally organised into teams specialising in different areas of computing.

Those errors which occur regularly with a particular piece of hardware or software may be stored on a database. These systems make use of keywords describing the problems, so that entering a keyword will automatically bring up the appropriate remedy from the database. Some help desks make use of expert systems where fairly inexperienced help desk staff can

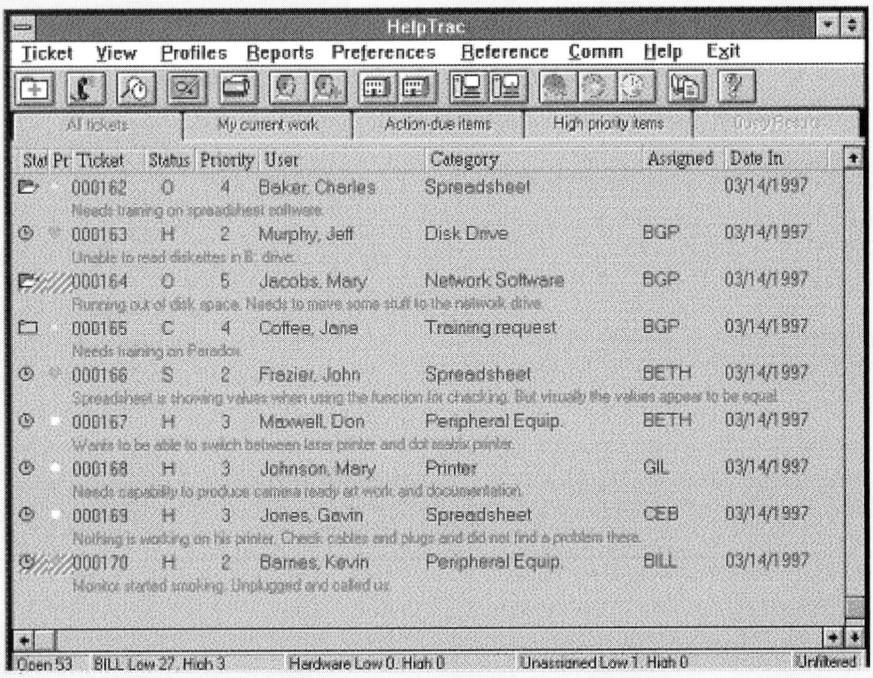

Figure 15.1 *Typical help desk management*

use a body of knowledge stored on a system which gives them a series of questions to ask the users over the phone. The replies are typed in and the system comes up with the best solution to the problem. After a while, the help desk staff build up their experience and rely less on the expert system.

Troubleshooting a user problem

The use of a clear, structured set of questions is vital in troubleshooting user problems, since in most organisations, the help desk is not in the same location as the user, and the help desk staff cannot necessarily see what the user sees. Accurate communication over the phone is therefore paramount.

Questions asked will obviously vary from one organisation to another and in some cases the help desk will have clear descriptions of hardware and software available to the user that will cut out some of these questions. Most procedures will usually include the following questions:

- What hardware is being used?

- What applications software is being run? (This usually includes the version of the software being run.) In some cases the help desk staff may have descriptions of all the software on the user's machine loaded into a database.

- What operating system is being used?

- Give a concise explanation of what the problem is and also what the user was doing prior to noticing the problem.

- Describe the current state of the computer; is the computer displaying any error messages, or has it crashed?

Activity

Imagine you are working on a help desk for a large organisation. A user rings you to report a problem they are having with a printer that according to them is not working. What general questions will you need to ask to enable you to sort out their problem?

(Remember that many novice users can make fairly obvious mistakes, so your trouble-shooting should start off with simple questions.)

How is the performance of the help desk assessed?

It is easy to assess the performance of some departments in an organisation. For example, for a sales department you can compare the actual sales made against targets set. But how would you assess the quality of work of a help desk?

Here are some factors which can be examined to help assess the quality of the service provided by a help desk.

- The number of calls logged over a certain time period (e.g. per day, per week, etc.) could indicate how busy the service has been. We could also record the time between the phone ringing and its being answered (called the response time) as significant delay is often an annoyance to users.

- The time taken to resolve the user's problem (called the resolution time) could be measured. Occasionally, with more technical problems, the help desk staff may not be able to resolve the problem immediately and have to get back to the user later on. Some problems may need the advice of the organisation that supplied the hardware or software.

- The quality of the help desk may be assessed by examining users' satisfaction with the quality of the service they have received. There needs to be some way of finding out whether the calls have been resolved to the user's satisfaction and one way would be to send a questionnaire to the users with a variety of questions about the way their problem was dealt with and eventually resolved. Since this would be subjective (i.e. what one person may think good service, another may not) the questions need to be carefully constructed.

If a user cannot resolve the problem using the advice received from the help desk, he may make a repeat call about the same problem. The user may refer to the same person if they want a further explanation or they may hope to get someone else to answer their query who can explain it better. That the user cannot resolve the problem with advice could indicate a number of things: that the user is unable to follow instructions; that the help desk's advice was not clear enough or that the advice given to the user was wrong. All these decrease the efficiency of the help desk and steps need to be taken to overcome these problems.

Help desk targets may be set which have to be met or improved upon. For example, a target may be that 90 per cent of the problems should be solved with a single call, or that all complex technical problems are resolved within 24 hours.

How can users contact the help desk staff?

Anyone who has tried to contact a help desk will know how difficult it can be to make contact by phone. Some help desks appear to take their telephones off the hook since it seems impossible to contact them at any time of the day. These help desks tend to be those of the hardware and software manufacturers who offer free user support. If the user has to pay for this support, the situation is usually much better. In-house help desks obviously have a vested interest in returning the user to productive work, so tend to respond more rapidly.

There are various ways users can contact help desks. They include telephone, voicemail, e-mail, company intranet and the Internet.

Because of the problems experienced in contacting help desks by telephone, most help desks allow users to send their problems in the variety of formats shown above. Sometimes the help desk will send the reply back to the user in the same format in which it was sent. If the problem is vaguely described, it may be necessary for the help desk staff to speak to the user. Since most users are connected to a network, it is usually possible for the help desk staff to see the user's screen display on their own workstation so that they can see what they are trying to do. In some cases, the help desk staff can work at home as this is a task ideally suited to telecommuting.

Help desk software

As you will have seen in the last section, keeping track of all the calls, details of users and their problems is a necessary part of the quality control for any help desk. It is therefore not surprising that software tools have been developed to manage the calls and allow the user's problems to be solved as quickly as possible.

Help desk management software has the following features:

Figure 15.2

- There is usually a database at the heart of the software, containing outlines of problems and their solutions; this reduces the need for the help desk staff to rely on memory.

- Since help desk staff access the same database of solutions, they should all use the same approach, regardless of the member of staff giving the help.

- The system keeps track of each call until the problem is resolved.

- Once the problem is resolved, it is added to the database so that if a similar problem occurs, the same solution can be given to the user. This means that many of the calls to the help desk are routinely solved in minutes rather than the two to three hours it used to take.

- The help desk staff can call up the user's history of problems which helps them offer a level of help tailored to the user's ability. Repeated requests for simple help indicate a novice user.

Activity

Using the Internet, investigate the facilities offered by two different pieces of help desk software. Present the results of your investigation as a series of bulleted points for each package.

To start you off, here is the web address of a company that produces help desk management software:

www.helptrac.com

There is even a demo version of the help desk software at this site so you can get the feel of this type of software.

You may be able to find other websites. Make a note of their web addresses in your answer.

User support from software houses

Software houses (companies who write specialist application software) and software manufacturers such as Microsoft, Lotus, etc. provide user support via telephone help lines or over the Internet. Many producers of software provide users with a period of free advice over the telephone and after this period they usually have to pay for the support. Other software companies use help desk facilities to boost their income since sometimes the customer has to dial a premium rate telephone line and pay for the service by the minute.

Help desks are usually very busy just after a new version of the application software or operating system has been launched, since users may have queries which the manual or the on-line help does not deal with. As more books and training courses are released supporting the new software, and the experience of the user is built up, so the less experienced user is able to get help without resort to the help desk. It is important to determine in advance of buying software, what sort of support is available, whether it is provided free and if so, for how long.

Many support problems arise when one company is taken over by another since they may no longer want to support the older company's products. A similar problem can occur when there is a new release of software and the organisation is still running the previous version. Eventually the software house may no longer

support the older software and it becomes necessary for the organisation to change software.

Support articles

Another source of help is from computer magazines produced by the supplier or articles in the computer press addressing common problems and outlining what the user can do to solve them. Similar to these are the plethora of computer books that explain how to use a particular package. Many of these books are aimed at a particular level, so if you are a very advanced user and want to develop applications using the software, it is possible to find a book which assumes your prior knowledge so that you do not waste time starting at the beginning again.

Many paper-based or on-line articles include a section called FAQ (frequently asked questions) and which deals with many of the more common problems.

Utilities

Help utilities are a feature of most software packages; their purpose is to supply the user with on-line help if they get stuck. In many cases, the user needs to be quite knowledgeable about IT to be able to use the help facilities, since they must understand the nature of their problem and be able to describe it using a word or combination of words. Some packages make use of on-line tutorials which instruct users in how to perform certain tasks such as doing a mail merge using a word processor. Many problems can be resolved using the on-line help and all users should be aware that this facility is available to them and know how to use it.

Specialist bulletin boards

Specialist bulletin boards are a useful place to go to for support from other computer professionals. Most computer staff will use the Internet on a day-to-day basis and it is the natural place for them to look if they are having any problems with hardware or software. Since this advice is free and often impartial, it is very useful. Many experienced computer professionals are keen to impart advice on problems which newer users may come across.

The management of change

When organisations introduce new information systems, there is the likelihood that they will cause a change in the working practices of the organisation and that the change will affect staff in some way. Managers who oversee the development of the new system need to be skilled in the management of change and so able to gain the full co-operation of all the staff concerned.

There is no doubt that many people are resistant to change until it can be shown that the change may be to their advantage. After all, many staff will have seen the reduction in the workforce as many of their jobs were computerised in the past.

The adverse reaction of staff to the introduction of new systems is typified by the following:

- **A fear of redundancy**
  Some systems are introduced to reduce the number of people needed to do a particular task, as often the greatest cost is staff wages.

- **Fear of reduction in status and job satisfaction**
  With the help of the management information supplied by computerised management information systems, managers are able to get through more work and fewer middle level managers are needed. Job satisfaction can be eroded owing to many of the tasks being monitored by the computer. Some managers could lose power if data for the whole organisation is held centrally, as is the case if the organisation uses a data warehouse. This means that the data in the system, although originally supplied from their department, no longer belongs to them. Subject to the relevant security clearance, the data can be used by anyone in the organisation.

- **Fear of looking ridiculous**
  Some staff, especially older members of staff, may feel that their lack of IT knowledge could cause them to be ridiculed by the younger staff who are more aware of IT.

- **Health fears**
  There are often programmes on the television and articles in newspapers or magazines which raise health concerns about working with IT equipment. These are usually quite alarmist, to attract the reader's attention, and are often without substance, but they do fuel people's worries. Radiation from monitors seems particularly to worry pregnant women who may be concerned about it affecting their unborn children. These fears should be addressed by the managers who are implementing the change and they may need to change working practices to alleviate some of these concerns.

- **Changes to organisational structure**
  When a completely new system is introduced into an organisation, it will often be seen as an opportunity to alter the structure of the organisation so that it fits in better with the new system. The introduction of new systems frequently means the boundaries between functional areas become more blurred and staff may be asked to do a greater variety of tasks. For example, a customer may place an order with the sales staff and at the same time ask about the balance of their account, which would normally have been dealt with by the accounts department. The sales person may now have to do both tasks.

- **Changes to internal procedures**
  Staff members are often asked to take on more responsibility and do a wider variety of tasks when IT systems are introduced. For example, some staff who previously would have performed a purely administrational role, now get more directly involved with customers, and may be asked to sell goods or services. With the new IT system their traditional job may take much less time, so they now have time available to devote to other profitable activities.

  Ways of doing things must be reviewed and changed if necessary, since the systems analyst will not usually fit the IT system around the existing system, preferring always to consider the best method of performing the task. Working procedures frequently change and this can cause stress to some staff unless they are consulted about the changes and properly trained to deal with the new procedures.

- **Changes in employment patterns**
  Increased use of IT usually means movement towards the paperless office as more transactions are performed electronically. This means that the office space requirements are smaller. In some cases this will result in the organisation moving to smaller premises to reduce costs (rent, heat, light, etc.) and sometimes this requires a move away from the original location. Clearly any move will affect the staff who will need to be kept informed of proposed changes.

In some organisations, it may be possible for staff to work from home using a terminal connected to the company's computer system.

Increased use of IT usually means that there is an increase in the number of skilled workers (network managers, project managers, programmers, computer engineers, etc.), usually at the expense of less skilled jobs.

- **Changes to conditions of employment**
  With the increased use of computers and easier communications, many organisations now operate in global markets and have to be able to react to customers' requests. This necessitates some operations running 24 hours a day. Flexibility can mean that more part-time work and work outside normal office hours is available.

  Many staff who work with company data and information have restrictions in their conditions of employment regarding what they can and cannot do with the IT system. Most companies forbid the running of unauthorised software on company machines to protect their software and data from viruses. There will usually also be some conditions relating to disclosure of company data.

Overcoming the resistance to new IT systems

Fear is one of the greatest psychological problems facing the introduction of new information systems. The greatest fear is usually that of job loss. Many staff may also be frightened that their conditions of service will worsen. Since these fears can lead to low moral and poor co-operation by the staff in introducing new systems, managers should identify the fears and be honest about the consequences of the damage. There are many steps that can be taken to reassure staff, and some of these are outlined below.

- All staff should be made aware of the need for the new system and should be involved, even if only in a small way, with the introduction of the new system. If the staff see the genuine advantages of the system and can input their own ideas they are less likely to oppose it. Managers should positively encourage staff to provide advice on the new system and their contribution should be acknowledged.

- The learning process should be made easy for staff, and comprehensive training and retraining offered. Many of these training sessions can be arranged off-site so that staff can stay in a comfortable hotel and the training becomes a social thing as well. Some companies make use of multimedia computer-based training (CBT) and this can be conducted at the company's premises to minimise disruption to the day-to-day business operations.

- Managers should explain the advantages that the new system has over the old system. Staff may well be pleased that irritations they felt within the old system will be eliminated or reduced in the new system, thus improving their job satisfaction.

- Top management should spell out the implications of the new system before rumours start, particularly with relation to job security, pay, changes in contracts of employment, promotion prospects and, changes in working conditions. Above all, information about the new system must be communicated fully and frankly.

- Point out how many staff using the new system will learn new skills which will improve their promotion prospects. Such skills may also enable them to move to a better job outside the organisation if they so wish.

- Friends who have worked together for many years should be kept together if possible since people who enjoy each other's company work better as a team.

- Management should be willing to accept criticism of the new system and should be prepared to act upon it.

- New systems should not be developed in a rush. Users need time to adjust to changes and should be given time to get used to them. Confidence in a new system usually rises with time and users start to accept it.

Project management and effective IT teams

An IT project is an activity which is conducted for a fixed period by a project team to meet certain, stated objectives. A project normally ties up resources such as equipment and people whilst it is proceeding.

Dividing the overall task into small sub-tasks

The majority of IT projects cannot be undertaken by a single person, mainly because they are so large they could never be completed in an acceptable time, and the technology might change in the intervening period. It is common to talk about the size of large IT projects in 'man years' it takes to complete them. The largest IT projects can take around 200 man years to complete and this means that it would take one person 200 years, two people 100 years, four people 50 years, and so on.

Each smaller task, called a sub-task, can then be allocated to the person to whom it is most suited. Most project teams consist of between five to seven individuals as this has been found to be an optimum number. If the project is very large, several project teams will be needed, each working on a small part of the project. The project managers of these teams will all meet to co-ordinate the overall project.

Working in teams

One reason for staff working in teams, is that it brings together people with a wide range of experience and skills in different areas of the organisation. When designing and building a new system, technical knowledge is important since it is important to determine what is technically possible. Systems analysts should have had experience of similar large projects but this may not always be possible since large projects are not undertaken very often. Sometimes, to get the level of technical expertise right, it might be necessary to look outside the organisation for contract staff who might have worked on similar projects in similar organisations.

Many contractors specialise in a particular area of work, so you could, for instance, find a contractor who has an in-depth knowledge of system testing for large insurance companies. Such expertise does not come cheap, with many contractors earning over one thousand pounds per week, so this option could increase the cost of the project significantly, but the benefits may far outweigh the costs.

Teams are assembled by team leaders or senior managers to accomplish a particular task, so team members do not necessarily know each other, yet to work together successfully it is necessary for team members to get along. One of the most common problems team members have to overcome is working with people they dislike, which can cause tension within the group.

Interpersonal skills are all about a team member's ability to mix and get on with the other team members. Some team members may exhibit skills of leadership by offering to take over meetings or perform some of the co-ordination activities of several team members. Some members may be enthusiastic about the project and this may mean that they are popular within the group. Any group of people is likely to contain some members who have a positive attitude to their work and get on with the job while others sit around moaning about their colleagues, the management or the way the project is being developed. Such people always see the disadvantages rather than the advantages of doing a particular task and can be quite disheartening to work with. Good team members participate in the project and are active members of the group.

A summary of the reasons for working in a team

Why work as part of a team?

- Many IT tasks or projects are far too big to be performed by a single person.

- A team brings together people with expertise in different areas.

- Members of the team are able to 'bounce' ideas off each other and this can produce better solutions to IT problems.

Figure 15.3 *Working as a team has its advantages*

- An effective team can produce work which is far superior to that which could be produced by any individual member of the team.

Team leadership

Responsibility for the success or failure of an IT project rests with the project manager, so it is extremely important to ensure that managers are of the highest calibre. A good project manager will have worked on many similar projects before and therefore built up skills and experience directly applicable to the project in hand. A good project manager will have excellent leadership skills, be good at communicating (both in writing and in speech), at delegating work, listening and decision making, and be able to work under immense pressure.

Many of the team members may be given a free rein to use their time effectively, so these staff will manage their own time to some extent. Contractors are often 'results orientated' and tend to work well with little management. The main responsibilities of the project manager should therefore be co-ordinating activities and dealing with problems.

Costing

At the inception of the project, the team will need to assess its cost. It is often thought that the cost of the hardware will be the most expensive part of developing a new system. Although this may have been the case until the early 1990s, hardware costs have fallen and the wages of computer development staff have risen, so staff wages are now usually by far the greatest part of the cost.

Estimating costs can be quite difficult, and can only be done accurately on the basis of a similar project. Yet costs do have to be estimated accurately for a decision to be made as to whether the project should proceed, and if so, for a budget to be allocated. The time taken to complete a project also needs to be estimated quite accurately, since if it runs over the allotted time, costs can rise owing to increased staff wages, etc.

A good project manager should have experience of a number of projects, and thus be able to estimate fairly accurately the time a project is likely to take and how much it will cost. However, unexpected problems can still arise, that no amount of experience or planning can allow for.

Monitoring a project

Monitoring a project means comparing what is actually happening with what was planned. All projects should be carefully planned before inception and the plan agreed with all members of the project team and the senior managers/directors of the organisation. Part of this plan will relate to timescales, costs and quality, and at various stages in the project, its progress should be compared with that of the plan. If any areas that deviate from the plan are identified, steps can be taken to bring it back on course again. Many projects run late, sometimes due to influences beyond the team's control (such as the unexpected sickness of a key member), and sometimes because of the inexperience of the project manager or the team. If a project starts to run late, it is important that this is noticed at an early stage when corrective action can easily be taken. For example, the project manager may decide to take on extra staff (e.g. contractors) or to introduce overtime for existing staff. Either of these options will, however, start to increase the costs of the project and the project manager will need to look at the implications of this carefully.

Controlling a project

To control a project it is necessary to produce a plan and time schedule for the various activities that make it up. Various aids exist to help a project manager to do this. Co-ordination of the various interdependent activities is an important part of project control. If all the staff involved in the project are employed by the organisation, then co-ordination is usually easier than if contractors are involved because the latter may have different methods and styles of working. To co-ordinate the various activities, regular team meetings should be held. At these meetings, various strategies are looked at, such as re-deploying staff or bringing contractors in to help bring back on target any activities that are starting to fall behind schedule.

Cost control is important since projects are allocated only a limited amount of money, called a budget. Most organisations include all costs (staff wages, rental of accommodation, use of consumables, etc.) in the overall cost of a project. It is important to keep a careful check on the project costs and monitor them throughout its duration. The project manager needs to keep accurate records of the costs and this is usually done using a special software package or sometimes an ordinary spreadsheet.

Time control is monitored using a variety of techniques such as Gantt charts, PERT (project evaluation and review technique) or critical path analysis (CPA).

Gantt charts are horizontal bar charts, used to plan and schedule the tasks which make up the whole project. Project evaluation and review technique (PERT) involves charting out the time and other resources needed to complete a project. Although you could perform PERT using only a pen and paper, there are now many project management software packages which contain PERT features. Critical path analysis (CPA) is a system developed to find the minimum time necessary to complete a project. The techniques for CPA are simple and can be performed without a computer, although for larger projects it is best to use the software packages that are available.

Adherence to standards

There are various standards which lay down rules about the way data are encoded and transferred and it is important, particularly in the area of communications, that these standards are met in order to prevent incompatibility problems. Unfortunately, there are many different standards in use, although there is now movement towards a single common standard. When this happens, it will lead to 'open systems' in which all computers and equipment will be able to communicate with each other.

Activity

If you look though the computer press (e.g. the paper *Computer Weekly*), you will see that there are a large number of advertisements for project managers. The importance of the post is reflected in the large salaries that these people earn.

Your task is to research project manager posts in the computer press or using the Internet (many computer staff agencies have websites) and produce a report outlining the following:

1 The tasks a project manager must be capable of performing

2 A brief description of the general management skills which a project manager must possess

Activity

There is a variety of standards in use worldwide and your task is to determine what the following standards authorities cover:

(a) CCITT

(b) IEE

(c) ISO

(d) ANSI

Critical path analysis (CPA)

To find the minimum time for the completion of a project, one must find the 'critical path'. The critical path is the sequence of activities that takes the longest time from beginning to end. The critical path is determined by time alone; it does not assume that any one activity is more important than any other. If any activity, or activities, along the critical path are delayed for whatever reason, the whole project will be delayed.

To calculate the critical path, you need to take the following steps:

1 Break the project down into its component activities.

2 Arrange the activities in a logical sequence, each being represented by an arrow. This is known as a network diagram.

3 Estimate the duration of each activity.

4 Identify each path through the network and calculate the time for each path. The path with the greatest duration is the critical path. The difference between the duration of the critical path and that of the other paths is the spare time or 'float' for the other paths.

The advantage of the critical path method is that it highlights those activities that have a direct effect on the timing of the whole project.

Let us now take a look at the symbols used in network diagrams.

Arrows

Arrows are used to represent activities (see Figure 15.4). If the arrow is long enough, the activity can be written along it, or you may prefer to letter each arrow and have a key at the side. Note that the length of an arrow is not related to the duration of the activity it represents.

Figure 15.4 *A network diagram arrow*

Circles

Circles, called nodes in the critical path analysis diagram, are used to denote events which mark the end of one activity and the start of another (see Figure 15.4). They are divided into quadrants and a number is placed in each quadrant (this will be dealt with in more detail later in the chapter).

Figure 15.5 *A network diagram node*

Deciding on the sequence of arrows

To draw the arrows in the correct sequence, it is necessary to determine the activity done directly before each arrow, in other words, to determine the preceding event. In Figure 15.6 you can see that activity B cannot be done until A has been carried out.

Figure 15.6

In Figure 15.7, activity C can only be started when both A and B have been completed.

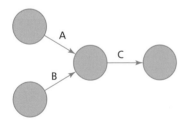

Figure 15.7

Activities B and C in Figure 15.8 can only be started after activity A has been completed.

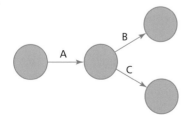

Figure 15.8

Dummy activities

Dummy activities use broken or dashed arrows and show an activity that takes no time to complete and uses no resources. They are used because in critical path analysis diagrams, two activities may not have the same start and finish nodes. Take the following example. Activity A precedes activities B and C; in their turn, activities B and C both precede activity D. You could draw a diagram like Figure 15.9. However, this is not allowed because activities B and C both have the same start and finish nodes, so instead you have to use a dummy activity and draw the diagram as shown in Figure 15.10. Activity E is the dummy activity, which takes no time, and consumes no resources. It is shown as a dashed line.

Figure 15.9 *This representation is not allowed, as B and C have the same start and finish node*

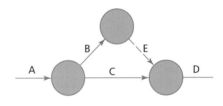

Figure 15.10 *The problem in Figure 15.9 is solved by inserting the dummy activity E*

Node number

The nodes should be numbered, preferably sequentially in the order of the events, but do not worry if this is not possible, since the main purpose of the node number is as a reference point.

Earliest start time

This gives the earliest time an activity can start, measured from the beginning of the project.

Latest start time

The latest start time is the latest time the previous activity can finish or the latest time the next activity can start, if the total duration of the project is to be unaffected. Any delay in this time will result in the whole project being delayed.

Float time

The float time is found by subtracting the earliest start time from the latest start time. It gives you the amount of time by which the start of an activity, or the finish of the previous activity, can be delayed without it affecting the duration of the whole project. If the float time is zero, this means there is no float, and any delay in the activities connecting nodes that contain zero float times will cause a delay in the completion of the whole project. The path which joins up the nodes with zero float times is called the critical path.

Activity tables

An activity table breaks down the whole job into a series of smaller activities and shows the estimated duration of each activity, and the activity (or activities) that have to be completed directly before each activity can be started.

Example 1

An old tarmac drive is starting to break up and needs replacing. Sarah, who is a systems analyst and keen on DIY, decides to do the job herself. The activity table for doing this job is given below.

Figure 15.11 shows a network diagram for the task. It is quite a simple network diagram because Sarah is working on her own and the only time she can do things in parallel is when she is awaiting delivery of the skips or materials. Most of the activities are therefore performed end to end. Times can be inserted on the diagram underneath the activity letters.

Example 2

You are investigating a computer project and have drawn up an activities table like the one at the top of the next page.

The next stage is to work through the activities table and prepare a sketch as you go along. The nodes (i.e. circles) are not put in at this stage, since the diagram will probably need changing.

1 Activity A has no preceding activity so it must be the first activity. It is therefore represented by a single horizontal line (Figure 15.12).

A

Figure 15.12

Activity	Preceding activities	Estimated number of man days
A Measure job and estimate materials	None	0.25
B Find cheapest suppliers	A	0.5
C Order skips and await delivery	B	1.0
D Dig up old drive	B	2.0
E Order materials and await delivery	C	1.0
F Dig trench for edging stones	D	0.5
G Lay and cement in edging	F and E	1.0
H Spread sand, compact and level	G	1.0
I Lay blocks	H	3.0
J Compact paving	I	0.5
K Brush sand into cracks	J	0.5

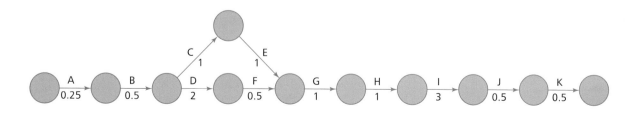

Figure 15.11 *Sarah's network diagram for laying a new tarmac drive*

Activity	Preceding activities	Estimated duration in weeks
A Feasibility study	None	3
B Decide on computer equipment	A	2
C Prepare site	B	1
D Order and await delivery of equipment	B	2
E Decide on staffing	A	1
F Order consumable materials and await delivery	E	1
G Train users	C	2
H Install equipment	F, D and G	1
I Test system	H	1
J Implement system	I	3

2   Activities B and E are both preceded by A, so you now have a branch (Figure 15.13).

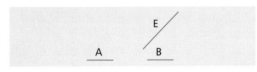

Figure 15.13

3   Activities C and D are preceded by B, so you need another branch (Figure 15.14).

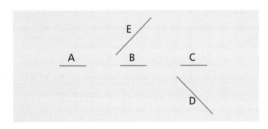

Figure 15.14

4   Activity F is preceded by E, so you draw a horizontal line (Figure 15.15).

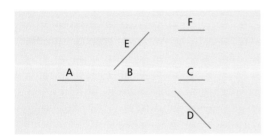

Figure 15.15

5   G follows C, so you draw another straight horizontal line (Figure 15.16).

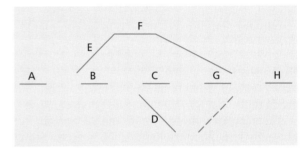

Figure 15.16

6   Activity H is preceded by the three activities, D, F and G. You now have to bend the line for F around to join to H, and activity D will need a dummy activity (Figure 15.17). Don't worry about the curved line at the moment; you can straighten it later.

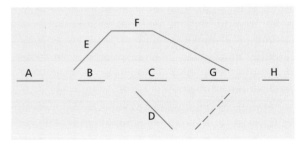

Figure 15.17

7   I is preceded by H, so a horizontal straight line is drawn (Figure 15.18).

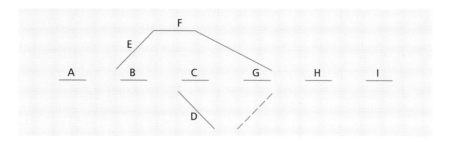

Figure 15.18

8 J is preceded by I, so you draw another a horizontal line (Figure 15.19).

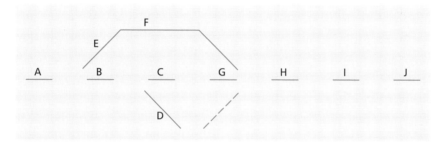

Figure 15.19

9 You can now draw the neat diagram using straight lines, and putting in the nodes, arrowheads and duration of each activity. Figure 15.20 shows this.

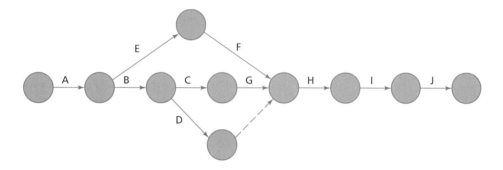

Figure 15.20

10 You now need to add other details before you can use the diagram. Each node is divided into quarters, as shown in Figure 15.21, and these quarters are used to contain the numbers described below.

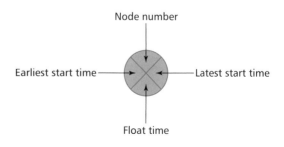

Figure 15.21

Completing the diagram

11 The earliest start times are put into the left-hand side of the nodes as follows. First place a zero in the first node since this node marks the start of the whole project. Activity A takes three weeks, so in node 2 you place the number 3. Activity B takes five weeks, so you add this to the value of the previous node and enter the earliest start time of five into node 4. Activity C takes one week so you insert six into node 5. This process is continued until you come to a point where several different paths join. When this occurs you always put the *latest* of the 'earliest start times' in the node. The reason for this is that the next activity cannot be started until *all* of the preceding activities have been completed, so it is necessary to wait for the latest of them.

When the last node is reached, the number you insert here is the earliest time for the completion of the whole project, which in this case is 13 weeks.

12 You now start to enter the latest start times, working from the end of the diagram back towards the start. In the end node, you place the same value as the earliest start time into the 'latest start time'. You now start to work from right to left, subtracting the times for each activity. When you reach a join you insert the *earliest* of the latest start times. In other words, the whole process is calculated in exactly the opposite way to the way the earliest start times were calculated. When you get to the first node in the network, you should get a value of zero. If not, you need to recheck your work.

13 The float times are now inserted and these are easily calculated. For each node, you

simply subtract the earliest start time from the latest start time and insert this number into the appropriate space in the node. Nodes with zero float times mark the critical path and any activity along this path which is delayed will delay completion of the whole project. In this example, the critical path is A to B to C to G to H to I to J, and the earliest time in which the whole project can be completed is 13 weeks. Figure 15.22 shows the completed diagram with all the numbers inserted into the nodes.

Gantt charts

Gantt charts are horizontal bar charts used to plan and schedule jobs. They show diagrammatically when the tasks that make up the whole job start and finish. They have a timescale going across the page and a list of the activities to be done, going vertically down the page. The blocks that show the duration of the activities are shaded to show the time taken on each task.

Gantt charts are usually constructed on squared paper so that times can be read off accurately. By placing a transparent ruler vertically at the point on the chart representing the present time, it is possible to determine easily which jobs are behind schedule and which are ahead.

The main problem with Gantt charts is that they fail to show the dependence of one activity on another, but combined with critical path analysis, they can be a useful aid to project management. Most project management software makes use of Gantt charts in some way. An example of a Gantt chart is shown in Figure 15.23.

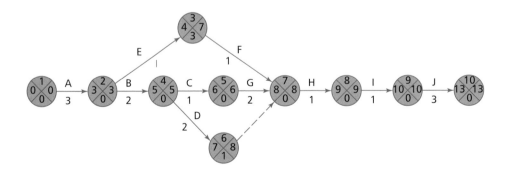

Figure 15.22 *Completed activity diagram*

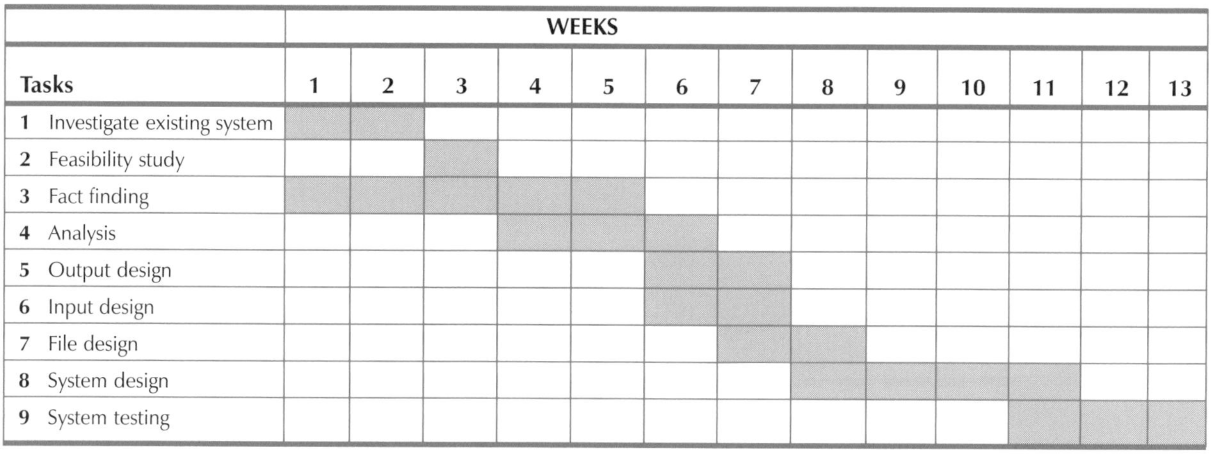
WEEKS
Tasks
1
2
3
4
5
6
7
8
9
10
11
12
13
1 Investigate existing system
2 Feasibility study
3 Fact finding
4 Analysis
5 Output design
6 Input design
7 File design
8 System design
9 System testing

Figure 15.23 *Example of a Gantt chart*

Activity

You have been asked to investigate project management software such as Microsoft Project. Your task is to evaluate the use of this software for managing ICT projects.

How does the software compare with doing the same task manually? How easy is it to use? What are the main advantages in using this software?

Produce a brief report outlining your findings.

Training

Any change which an organisation makes to its IT systems needs to be supported by training which will allow users to implement the changes smoothly without any major problems. Training sessions should suit the type and level of each user, so a senior manager would have different training requirements compared to a data input operator. There are two types of training: skill-based and task-based and their differences are outlined in the next section.

Skill-based and task-based training

Skill-based training teaches a variety of skills which can be applied to any task. For example, an important skill in IT is being able to produce documents that look professional using a word processor; once learned, staff can apply this skill to any suitable application they come across in their employment.

Task-based training is different because here the user is trained to perform a certain task which may not be transferable to other situations. For example, many organisations do business directly with customers over the telephone. Applications making use of the telephone include those for insurance, loans, mortgages and mail order goods. A company usually adopts an approach to be used consistently by all telephone-based staff, and for this they need to be trained. Task-based training is more often performed by the organisation's trainers in-house (i.e. within the organisation), and tends to concentrate on a particular job rather than a range of skills which can be applied to different situations.

Activity

For this activity you need to differentiate between skill-based and task-based training. In some of these situations it is quite hard to decide which is being described. You need to ask yourself whether the skill learned is transferable to other applications.

1 Learning how to scan a photograph into a DTP or word-processing package.

2 Being shown the need to proof-read what has been typed into an order screen against the customer's order on paper.

3 Learning how to access the corporate intranet remotely, from a laptop computer attached to a mobile telephone.

4 Learning how to use the organisation's templates for memos, agendas, letters, quotations, etc.

5 Learning the procedures to be employed when taking a customer's order over the telephone.

6 Being shown how to interrogate the organisation's data warehouse using Boolean search criteria.

7 Learning how to install software from CD-ROM onto the hard drive of the computer.

8 Learning about the company's security procedures.

The need to continually update and refresh skills

Organisations are continually looking for improvements in their information systems to make them more competitive or efficient and this usually involves changes in operating procedure, changing hardware and software, and bringing in the latest technology. All of these need staff to update their skills and learn new things. Most staff are happy to do so because it gives them a sense of achievement and also improves their promotion prospects.

The following changes would result in staff needing to update skills:

- a change in a version of the software

- the introduction of new software which had not been used before

- a change in the operating system being used

- the introduction of new technology such as EDI (electronic data interchange), intranets, data warehouses, websites, etc.

- the introduction of new hardware.

Computer-based training (CBT)

Computer-based training uses the computer as a trainer to instruct a person interactively. This may be working towards a qualification. Although CBT courses come on a variety of media, the majority are on CD-ROM. They differ considerably in quality and many utilise the multimedia capabilities of the PC. There are packages covering most generic applications software, other specialist software and all the main operating systems. CBT material is also available for helping to obtain Microsoft or Novell certification. These are industry standard qualifications which specialists are advised to secure.

Computer-based training is popular with computer and personnel managers for the following reasons:

- it has a high rate of success

- it is relatively cheap compared with other methods of training.

Suppose an organisation you are working for has decided to change from their present operating system to Windows 2000. Relevant staff could be sent on a five-day training course costing around £1000 or use CBT that would cost about £1500 to licence for a certain number of users. If there are 15 staff who need to be trained, the CBT course will only cost around ten per cent of the more traditional training course. Although you may think that with the CBT course you are only interacting with the computer, many CBT courses also incorporate features such as on-line discussions, self-study material, and e-mail exchanges with the tutor responsible for the course. CBT can be good for those people who do not like asking questions in a classroom situation. Also, if there is a point in the course that the student does not grasp, they have the opportunity to go over that part again. If the problem is still unresolved, then they can send an e-mail query to their tutor.

The main drawback of computer-based training courses is that the trainee can get the feeling that they are working in isolation since they do not interact with other trainees as in a classroom. The use of e-mail and videoconferencing, if available, goes some way towards addressing this problem. Another problem with CBT is that the person being trained using this method does need to be well motivated, whereas with a traditional course they are taken away from their normal activities to attend the course. With CBT most people have to fit it in around their normal activities, and find the time to study. Of course, this can also be one of the advantages of CBT, since staff do not need to leave the office. You may say that learning with CBT is like learning from a book, but a CBT course is a lot more interactive and, on the whole, a better training medium.

✓ Advantages of CBT

- You can work at your own pace and do not have to keep up with the rest of the class.

- You can train yourself when you have the time, such as during a slack period at work.

- CBT courses are much cheaper, particularly if they are mass produced.

- There is no need to leave the office to take the course.

☒ Disadvantages of CBT

- There are not always CBT courses available for training in more specialist areas of work.

- If the organisation has to develop its own CBT courses this can make them expensive.

- The organisation may not be sure that the person is taking the course seriously.

- The delivery of some CBT courses can be boring.

CBT is useful as support for more hands-on forms of training and it can be used to brush up on new skills learnt from traditionally taught courses. However, unless the training needed is quite simple, as the sole method of training, it suffers from the main drawback that a lot of motivation is needed by the trainee to learn in this way.

CASE STUDY

Computer-based training

Computer-based training (CBT) has changed greatly, and is no longer the inferior and cheap alternative to classroom-based training. Many of the large training providers such as IBM, ICL and Oracle are using web technology to bring the benefits of instructor-led training to the desktop. Instant backup is provided by tutors using e-mail or audio visual links (e.g. videoconferencing). ICL is providing training on Microsoft products with 24-hour access to a tutor's expertise. The whole idea behind these new training strategies is to replicate all those parts of the classroom-based course that enrich the learning process. One of the main advantages in using a combination of CBT and web-based support, is that if a person needs to know about only *part* of a course, then it is not necessary for them to sit through the whole thing.

Interactive video instruction

This should not be confused with the type of video which you simply watch to find out about certain aspects of computing or particular packages. *Interactive* video involves the use of CD-ROM and videodisk controlled by the computer and allows interactive training and education. Many organisations make use of this type of training, although it is fair to say that it has been superseded by the use of CBT on CD-ROM because the equipment is more readily available.

On-line tutorials

Many packages come supplied with an on-line tutorial from which you can gain experience of using the package. In most cases, the tutorial is fairly limited and most users find it little more use than a general introduction to the main functions of the package and some of its main features.

Activity

Using a package of your choice, which contains an on-line tutorial, produce a short evaluation outlining the ease with which a beginner could gain experience using the package from just the tutorial.

In your evaluation you should include the following:

- How easy is it for someone with no prior knowledge to learn using the tutorial?

- Is the pace of the tutorial right (i.e. did it go too fast or slow or was it about right)?

- Was the tutorial made interesting with the use of graphics and animation?

- Did the tutorial make use of any multimedia capabilities?

- Did it cover only the introduction to the package or did it cover some advanced features as well?

Activity

A PC user who needs to learn about databases wants to train in the use of Microsoft Access. There are a variety of options open to her and she has listed these below:

- computer-based training

- interactive video

- using the on-line tutorial which comes free with Microsoft Access

- reading through a 'step-through' guide

- attending a formal training course.

Your task is to evaluate the strengths and weaknesses of each of these options.

Formal training courses

Formal training courses make use of a trainer who instructs staff in a structured way, just like the way you are probably being taught now. The trainer will probably use overhead projector slides to reinforce the main points contained in the training session and these are usually elaborated upon in notes given to each trainee. Feedback is obtained through question-and-answer sessions. Hands-on sessions may be incorporated into the training where appropriate and in many cases the user will be given a hands-on guide, which they can use to work through a series of exercises at their own pace. The trainer is normally available during these sessions should the trainee encounter any difficulties.

Formal training can be performed by an organisation's own employees if there is a specialist training department, or companies may buy courses from training consultants brought in to cover such needs. Alternatively, there are outside organisations who use their own facilities and premises for the training. These are ideal, although they can be quite expensive and usually cover only a range of the most popular packages.

Sometimes, the company who has developed the software or hardware will supply formal training for a certain number of users as part of the overall package.

Whichever training method is used it should be purposeful, stimulating and interesting.

Activity

There are a variety of training methods available depending on the task or skill the user is trying to develop. Which one is chosen depends on the ability of the user and the skills or tasks they are trying to learn. The following training methods may be available:

- interactive video instruction

- computer-based training

- on-line tutorials or help

- step-through guides

- a formal training course (i.e. one that is instructor-led)

Here is a list of staff who require training. Your task is to pick for each the single method of training you feel would be most suitable. When you have decided on the method, you should briefly explain why it is the best option.

1 John, who has never used a computer before, needs to learn word processing.

2 Kevin, who has been using Microsoft Office for the last four years on a day-to-day basis, is to install the latest version of the software. The user interface is quite different and he will need to learn quickly the similarities and differences between this and the previous package.

3 Sabrina works as a data input clerk taking customers' orders over the telephone and inputting them at a terminal. A major new system has been developed and all data input clerks (30 of them) need to be trained to use it.

4 Jackie has just graduated with a degree in Information Systems from a local university. She works in the computing department but finds her post as a junior programmer boring and would like to build up her knowledge of Windows 2000 to make her more employable should she choose to leave.

5 Karl is a busy sales executive and is constantly visiting customers on their premises. He needs to know about e-mail as he would find it useful when away from the office.

6 The company keeps a lot of personal data on its system so all staff need to be aware of the implications of the Data Protection Act.

7 A user has forgotten how to set up a relationship in a relational database package. The user has occasional problems but is, on the whole, an experienced user.

8 An experienced programmer who can program in three languages wishes to learn Java (another programming language) to improve her promotion prospects.

CASE STUDY

Training

Here is an abridged article that appeared in one of the weekly computer newspapers.

With the shelf life of most software packages diminishing all the time, barely as the user base has learned to master the existing version, a new version is released. To narrow the IT educational gap there is now a huge and growing industry developed to help computer users. There is a wide variety of training methods and options to choose from, covering formal instructor-led training, computer-based training, the use of step-by-step instructional guides, video tapes, and multimedia guides. There are also some firms offering training over the web.

The training method to use depends on a number of factors that include:

- whether the training is for a single person or an entire corporation

- the budget available for training

- the skill level of the student

- the subject matter of the training.

The nature of employment is changing. People now know that they are not going to work for the one company for their entire careers, so they must take responsibility for their own training. There is no doubt that the training needs of users are becoming more advanced and complex. For example, a couple of years ago staff would be taught about how to boot-up their computers and insert their work disks. Now they are taught the latest sophisticated software packages or how to use the organisation's intranet.

Although the costs involved in training large numbers of employees in an organisation are very high, the cost of not doing so can be even higher. For example, users who have not had proper training will experience more problems with hardware and software leading to lost productivity and more expense in needing greater numbers of help desk staff.

In America, they call the peer support system the 'hey Joe' support system. Here a peer (a person you work with) is asked to help you with a problem. The drawback with this is that two people are now not getting their work done and if Joe does it the wrong way we now have two people using the wrong method to solve the problem. In the meantime, the help desk staff who are paid to sort out the users' problems are lying idle because no one has called them.

Other methods of training make use of the technology itself, such as computer-based training, training over the Internet, interactive video instruction and ordinary video instruction. This type of learning has the advantage that the user can set their own pace. There is also another type of training called JITT, just-in-time training, which provides simple training on a focused task on the user's computer. You may already have come across JITT if you are a user of Microsoft Office where Wizards are used to provide simple advice regarding how to perform a simple task.

Questions

1 Why might instructor-led training be more appropriate for staff who are beginners whilst more experienced staff might use CBT?

2 Many types of training are mentioned in the passage above. Most organisations use a variety of training methods when training their staff. What are the advantages in this approach to:

(a) the employee?

(b) the organisation?

3 Here is a statement which appeared recently in an article in the computer press on training methods:

'Computer-based training is little more than an electronic page-turning exercise that is hardly any different from reading a manual.'

From your experience of CBT packages, write a short piece in reply to the above argument, saying whether you agree or disagree with the statement and supporting your argument with examples of CBT which you have used.

Developing training strategies

As time goes on, the number of people without any experience of using computers will diminish and the training needs of staff will change. It is unlikely, for example, that you would now find a 16–20-year-old who did not know how to turn a computer on and load a program, although ten years ago things would have been quite different. Young people have been brought up with IT around them and adapt a lot better to change than older people. IT is a compulsory subject in the National Curriculum meaning that all school-aged children will have used computers and software, such as word-processing, database and spreadsheet, and most will also be familiar with multimedia and the Internet. Younger members of staff are usually much quicker at picking up IT skills and any training needs to take this into account. Many users are quite demanding in what they want out of their desktop PC and so any training courses need to reflect this.

Employee code of conduct

As we have seen in earlier chapters, an employee code of conduct consists of rules drawn up by senior management or their advisors setting out how an employee should behave in the course of their employment. It also details the sanctions which will be applied should the employee not obey the rules. The code of conduct is usually set out in the corporate information technology security policy, but sometimes the code is contained in a separate document which the employees have to read, agree to and then sign.

An employee code of conduct would usually include the following:

Responsibilities

All members of organisations who use the IT facilities must act responsibly and each user is responsible for the security and the integrity of the resources under their control.

Users must respect the rights of other users, respect the integrity of the physical facilities and controls, and comply with all the pertinent licenses and contractual agreements.

Since computers and networks can provide access to resources both inside and outside the organisation, such open access should be treated as a privilege and requires that all individual users act responsibly.

Authorisation

Access to the organisation's information resources, without the proper authorisation from the security manager, unauthorised use of the organisation's facilities and intentional corruption or misuse of the information resources will usually be a violation of the policy.

Security

The security policy could include the following:

- non-disclosure of passwords
- non-disclosure of company data to any third party
- security measures to ensure that printouts of company data are not left lying around
- provision that any unwanted documents will be disposed of with care
- responsibility placed on users and system administrators to guard against abuses that disrupt or threaten the system's viability.

Penalties for misuse

Alleged violations of the employee code of conduct will normally be investigated further, and should there be any substance to the investigation, further action will be taken. In some instances this could include criminal or civil action.

Minor infringements of the policy could be committed unintentionally. Examples include badly-chosen passwords and excessive disk space consumption due to bad file housekeeping, etc. These unintentional breaches of the code of conduct are best dealt with informally by the user's line manager.

More serious infringements need to be dealt with in a more formal manner in case further action needs to be taken. Such infringements would typically include sharing accounts or passwords or leaving documents lying around on the desk. Serious infringements are usually dealt with formally, by issuing a written warning for the first infringement and followed by dismissal if repeated.

Serious infringements are likely to include the following:

- unauthorised use of terminals
- attempts to steal data or passwords
- unauthorised use or copying of software
- repeated minor infringements.

Very serious infringements could incur immediate dismissal and if the actions the employee took were illegal, police involvement could result in a criminal prosecution. Although many organisations would shy away from police involvement because of bad publicity, the seriousness of an offence may mean that there is no other choice, particularly if the employee's actions had caused a serious loss to the organisation. Infringements of this kind would include theft of software or data, fraud, infringement of the Data Protection Act and downloading pornography off the Internet.

Activity

Here are some examples of misuse of IT facilities likely to be prohibited by the employee code of conduct for an organisation. Your task is to decide on the seriousness of the infringement (minor, serious or very serious), and then to decide on appropriate action for the organisation.

1 Using the organisation's network to gain unauthorised access to other computer systems.

2 Knowingly, or carelessly, performing an act that will interfere with the normal operation of computers, terminals, peripherals, or networks.

3 Attempting to circumvent data protection schemes or uncover security loopholes.

4 Violating the terms of software licensing agreements or copyright laws.

5 Using electronic mail to harass other people.

6 Moving large files across the network during peak use periods, thus slowing the network down considerably for other users.

7 Posting on the Internet information that may be slanderous or defamatory in nature.

8 Displaying sexually explicit, graphically disturbing or sexually harassing images on the organisation's computer systems.

9 Bringing games disks into the company and running them on company machines.

10 Using the organisation's IT facilities for doing private work for which payment is accepted.

11 Extracting data from a database in a way that violates the data protection laws.

12 Not changing passwords regularly enough.

13 Leaving a terminal with personal data displayed on it without the user being at the terminal.

14 Not scanning data disks before using them in the organisation's system.

15 Copying software owned by and licensed to the organisation and then re-selling it at car boot sales.

Activity

Definition of terms

A variety of terms is introduced in this chapter, many of which may be new to you. It is important that you build up vocabulary that can be used when writing essays or answering questions. Write a definition for each of the following terms used in the chapter:

help desk

bulletin board

Gantt chart

PERT

critical path analysis

CBT

on-line tutorial

JITT

1 It is not uncommon for designers involved in the introduction of information systems to encounter resentment and opposition from existing employees.

Discuss the reasons for this response and describe steps that can be taken by the system designer to reduce this resistance. *(10)*

(NEAB, Module IT04, Specimen paper, q10)

2 An information system was introduced into an organisation and was considered a failure. The failure was due to the inability of the organisation to manage the change rather than for technical reasons.

With the aid of examples, describe **three** factors which influence the management of change within an organisation. *(6)*

(NEAB, Module IT04, May 97, q10)

3 Each day a software house logs a large number of calls from its users to its support desk.

(a) Describe how the support desk might manage these requests to provide an effective service. *(3)*

(b) Describe **three** items of information the support desk would require to assist in resolving a user's problem. *(3)*

(c) The software house receives complaints from its users that the support desk is providing a poor service. Describe **three** reports that the software house could produce in order to examine the validity of this claim. *(6)*

(NEAB, Module IT04, May 97, q7)

4 You are asked to advise an organisation on the introduction of a new software package.

(a) With the aid of **three** examples, explain why different users may require different levels of training. *(6)*

(b) Following the initial training you advise subsequent training for users. Give **two** reasons why this may be required, other than financial gain for the training agency. *(4)*

(NEAB, Module IT04, May 97, q9)

5 (a) Describe **three** items of information a user support line would log when taking a call from a user. *(3)*

(b) Many user support lines need to share problems and potential solutions between a number of operators who are answering calls. Describe **one** method of achieving this. *(3)*

(c) Some user support lines also offer a mailbox facility to enable users to log their problems using e-mail. What advantages does this have for:

(i) the software user

(ii) the user support staff. *(4)*

(NEAB, Module IT04, Specimen paper, q8)

6 A firm is creating a team to plan, design and implement an IT project. Describe **four** characteristics of a good IT project team. *(8)*

(NEAB, Module IT04, May 98, q7)

7 A multi-site college is considering the introduction of an IT-based system to log visitors. The current system is based on a manual log at reception. The new system will capture visitors together with details of their visit. The introduction of this system will cause considerable change for staff and visitors.

In the context of this example describe **four** factors that the management should consider when introducing this change. *(8)*

(NEAB, Module IT04, May 98, q4)

8 A range of software packages can be described as 'Project management software'. What is project management software and what does it do?

(NEAB, Module IT04, Specimen paper, q3)

9 A software house has a user support department that provides a range of services to customers including telephone advice and the supply of data fixes for corrupt files. The department uses a computer-based logging system to store details of incoming telephone calls from users (a call management system). The system is capable of producing a variety of reports via a report generator.

(a) The software house receives complaints from its users that this department is providing a poor service. Describe **three** reports that the software house could produce to examine the validity of this claim. *(6)*

(b) The department currently uses traditional mail to receive disks containing corrupt files and to return them with the data fixed. However, the department now wishes to use electronic communications based on ISDN. Describe **two** potential advantages and **one** potential disadvantage to the customer of this proposed change. *(6)*

(NEAB, Module IT04, May 99, q7)

16 Implementing IT Policy and Strategies

Policy and strategy issues

Strategy issues in IT are those issues connected with how the organisation can best achieve its objectives using IT resources. The strategy normally takes into account the strengths and weaknesses of the organisation so that any plans can build on the strengths and minimise the effects of any weaknesses. The organisation needs to consider within its IT strategy any constraints placed on IT development. Some constraints are shown in Figure 16.1.

Once the strategy has been decided, the organisation needs to set it out in a document. The contents of this document are agreed upon and adopted as IT policy for the organisation.

The information management policy

All organisations making use of IT need to have an information management policy that sets out objectives on the use of information technology in the organisation. As part of this strategy, the organisation will take a short-term and a long-

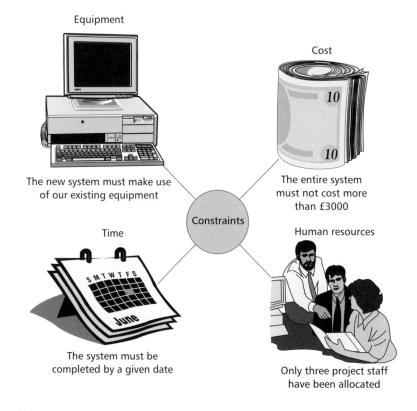

Figure 16.1 *Some of the constraints placed on IT development*

Equipment

The new system must make use of our existing equipment

Cost

The entire system must not cost more than £3000

Time

The system must be completed by a given date

Constraints

Human resources

Only three project staff have been allocated

term view as to what it should be doing about IT. Everyone can then take the steps necessary to achieve the objectives set.

Many organisations are still using systems developed in the 1980s and 1990s, and these systems were usually developed in a piecemeal fashion. At this time problems were solved by changing the hardware or software, and when another problem cropped up it was solved in a similar manner. Such systems were therefore often made up of equipment and software purchased from a variety of different companies, and often these were unable to communicate with each other and gave conflicting information.

Recently the tendency has been to have a single store of all the company's data (called a data warehouse) with this store accessed by all the other applications. EDI (electronic data interchange) has also become popular as a way of avoiding paperwork since all the transactions are performed electronically.

Many organisations have now decided to out-source their computing facilities to management companies, arguing that these companies provide a cheaper and more efficient service than running the computing facilities in-house.

Although the nature of IT changes with time, without a coherent information management policy, an organisation might develop new systems that are incompatible with existing systems and the whole management of the resources could become a nightmare. To develop a streamlined and efficient system, one must set out with a long-term view of what is wanted and put all the parts in place gradually.

The strategic implications of software, hardware and configuration choices

Although many IT developments are hard to anticipate too far in advance, all IT staff need to be aware of the organisation's overall IT policy as regards hardware, software and the configurations used. There are strategic implications surrounding the choice of the hardware, software and configurations and in the following sections we look at these.

Hardware

It is always preferable to choose software first, and then find hardware capable of running it.

This is frequently not possible in reality since the hardware has often been bought for other purposes and the new task could not have been anticipated at the time it was purchased.

In some cases extra hardware may be needed as more applications are added. At one time, once one manufacturer's equipment was bought you were tied to using the same kind in the future because different makes of computer could not communicate with each other. With the introduction of open systems (where the computer manufacturers have standards that allow mixing of equipment), organisations are no longer tied to a particular company's products. If the organisation has the most up-to-date computers, it will always be in a position to take advantage of the latest applications that exploit this technology.

Most organisations want to standardise the kind of PCs used, if possible. This is because staff are then not tied to using a particular machine for a particular task. Having all the computers the same might be ideal, but would be impossible to achieve as the cost would be too great. It is a waste to get rid of older PCs since these can be used for basic tasks such as wordprocessing or for use as intelligent terminals in client–server networks.

Organisations usually have a preferred supplier as part of their hardware strategy. The reasons for choosing a supplier include reasonable prices, service and a sound financial status (so that they are unlikely to go out of business).

Software

Organisations need a strategy covering how software is to be developed and bought. An organisation needs first to decide whether it wants to develop its own software using in-house staff (programmers and analysts), or whether, like a lot of organisations, it is going to out-source all software development. Smaller organisations would probably use software houses or buy specialist off-the-shelf software. Whatever choice is made there needs to be a strategy behind it.

It is important that organisations have a consistent approach to the software they use. This starts with the operating system. Many organisations are moving towards Windows 2000 as their operating environment because of its better networking capabilities and increased stability. The use of a single operating system may not get full support from all the staff since many of them will be familiar with other operating systems and the one that is understood best is usually the one preferred. In some circumstances, it might be necessary for some staff to use a different operating system, such as where the software they need does not work with the company-wide operating system. Such requests need to be considered carefully, as support costs (such as help desk costs) will rise with the greater range of different software used. Desktop publishing is an area where Apple Macintosh computers are preferred to PCs and organisations may be forced to concede that this is a special case and allow it.

The organisation will also need a strategy to choose generic office packages (i.e. software for wordprocessing, spreadsheets and databases), and all staff should normally be allowed to use only the chosen package regardless of their expertise with other packages. If the package is available over a network, then a standard version, with certain settings and configurations already made, will be loaded up on each terminal. Staff are still able to change settings (page settings, toolbars, etc.) while they are using the software, but these are not saved when the session concludes and a standard version is

always loaded. Staff should not be allowed to obtain software on their own initiative because of the problems this raises with licensing arrangements and support.

Configuration choices

Configurations, particularly network configurations, grow and change as the nature of the organisation changes. Many organisations diversify into areas that they could not have anticipated a few years earlier. For example, Tesco now sells financial services such as loans and pensions, and British Gas offers home insurance. Any configuration needs to be flexible enough to cope with these unexpected business demands.

It is very important to choose a network configuration that will enable the network to grow and service the business needs into the future. Although you may be happy with the number of terminals used by the network at present, you also have to consider the possibility of future expansion. As the network grows and as upgraded applications packages are installed, the hardware will become increasingly obsolete and will need upgrading as well. However, if the

Figure 16.2

organisation chooses the right cabling for the network, this may be sufficient to cope with the increased bandwidth needed to send graphics, and even video, across the computer network.

Methods of enhancing existing capabilities – future-proofing

One of the main problems in devising any strategy for IT in an organisation is that new developments seem to happen so quickly. New operating systems and applications software are constantly placing demands on the hardware that runs them. Couple this with new technology such as videoconferencing, voice recognition, etc. and the situation becomes quite difficult to manage. In an organisation with several hundred computers, the cost of upgrading to a new version of the operating system can be substantial. This includes not just the cost of the new software and licences, but also training costs. A software upgrade often demands a corresponding hardware upgrade, such as more memory or a faster processor.

Activity

A company is using the operating system Windows 98 on ten stand-alone PCs. A few of the staff have ordered their own versions of Windows 2000 but the manager in charge of IT is in favour of Windows NT as an operating system. What would be the problems in having all three operating systems in use within the organisation?

Any future-proofing plan should assess the total cost of computing facilities to an organisation. This is the sum of the costs of the hardware, software, development (or customisation), maintenance, help desk and other support, installation and training costs. These costs are often referred to as the 'total cost of ownership' and most organisations are trying to reduce this (see Figure 16.3).

Reasons for upgrading

There are a variety of reasons why organisations may wish to upgrade hardware/software provision and these include the following.

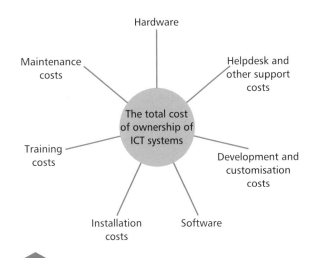

Figure 16.3 *The total cost of ownership of ICT systems (TOC)*

Hardware/software development

New IT equipment and software may need to be bought to facilitate the development of new systems such as videoconferencing, company intranet, the creation of company websites, data mining, etc. When purchasing hardware, organisations should look for potential growth of the system and only buy hardware that may be upgraded at low cost.

A need for more powerful PCs

More powerful PCs have greater memory and processing speeds and such power is needed for power-hungry applications such as data mining, CAD and videoconferencing. Powerful PCs, as well as being able to cope with demanding applications, also speed up simple tasks.

Organisational ethos

An organisation's image is of huge importance, and most want to be seen as innovative and keeping abreast of all the latest developments in information technology. You would not, for example, be impressed with a facilities management organisation or software house if, on a visit, you saw they were using old hardware and software.

Task-driven change

There are many computer applications that could not have been envisaged several years ago. One example is the use of loyalty cards to collect information about customers and their buying habits. New software needs to be developed for these new applications. These new applications drive the need for change in both hardware and software. Increased use of networks for communication of data, voice, pictures and video has driven the need for faster networks, making use of fibre optic links with high bandwidths (i.e. which are able to pass large volumes of data quickly).

Software change

Software is always being improved and new versions are produced at regular intervals. To take advantage of the improvements, companies may move to new versions immediately or wait a while and jump a few versions at a time. If they react to each new version as it becomes available, it could mean that staff are continually subject to change and this could increase the total cost of ownership as training costs will be high.

Activity

You are buying a computer for both business and home use. Since you are investing a lot of money in your machine, you want it to last for some time and be upgradeable. What things will you look for in order to future-proof your purchase?

When you are buying a personal computer for either business or home use, the main thing you need to consider is the choice of processor at the heart of the PC. If you make the wrong choice, you may be faced with having to upgrade the processor a lot sooner than necessary to run your future applications. It is reckoned that an average business computer has a useful life of around three to four years. After this technology growth means that upgrading is no longer a useful option; also the computers become less reliable and the repair costs rise.

When you buy a computer, you normally want to buy one with the highest specification you can afford. This is acceptable if you are buying just one machine, but when an organisation is purchasing several hundred machines, it will probably choose one that is just capable of doing the job at the moment but which can be upgraded in the future. This keeps the cost of the initial investment down and avoids paying for features or power that are not currently needed. Whatever is bought now will almost certainly be superseded by something faster and cheaper in few months, so there is not a lot of

point in buying a higher specification machine than is really needed.

When looking at large systems for use with networks, the situation is slightly different. The ideal system is scalable (i.e. it is easy to change its size), low-cost, easy to manage and maintain, quick to implement and simple for users. Most organisations with large systems are now trying to get those people who create the information closer to the systems which process it, and at the same time reduce the number of intermediate steps. There are many technical problems in future-proofing large systems, because when networks become very large, they become slow and may have to be divided up in some way. One way around this problem might be to use two file servers rather than one, but this approach causes fragmentation of the system and increased complexity.

Strategies for achieving upgrading

Keeping up with the latest developments in IT means taking advantage of the commercial benefits available. All organisations review new developments from time to time to see what advantages they offer. However, too much change in an organisation means that staff are constantly having to learn new ways of doing things, and they may feel that it is not worth learning to use a particular piece of software thoroughly if there is to be another release soon.

Upgrading may also be done when an old piece of hardware becomes unreliable and the maintenance costs start to rise. It is a bit like having a washing machine at home that regularly needs repairing. Eventually you get fed up with the trouble and unexpected repair bills and decide to replace it with a new machine.

Older computer hardware, which many companies still use, has expensive maintenance agreements and since the hardware producers are the only people who can repair it, this can be very costly. Some maintenance contracts can cost several hundred thousand pounds annually. This is probably now more than the cost of new, up-to-date hardware.

The upgrade path needs to be part of the overall IT strategy and it is important that all equipment is bought with this in mind. Most modern PCs are capable of being upgraded easily but some older models may need so many components upgraded that it is no longer feasible and it would be cheaper to buy a new computer.

Activity *KEY SKILLS N2.2, N3.2*

You have an old Pentium II 233 MHz computer with 32 MB of RAM, a 4 GB hard drive, quad speed CD-ROM and a 14 inch monitor; it uses Windows 95 as its operating system.

The monitor is old and unbranded and gives a poor picture when compared with branded, higher quality products. Staff, when working with Windows 95, are finding the information on the screen too small to see, so they would prefer to have a 17 inch monitor.

Your task is to cost the upgrade to a Pentium III 600 MHz with 128 MB of RAM, a 12 GB hard drive, 40 speed CD-ROM and a 17 inch branded monitor.

Emulation

Although PCs dominate the computer market throughout the world, there are other computer manufacturers, such as Apple, that many people prefer to use. This can cause problems when data needs to be transferred or if the same software needs to be used on both types of machine. Apple computers use a different operating system from PCs and to run PC software on these machines, special software, called emulation software, is needed which enables the Apple computer to behave in the same way as a PC.

There are some problems with software emulation. Part of the processing power is being used to make one computer behave in the same way as another. Behind-the-scenes software is converting the machine code instructions for one machine into the machine code of another and this inevitably slows the machine down.

Buying a machine containing emulation software might be the answer if some members of staff need the capabilities of a 'non-standard machine' yet still need to run the occasional application only available for a PC.

Activity

There are other small, desktop computers that compete for the same market as the PC. Your task is to find out what other makes of computer there are to choose from and what are their particular strengths in the market. Also investigate the software available to allow the other computers to emulate a PC.

Produce a report outlining the above.

Backup strategies

Part of the policy and strategy issues in an organisation is to look at the backup strategies for protecting data and software. There are several backup strategies that an organisation can adopt and the one chosen depends on a number of factors. One of these is the amount of data and its importance. Another is the time needed to restore the data from the backup copies. If several hundred terminals are used to access the data using a network, then the loss of this data may be intolerable, even for the short period needed to restore data from backups.

There are special backup procedures for company-critical data on networks.

The simplest backup strategy is to copy the files onto another disk, and if the amount of data is small, this can be achieved cheaply by copying onto floppy disks. This was OK several years ago, but now file sizes have increased and this is not an option in most situations, so another type of hard drive is used instead. Most operating systems have special backup commands and help the user to maintain a systematic backup schedule. Backup commands normally mark the time and date of the backup, so the user can find out when files were last saved.

Although you can have more than one hard drive attached to a PC (you can even buy ones that can be removed), most users prefer to use a tape drive (called a DAT drive) because it is much cheaper. The best forms of backup use removable storage media in case the computer is stolen or damaged in a fire. DAT drives can typically hold much more data than a traditional hard drive. The tapes used in DAT drives may be removed and stored away from the computer and can even be moved off-site, thus guarding against many disasters such as fire or flood. One backup strategy might be to take two backup copies each night and store one near the computer and the other off-site.

There are two main types of backup, full backup and incremental backup. These are discussed more fully in Chapter 8, page 131.

Activity

You have been asked to present a talk at a local computer club about the importance of taking backup copies and also how it should be done. As part of the talk you are expected to show some slides made using a presentation graphics package such as PowerPoint.

In your talk you will be expected to cover the following:

- The meaning of the word backup.
- How often backups should be taken.
- Where backup files should be kept.
- The best strategy for taking backups.
- What forms of backing storage media there are and the drives to go with them.
- A comparison of the speeds and transfer rates for different devices and some examples of the times taken to save different amounts of data.

The backing up of data

Data files change regularly, so backups must be taken frequently. To encourage users to take backups, producing them must be fast and simple. The average file (database, wordprocessing, spreadsheet, DTP) has become much larger over the years and this has meant that the use of floppy disks as a backup medium is no longer suitable. Far too many of them would be needed and the inserting and removing of disks would make the process tiresome and off-putting. Any method that makes taking backups too complicated or time consuming could deter people from taking them, which is a potentially dangerous situation.

Most organisations operate around a corporate data warehouse, which is a centrally held store of all the organisation's data. Since this will be connected to a network and have many users, the rapid recovery of any data lost is essential.

Incremental dumping of data files onto backup media is the main method of backup and this can occur automatically so that no one has to remember to do it. The network manager is the person who usually decides on the method and the frequency of backup.

The backing up of program files

Program files present less of a backing up problem since their contents do not change as regularly as that of data files. However, if the company has gone to the expense of producing its own software, or has paid a software house to produce it, it will have a great deal of money invested in program software.

If generic software is being used, it probably came on a CD-ROM, so this will be available to re-install should any problems occur with the hard drive of the PC. This sounds easy in theory but more difficult to do in practice, because most programs will need some configuration before they can be used with the organisation's particular hardware components. Configuration of programs takes time and needs repeating if the programs are re-installed from CD-ROM. Also, some special upgrades may have been added and patches used to repair some bugs may have been downloaded off the Internet; these would disappear if the program were re-installed from the original disks. These are the reasons why you should never rely on the original installation disks but do a proper backup of program files.

One strategy to adopt to protect program files is to periodically dump the contents of these files onto tape. The ancestral file system can be used where a series of generations of the tapes are kept; grandfather, father and son (see Chapter 6.)

One of the problems in losing the use of program files is that it can take some time to recover these files from the backups and the time delay, particularly if the programs were on a file server, may be unacceptable. While recovering the files it is usual to close the system down, which in turn could shut down hundreds of terminals and wreck productivity. Many companies try to avoid this by using disk mirroring systems or distributed systems where entire computers are duplicated. Such systems are expensive but necessary in critical business systems where the loss of a network, even for a short time, would be unacceptable.

Activity

Can you think of a list of applications where loss of the network facilities, even for a short period, would be unacceptable? Name all these applications and say what problems the loss of the network for a short period would cause.

When should program files be backed up?

The regularity with which program files should be backed up depends on the type of program files. For example, if a new application is being developed and the programs are being customised, they need to be backed up regularly. If, however, the programs are not altered, then after the initial backup no further backing up is needed until changes are made to them or they are in danger of being lost or corrupted. System maintenance performed by an inexperienced member of staff could cause certain files to be deleted, so it is always wise to take a backup first. One situation that could lead to files being lost is when hardware is upgraded; it is as well to take a backup prior to any such activity.

What media should be used for backing up program files?

Floppy disks are not used for backup storage because even with compression, their storage capacity is too small and the number needed to back up an average program is too great. Also, the backup process would take too long.

In most cases, tape drives with removable tapes are used. Read–write CDs can also be used.

The storage of backups

Most organisations make use of networks. In a client–server architecture network, the tape drive is normally attached to the server and this is used to back up the programs and data stored on the server. Networks in large organisations often make use of more than one server and because it becomes complicated backing up data in several locations (i.e. at each server), centralised backup is used. The disadvantage is that in backing up, the entire contents of all the other servers are sent over the network thus generating a lot of network traffic. This huge amount of data can really be sent only when the network is not being used for normal day-to-day tasks which usually means backing up at night.

Stored backups (either tapes or disks) should be:

- kept away from the computer
- preferably kept on a different site; you do not physically need to move them since you can send them over a communication line
- kept in a safe place (away from extremes of temperature and away from magnetic fields in the case of magnetic media); they could be kept in a fireproof safe in the same building
- clearly marked with a description and the date/time the backup was made.

Questions

1 Data stored on the server for a network is extremely important. The security of such data is achieved by using a redundant array of inexpensive disks (RAID).

 (a) The RAID system is a fault-tolerant disk scheme. Explain what this means.

 (b) There are levels of RAID from 0 to 5 with levels 0, 1 and 5 being the most popular.

 Explain the main features of RAID 0, 1 and 5.

2 RAID 1 makes use of disk mirroring. Explain what disk mirroring is and what its advantages are.

CASE STUDY

Here is part of the corporate computer strategy for a large organisation that deals with the future plans and needs of the company.

At present, all the company's PCs are connected via an ethernet LAN running Novell Netware. All of these networked PCs can access the Microsoft Office Suite of software with the package stored on a file server. Each of these terminals is also able to access the central host computers in terminal emulation mode to access all the company's specialist applications.

In the future, the company will use a data warehouse as a central repository of data and this will mean that users will not be faced with conflicting views of the same data from the many different information stores at present. All the data for all the major applications the company runs will be stored on this data warehouse. The warehouse will be Oracle-based and will be the company's first client–server implementation. This system will be up and running within the next two years.

A review of the PC network and its software will take place within the next two years. The electronic mail facilities will be upgraded and conversion will take place from Windows 95 to Windows 2000 as the main operating system for PCs. At present there are 234 PCs with a mix of 486 and Pentium models. Within the next year, all the 486 machines will be replaced by Pentium computers and we will be looking at a minimum specification for all the machines of Pentium III 450 MHz computers with a minimum of 128 MB of RAM. There are some major applications, such as the company payroll and personnel systems on the PC network, and to these will be added a PC-based customer complaints application written in DataEase.

The company will also be developing EDI as a way of trading with the large multiple stores. As all companies will have to use such a system in the future, the company will need to review their networking needs and to build a platform on which EDI may be implemented.

Data management concepts

All organisations have to manage the data they hold, and the usual way of doing this is using database software.

Database software

Database software allows data to be entered and stored in a structured way that aids its retrieval. Databases may either be flat file, which are simple to set up since they resemble a card-box file, or relational, which are much more flexible but require specialist knowledge to set up.

Many packages incorporate a special programming language so that a whole application can be built around the database.

Database management system (DBMS)

Database management systems are applications packages based around the need to hold a collection of centralised and structured data suitable for further manipulation. DBMSs allow the user to set up their own databases and most packages are fairly flexible in how this is done. Database management systems keep the data separately from the programs and this means that any programs developed are independent of how the data is stored.

Since most commercial databases are relational databases, this type of software is often referred to as a 'relational database management system' (RDBMS). Such a package allows:

- the database to be defined

- users to query the database

- data to be appended (added), deleted and edited

- the user to modify the structure of the database

- the user to import and export data

- provision of adequate security for the data held.

A DBMS consists of two parts: the data description language (DDL) and the data manipulation language (DML). The DDL specifies the data to be included in the database while the DML is used to access the required data. Data is usually accessed using a series of statements in query language, although a programming language such as Cobol can be used to write statements and extract data. The query language used is usually structured query language (SQL) and this is the agreed language for the interrogation of information contained in databases.

Database management system (DBMS) and relational database management system (RDMS)

Database management systems can be found on all sizes of machine from small microcomputers to large mainframes. They can be single-user systems in the case of stand-alone machines, or they can be multi-user systems, where each user has access to the same data. If the database uses data contained in tables with relationships established between them, it is called a relational database management system (RDMS).

In some cases data is held centrally on one machine. In other cases, where the data is shared over several databases on different machines, it is called a distributed system. Many organisations now use a data warehouse where all the data needed to run the organisation is stored centrally, and used by various different applications. This data is held separately to the applications, which means that if applications change over the years, the data can still be used.

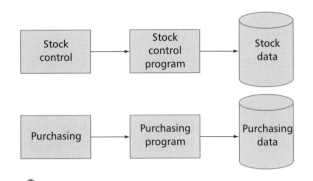

Figure 16.4 *The applications with data approach*

Figure 16.5 *The relational database approach*

Figure 16.4 shows the older method of storing data, where the data for each application is stored separately and the applications programs used to access their own data. Problems may occur when the same data is used by different applications. In such a case each application will need to be updated when changes are made, otherwise data about the same thing will no longer be consistent across the different applications. Figure 16.5 shows the relational database management system approach, where all the data is held in one place and various applications have access to it.

We now look at the advantages of the relational database management system.

☑ Advantages in using a RDBMS

1 It makes people think about the data being stored and stores it in a logical and structured way.

2 Data can be kept separate from the applications using it (data independence). This is useful if the database program or other application programs are changed as it is not necessary to re-input the data (although you usually have to convert it using a special program).

3 It avoids data redundancy. Data is only entered once and stored once no matter how many applications use it.

4 Because the data is held centrally it can be used as a corporate resource by all departments rather than belonging to a single group or department.

5 Data integrity is maintained. An update of the data in one place ensures that the data is up to date in all other applications.

6 Increased security. Centralised access is easily established and so security is easier to maintain than when the data is fragmented around the system.

7 Data definitions are standardised. Before the advent of database management systems, it was common to find different applications using different names for the same item of data. The data dictionary provided with most DBMS eliminates this problem because everyone uses the names and definitions established in the data dictionary.

☒ Disadvantages in using a DBMS

1 Learning how to use a DBMS can be difficult and slow. DBMSs are quite complex and need a lot of knowledge about analysis and design before they can be successfully implemented.

2 Costs for the development of a DBMS can be very high.

3 All the data is stored in a central location and this makes it more vulnerable than when it is distributed around the system. A centralised system needs good security and a disaster recovery plan should be tested from time to time.

The database administrator (DBA)

The database administrator (DBA) is the person who is given overall responsibility for an organisation's database. Since most organisations have a central pool of data and all the other systems make use of this data, looking after the database and its contents is an extremely responsible job.

The job of a DBA would normally involve some or all of the following:

The creation of the database

This requires knowledge of the techniques of systems analysis. Once tables and relationships have been created, the DBA would be responsible for the conversion of existing data into a form appropriate to the new database.

Monitoring of the performance of the database

Users may want fields added to the database that were not envisaged at the time of creation. As more users use the database, its performance may be degraded and a new system will have to be investigated.

Keeping users informed about changes that affect them

As the organisation's data requirements change, changes to the structure of the database will need to be explained to the users. They may be able to extract more useful information from the modified system.

Specifying database access rights

Users are allocated certain access rights to the data held on the database. Someone in the sales department should not be able to access personnel details stored on the same database as their sales information. Some users are given access rights so that they are able only to see the data and not alter it. The database administrator is also responsible for allocation of passwords to each user.

Maintaining the data dictionary

The data dictionary ensures that the names of all fields and tables are communicated to all users of the database. It ensures that everyone is using the same terminology so that there can be no misunderstandings about the meaning of a field name or table.

Assessing and organising training for users

Users need to be trained in how to access the data held in the database. The DBA either provides training themself or briefs trainers on what training is needed.

Data integrity

Data integrity means the correctness of the data. As soon as some of the data contained in a database is discovered to be inaccurate, users start to lose faith in all the data held. There are a number of steps that can be taken to ensure integrity of the data and these include the following.

Making sure errors do not occur during transcription of the data

In some systems, someone has to fill in a form from which the details are then entered into the computer. The filling in of the form is called transcription, and the mistakes that occur during this process are called transcription errors. Transcription errors are hard to eliminate altogther but careful checks by the management and thorough training of the staff who do the transcribing can reduce their occurrence. Transferring the data from the form to the computer is also transcription and transcription errors often occur in the process.

Using verification methods

When source documents are used (invoices, application forms, orders, etc.), the data is read off and then typed into the computer. Verification methods are methods that ensure that the data being typed in is identical to that on the source document. Such checks compare what has been typed in against what was on the original document. It represents a form of proof-reading.

Using validation methods

Although verification checks that no errors have been introduced during the typing of data, the source document may have been incorrect to start with. Validation is performed by the database. It checks the correctness of the data by the use of data type checks, range checks, etc.

Ensuring there are procedures in place for regular updating

Databases need to be regularly maintained. This maintenance involves continual updating of information. For example, in a school or college, a form is filled in every year so that each pupil/student can inform the school/college of any change in their details.

Making sure that there are no errors in operating procedures

The wrong file could be used to update a master file resulting in the wrong details being stored.

Data consistency

In some organisations, the same data can be found in different files. This is wasteful because the data may have been input several times. If the data changes or additions are made, this must be repeated for each file to ensure consistency. If this is not done, the situation will arise where the data provided depends on the file you use! This is clearly unacceptable.

Data redundancy

The whole point of producing a central pool of data is that once created, this data can be shared between a number of applications. The main advantage in this approach is that data need not be duplicated.

Most organisations now keep data separate from the applications used to process it, which means that if the applications software is changed, the data can be used with another application.

Using a centrally stored pool of data with a database does reduce most of the duplication but it is impossible to eliminate duplication completely. Data which is repeated unnecessarily is called redundant data.

The analysis and production of a data model

It is important that a database is well designed so that it can be used to extract the stored data in any way the user requires. The first stage in producing a database is to analyse the information requirements of the organisation and then produce a data model. The purpose of a data model is to make sure that data needs have been thoroughly investigated. The data model produced can be called a logical model and this means that it will be independent of how the data is to be stored or the technologies involved. The data model for a manual system would be the same as that for any computerised system.

Like all models, data models can be refined until the model reflects the real system as closely as possible. Not all data models can be implemented using a database approach, so the model may need adjusting to produce a model from which a database can be produced. Two techniques are used by the analyst for this: entity relationship modelling (ERM) and normalisation. Both techniques ensure that the model produced is one that directly reflects the structure of the database. Many analysts choose to do both entity relationship modelling and normalisation, although only one is really necessary. The necessity of doing one (or both) exercises cannot be overemphasised, as it is much the easiest way to ensure that the resulting relational database will work as expected.

Producing an entity relationship model

Entities and attributes

An entity is the existence of a thing as opposed to its qualities. Take for example an ORDER in a sales processing system. An ORDER could exist without us knowing anything about who placed the order, what items were ordered, the date of the order, etc. All the facts about the order add further detail to the entity, ORDER; these additional facts are called attributes. For example, the entity ORDER may contain the following attributes:

ORDER entity

order number

order date

items ordered

customer name

customer address

quantity

Entity relationships

Relationships between entities may be shown in a diagram called an entity relationship diagram. Entities are represented by rectangles and the unique name of the entity is placed in capital letters inside; it is always shown in the singular (i.e. ORDER not ORDERS). If we were to use a plural for the entity name we would be implying a certain type of relationship that should only be shown by using a line connecting the boxes as in Figure 16.6.

Figure 16.6

Notice in Figure 16.6 that the line joining the entities is labelled with the name of the relationship, and that it is named in both directions.

The above entity diagram shows that a customer 'places' an order and that an order is 'placed by' a customer.

Activity

Look at the entity relationship diagrams in Figure 16.7 from both ends and write down the two descriptions for each diagram.

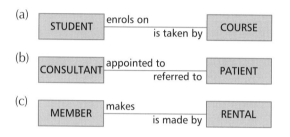

(a) STUDENT — enrols on / is taken by — COURSE

(b) CONSULTANT — appointed to / referred to — PATIENT

(c) MEMBER — makes / is made by — RENTAL

Figure 16.7

There are some things that these simple entity diagrams do not tell us, which it would be useful to know, such as whether there can be a customer without an order or whether a customer is allowed to make many orders. We need to add two things – degree and optionality – to these diagrams.

Degree

The number of occurrences of each entity type in a relationship is denoted by the degree of the relationship. The diagram below shows the three types of degree a relationship may have.

One-to-one (1:1)

One occurrence of A is only ever associated with one occurrence of B.

One-to-many (1:m)

One occurrence of entity A is associated with many occurrences of entity B.

Many-to-many (m:m)

Many occurrences of the entity A are associated with many occurrences of the entity B.

To understand the above, let's look at the following entity relationship in a video rental system.

VIDEO — available for / consists of — RENTAL

Looking at the above, it suggests that for each rental there is a single corresponding video. But if we define RENTAL as the loan of one or more videos by a customer, then this diagram needs to show this. Because one person can rent one *or more* videos at a time, it is properly shown as a one to many relationship.

VIDEO — available for / consists of — RENTAL

Optionality

Suppose that, as well as renting videos, the video hire shop also hires out games for consoles and computers. This means that a rental may not always be for a video, because it could be for a game. We need to include this optionality in the diagram. Optionality is indicated by a solid line to indicate that half of the relationship is mandatory (must be) and a broken line to indicate that half of the relationship is optional (may be). The entity relationship now becomes as follows:

VIDEO — available for / consists of — RENTAL

From this diagram we can now say the following:

- Going from left to right: one or more videos must be available for a rental to take place.

- Going from right to left: a rental may be for one or more videos.

As you can see, a single diagram can convey a large amount of information about the entities and their relationships with each other.

Activity

1 Explain in words what each of the following entity relationship diagrams show.
   Remember, you will need to look at the relationship from both ends and you should also state the degree and optionality.

(a)

(b)

(c)

(d)

(e)

2 For this activity you have to look carefully at each entity relationship and then describe the relationship from both ends. Remember to include degree and optionality in your description.

(a) Each item of stock may be stored in a depot.

   A depot must be the store for one or more items of stock.

(b) A customer order may be placed by a customer.

   A customer must be the orderer of one or more customer orders.

(c) A reader must be the maker of one or more reservations in a library system.

   A reservation may be made by a reader.

The problem with many-to-many relationships

Many-to-many relationships cause database problems and it is therefore necessary to deal with them in the following way when designing a database.

Suppose we are looking at the entities ORDER and PRODUCT in an order processing system (see Figure 16.8). Since an order is for one or more products and a particular product is in one or more orders, there is a many-to-many relationship between the two entities.

Figure 16.8

To solve the problem, we split the relationship and form a new entity that has some characteristics of the original two entities. Each product in an order would be on a separate line so ORDER LINE could be a suitable new entity. The entity can now be split as in Figure 16.9.

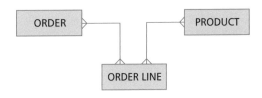

Figure 16.9

This would have the details of the goods being ordered on one line of the order and so could include product number, product description, product price and also the order number.

Activity

Many-to-many relationships may be encountered in a hospital or GP system as shown in Figure 16.10.

Figure 16.10

This entity relationship shows that one doctor deals with many patients and that one patient sees one or more doctors. It is therefore a many-to-many relationship.

1 Explain the reason why many-to-many relationships cannot be implemented on a database.

2 Re-draw the diagram by including a suitable intersection entity and give this new entity a suitable name.

The reasons for drawing entity relationship diagrams

The whole purpose of drawing entity diagrams is that they enable the systems analyst to analyse the data, and once this is done, design the database and implement it. Drawing these diagrams brings to the attention of the analyst any problems with many-to-many relationships, and so they can ensure that their final data model is valid. The technique called normalisation, that we look at next, also ensures that the data model is valid. The main difference between the two techniques is that entity relationship modelling is a top-down process because entities are looked at first and then decomposed to their attributes. Normalisation is a bottom-up process because it looks at the attributes first and then seeks to put the attributes into entities. The main thing is that the data model is valid, so that the resulting database will work.

Entity descriptions

When developing a system, it is important that everyone concerned with the development should use the same definition for each of the entities. To avoid misunderstandings, entity descriptions should be established and each person should use the same definition. For example, in a college enrolment system everyone should know how the college defines the entity STUDENT. A definition of the entity STUDENT might be as follows:

STUDENT – a person taking an approved programme of study at the college that could involve taking one or more courses.

Other entity definitions include:

CUSTOMER – a person or organisation who has ordered and paid for goods before or is in the process of making an order at present.

ORDER – a request for the supply of goods or services.

PAYMENT – a payment made by cash, cheque, credit card or electronic funds transfer reducing the overall outstanding debt. Payments are recorded against a specific invoice.

When designing a database system you should include a list of the entity descriptions as part of the overall documentation.

TASKS

Individually produce a brief, clear description for each of the following activities. The context in which the entity appears is outlined in brackets after the entity.

1 PATIENT (as applicable to a general practitioner)

2 VIDEO (in a video hire system)

3 RESERVATION (in a seat reservation system for an airline)

4 STOCK (in a warehouse system)

Scenario: a college/school library system

Your college/school library operates a manual system that is to be computerised. The systems analyst has investigated the system and found the following:

> The library is divided into sections and each book belongs to just one of the sections. If a book has more than one author, then only the first author's name is stored on the system. Borrowers may borrow any number of books.

From this information the analyst has identified the following entities as appropriate for this system.

BORROWER
LIBRARY
AUTHOR
SECTION
BOOK

TASK 1

From the information describing the system you have been asked to describe the relationships between those entities where a relationship exists. So that you get the idea, the systems analyst has done one for you:

Now do the other diagrams.

DEBRIEF

For this task you will need to establish which of the entities have relationships between them. For example, there is a direct relationship between a book and a section because many books are contained in one section. We do not therefore need any direct relationship between BOOK and LIBRARY because there are many books in a section and many sections in the library.

TASK 2

Having drawn all the pairs of relationships which exist between entities, the analyst has now asked you to join these and draw an entity relationship diagram for the whole library system.

DEBRIEF

Do not worry if you don't get the diagram right first time. It is much better to draw it in rough and then re-draw it neatly, repositioning any of the entity boxes so that none of the relationship lines cross.

BOOK is the main entity in a library system, so it is best to put it in the centre of the diagram since it is the one that is likely to have the greatest number of relationships with other entities.

Normalisation

Suppose we want to design and build a new in-patient database for a hospital. Before we do this we need to find out about the existing system and do a certain amount of initial analysis. This initial exercise reveals the following facts about the system:

Each ward in the hospital has its own name and a unique reference number. The number of beds in each ward also needs to be recorded along with its name and reference number. Each ward has a complement of nurses who are given unique staff numbers which are recorded along with their names. Each nurse works in only one ward.

In-patients are given a patient number when they arrive and this is recorded with each patient's name, address, telephone number and date of birth. When admitted to a ward, each patient is assigned to one consultant who is responsible for medical care. Consultants have their own unique staff numbers recorded with their names and specialisms.

Suppose we decide that we can attach all the details to a single entity and that this entity is **PATIENT**. We can list the following attributes:

PATIENT
Ward_number
Ward_name
Number_of_beds
Nurse_name
Nurse_staff_number
Patient_number
Patient_name
Patient_address
Patient_tel_no
Patient_DOB
Consultant_number
Consultant_name
Consultant_specialism

The above represents the data in its un-normalised form.

Going from un-normalised form (UNF) to first normal form (1NF)

The collection of data is in first normal form if it contains no repeating data item groups. We therefore need to remove the repeating groups from the above list and put them in their own list. Examining the list we can see that the attribute Patient_number does correspond to just one Nurse_staff_number and Nurse_name, since many nurses work on the same ward and will look after the same patient. This makes these attributes a repeating group and therefore to reach the first normal form we must remove this group and place it under its own entity, giving the entity a name that reflects what it holds.

PATIENT–NURSES is a suitable name in this case. To obtain the details of a particular patient's nurses, one needs to know the Patient_number as well as the Nurse_staff_number. Both of these fields need to be primary keys since they are both needed for identification purposes.

We now have the following:

PATIENT (Patient_number, Patient_name, Patient_address, Patient_tel_no, Patient_DOB, Ward_number, Ward_name, Consultant_number, Consultant_name, Consultant_specialism)
PATIENT–NURSES (Patient_number, Nurse_staff_number, Nurse_name)

Going from first normal form (1NF) to second normal form (2NF)

Here we look at the entity with two keys to see if each of the attributes in this entity depends on both of the keys. If an attribute depends on just one of the keys then it should be removed with its key and grouped in a new entity.

In our example we need to look at the entity PATIENT–NURSES because this entity contains two keys (remember the primary keys are underlined). We need to check that the attributes which aren't underlined depend on both of the keys (i.e. the underlined attributes). The only non-key attribute we have is Nurse_name, which although it depends on Nurse_staff_number, does not depend on Patient_number. We need to take this and put it with a copy of its key into a new entity which we will call NURSE. On doing this, the data is now said to be in second normal form (2NF).

PATIENT (Patient_number, Patient_name, Patient_address, Patient_tel_no, Patient_DOB, Ward_number, Ward_name, Consultant_number, Consultant_name, Consultant_specialism)
PATIENT–NURSES (Patient_number, Nurse_staff_number)
NURSE (Nurse_staff_number, Nurse_name)

Going from second normal form (2NF) to third normal form (3NF)

To go to third normal form, it is necessary to look at the attributes in each of the entities to see if any of the attributes are mutually dependent. If they are, they must be moved to a separate entity. When moving attributes it is necessary to leave one of the attributes in the original entity to use as the key for the newly created entity.

For example, in looking at the entities and attributes in second normal form, we can see that Consultant_name and Consultant_specialism are mutually dependent on Consultant_number. We now move this group to a new entity called CONSULTANT and leave the attribute Consultant_number behind to provide a link between the tables.

In addition, Ward_name is mutually dependent on Ward_number so these can be removed and placed under a new entity. Again Ward_number is also left in the original entity to provide the link for the relationship.

The data now is in the following third normal form:

PATIENT (Patient_number, Patient_name, Patient_address, Patient_Tel_no, Patient_DOB, Ward_number, Consultant_number)
PATIENT–NURSE (Patient_number, Nurse_staff_number)
NURSE (Nurse_staff_number, Nurse_name)
CONSULTANT (Consultant_number, Consultant_name, Consultant_specialism)
WARD (Ward_number, Ward_name)

The attributes are now in third normal form and are said to be fully normalised. If we wanted, we could now use the entities as the names of tables and their attributes as the fields. The purpose of normalisation is to organise the data model into a form that may be implemented directly using a relational database.

Activity

Normalisation practice activity

The following data items are in un-normalised form and need to be fully normalised (i.e. converted to 3NF) so that tables can be created which minimise the data duplication across the tables, thereby solving many of the problems associated with data redundancy.

The entity is in bold and all the data items that are attributes of this entity are enclosed in brackets after it.

CUSTOMER ORDER (<u>Customer_order_number</u>, Customer_number, Customer_name, Customer_address, Customer_tel_no, Depot_number, Depot_name, Product_number, Product_name, Product_quantity, Product_price)

(Remember, primary keys are underlined.)

Go through the process of normalisation showing the various stages (1NF, 2NF and finally 3NF). To help you through the processes, here are a few reminders:

1NF

A table is in first normal form if it contains no repeating groups.

2NF

The table must be in first normal form and then contain no non-key attributes which are dependent on only part of the primary key.

3NF

The table must be in second normal form as well as there being no non-key attributes which depend on other non-key attributes.

Convert the data into third normal form, showing the intermediate steps.

Tables and relationships

Relationships can also be checked after normalisation by considering the data arranged in tables. Take the following example. Since a customer may make many orders, a single line in the customer table could correspond to several lines in the customer order table. This is a one-to-many relationship.

CUSTOMER table   ORDER table

Customer_number
1000
1001
1002
1003
1005

Customer_number
987
1000
1004
1000
1003

ONE   to   MANY

Since just one item of stock is on each line of an order, this may be shown on the diagram as a one-to-one relationship between the tables.

STOCK table   ORDER_LINE table

Item_number
3447
2345
3423
3400
1459

Item_number
3447
3400

ONE   to   ONE

In many-to-many relationships, one line in one of the tables would correspond to many lines in the other table and vice versa. You should not come across this when the entities are changed to tables and the attributes to fields (i.e. columns) since the whole point of normalisation is to prevent this situation from arising.

Questions

Here is a question to give you some practice at normalisation.

A car hire company uses a manual system at present, but because of an increase in vehicles and rentals, it has now decided to store the data using a computerised database.

Someone in the company has been on a course at the local college but they only know about flat-file databases and have decided to store all the data in the one file which they intend to call **VEHICLE**. The fields that need to be stored are shown below the file name **VEHICLE**.

VEHICLE

Registration_number
Make
Model
Year
Customer_number
Surname
Initial
Address
Date_hired
Date_returned

Sometimes one customer may hire many cars at the same time so you will need to bear this in mind when going through the normalisation process.

1 The person who has been on the college course has suggested that a flat-file database could be used to hold the data but you disagree. Present a written argument, containing examples showing the likely problems, why storage of the data in a flat-file database would be unsuited to this application. Also, explain the advantages of storing the data in a relational database.

2 You now have to go through the normalisation process until the fields have been placed in third normal form. You should explain and show how you arrive at your final arrangement.

Creating the database structure

After the normalisation process, we end up with several entities where previously we had just one; each entity has a list of associated attributes. Once this is done we are in a position to construct the tables used to store data. Each table can be given the same name as the entities and the field names can be the same as the attributes. We then have to plan the structure of each table separately.

In Microsoft Access this is done using the table definition window.

A client–server database

A client–server database makes use of a network with client–server architecture. client–server architecture employs one more powerful computer, called the server, to look after printing, file maintenance and any other peripherals connected to the network. The less powerful computers, called clients, are connected to the network and can use the services offered to them by the server. The server is a dedicated machine, so it is not used as a client. Both the server and the client require network interface cards and also software to supply the protocols (sets of rules) to enable communication between the two.

To understand the concept of client–server it is best to look an example involving a database. Suppose we are using a database on a stand-alone machine for running a query such as 'producing a list of members whose membership has expired'. When a query like this is run, the database program opens the file where the data

is stored and then reads each record to see if it matches the criteria set in the query. If it does, then it is stored in memory, and if not, it is discarded. In this way the data for the query report is built up.

Figure 16.11 shows a single server client–server network which might be used in a local area network of a small office with between ten and 50 users.

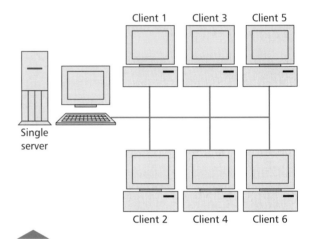

Figure 16.11 *A single server client–server network (10–50 users)*

If the same user had employed this same system but using a network, the file containing all the data would need to be stored on a central file server. This would enable everyone in the same organisation to access the same data. When one of the PCs connected to the network wants to run the same query as before, every record will have to be passed from the server to the PC, which will create a huge amount of traffic on the network and slow all the other users of the network down. Most of this traffic is unnecessary as many of the records passed to the PC will be discarded since they do not meet the criteria imposed by the query.

Using a client–server network, the problem is solved by allowing the server part of the application to be run on the applications server, and the client part of the application to be run on the terminal. It is now the client part that directs the server program to interrogate the database to extract the data that meets the search criteria. Once found, the server program sends only the data that match the criteria back to the terminal (i.e. the client). This therefore reduces any unnecessary data passing through the network.

Client–server architecture is the preferred network option for most large companies because each terminal can access all the network facilities without losing any of its own processing power.

The main disadvantage of client–server architecture is that the network is entirely dependent on the server for its operation and if the server breaks down, it affects every PC to which it is connected. However, if the network is properly run and the files are regularly backed up there should be no serious problems with this type of architecture.

The server

To run a client–server network, a powerful computer is needed to act as the server responsible for the storage and distribution of the data around the network. Along with the less powerful client workstations, a special electronic switching box (or hub) is needed to control the flow of data traffic around the network. Another purpose of the hub is to allow machines on the network to operate without interfering with each other, so if a fault occurs with one client machine the others will still operate normally.

Many desktop PCs are now capable of acting as servers, but it is better to use a specially designed server. Many specially built servers include network cards as standard and they often contain an internal hub and the wires to connect up to the workstations (i.e. terminals). Software is usually included and this typically includes Internet gateway software and server management software which helps improve the reliability and the overall running of the network.

Many servers come with more than one CPU and it is now possible to buy PC servers with eight CPUs. They usually have more RAM than a standard PC would need. Because most applications will be run using software stored on the storage devices connected to the server, the server needs a large amount of reliable backing storage for system software, applications software and the data needed by the applications. The backing storage devices can be high capacity, fast hard drives or a RAID system could be used. Most servers have controllers that allow backing up devices, such as external tape drives or optical disk drives, to be connected.

Activity

Definition of terms

A variety of terms is introduced in this chapter, many of which may be new to you. It is important that you build up vocabulary that can be used when writing essays or answering questions. Write a definition for each of the following terms:

future-proofing	RDMS
emulation	entity
differential backup	attribute
full backup	normalisation
DBMS	client–server databases
incremental backup	

1 A computer user has bought a large number of packages for a NEAB PC computer. Due to increasing workload it is necessary to replace this model with a more powerful computer. The user has a choice of

either: buying an NEAB SUPERPC machine which is compatible with the NEAB PC,

or buying a MEGAMACHINE which is a completely different piece of hardware but provides the software emulation of the NEAB PC.

(a) (i)   Why does the user need to relate the new machine to the NEAB PC?   *(2)*

(ii) Explain the terms 'compatible' and 'software emulation'.   *(2)*

(b) Discuss the relative merits of adopting one choice of computer as compared to the other.   *(4)*

(NEAB, Module IT05, Specimen paper, q6)

2 A hospital information system holds program files which are rarely changed and large database files which are constantly changing.

Describe a suitable backup strategy for this system, explaining what is backed up and when, together with the media and hardware involved.

(NEAB, Module IT05, May 97, q9)

3 You are the IT manager of a college. Your principal wishes to implement a computerised student identification card system. One way of providing the software for this system is to use a generic applications package, and to customise it to meet the specifications.

(a) Describe **two** ways of providing the software other than using a 'generic applications package'.   *(4)*

(b) The college has a clearly set out IT strategy; however, this project has not been included. Identify and describe **four** issues that should be considered when making a final choice from the above three methods.   *(8)*

(NEAB, Module IT05, May 98, q5)

4 A company has been running a large number of application packages on a personal computer. Although the computer works and has no hardware faults, the manager of the company now wishes to upgrade to a more powerful computer to run the same type of application packages.

(a) Give **four** distinct reasons why the company may wish to upgrade their computer. *(4)*

(b) The company could buy a computer which is 'compatible' with the current machine in use. An alternative is to purchase a different type of computer, with 'software emulation' of the current hardware. Explain the terms 'compatible' and 'software emulation'.   *(6)*

(c) Identify and describe **three** additional evaluation criteria that you might also expect the company to include.   *(6)*

(NEAB, Module IT05, May 98, q7)

5 A company sports centre uses a database management system to operate a membership and fixture system. Normally members register for at least three sports, although they can play any of the sports offered by the centre. Fixtures against many other organisations are arranged in a wide range of sports involving a large number of teams.

(a) Name three database files you would expect to find in this system. (3)

(b) For each of the database files you have named, list the fields required to enable this system to be maintained with minimum redundancy. (6)

(c) Draw a diagram to show the relationship between the database files named in part (a) (3)

(d) Describe three database reports that the system might be required to produce. (3)

(e) The manager of the centre intends to send out personalised letters to each of the members. This is to be done using the mail-merge facility offered by a word-processor in conjunction with the database. Explain how this is achieved. (4)

(NEAB, Specimen Paper, q10)

6 A college library uses a relational database management system to operate a membership and loans system. Staff and students can borrow as many books as they wish at any given time.

(a) Name **three** database tables that you would expect to find in this system. In each case, identify the columns and keys required to enable this system to be maintained with minimum redundancy. (6)

(b) Draw an entity relationship diagram to show the links between the database tables named in part (a). (3)

(c) Describe the capabilities of the relational database management system that might be used to identify and output details of overdue loans. (6)

(NEAB, Module IT02, May 97, q7)

7 A company makes use of a computerised flat-file information storage and retrieval system. The company is experiencing problems due to the use of this flat-file system.

(a) Describe **three** benefits that the company would gain by using a relational database as opposed to a flat-file system. (6)

(b) The company currently has three files in use; customer, stock and orders. During conversion to a relational database system these files would need to be normalised. Explain clearly what you understand by the term normalisation. (2)

(c) Examples from the three files are shown below. Normalise these files explaining any assumptions or additions you make to the files. (5)

Customer File

Surname	Forename	Street	Town	City	Postcode
Smith	James	11 The Avenue	Bemersley	Ruston	RS12 5VF
Penfold	Jayne	67 Bathpool Road	Outclough	Wignall	WG5 6TY

Orders File

Surname	Forename	Postcode	Order date	Item ordered	Quantity bought	Price	Total cost	Paid
Smith	James	RS12 5VF	6/5/98	Magic Duster	2	£10.99	£21.98	Yes
Penfold	Jayne	WG5 6TY	1/6/98	Banana Rack	1	£12.50	£12.50	No
Smith	James	RS12 5VF	12/5/98	Winsor Doormat	1	£29.95	£29.95	Yes
Smith	James	RS12 5VF	12/5/98	Easee Food Grater	1	£11.99	£11.99	Yes
Penfold	Jayne	WG5 6TY	1/6/98	Winsor Doormat	1	£29.95	£29.95	No

Stock File

Item name	Price	Quantity in stock
Winsor Doormat	£29.95	11
Magic Duster	£10.99	34
Electric Potato Peeler	£39.00	0
Easee Food Grater	£11.99	9
Banana Rack	£12.50	1

(NEAB, Module IT02, May 98, q10)

8 A manager has upgraded his desktop computer to take advantage of his company network environment.

State **two** changes that you would expect him to see as a result of such an upgrade. *(2)*

(NEAB, Module IT05, May 99, q1)

9 A hospital information system holds program files, which are rarely changed, and large database files, which are changing constantly. At present, the backup strategy uses a tape storage device, and has the following characteristics:

Each evening the information system is taken off-line and a full backup is made of the entire system. Three sets of tapes are in use and are referred to as sets A, B and C.

Set A is used one evening,

Set B is used the next evening,

Set C is used the following evening.

This sequence is then repeated, starting the next evening, with Set A again.

An advisor has suggested a change is required to improve this strategy. Give, with reasons, **four** changes that could be made. *(8)*

(NEAB, Module IT05, May 99, q5)

17 *Software*

Evaluation of software

When an organisation buys software it is committing a lot of time, effort and money, so it is important to be sure that the package chosen is the best one on the market for its purpose. To make sure that the software is suitable, organisations must evaluate it before they make a final decision to purchase. Sometimes an organisation will be looking for a generic package, such as a suite of integrated software that includes wordprocessor, spreadsheet and database; at other times it will be looking for a specialist application package.

Most software manufacturers have broadened their product ranges, as software now performs more functions than it did in the past. Business software would usually have dealt with accounts payable and receivable, general ledger management and payroll processing, but current software often ties the accounting functions with sales management, the Internet, EDI (electronic data interchange), document imaging, workflow and many other applications. This increased functionality makes it more difficult to select the right software.

Many organisations and users have experienced software failure, where software has not lived up to the promises made by the salesman or the hype in the advertising material. Perhaps bugs were found in the programs once the package was purchased, for instance, and the company received very little support from the software developers.

If you are an individual and want to get the feel of a package before you purchase, then evaluation copies can be found on the CD-ROMs that come free with many of the popular computer magazines. These are usually almost complete versions, but without important functions such as printing. These demonstration/evaluation versions give users a chance to see the capabilities of the package. Another source of software for evaluation is the Internet. All software companies have websites and most of these will allow users to download software for evaluation purposes. The evaluation version may be a complete or partial version and will usually be time-limited, which means that the package can be used for about a month and then will erase itself or prevent itself from being used in some way.

To match the user or client with the best software for their particular application, it is necessary to determine the user needs and then match the capabilities of the software with these needs. Sometimes, an organisation will already have software suitable for the task they had in mind but not be aware of it because they do not understand or use the full capabilities of the existing package. For example, many wordprocessing packages have desktop publishing features which may be adequate without buying and learning specialist (and more complex) DTP software. Organisations frequently do what is called a software audit (see Chapter 14) to determine what software they have and the licenses that go with it, and this can be used to see if suitable software is already in place.

When purchasing industry-specific software, that is, software for running a specialist application, it is important to look at the credibility of the supplier. Their financial status is important because many software companies go out of business and this could lead to the software not being supported. Some software developers may be taken over by others and the new company may not be prepared to support old software. The buyer needs to be sure that the software is backed up by experienced and trustworthy software manufacturers, trainers, and support staff.

Steps for evaluating software

Here are a series of steps you should take when evaluating software:

- identify software packages for consideration
- research these software packages
- look at the demonstration/evaluation versions
- check references from people who have used the software
- make your final selection.

The methods of evaluation

There is a variety of methods you can use to evaluate software, to find out if it is suitable for your particular task or tasks. To some extent the method used depends on the type of software being evaluated.

Evaluation/demo versions are ideal if you want to actually use the software for a while before deciding to buy it. You can ask the users to run the software on a day-to-day basis and then ask them to fill in an evaluation questionnaire.

Demo versions are mainly available for the popular packages; when large companies are buying very expensive packages, costing several hundred thousand pounds, another method is often used. In large installations, the software supplier will often take the potential buyer of the software to see customers who have bought the software and have been using it for some time. It may even be possible to find a company using the software in the same line of business. For example, if you were the operations director for a large charter airline, then because it is such a specialist field, the software supplier is likely to have sold this package to several other charter airlines, maybe in other countries. These may be visited to see how they find the software. In such specialist areas, the companies do not often have to contact the supplier to find out what is available; usually the software developer will contact them instead. Trade magazines are often a source of information about specialist IT applications. Surprisingly, many IT directors from companies that are actually competitors, will help each other in this way if they can.

Evaluation criteria

Before evaluating any software, you need to know clearly what you are looking for. You need to decide on a set of evaluation criteria. The criteria for evaluation should be agreed with the user/customer if applicable. Evaluation criteria might include some or all of the following areas.

Agreed problem specification

In many cases the organisation may have an outdated manual or computer system that is showing strain and not providing users with the information they want. It may be decided that they need new software that will produce important management information that the present system does not supply.

Functionality

Some packages, particularly databases, can be customised so that an entire application can be built around them. Although programming is not usually needed to do this, a fair amount of systems analysis knowledge and knowledge of the package is required if the system is to be successful. Functionality looks at the capabilities of the software.

Are import/export facilities provided by the program?

Is it possible to save the files in an industry standard format? This is particularly important if files need to be sent to another company where they will be loaded into a different system, using different applications software. Database files need to be transferable because if the organisations decided to use new software they do not want the expense of having to re-type the data. To see if import/export facilities are provided, the manual or books on the software could be referred to.

The amount of data that can be stored may also be limited, e.g. the size of the spreadsheet, the number of records stored by a database, etc.

Performance: the use of benchmarks

Benchmarks are special tests that measure the performance of either a program or hardware against a standard. There are two main categories of benchmark tests, application-based and playback tests.

Application-based tests

Application tests are where real applications (such as wordprocessing) are run and timed. These tests give you a good measure of how your system will work in use. You may have heard of Winstone; it is a popular benchmark which runs about twelve applications in the Windows environment.

Playback tests

Playback tests involve lots of system calls made to access the disk drives or calls to manipulate the graphics. Winbench is a popular benchmark to test graphics, CD-ROM and hard drive systems.

Usability and human/machine interfaces

Usability is a measure of how easy the software is to use. To be really usable, software should be intuitive, which means that it is easy for the user to figure out what to do without having to look it up in a manual or use the on-line help. Most, but not all, software makes use of a graphical user interface which is easier for new users since this type of interface is generally familiar.

It is hard to evaluate usability if you are experienced since what you may find easy might be difficult to a new user. If software is difficult to use, there will be increased support costs as more training is needed and more calls will be made to the help desk to sort out problems.

Compatibility with the existing software base

In many cases, the operating system that the organisation runs will determine its range of application software. Very popular packages are available in versions for a variety of operating systems. The situation is different for more specialist applications, many of which can only be used with one operating system.

Often the organisation will be buying a program module, so it is important that this fits in with existing modules and that data can be exchanged between them. Software upgrades usually allow previously stored data to be read by the new version, but there are usually difficulties with the old version reading data created in the new version. For this reason, it is not a good idea to use different versions of the same software within an organisation.

Transferability of data

How easy is it to transfer data to another package? With packages produced by the same manufacturer there is usually little difficulty, but if the software comes from different

manufacturers the ease with which data can be exchanged can vary.

Robustness

Are there any bugs in the package? There frequently are if it is a completely new package or a new version of an existing package. There is usually a financial incentive for software manufacturers to bring software to the marketplace before it is fully tested and this frequently means that early versions of the software contain bugs. These bugs can cause programs to crash and users to lose data.

User support

User support is extremely important because if there are problems, they can reduce the efficiency of the system and waste both time and money. Just like a new TV or car, software has to be 'fit for the purpose', so if it does not do what it is supposed to in an efficient manner, the software developer can be sued.

Support also includes the documentation that accompanies the software. It is important to ask questions such as:

- What is the quality of the documentation that accompanies the package?

- Is the package easy to learn? Some packages are notoriously difficult to learn and can take many months of use to master. In some packages on-line help is included but the quality of the help provided can vary widely and users could end up more confused.

- Are there lots of existing users of the package? If there are, then the likelihood is that they have discovered most of the bugs and had them fixed. More users also means that there will be plenty of books, training courses, CBT courses, software manuals, user groups and websites. There are lots of users of the integrated package Microsoft Access, so many of the staff in a large organisation will have some experience of it.

- How good is the technical support? Most software companies have a help desk that you can telephone or e-mail with technical problems, but the quality of the service and advice can differ widely. Sometimes this support is free but if not it can be quite expensive (see Chapter 15).

Resource constraints: hardware, software and human resources

One hardware constraint might be that the software being evaluated must run on existing hardware. A software constraint may be for a Windows-based package. A human resource constraint for the new system may be that it will operate successfully without needing new staff with particular expertise.

Upgradability

Software is continually being improved upon and it is in the software manufacturer's interests to provide periodic upgrades for the user to purchase. When software is first put on the market it frequently contains bugs or has important features missing and these upgrades allow the manufacturer to address these deficiencies. Problems can arise if the software manufacturer goes out of business. When this happens there will no longer be any upgrades (unless they are taken over by another software company) nor user support. It is therefore important that the software developer is chosen carefully and their financial standing investigated before dealing with them.

Portability

Portability means the ease with which the data can be transferred from one package, or module of a package, to another. If the software needs to be changed in the future it is important that data can be transferred (or 'ported') to the new package. This is especially important with databases where a large amount of data could have been collected over many years. (Portability is discussed in more detail later in this Chapter.)

Licensing arrangements

When software is bought for use on a network, a single copy is provided and a licence to use it on a certain number of machines. It is usually much cheaper than buying individual copies. It is therefore important to ask such questions as:

- What licensing arrangements are there?

- Am I allowed, under the licensing agreement, to make a copy for my laptop computer?

- Can site licences be bought?

- Are upgrades to the software sent regularly and are they free or is a charge made?

Financial issues: development cost and development opportunities

The cost of developing a software solution is not just the cost of the software since in many cases the software needs to be configured to the needs of the organisation. Staff must be trained, data transferred to the new system and staff will need support during the changeover.

Reviews of popular packages are freely available in computer magazines or over the Internet. It is harder to find reviews of specialist software but there are companies who provide evaluation reports for such products. These reports usually compare a range of possible software. They are the result of a lot of research and work by the publisher and are therefore relatively expensive. Making the wrong software choice can be very expensive, so such evaluations are probably money well spent. Using this type of review can also reduce the time and costs associated with selecting software.

You can ask the software producer for references but you need to bear in mind that they will only give you the names of satisfied customers and there could be many more dissatisfied ones. Alternatively, you could ask for a customer list and then pick out those you contact at random. Rather than getting a reference over the telephone, it is best to go and see the software being used in an environment similar to yours.

Activity

1 'The wrong software costs about the same as the right software – until you try to use it.'

Explain the meaning of the above statement.

2 You are required to evaluate virus checkers for your school/college. At present the virus checkers are old and staff have reported that there are viruses on the computers that are not being spotted by the present virus checking software.

Before you start, you have decided to draw up a number of evaluation criteria.

(a) Explain what is meant by 'evaluation criteria' and explain why it is important to have them.

(b) As part of the evaluation criteria you should consider the following:

- the functionality of the system
- the user support provided by the software developer
- the hardware resource requirements for running the software.

Explain what you would be looking for under each of the above headings when you are evaluating three different virus checkers.

(c) Besides the evaluation criteria outlined above, there are several other evaluation criteria you could use. Bearing in mind that this software is to be used in a school environment, describe three other evaluation criteria you could use.

Evaluation report

The main function of an evaluation report is to make clear the results of the evaluation and to make recommendations on which a decision can be made. Such a report usually contains the following headings:

- methodology used
- actual evaluation
- recommendations
- justifications.

Software to support specialist applications

A whole range of software exists to support specialist applications. Such software tends to be quite complex because, unlike generic packages such as wordprocessors and spreadsheets, an understanding of the subject area to which the package is applied is needed, as well as skills in using the package. For example, to use music software successfully you need to understand a fair amount about music and preferably be able to play a musical instrument.

Some examples of specialist applications are outlined in the following sections.

Geographic information systems (GIS)

The geographical information system is an example of a specialist software application that is gaining popularity.

We are constantly making decisions based on spatial data; you will, for example, have worked out the quickest route to get to your school or college. You know where your friends live and how best to get there and when you go shopping you have an idea of where the goods you want can be found. When you go to the toilet in the middle of the night, the spatial data held about the location of the furniture in your room and the location of the door can be very useful!

Sometimes we are asked a question that depends on the spatial data we hold. For example, a motorist may stop and ask us the best route to the Dog and Gun, or someone may ask us what bus they need to get into town. The spatial database we have in our brains is developed over a period of time and needs to be regularly updated as things around us change. If you move to a new area this human store of spatial data needs to be developed from scratch, with new details about the locations of shops, banks, bus stops, railway stations, schools, etc.

Computerised sets of spatial data and the tools required to manipulate them are called geographical information systems.

When databases have the spatial element added, they become very useful indeed. The data in an ordinary telephone directory is ordered according to surname, with the address and telephone number alongside. Although there is spatial data held (the person's address), the data is referenced through the surname. If you want a list of the telephone numbers of everyone in your street, the only way to do this is to look through the whole telephone directory noting phone numbers corresponding to addresses in your street. With a computerised GIS this would be an easy task.

A geographic information system is an organised collection of hardware, software, geographic data and personnel designed to efficiently capture, store, update, manipulate, analyse and display all manner of geographically referenced information. They combine the essential elements of a relational database with computer cartography (computerised maps). One important characteristic of such systems is that every feature on the map is linked to a record in the database and may be related to other databases as well. In some ways, geographic information systems may be thought of as 'intelligent maps' and used to provide answers to spatial queries such as 'which is the quickest way from A to B?'. The data for graphical information systems is organised into layers, each layer containing one particular type of information about the area in question. For example, one layer may contain information about the soil (type, texture, permeability, pH, etc.) and another layer may contain information about roads (width, number of lanes, type of surface, pavement material, etc.). All of the layers refer to the same geographic area (i.e. the same computerised map).

Geographic information systems organise data according to a location based on a map. They originated with local authorities who used them for keeping track of lamp posts, manhole covers, holes in the road, etc. With the aid of a GIS many commercial organisations now examine customers' postcodes to see in which areas the sales force is strongest and where more effort needs to be put. GISs are also used for finding the best sites for certain shops and by the police to investigate the distribution of crime. Where a town is close to a river which tends to flood, the emergency services can use a GIS to identify those premises most at risk.

One of the advantages of a GIS is that the data can be searched in two different ways. The query can be addressed to the data in the tabular database and the results displayed on the map; for example, it could show all the towns with a population over 20,000. Alternatively, a query can be addressed directly to the map and the results displayed in tabular form; for example, we could construct a query such as 'show me the population of all the towns I point to'.

Geographic information systems demand high specification hardware and are quite expensive, a typical package costing around £1000. Users of GIS packages need quite a lot of training before they can use the system successfully. The data needed to set up the system also costs a lot to collect. Maps linked to postcodes are bought from the Ordnance Survey and these are very expensive, costing over three thousand pounds for the whole of the UK. The alternative to this system is to use paper maps with people paid to add information to the maps, but this causes all manner of problems and is seldom used now.

Modelling may be performed using a GIS. Before any system can be modelled it is necessary to identify and collect the data on which the model depends. For example, if we want to model how a forest fire spreads, we first need data on forest type and density, the amount of dead fuel, slope, moisture in the soil, wind speed and direction and many other variables. Once these have been collected, the relationships between the factors needs to be established and defined. We can then refine the model until it behaves like the real situation. Once this is done, the model can be used for making predictions, e.g. how best to fight a forest fire on the basis of how it is likely to spread.

Utilities companies (water, gas, electricity and telephone)

The utilities companies use GISs to determine the location of pipes or cables above and below ground. GIS can also be used to decide where best to lay new pipes or cables.

Police forces

The police use GISs for:

- displaying maps showing incident locations
- real-time monitoring of police resources
- holding the burglar alarm and key holder index
- holding details for boarding-up services.

Archaeologists

Archaeologists may use GISs for determining the five or so environmental variables that most often correlate with an archaeological site. In this way sites with similar variables to known sites can be located and investigated. This is an example of using a GIS for modelling.

Local authorities

Local authorities use GISs for:

- keeping data on pavements, lamp posts, traffic lights, road signs, etc.
- planning routes for the emptying of bins, street cleaning, etc.
- keeping track of planning applications
- recording details of land use.

The emergency services

The emergency services need a detailed address database to direct vehicles to emergencies using the fastest route.

Cemeteries

Cemeteries can use GISs to store the locations and occupants of the burial plots.

CASE STUDY

Using a GIS in a local authority

At one time local authorities made continuous use of paper maps which used to get dirty or rip; in any case the place referred to always seemed to be in the corner of a map so several maps had to be joined together! When a planning application is made, the council has to write to the owners of neighbouring properties to see if they object to the proposed development. A GIS makes this simple. All the council employee has to do is type in the address of the proposed development and a map is produced on screen, centred on this property. All he or she then has to do is point to surrounding properties on the screen and the system will automatically list their addresses and can even send them standard letters. By using this system, councils have managed to save a lot of staff time and expense.

CASE STUDY

Using a GIS for the analysis of road crash data

In the USA, an average of 100 people are killed each day in vehicle accidents and around 2.3 million injuries per year are caused. A GIS has been developed based on all the accident data for the last ten years and this provides spatial display, query and analysis capabilities for users in highway safety, law enforcement and health services.

Crash analysis requires information on the characteristics of crashes and potential contributing circumstances. The data connected with an accident is recorded using the GIS. The data recorded includes details of the event (number of crashes, severity of crashes and the number of fixed objects struck), data about the highway features (geographic locations, roadway classifications and surface types), vehicle characteristics (type, size and age of vehicles), human factors (age, gender, licence status) and environmental conditions (weather and light conditions).

The crash data is used to provide a statistical analysis of those sections of road that have a high incidence of accidents, and to decide what might be done to decrease the accident rate. Such improvements might be to remove telegraph poles or trees, straighten curves, reduce speed limits or widen lanes etc.

The software itself uses pull-down menus to make it more user-friendly. Users can query the database for crashes of a certain type, at a certain time or involving drivers with certain characteristics. The results of the query can be viewed on-screen, saved to a file or printed out. The GIS enables users to point to a section of road on a map and then specify their query asking for the results in table or map form.

The system is also used to analyse the implications of the response to emergency calls. Response time is critical in crashes that involve an injury; timely arrival of the emergency services can mean the difference between life and death.

The GIS can be used to analyse the relationship between the location of emergency services and the distribution of crashes, which is a crucial determinant of the final outcome of highway crashes.

If, for instance, the emergency services aim to reach 95 per cent of crashes within ten minutes, travel time area analysis can reveal the number and types of crashes that are reached within this threshold. The results of this analysis are used to detect high crash zones with unacceptable response times, and if necessary, allocate additional facilities in these areas.

Activity

Here is a definition of a geographic information system.

'A geographic information system is a collection of spatially referenced data (i.e. data that has locations attached to it) and the tools required to work with the data.'

This definition is quite complex and you have been asked to supply an easier explanation, along with a description of some applications that make use of such systems.

Project management software

Project management software consists of tools which help the user schedule tasks, manage resources, monitor costs and generate reports for analysis and presentation. The most popular project management software for PCs is Microsoft Project and it includes the following features:

- support for multiple projects, resources and schedules

- project information can be viewed in a variety of different formats including calendar, Gantt, PERT and resource usage

- automatic critical path analysis

- complex tasks may be broken into small tasks

- project information can be shared via a network such as over the Internet.

With most project management software, the user has to input the length of time each activity is expected to take, the logical relationship between the tasks, what resources are available and when.

Music software

Before the advent of synthesiser technology, musicians were limited because they only had two hands and two feet. Although it was possible to layer music together (put two sounds together), a multi-track recording studio was needed, where sounds could be put on different tracks on a tape and then played back together. One problem was that you could do this only in a recording studio and the equipment could not be taken on the road.

Then music was revolutionised when a synthesiser manufacturer connected two synthesisers together with cables, so when one of the synthesisers was played the other one sounded as well. In other words, the synthesisers were able to communicate with each other. This then led to the development of the MIDI system. MIDI stands for musical instrument digital interface. Hardware and software designed to MIDI standards are able to send electronic messages to MIDI devices such as keyboards, musical synthesisers and drum machines.

Mathematical software

There is a whole range of software whose purpose is to deal with mathematical problems which cannot easily be solved using spreadsheet software.

MathCAD is an example of one such package used to display, calculate and analyse equations in standard mathematical format. This particular package has capabilities such as solving simultaneous equations, systems of equations or inequalities, evaluating complex expressions from algebra, trigonometry, calculus and statistics. It can also be used to prepare tables and graphs of functions.

MathCAD can be used just like an ordinary calculator, so to perform the calculation:

$$3^6 \times 8.7 - \frac{1}{2}$$

we would type:

$$3 \wedge 6 * 8.7 - 1/2 =$$

Computer-aided design (CAD) systems

Because changes in design are so easy to make using a computer, it is hard to find any aspect of design that is still performed manually. CAD packages are used to manipulate designs of buildings, cars, engineering components, structures (bridges, tunnels, etc.) and computer chips. Designs can be made up from previously stored shapes and drawings in a fraction of the time it would take to do a manual drawing. In addition, alterations may be made rapidly without the need for re-drawing.

The most popular CAD package is called AutoCAD and this software can be run on desk-top computers and more specialist graphics workstations. AutoCAD is an interactive drawing system designed to permit a user to construct or edit a drawing on a display screen. It is rather like a wordprocessing system, except in this case the thing processed is a drawing. Each drawing is stored as a disk file and AutoCAD is able to edit one drawing (or file) at a time. The principle functional component of AutoCAD is the drawing editor that is the working area on the screen. AutoCad has many advanced features. For example, you can draw a line and then turn it automatically into a cavity wall showing the inner and outer walls. Floors and ceilings may be added and there are even pre-drawn shapes for all sorts of features, such as toilets and washbasins, that may be added.

The main advantages of using CAD rather than drawing with a drawing board and pencil are as follows:

- The quality of the drawings is consistent.

- Alterations are readily made without the need for re-drawing.

- Diagrams can be multi-layered so that you can, for example, take just the heating system and display that, or just display the lighting circuits, and so on. Some diagrams can have ten or more layers that can be shown together or separately as required.

- Many buildings are now multi-storey with the plan for each floor the same shape. By copying the external walls of each floor and any services that do not change from one floor to another, a lot of time can be saved.

- When drawings are finished with, they may be kept on a floppy disk and stored for reference thus saving valuable space.

Using a CAD package, it is possible from a two-dimensional plan to produce a three-dimensional impression. You can then use the package to act as a person in the building. Point them in different directions and the package will show on the screen the view that would be seen. By moving the 'figure' from one room to another, you can also see exactly what the whole building would look like viewed from the inside.

Hardware used by CAD systems

CAD software places high demands on any computer system and it is important to choose a fast processor such as the Pentium III with a high clock speed. Some drawings are very complex indeed and can come in many layers and therefore take up a lot of disk space when stored. CAD systems should therefore have high hard disk capacity and, like any serious application, there should be some backup system in use.

When producing diagrams, plans or drawings, the screen display can become very cluttered so CAD workstations usually have larger screens (typically 19 or 21 inch) compared to other applications. Very high resolution screens are used for the sake of the user's eyesight and this, along with their size, means that screens are quite an expensive component of CAD systems.

Since the working area of the screen needs to be as large as possible, the user does not normally want it cluttered with menus and toolbars, so a CAD system usually makes use of a graphics tablet (sometimes called a digitising tablet). Graphics tablets are input devices with a tablet overlay, the exact features of which depend on the particular CAD software being used. Each of these items on

the tablet is the same as if it were on the screen. To select an item, you simply move the hand-held puck until its cross-hairs (in its perspex viewing window) are positioned over the required item and then press the pick button to make the selection.

Many companies involved in CAD work act as consultants and have to send their drawings to clients, such as architects, engineers and builders, etc. who use the data as input to their own systems. To save time sending disks through the post, many organisations use the Internet to send files to their clients.

Because there is so much detail on each diagram, plans have to be produced on a large scale, typically 1:50, and this means printouts require a special plotter. These drum plotters use an ink jet technique to spray the image onto the paper as it moves up and down over the drum. Some companies use flat-bed plotters but because they take up a large amount of office space, they are much less popular.

Computer-aided manufacturing (CAM) systems

Computer aided manufacturing (CAM) is used in modern factories where, once a part has been designed using CAD, the data is sent to the factory floor (usually via a network link) where the CAM program instructs the machine how to make the part. There needs to be an interface to enable the computer supplying the instructions to communicate with the machines making the parts.

Software development

In this section we look at the various ways of providing a software solution as well as the criteria used when selecting software solutions to specialist applications.

Sources of software solutions

If software needs to be developed or bought to solve a particular problem, there is a variety of ways in which this can be done. The main ones are to use:

- **a generic package** (database, spreadsheet, etc.) that could be customised to an organisation's needs

- **specialist software**, that is, software developed for a particular application that usually still needs customising to suit an organisation's operating procedures.

- **an external software developer**, called a software house, to write bespoke (i.e. tailor-made) software to an organisation's specifications
- **in-house staff** (systems analysts and programmers) to design and then write software tailor-made to their needs.

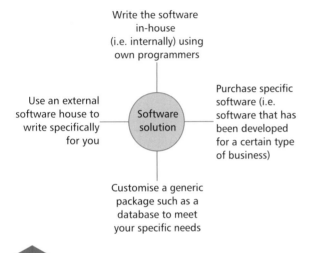

Write the software in-house (i.e. internally) using own programmers

Purchase specific software (i.e. software that has been developed for a certain type of business)

Software solution

Use an external software house to write specifically for you

Customise a generic package such as a database to meet your specific needs

Figure 17.1 *Ways of providing a software solution*

Choosing specialist applications software

When any organisation chooses new specialist applications software, it needs to be quite clear what is required. A variety of staff will be using this software, so ideally everyone should play a part in deciding which package to choose. There are many reasons why the choice of a package should not be left to a single person, some of which are outlined below:

- The person choosing the software may have different requirements to the other potential users and although it may be capable of performing his tasks, it may be unsuitable for others.

- A particular package may be chosen because the buyer has used the software before and will not have to learn to use new software.

If the organisation does not employ any specialist IT staff able to oversee the choosing of a package, then consultants should be brought in who have expertise in this area.

Figure 17.2

Sometimes there is a tendency for staff to develop their own systems and buy software as and when they need it without any consultation or indeed the knowledge of the IT department. Such informal acquisitions are frowned upon by IT departments for a number of good reasons which include:

- The software being bought may be incompatible with existing hardware.

- The software being bought may be incompatible with existing software (usually the operating system).

- Help costs may be high because staff will not have been properly trained in using the software. The staff involved in introducing *ad hoc* software may not be aware of the cost of software support.

- If software is brought into the organisation in this fashion, it is hard to be sure that the organisation has the correct site licences and it could unwittingly be in breach of the law.

- If such software is used to hold personal data, users will need to register its use with the Data Protection Commissioner.

Providing software solutions

Ten years ago, if a large company wanted some software to do a particular specialist task they would probably have considered writing it themselves using their specialist programming staff or getting an outside software house to write it for them. Now, very few companies will consider this and instead look to buy specialist business applications software. Companies are very diverse in the way they are structured and do business and in their different information flows and operating procedures, yet they are still able to buy a package to suit them. The reason for this is that modern packaged software is very configurable; it can be altered to suit the particular needs of an organisation. The potential for configuring packaged software makes it quite complex, so selecting the right package for a particular organisation is quite difficult. Once such a package has been bought a lot of expertise is needed to configure it to suit the organisation.

Companies are now turning to packages to run their key applications, such as process control, capacity planning, accounts, project budgeting, etc. Such software was first used in the manufacturing industry but has now spread to all business areas. The software is sometimes

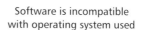

Software is incompatible with operating system used

Software bought is incompatible with existing hardware

Increased costs because staff have not been trained in using the software properly

If the software is used to hold personal data, they will need to register its use with the Data Protection Commissioner

Use of software could cause the organisation to be in breach of the law

Figure 17.3 *Problems due to informal acquisitions of software*

referred to as enterprise resource planning (ERP) software. ERP software is usually fully integrated and uses a single database which stores all the company data regardless of its origin. The advantage with this is that all staff use the same database and interface to get the information they need for their particular jobs. Sometimes it is necessary to look to other software developers for modules. When this happens, compatibility becomes an issue; software is less likely to be as integrated and problems may arise sharing data.

Buying a specialist package is different to buying an office package, such as a wordprocessor, because office packages need little doing to them before they can be used. It is necessary to spend a lot of time and money configuring specialist packages, but this is still much quicker than writing a program from scratch.

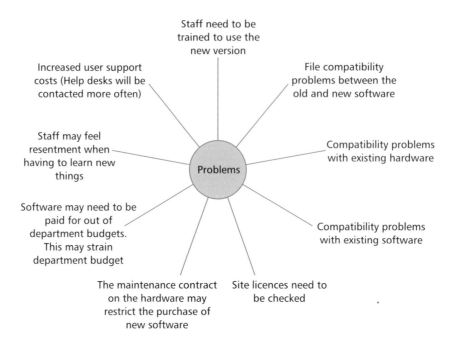

Figure 17.4 *Changing software for a whole organisation is not simple*

Issues in choosing a software solution

There is a variety of issues an organisation should consider before deciding which of the above options to choose when a software solution is required.

Cost

Projects are always given a budget and this on its own can determine which method is adopted. Generic packages are usually cheap, as these packages are mass produced and the costs are shared among the many users. Both generic and specialist software need customisation and this increases the cost because someone must be paid to do this. If extensive customisation of the software is needed to fit it to the organisation, it may be worth changing the operating procedures to fit in with the software, or alternatively to opt for tailor-made software whether produced in-house or not.

Writing software from scratch can be very expensive, but many organisations still do this because they get a perfect solution to their problem and not a compromise. This method may not be an option for many organisations because of the cost.

There are costs other than those of development which may need to be considered. Training and support costs are likely to be much

higher if bespoke software is developed, whereas with generic packages these costs are likely to be quite low.

User support

User support is likely to be much better if software is developed in-house, but if the organisation decides to go outside for its software, quality of support is more variable. When generic packages and specialist software have a wide user base, the user support tends to be better because suppliers are able to cope with the higher support costs. Small software houses may go out of business or be taken over by larger companies who may decide not to support the existing software.

Compatibility with existing software

New software may have to be compatible with existing software so that files and data can be transferred between packages. The ease with which this may be done could be a deciding factor in the choice of software.

Compatibility with existing hardware

New software frequently places greater demands on the hardware running it, so it is necessary to add extra memory, faster processor chips, etc. to the machines, which increases the overall cost of development.

Upgrade paths

Software frequently needs to be upgraded, sometimes because of necessity (e.g. changes in tax, National Insurance, VAT) and sometimes to iron out bugs or include some new features. Upgrade paths depend on the original supplier still being in business, so any outside supplier of software should be carefully chosen.

Ease of use

Generic software has a huge user base and this means that more time and attention can be devoted to the development of features that make the software easy to use. Generally, the human/computer interface is much better with generic packages and frequent upgrades mean that problems are soon ironed out.

Development time

Sometimes only a certain time is allowed for development of new software and this can be a deciding factor in which method to use. Developing software from scratch, either internally or externally, takes longest, whereas generic packages are quick to implement. The more customisation needed, the longer needed for development.

Testing also takes time and some software is brought to the market before testing is complete which means that new software can contain bugs. Generic packages tend to be more thoroughly tested than other types of software.

The appropriateness of the solution

The best solution to an IT problem may not always be the one chosen. There may be constraints imposed, such as money, resources, time, etc., so often a compromise is needed. The appropriateness of the solution is a measure of how good the solution to a problem is.

Activity

An organisation has been using the integrated general purpose package Lotus Smartsuite for around four years. It has 30 staff who make use of parts of the package in doing their jobs. A new IT manager has been recruited and since he knows little about this package, is eager to change over to a package he knows more about. He gets all the staff together and explains to them that Microsoft Office (another integrated package) is much better and he intends to buy it for the organisation and everyone must start using it.

1 Explain what likely costs there will be in changing over from one package to the other.

2 The IT manager has made a unilateral decision to change to a new piece of software. What problems might he encounter with this approach?

Software reliability

Testing the reliability of software is performed either by the supplier or the software producer. Testing ensures that the software does not contain any errors, or bugs as they are called. If bespoke software has been developed, it is checked to see that what has been developed meets the criteria of the specification.

Software testing is all about the process of executing (i.e. running) software in a controlled manner to answer the question 'does the software behave as specified?'. If a software house has been contracted to write software to a customer's specification, then testing should show that it conforms to the specification.

Debugging is a slightly different process to software testing, since it looks for parts of the program code which are responsible for the software not behaving as expected. Debugging supports software testing but no amount of testing is likely to uncover all the bugs because many will only occur when the software is used in an unusual or unexpected way. Bugs in a program are a bit like land mines; they are hard to find, they don't cause a problem until you stumble across them, but when you do you are in serious trouble! Software testing, then, is a little like an engineer clearing a road through the minefield. After this is done, you are safe because someone has been there before. If, however, you go along an untested route then it may be dangerous.

Thorough software testing costs a lot of money and takes a long time; the amount of testing needed depends on the potential consequences of any undetected bugs. Obviously in a fly-by-wire, computer-controlled aircraft, any bugs could have fatal consequences. Failure in most applications is not so serious, fortunately. Bugs can, however, cause a loss of credibility to a software company and result in fewer orders. If, on the other hand, a software company is known for reliable software then they will get a lot more orders as a result.

One method of testing is to look at the program code and identify any part of it that is likely to cause a problem. Testing also involves analysing the software as it is being run using a variety of techniques such as traces.

The main objectives of testing are to:

- make sure the software is compatible with other systems with which it should communicate

- eradicate faults in the software by looking at how it will be used, predicting what errors are likely to occur and then designing tests to expose these errors

- test portability; this means checking that the software can be ported to specified hardware and software platforms

- review the software, usually by presenting the software to project personnel, managers and other interested parties for their comments.

Alpha testing

Alpha testing is the first stage in testing computer products such as software, before they are released for public use. Alpha tests are usually co-ordinated by the hardware manufacturer or software producer. They are usually performed at an in-house site that is not normally involved with the software developers. Alpha testing uses data that is selected by the software producer. When bespoke (i.e. tailor-made) software is tested, the alpha test is normally carried out to test the implementation against the design specification and check that it does what it is supposed to. Larger tests (called beta tests) are conducted by users selected by the producer.

Beta testing

Beta software is the name given to the preliminary version of a program that is widely distributed to users before commercial release. These customers test the program by operating it under realistic conditions. Often, heavy duty,

demanding users are chosen so that any bugs or shortcomings are exposed before final release. With bespoke software, this will be the first time that the software is tested off-site using real 'live' data. It is difficult for software developers to test software in all the environments in which it will be used, so this is a very important stage.

When bespoke software is developed, the developer needs to reach agreement with the organisation for whom they are developing software, about how testing is to be done. Because of their specific needs, testing will usually take place on the customer's premises using their hardware, operating system and data.

Maintenance releases

Maintenance releases of software provide additional functionality and improve the quality of the original package. They are also an opportunity for software manufacturers to provide the patches of code which enable software to work with new hardware or peripheral devices which were not around when the software was originally developed.
The websites of software developers are useful sources of these releases and if you have software that does not work with your hardware, it is the first place to look. Bulletin boards are similarly useful.

Maintenance releases may also be sent direct to the customer by the software supplier and this is another important reason for sending the registration form back to your supplier, otherwise they have no way of knowing your address. Maintenance releases may be sent on floppy disks or CD-ROM/DVD to all licensed software users.

Maintenance releases usually address the following:

- They are used to perfect the software in some way, by, for example, improving the speed with which certain operations are performed and hence improving the use of main memory.

- They may also be corrective, which means that they correct bugs that come to light after the software has been released.

Activity

A review in a magazine made the following statement:

'Like accounting software, project management packages have the reputation of stressing functionality over usability'.

Explain what this means.

Activity

'It is almost impossible for software to be tested in a way that would eliminate all the bugs.'

A computer professional who specialises in software testing makes the above comment.

1 Explain why, in reality, it is hard and if not impossible, to produce software without any bugs.

2 There are three ways in which software is tested:

(a) alpha testing

(b) beta testing

(c) testing on the customers premises for bespoke software.

Explain the essential features of each of these testing methods.

Activity

KEY SKILLS C2.2, C3.2, IT2.2, IT3.2

For this activity you have to evaluate a range of screen capture programs. Many of these programs are available as shareware or public domain software. You will have to download any promising ones off the Internet. There may also be some demo versions of screen capture software that you are able to download for evaluation purposes.

Screen capture programs can prove very useful for doing the documentation for your project work. Using this software you are able to capture any screen, windows, icons and toolbars. You are also able to cut out part of the screen

and save it as a separate file. Screen capture software is ideal for producing user or training guides.

You need to obtain two or three promising pieces of screen capture software and evaluate them, with a reasoned recommendation for one of them.

Your task is to produce an evaluation report including some or all of the following:

* **The methodology used** (i.e. how you have decided to do your evaluation)

    Make sure that you explain the name of the software and where it was obtained.

* **The evaluation** containing comments under the following evaluation criteria:

    – the agreed problem specification (what problems the software should solve)

    – the functionality of the software (i.e. the features it has that enable it to do the job)

    – import/export facilities (how easy it is to put the screenshots into other software e.g. wordprocessing or DTP)

    – usability and the human/machine interface (how easy it was to use; whether the menus and screens were well laid out)

    – robustness (whether it crashed when you were using it)

    – user support (what it offered if you had a problem with the software; whether the documentation provided with the software – on-line or otherwise – was easy to use)

    – licensing arrangements

    – financial issues (the cost of the software and licences).

* **The recommendations**

    Which (if any) of the packages do you recommend?

* **Justifications**

    Provide a summary of the strengths and weaknesses for each package and a justification for your choice of software.

Your evaluation report should be word-processed and you could include some examples of screen captures that you have managed to make using the software. These can be inserted into the wordprocessed document.

Portability of data

Portability of data is the ease with which data can be transferred from one computer system to another. There are a number of factors that affect portability, including:

- the operating system on each machine

- the application package (and its version) being run on each machine.

There are many situations in which portability is an issue and these include:

1 **If you want to transfer a file that has been created using one package to a completely different package.**
   This might be the case if a person has created lots of document files using one wordprocessor (say WordPerfect) and wants to transfer them to another wordprocessor (say Microsoft Word). Some wordprocessing software is able to recognise the different file format and is able to automatically load the files from the other package. Most wordprocessors can save text in a variety of different formats, such as ASCII and RTF (rich text format), and using this facility can aid the movement of document files between packages, although often the formatting is destroyed in the process. Failing this, there are special file conversion programs (a type of utility program) that can be purchased to perform file conversions.

2 **Where the files created using one software package run on one type of hardware need to be transferred to the same package running on different hardware.**
   This is often called using files on different hardware platforms. You might, for instance, want to transfer files from a wordprocessor on an Apple Macintosh to the same wordprocessor on a PC.

3 **Where the files were created by different versions of the same package.**
   Suppose you are working on your project at college and at home and you have a more up-to-date version of the software at home. Although it is easy to move up to a higher version of the same software, it is sometimes difficult, or even impossible, to make the transfer from the new to the old version. You

may need to bear this in mind when you are working on your projects.

4 **Where a file in one type of software needs to be transferred or used by another type of software.**
   This could be the case if you have created a picture in one package and then want to transfer the file to a desk-top publishing or wordprocessing package. It is often necessary to import a graphics file into a wordprocessed document.

Why portability is important

Being able to transfer files is extremely important because not everyone uses the same hardware and software. Book publishers usually ask all their authors to supply manuscripts on disk to avoid the keying costs of typing directly from the manuscript and the possible errors that would be introduced in the process. Authors use different wordprocessing software and possibly even different hardware (e.g. Apple Macintosh or PC). The publisher needs either to convert these files using special conversion software, or use a DTP package that can read the files directly.

Some people work with different platforms (a platform is a combination of hardware and software), so file portability is important to enable data to be exchanged between platforms. A college may still be using an older version of Windows (e.g. Windows 95), whilst its students, with their more up-to-date home computers, use Windows 98 or Windows 2000. Since many of these students will be working on computers both at home and at college, it is important that their files can be ported between the two computer systems. They may also be using different versions of the same package, for example, Word 97 at college and Word 2000 at home.

Many organisations use different versions of the same software, despite the problems it can cause. This usually arises when new machines are bought and they come with the latest version as pre-loaded software. The problem with using different versions is that it is necessary to transfer files up to the new version as well as back down to the old version. Moving up a version is easy but going the other way can cause problems and not all software is capable of doing this.

An organisation uses two different operating systems and two different versions of an integrated package, consisting of wordprocessing, spreadsheet, database and presentation graphics software, on their 100 or so PCs. What particular problems are they likely to experience in using different versions of the same package?

You may have lots of files (particularly database files, that have been created over a long time) that need to be kept and used. If you change your software you will need to ensure that the new software can read these files. The alternative, which is re-keying all the data or possibly printing it out first and then using a scanner to scan it in, would be too costly, time consuming and error-prone.

Producers of new versions of software, or completely new software, need to make sure that the features offered are an improvement on the old version. From a sales and marketing point of view, it pays for software producers to make it at easy as possible for users to transfer files from other versions or packages.

The emergence of standards

In the early days of computing, there were only a handful of computer manufacturers around and each had its own set of standards. This meant that once an organisation had bought a computer, they were also forced to buy any peripheral devices they needed in the future from the same manufacturer. The manufacturers were quite happy with this situation since they did not have to try too hard to get extra sales. It also meant that organisations had to take out expensive maintenance contracts with the manufacturers. Things changed when other manufacturers came onto the scene and offered compatible hardware, software and computer services such as training and maintenance at very attractive prices. More companies started to manufacture similar hardware and the whole computer industry became a lot more competitive. To enable their hardware to have as wide a market as possible, these new manufacturers made their equipment compatible with a wide variety of manufacturers' computers. Standards between manufacturers became a marketing issue and it became

important that hardware from one manufacturer could be used in combination with that of another manufacturer.

Computers became more popular with the development of the personal computer and the widespread use of networking. At this stage, the haphazard approach to compatibility could not be sustained and co-operation was needed between manufacturers to ensure that computer operation was standardised. So, as users became more demanding and knowledgeable, the major computer companies decided that standards were needed so that all computer equipment could be connected together.

Protocols and standards

We now take the transfer of data between machines for granted and that the wordprocessed document produced on your PC at home can be brought into college and loaded into one of the college's computers running the same software. We therefore do not need to worry about the brand of computer, since all PCs are designed to behave in a similar way and therefore the data on one machine can be read by another.

There are still some problems to resolve. It is in everyone's interest for software to be continually developed and improved, and as the memory capacity and speed of chips has increased enormously in recent years, software is needed which takes advantage of these capabilities. Within the same organisation, many different versions of the same package may be used and this can cause problems if data needs to be saved off one machine then loaded onto another running a different and more recent version of the same software.

When a new version of software is developed, the manufacturer will usually try to encourage existing users to convert to the new version. The way they normally do this is to offer an upgrade at a special price which is much cheaper than that offered to new users. There are some serious disadvantages when companies change versions of software. First, users need training in the new version and this costs money. Secondly, customers have to purchase the upgrade copies or licenses in the case of a network. Additionally, they may experience problems with the new version and have to set up a special help line. Upgrading the software in a company is generally more problematic than upgrading your computer at home and to some extent this is why it is common to find that software on home computers is often more up to date than that of many large companies.

File conversion is a very important part of computing and it is imperative that software is capable of reading files created using different software. Suppose you are using an existing database system and your files, which have been set up over a period of ten years, contain tens of thousands of records. To type these into a new system could take years and would be very costly. File transfer is always possible if the new software is an upgrade of the existing software. If the existing software is from a different manufacturer, then transfer is usually still possible. There is more of a problem if the original software developer is no longer in business or if the manufacturer was a little known one. Therefore, when moving to new software, it is important to determine how easy it is to transfer the data from your old package.

Transferring files between different wordprocessors

The most common type of file transfer is between different wordprocessors. Even within the same organisation, staff will choose the wordprocessor they are the most familiar with despite the IT department trying to standardise wordprocessors to just one.

Activity

A large organisation has an IT department responsible for computing facilities across all departments. It has recently become clear that departmental managers and individuals are buying (using the company's money) their own preferred wordprocessing software for use in the organisation. The argument they put forward for doing this, is that they have this software at home and are more used to it, or that it is better and more up-to-date than the one the organisation supplies.

The computer manager is concerned about this pattern and she has decided to write a short letter outlining why it is important that everyone in the organisation uses the same wordprocessing software.

You have been asked to produce a single page for this manager outlining the reasons why only one type of wordprocessing package should be used.

Object linking and embedding (OLE)

Because users often want to transfer numerical, graphical and textual data between applications, many application packages make this as easy as possible. The transfer of data is usually easier if all the applications used are produced by the same software manufacturer. This is why many people decide to use integrated packages rather than separate applications.

You may, for example, be producing a wordprocessed report, using data from a database package, a spreadsheet and a graph from a spreadsheet package and some clip art which you have altered using a drawing package. All this data needs to be incorporated into the same wordprocessed document.

Windows software makes use of object linking and embedding (OLE), using which you can easily pass data from one application to another. Before looking at how it works, we need to understand a few terms. An **object** is simply any piece of data in one application (it might be a drawing), that is capable of being transferred to another application. The source document is the document from which the object comes and the destination document the document into which the object is to be placed.

When you embed an object, you are inserting data created in the source document into a destination document created in a different application. Once the object has been embedded in the destination document, there is no link back to the source document, so if changes need to be made, they are made to the destination document.

If an object is linked, the situation is slightly different: you are not making a copy of the data and putting it into the destination document. Instead a link is being created between the destination document and the source document. This means that when you edit the source document, the destination document will change to reflect the alteration.

OLE is useful, for instance, if you want to include a picture in a database. If pictures are placed in the actual database file, then because they are usually very large, they would make the database run very slowly and take up a large amount of disk space. Instead it is much better to use OLE.

Protocols

For one computer to talk to another there needs to be a communication link between them, as well as a suitable protocol for the communication. Having a physical communication link is not enough on its own. An analogy is phoning someone who lives in Japan; the communication line may be in place but unless you can speak Japanese or the other person can speak English, you are not able to communicate. A common method of communication is needed and in the case of computers, this is called a protocol.

A protocol can be defined in the following way:

A protocol is the formal specification that defines the procedures to follow when transmitting and receiving data. Protocols define the format, timing, sequence and error checking used in the network.

Protocols are basically agreed ways of doing things, and it is essential to have them if computers are to communicate properly.

Protocols and addressing mechanisms used to support the World Wide Web

There are several protocols used when communicating using the Internet, and these are described below:

- TCP/IP (transport control protocol/Internet protocol)
  TCP/IP is a set of protocols that allows computers to share resources over the Internet.

- FTP (file transfer protocol).

File transfer protocol is used when transferring files over the Internet. FTP obtains the files from where they are situated and places them on your access point. You can then download them from this point. This means that there are two downloading procedures needed to get the files into your computer. FTP has the capability of transferring files between dissimilar computers because it works independently of a particular operating system.

Web addresses

The web uses TCP/IP, the protocol for sending documents across the Internet, with another method of locating and accessing documents on different networks. This other method uses a string of characters (e.g. www.yahoo.com) called the universal resource locator (URL). The URL identifies the name and address of each document available on the web.

The URL identifies the type of server protocol used where the document is located. Some servers are specifically set up for Internet use and these servers handle documents using Hypertext Transfer Protocol (HTTP).

The URL also identifies the type of site. A World Wide Web (WWW) site uses file transfer protocol to transfer files from one computer to another. Sometimes a program called Gopher organises the files on a server. Using Gopher means that you do not need to know or enter the exact file name to access the data.

The URL also identifies the domain address that consists of the name of the major server or site. The domain address usually contains the name of the company or organisation and a two- or three-letter extension to signify the type of organisation (e.g. com, org, gov, edu and net).

The URL also identifies the specific location of the document on that computer's network such as its folder, subfolder and the document's name.

Web addresses can be long and cumbersome to type in, but once the first one has been typed you can usually use the links that have URLs encoded into them. Web browsers usually have bookmarks or favourite places where you can store the URLs of useful sites for future use.

The two types of standards used in IT

There are two types of standard used in the computer industry: *de facto* standards and *de jure* standards.

De facto standards

De facto standards have been developed through commercial use. These standards are developed by individual companies and are not always available for other companies to use. *De facto* standards are unpublished and not made available because the companies who develop them want to protect their commercial interests. Some *de facto* standards are not closed system standards. The Windows operating system is an example of a proprietary, open systems standard. Windows is also an example of a *de facto* standard that has been developed by one company and due to the sales success of the standard has become a widely accepted standard.

De jure standards

De jure standards are non-proprietary, meaning that no single company has created them or owns the right to use them. *De jure* standards have been created to enable computer equipment suppliers to connect to each others' equipment. This enhances connectivity and interoperability. Any supplier can use *de jure* standards as specifications are publicly available. TCP/IP is an example of a nonproprietary *de jure* standard.

Activity

Write a short article entitled 'Protocols, their importance in network communication'. The article, which should be no more than three A4 pages in length, is to be printed in a computer magazine aimed at their general readership (i.e. experts and non-experts).

You are best aiming your article at the novice reader, so all specialist terms should be carefully explained. Technical accuracy is also important since the expert reader will pick out any mistakes that you make.

Use the Internet, computer magazines, books, etc. for your reference material and include a bibliography showing the sources of your reference material. Include a list of useful web addresses readers can use to find further information.

Activity

A variety of terms is introduced in this chapter, many of which may will be new to you. It is important that you build up vocabulary that can be used when writing essays or answering questions. Write a definition for each of the following terms used in the chapter:

import/export facility

portability

upgradability

GIS

bespoke software

generic software

integrated package

alpha testing

beta testing

maintenance release

software house

de jure standards

de facto standards

proprietary

URL

FTP

HTTP

1 A software company is preparing to release a new application program. Describe **two** types of testing carried out before the final release of the software. Explain why both are needed. *(6)*

(NEAB, Module IT05, May 97, q5)

2 The management of a local college has decided to buy a computer-aided-design (CAD) package to help to plan the best use of available space in the college.

(a) Describe suitable hardware to support the use of the package. *(4)*

(b) Identify **two** features available in a CAD package that are not generally found in a simple drawing package. *(2)*

(c) Give, with reasons, **three** advantages of using a CAD package rather than manual methods for this application. *(4)*

(d) At various times the management is required to produce statistical reports using a spreadsheet with data currently held in the CAD package. Describe the functionality required by the CAD package to allow this to happen. *(2)*

(NEAB, Module IT05, Specimen paper, q5)

3 An examination board is considering developing a system which is to be used for maintaining and processing module test results of candidates.

• Describe the different ways in which the examination board may be able to provide a software solution.

• Discuss the issues the examination board should consider before choosing any particular solution. *(20)*

(NEAB, Module IT05, June 97, q9)

4 You are asked to evaluate a software package and produce an evaluation report.

(a) Describe **four** criteria you would use to evaluate the package. *(8)*

(b) What is the function and content of an evaluation report? *(4)*

(NEAB, Module IT05, Specimen Paper, q4)

5 Before releasing a new package the software company carries out alpha and beta testing.

(a) What are these **two** types of testing and why are they both needed? *(6)*

(b) Explain why, once the package has been released, there may be a need for maintenance releases and how these might be dealt with. *(6)*

(NEAB, Module IT05, Specimen Paper, q8)

6 'I don't care which version of a wordprocessing package the rest of the company uses. As a senior company manager I intend to upgrade my department to the latest version.' Give **four** potential problems this attitude may cause for other IT users in the company. *(4)*

(NEAB, Module IT05, May 98, q2)

7 A company is about to change its accounting software. In order to evaluate the different packages available to them, they have drawn up a number of different evaluation criteria.

(a) Why are such evaluation criteria needed? *(2)*

(b) Explain the issues involved with each of the three evaluation criteria given below:

Functionality

User Support

Hardware Resource Requirements *(6)*

(c) Identify and describe **three** additional evaluation criteria that you might also expect the company to include. *(6)*

(NEAB, Module IT05, May 98, q8)

8 A freelance reporter who regularly contributes to various newspapers and magazines is considering which wordprocessing package she should purchase. A friend has said that 'most modern application packages enable users to produce files which are portable'.

With the aid of specific examples discuss this statement. Include in your discussion:

- an explanation of what portability means in this context;

- why portability is important;

- how the Information Technology industry can encourage this portability. *(16)*

(NEAB, Module IT02 (now IT05), May 96, q10)

9 Two users are using two different versions of the same wordprocessing package. When user A sends a file on disk to user B there are no problems in reading the file. However, when files are transferred the other way, the transfer is not successful. Explain why this might happen and how to overcome this problem. *(4)*

(NEAB, Module IT02 (now IT05), Specimen Paper, q3)

10 A software company has notified customers of a maintenance release for its accounting package. The notification states that a programme of alpha and beta testing will be carried out to ensure that the maintenance release is reliable.

(a) State **three** reasons why a maintenance release might be necessary.   (3)

(b) What is meant by the terms:

    (i) alpha testing?

    (ii) beta testing?   (2)

(NEAB, Module IT05, May 99, q2)

11 A university has decided to buy a new payroll package. They are considering several options and have drawn up a range of evaluation criteria to help them select the most appropriate one.

(a) The criteria used by the university include:

    'performance'

    'robustness'

    'user support'

    For **each** of these criteria, describe **two** issues that you would expect the university to consider.   (6)

(b) Describe **three** other criteria you would expect the university to apply when comparing systems.   (6)

(NEAB, Module IT05, May 99, q8)

12 The rise of *de facto* standards due to commercial sales success can only benefit organisations and individuals'. Discuss this statement.

Particular attention should be given to:

    Operating systems;

    Portability of data between applications;

    Portability of data between different computer systems.

Illustrate your answer with specific examples.

Quality of language will be assessed in this answer.

(NEAB, Module IT05, May 99, q11)

18 Communication and Information Systems

Network services

Computers used in a stand-alone environment are very useful, but as soon as they are joined together as a network, a huge number of new applications emerges, such as e-commerce, e-mail and increased security. In this section we examine the uses of networked systems.

When intending to install a wide area network (WAN), organisations might consider using existing network services rather than starting from scratch. What we mean by 'network services' are the actual transmission channels along which the data signals are passed. Two commonly chosen systems are the public switched telephone network (PSTN) and the Internet. Using public network services, you can extend a network out of the office without having to install any additional transmission system. This helps to keep down the costs associated with installation.

Public switched telephone networks were originally developed for the telephone, but they have been extended to carry different kinds of data. Users pay to use these services and also for any hardware installed in the office to connect the company's network to the PSTN. Connection is made at the point where the telephone wire enters the building. Once data reaches the telephone company's wires, it can be routed along a variety of different media including high capacity coaxial cable, fibre optic cable and microwave transmission.

The Internet is the largest network of computers in the world. It consists of WANs, LANs and single computers, all linked together. Figure 18.1 shows the arrangement for a typical home computer connected to the Internet.

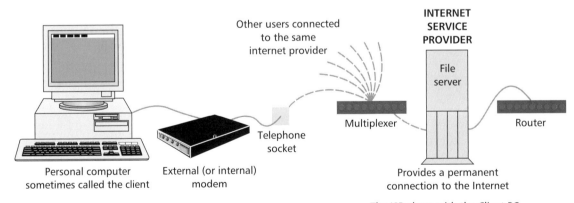

Figure 18.1 *The largest collection of interconnected computers in the world: The Internet*

What is the Internet?

The Internet is a global network of computers in government departments, businesses, schools, colleges and homes connecting hundreds of millions of people around the world. It enables the quick and easy exchange of information. It also allows people to speak freely about their ideas and opinions. It has been a major player in the creation of the 'Information Age'.

What is the World Wide Web?

The World Wide Web (WWW) is simply the multimedia part of the Internet. Using the WWW you can view graphics and video as well as listen to sound. There are also hyperlinks to other pages or media. The World Wide Web has its own protocol called HTTP (hypertext transfer protocol) (see page 307).

The network infrastructure required to support the World Wide Web

Most of you will log on to the Internet through an on-line service or Internet service provider (ISP). The Internet consists of a series of network access points (NAPs) which are situated in all the main cities of the world. All the networks are connected to each other via these NAPs and to fast land-lines or satellite communication links. Since there are so many lines, if a particular route goes down, data can simply be re-routed. Your ISP is connected directly or indirectly to one of these NAPs.

When you log on to the Internet the protocol TCP/IP is used. When you connect to certain web pages a string of numbers may appear; this string is the IP address of the web pages you are connecting to. Your own computer, when connected to the Internet, is given its own, unique IP address by the ISP. The IP address consists of a string of numbers separated by the odd dot here and there, and there is a piece of software on the server that turns the IP address into what is called a **domain name**. This software is called DNS (domain name service). Now instead of typing a long series of numbers, you can simply type a domain name such as http://www.thorneseducation.co.uk.

Before data is transmitted over the Internet, it is broken down into small 'packets' of data. These packets are sent and then reassembled into their original form. The data is sent using the best possible route available at that particular moment. Occasionally, the packets are lost or corrupted along the way and the computer has to send them again. When the Internet is busy, the likelihood of packages colliding and therefore of being corrupted is greater, and since the data then has to be re-sent, this means the network becomes busier still.

Intranets

An intranet is a private network that uses the same technology as the Internet to transfer data from one terminal to another and also to interrogate centrally held data. Intranets are becoming very popular with businesses because they offer a lower cost business network.

Selecting a type of network for a particular application

There are many ways that terminals and other pieces of equipment can be connected to a network. Links can be physical, as in networks that make use of cables, or logical, as in those which use microwave or radio links. They can be organised in many ways, called topologies (see Chapter 9, which covered the common network topologies). Although network topologies, such as bus, ring, star and mesh, are clearly defined, in practice many networks use a variety of topologies and are therefore called hybrid networks.

At one time networks were simply used to carry data, in the form of text, from one terminal to another. Now more demands are placed on them and they frequently carry sound, graphics and even video images. This has meant that networks need very careful design if the data is to arrive at its destination quickly and intact.

Activity

This chapter carries on from Chapter 9, so it is important that you remember what was written there. You will also have exam questions on the work in this chapter that will assume knowledge of the contents of Chapter 9. Have a look back at Chapter 9 and then answer the following questions to test your knowledge.

1 Explain the main features of a LAN and a WAN.

2 Briefly outline **three** of the main advantages in networking computers together.

3 (a) Explain the differences between a peer-to-peer network and a client–server network.

   (b) Explain the advantages and disadvantages of using peer-to-peer and client–server networks.

4 There are various devices that can be attached to a network other than the terminals/computers themselves. Explain what each device in the following list does:

bridge	router
gateway	hub.
multiplexer	

Backbone networks

Once a network starts to get large (typically 250 to 1000 users), it becomes harder to design a fast network. One problem might be the wide geographical area over which the clients are spread which usually means that a distributed network will be needed containing several servers each dealing with a particular network task. To provide the sort of speed such a large network needs, a high-speed backbone is required between servers.

Selecting a network system: peer-to-peer or client–server?

Before thinking about such things as protocols, network adaptors and transmission media a decision must be made as to whether a peer-to-peer or client–server network should be used.

The following questions should help to determine whether or not a peer-to-peer network would be suitable.

1 Are only ten or fewer terminals envisaged for the network?

2 Are the network users knowledgeable about computers and will they be able to perform simple file operations such as deleting files, creating directories, installing software and taking backup copies?

3 Can all the users of the network be trusted to take adequate security measures?

4 Is it envisaged that nobody will have overall charge of the network?

5 Will no extra hardware be purchased, such as a file server?

6 Are all the terminals to be situated near to each other?

If all or most of the answers to the above questions are 'yes', then a peer-to-peer network would probably be most suitable. If not, the following questions should help to determine whether a server-based network would be suitable.

1 Are there over ten terminals at the moment or more than this number envisaged for the future?

2 Do most of the users know little about computers and simply use them to run limited applications about which they have some knowledge?

3 Are there enough users of the software to make the purchase of one or more file servers cheaper than storing files and licensing applications on each client computer?

4 Is central management of the network essential?

5 Do all the users need to access centrally held data?

If all or most of the answers to the above questions are 'yes', then a client–server network would be most suitable.

Activity

A small business is thinking of networking five PCs together. They do not want to spend very much and would prefer not to give a single person complete charge of the administration of the network. Most of the users have very limited knowledge of operating systems although they do have knowledge of frequently used applications, such as wordprocessing and spreadsheets. The business will keep important data on the system and this needs to be kept safe.

The boss of the company has been told there is the choice between a peer-to-peer network and a client–server network.

1 In what ways would a peer-to-peer network be appropriate for this business and in what ways would it be inappropriate?

2 In what ways would a client–server network be appropriate for this business and in what ways would it be inappropriate?

Activity

A small company selling car repair manuals by mail order is setting up a network consisting of ten terminals. All the data is to be held in a database which all the terminals will need to access. It has two members of staff who are quite knowledgeable about computers and are taking part-time degrees in IT.

1 State, with reasons for your choice, whether a peer-to-peer or a client–server network would be most suitable for this company.

2 Explain why any other network is unsuitable.

Choosing the network topology

A topology is the way a particular network is arranged and there are many different types to choose from (see Chapter 9). Here are the types of network most suited to each of the topologies:

Bus

Bus topologies are most suitable:

- for small networks (especially peer-to-peer)
- where the cheapest solution is required
- where the network is likely to remain the same over a period of time (i.e. extra terminals will not be added).

Star

Star topologies are most suitable:

- for large networks
- where extra client computers need to be added
- where the network will need to grow as the needs of the organisation increase
- where easy troubleshooting is required.

Ring

Ring networks are most suitable:

- where the network needs to operate under a fairly heavy load
- where the network arrangement will not need to be changed
- where operating speed is important.

Although we have looked at each topology separately, it is possible to have combinations of the above networks, called hybrid networks. The main advantage of doing this is to produce a network topology that has as many of the desirable points as possible but without the disadvantages that normally go with a single topology.

Activity

You will need to use material covered in Chapter 9 as well as the material in this chapter for this activity. The following questions all refer to the diagram shown on the next page.

1 The diagram shows a number of LANs connected together to form a WAN.

What are the main features of

(a) a LAN?

(b) a WAN?

2 There are three LANs shown in the diagram, each with a different topology.

(a) Explain what is meant by the term 'topology'.

(b) Name the three network topologies shown.

3 The diagram shows a piece of hardware called a gateway. Explain the purpose of a gateway.

4 Explain the purpose of a bridge.

Distributed systems

In distributed systems, processing is spread over several connected computer systems that are able to share resources. One of the computers may contain customer information, whereas another may have data concerning sales. A distributed system is able to combine this data. In this way the workload is spread or 'distributed' over the whole network.

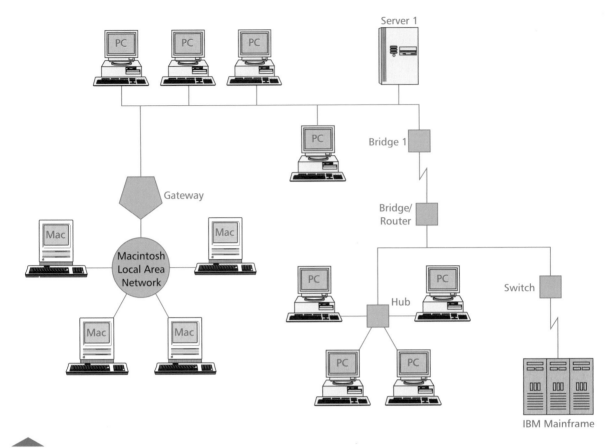

Figure 18.2 *A wide area network*

Another advantage of distributed systems is that security is improved since there are usually several servers on which data is stored and these servers are usually in different parts of the country, or even spread across the world. Data can be transferred easily using high-speed communication links between servers and this mirroring provides instantaneous backup should there be a problem with one of the servers or the communication links.

A distributed system can also be one in which control of the network can be from any of the terminals on the network, provided permissions allow. This is particularly useful if use of a site is lost, for example because of a fire or explosion, and all the computing needs to be transferred to one of the other sites.

Distributed databases

With a distributed database, portions of data in the database are stored on separate server computers situated at different locations. The database appears no different to the user, who will not be aware that the data comes from different places. The advantage of using a distributed database is that it can be replicated at different locations, which means that if the data is lost from one location it should not affect the data stored at the other locations. Since disaster is unlikely to strike at more than one location at the same time, security is improved. Users access the database via a LAN, so updating is faster than using the slower WAN connection to a centralised database.

Activity

Draw a diagram showing a distributed network.

Activity

1 What is meant by a distributed database?
2 What are the advantages and disadvantages to an organisation of using a distributed database?

Network security, auditing and accounting

The security problems posed by a network are a lot more complex than with stand-alone computers. This is because multiple terminals allow many points of access to important data. If a network is large, then many users will depend on the network and the loss of network services or data, even for a short period of time, will cause serious disruption to the organisation. Loss of data may be too much for an organisation to cope with and has been known to put companies out of business.

Access control

It is important to make sure that only certain people can access certain data, and the task of preventing unauthorised access is called access control. There are two types of access control: physical control and logical control.

Physical control

This type of control prevents the user from getting near the computer or getting it to work. It usually involves one or more of the following methods:

- control access to the room (use keypads, special cards)

- control access to the building (use guards, make visitors and staff wear security badges)

- put locks on computers which prevent them from being switched on

- lock computers away at night or put steel covers over them.

These are just a few of the many ways available and more detail on this can be found in Chapter 6.

Logical control

Logical control is used to prevent anyone without authority from accessing or changing certain information or doing damage to important files, whether accidentally or deliberately. Staff need to be able to alter certain files but there should be some way of preventing, for instance, a person who works in the sales section from accessing the payroll system. There are two main types of network security: user level security and share level security.

User level security

In user level security, each user is allocated a user name and a password, both of which have to be entered correctly before access to the network is granted. Once a user logs on to the network there are still further restrictions as to what can and cannot be done. For instance, say you set up a certain budget spreadsheet, and you have unlimited access to and can change it as you like. If company policy says that you are the only person allowed to update it, and your boss wants to see it on his or her terminal, this would be allocated on a 'read-only' basis. Any other users wanting to see it on their terminals would be denied access.

Share level security

Share level security means that each resource on the network, rather than each user, is given a password. In some cases two passwords may be used, one for full access and a different one for read-only access. The main problem with this method of security is that in certain types of network (particularly peer-to-peer networks) it can result in a larger number of passwords for each user to memorise. Writing them down on paper or not changing them very often means that users get to know each other's passwords and thus gain access to resources which the password was supposed to be protecting.

Some network operating systems give each user the opportunity to create a list of passwords they are allowed to use for each resource. To access this list it is necessary to input correctly both the user name and a password, so this is actually a combination of both user level and share level security.

Forced recognition of security

One of the problems with security is that users do not always appear interested in it or see the need for it since it presents an added burden to their daily work. To make users more aware of the importance of security, clauses can be written into their contracts of employment. For instance, there may be a non-disclosure clause which states that an employee is likely to be dismissed if they disclose their password or any confidential company information to another person and once the employee has signed this contract they are then bound by all the clauses and conditions in it. In government departments and the armed forces, members of staff have to sign the Official Secrets Act that makes it a crime to pass on information to any outside bodies. In addition, many of the staff in private companies who are working on government contracts may also have to sign the Official Secrets Act.

How does a company allow its business partners (suppliers, customers, delivery firms) and its own staff to have access to data over communication lines such as telephone lines, without exposing the company to unauthorised access by hackers? The main way is by using something called a firewall. If you look at Figure 18.3 you will see how the firewall filters out unauthorised requests for access.

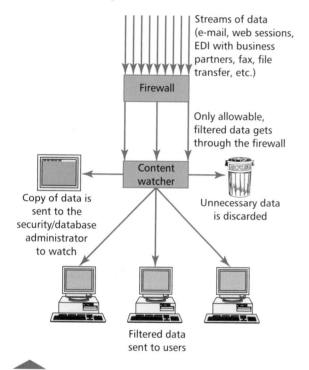

Figure 18.3 *How a firewall works*

Control of software

One of the main problems any person in charge of a network has, is checking to see if anyone has put unauthorised software on the system. Pirated software is theft and it is up to the organisation to make sure that none of its staff indulge in such activities. Ignorance of the law is not a defence; if pirated software is being used, it is the organisation's responsibility even if the company had no knowledge of it. An organisation funded by the software manufacturers called FAST (Federation Against Software Theft) is actively looking for companies who have pirate software on their machines and the penalties are large fines or even imprisonment, not to mention the adverse

publicity which results. How can the organisation know if there is any unlicensed software being used? One way is for the network administrator/manager to go along to see each user and examine what software is stored on the computer. They can then check with the company's software licences to make sure that only software for which they hold a licence is in use. A better method might be to use some of the software available for this task. Such software allows the person in charge of the network to examine from their own desk the hardware and software configuration of any machine connected to the network. As well as checking for the software on each machine, an audit of hardware and software programs is also useful for determining whether each user's computer is capable of running a new package being considered for the system. The software also allows you to answer such questions as 'which computers on the network are running Windows 2000 with less than 64 MB of RAM?' so that you can identify and subsequently upgrade them.

More information on software and hardware audit programs can be obtained from Dr Solomon's website on www.drsolomon.com or if you want to go direct to information about the hardware and audit package on:

www.drsolomon.com/products/audit/

Activity

A company uses 30 computers. The IT manager has been asked to conduct an audit of the company's hardware and software. Why is this much easier to do using a network than with stand-alone computers?

Security problems with networks

If viruses get onto a network they can spread like wildfire and have the potential to cause very expensive damage. This is not the case with a stand-alone machine. Viruses not only cause the loss of programs and data, they also cause loss of productivity. A virus attack can mean hours of painstaking work re-creating lost data and programs from backup copies, scanning disks for viruses and so on.

Viruses can enter a network in three ways:

- through the Internet

- through the intranet
- on disks brought into the company from outside.

Since prevention is better than cure, virus scanners need to be situated wherever data from outside enters the organisation. The ideal situation is to install virus scanners on every machine, but this is costly in terms of software licences. It is important that all staff should be made aware of the threats posed by viruses, and this will encourage them to check any disks they receive from outside before putting them onto the organisation's computer. Many companies go as far as to ban their employees from loading disks brought in from outside, although many employees still do so.

Although virus scanners are able to pick up most viruses, viruses are constantly under development so it is important that the latest release of a virus scanner is used. It is possible to get regular updates of most virus-scanning software off the Internet.

Firewalls are used to prevent unauthorised access but they do not filter out viruses. For example, if an e-mail were sent to a manager and had a virus attached, the firewall would still allow it to enter the company's network. There are some products now available which incorporate a virus scanner into the firewall and with this system any suspicious files are first sent to a server containing a virus checker.

User accounting

User accounts identify individual members of staff on the computer network. To open a user account you usually have to type in a user name and a password. Once a user has logged on, the network resources appropriate to the user are made available and work can begin. Sometimes, rather than allocate files and resources on a user-by-user basis, it is easier to group users who need the same resources together, and these groups are called workgroups. Workgroups are frequently set up based around the functional areas of a business, such as accounts, sales, marketing, stock control and personnel.

When a new user account is created, it must have a unique user name which identifies the user to the system. It is useful to bear in mind that many users do not work at a desk and may have to share a terminal. Without the user name system the computer would be unable to know who is working at the terminal and what

resources should be provided. Passwords which the user keeps secret (even the network administrator/manager may not be able to find them out) give the user a key to the network. It is important that the user does not invent passwords that are easy to guess, such as the names of their girlfriend, pets, etc. It is also important to remember the password and not write it down somewhere where it can be easily found, such as in a diary or on a post-it note stuck somewhere near the computer.

Creating user groups on a network

Setting individual user rights on a network can be very time-consuming so use is made of the user groups. As most organisations do not have different security requirements for every user, it is easy to group together those users who need to have the same type of access. A user group shares the same access permissions. For example, you could create a finance group, of which all the members of the finance department are members and have identical access.

It is possible for a user to be allocated membership of more than one group. Senior managers in an organisation may need to be members of the sales, finance, personnel and production groups, for example.

The accounting log

The accounting log is a log kept by the file server that allows the network manager/administrator to monitor each user's work on the network. It is possible from the log to see how each particular user has used the network. Here are some of the things that can be examined:

- **The identity of a user using a particular terminal** – users sometimes move from one terminal to another, perhaps even on different sites, so it is necessary for the accounting log to keep track of them.
- **The actual machine being used** – terminals are given an ID number by the operating system to identify them to the network manager; this is necessary because terminals can be moved or swapped around by the users without the network manager's knowledge.
- **Details of system crashes/system failures** – the network manager will need to know what program and data files were being used at the time of the crash and then investigate it further to see if it was due to a hardware or

software fault or perhaps some other problem. It is also possible that some data has been destroyed during the crash.

- **Disk space** – the amount allocated to each user and the amount they have actually used. Some users may use very little of their allocated space so it can be reallocated to other users who are running short of space.

- **The number of pages of printout produced** – useful information when the network manager is allocating printing resources on the network.

- **The amount of processing time used by each user** – the network manager can see who uses more processor time. This information is important when trying to improve the performance of a network.

- **Details of files used, stored, deleted and amended** – it is useful to know which user has used which file for security reasons.

- **Time the user logged on to the system** – it is useful to security to know at what time a user was logged on to the system.

- **Time the user spent logged on to the network** – this is particularly important if the company is using telecommunications companies that charge for time spent using the telephone network. It can be used to identify those users who have spent excessive amounts of time logged on to the Internet.

- **Any failed log-on attempts** – these attempts could be because a user has forgotten their password or because an unauthorised person is trying to gain access, in which case further investigation is needed.

- **Details of e-mail usage and storage** – some users may be using e-mail for all sorts of unauthorised purposes and saving the e-mails on their workspace. Some networks allow the network manager to read e-mails from outside the company, to make sure that the system is not being misused by members of staff.

- **The IDs of users logged on to the system** – useful if the system administrator needs to do something which will slow down the network response if there are lots of users logged on.

The purpose of the accounting log

As you can see from the above, the whole purpose of the accounting log is to enable the network manager to run the network effectively and efficiently. To this end, the log provides useful information about the use of network resources and provides statistics that can be analysed with a view to improving network performance. Improvements can be brought about by purchasing new hardware or software or by using a different transmission medium. Any upgrades need to be based on the information gleaned from the network log. Once a system is in place the log can be used to allocate devices such as printers to those users most likely to need them.

The accounting log is an important weapon in detecting misuse of the network. Because users know that a log is kept, it may make them less inclined to misuse the network, as there is a greater chance that they will be caught.

Sometimes the departments within an organisation are run like separate businesses and each department has its own budget and pays for its use of the networking facilities. It is therefore important that departments limit use of the network to reduce costs and help meet their department budgets.

Activity

A good network administrator is seldom seen by users, since he keeps problems from occurring. Describe some of the tasks a network administrator must do to keep the network running smoothly.

Uninterruptible power supplies (UPS)

Many networks use a single file server, so electrical power failure to this important piece of hardware can be disastrous. If the power fails when the server is in the middle of an important operation, such as copying data from hard drives onto a backup storage device, then data loss is likely. One way around this problem is to make use of a device called an uninterruptible power supply (UPS) which is like a powerful battery and maintains the power during a power failure until a generator can be started to supply power for a longer period. Many UPSs will tell the network operating system that the power has failed and instruct the server to immediately save its data.

Protecting network traffic against illegal access

As more and more business and daily routines involve electronically held data, the opportunity for misuse of data increases. Various methods are used to protect a network and these are outlined in the following sections.

Ensuring that passwords are kept private

Passwords are the first step in protecting a network against illegal access. Here are some key points to help protect your password. These have been covered before, but their importance cannot be stressed enough.

- Never give your password to anyone. Sometimes when you are on the Internet you may be asked for your password by someone masquerading as a network administrator from your ISP; do not give it to them!

- Never write your password down. Many passwords are written down in diaries or on bits of paper kept near the computer.

- Never let anyone stand behind you while you enter your password.

- Never e-mail your password to anyone.

- Never use for a password a word that can be found in a dictionary. It is best to use a password made up of letters, numbers and punctuation marks. As a further precaution you can use a combination of upper and lower case characters.

- Passwords should be changed on a regular basis (probably every three months).

- Never use your user ID as your password.

- Do not choose a password that relates to you personally, like a nickname or name of a pet.

Encryption

More and more business is now being conducted over the Internet but some users are still worried, particularly when they are asked to type in their credit card number or other personal details. The first step in protecting the privacy of on-line transactions is to ensure that the information remains hidden to anyone other than the person to whom it is sent. Encryption, which involves jumbling up the information before sending, is the main method used. Only a person with the secret encryption key can unscramble the information. You may have used encryption in its simplest form to send secret codes as a child. You could, for example, have

substituted each letter in the alphabet for one five places ahead, or used numbers for letters so that A is 1 and Z is 26. These are simple methods (called algorithms) for encryption. The key in the first case is the number of positions that the letters are shifted forward. The more complex the algorithm used, the harder it is to crack the code. Also, the longer the key, the harder the code will be to crack. All this sounds difficult, but you do not have to create your own algorithms and keys as there is software that does this for you. The software works invisibly and all the user sees is a small padlock on the screen which tells them that they are using a secure line. If you are interested in understanding the detail of encryption further then there are many sites on the Internet which cover this important subject. There is more about encryption on page 218.

Communication methods

The difference between digital and analogue transmission

Analogue signals have an infinite number of values between the smallest and largest possible. Digital signals jump between certain set values. For instance, a clock with a dial and hands can show an infinite number of times, whereas a digital one jumps from one minute (or one second) to the next. Digital signals consist of pulses of electric current which represent the information to be processed by a computer. The voltages in a digital system can be high or low, with a high voltage used to denote a 1 and a low voltage a 0. Data is thus represented as binary pulses (1s and 0s) consisting of high and low voltages. It is cheap to produce electronic circuitry to deal with digital signals and because of the binary nature of the signals (only 1 or 0 possible), noise is not so much of a problem; if the signal becomes distorted it may be regenerated and made like new again. With analogue signals this is not possible because of the complex nature of the waveform, so the effect of the noise is to continually degrade the signal.

Modems

When telephone lines are used to transfer data, they are being used for a purpose for which they were not really designed. In a telephone, the varying frequencies of the human voice are converted into analogue electrical signals that are then passed along the telephone wires. The earpiece of the receiving telephone converts the electrical signal back to sound. Sound signals are analogue signals because their waveforms have values that vary continuously. Since the electrical signals produced by the telephone are replicas of the sound, the electrical signals are also analogue.

'Modem' is an abbreviation for modulator/demodulator. A modem is used to convert the digital signals from a computer into analogue form so that they can pass along the telephone lines (Chapter 7 has more information about modems). When received, another modem changes the analogue signals back to their digital form. To look at, external modems are just small boxes with several indicator lights which flash on and off. Some modems, called internal modems, are situated inside the PC and these often display their flashing indicator lights on screen, to show what is happening. Modems plug directly into the telephone socket and if the lead isn't long enough (it seldom is) an extension lead can be used. Figure 18.4 shows two modems connected at either end of the telephone line.

Modems determine the speed at which you can interact with other computers over the phone lines. When a modem dials a number and connects to another computer, it first negotiates with the receiving modem a speed for the transmission and receipt of data. The speed of transmission is important since this determines the time it takes to transfer the data and hence the cost of the phone call and possibly the on-line charges levied by the service provider. There is more information on data transmission rates later in this chapter.

Some of the latest modems are able to deal with both voice and data at the same time using a single telephone line, a system called digital simultaneous voice and data (DSVD). This is an important issue during a videoconferencing session where you can speak and exchange data using an on-screen whiteboard at the same time.

Integrated service digital network (ISDN)

ISDN provides an alternative to the modem and the standard telephone line. When you use an ordinary telephone line, most of the circuit between you and the other party is digital, so your voice travels mainly as a digital signal. Only the initial and the final links in the chain (from the telephone to the local telephone exchange) are still analogue and it is for this small part that we need the modem. However, with ISDN these final links are changed to digital links which means that no modem is needed, although another device (an ISDN terminal adaptor) is needed instead. ISDN offers fast, clear and consistent communications between devices and also supports simultaneous transmissions over the same line, which is particularly useful for videoconferencing, where video and sound are sent together.

Activity

A researcher for a newspaper spends much of her time on the Internet either obtaining research material from libraries and other institutions around the world, or sending material via e-mail to her newspaper. Because she uses the Internet so much she is thinking of using ISDN. You have been asked to produce an outline of ISDN for this researcher. She would like to know what it is, what costs are associated with using the service, and its main advantages and disadvantages compared with using a modem.

Serial transmission

In this form of transmission each character is broken down into its binary code and the resulting series of bits (0s and 1s) are sent one after another down the communication line. When they reach the receiving device, they are

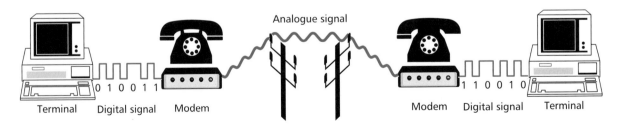

Terminal   Digital signal   Modem   Analogue signal   Modem   Digital signal   Terminal

Figure 18.4 *Using a telephone line to carry data*

reassembled to form the character again. Although serial transmission is slow compared with parallel transmission, it is the method of transmission used over all but very short distances.

Handshaking

Handshaking is the name given to the method of controlling the flow of serial communication between two devices so that transmission only happens when the device at the receiving end is ready to receive it. There are two methods in use, the hardware method and the software method. With the hardware method, a separate wire is used to send a signal to tell the sending device that the receiving device is ready. This method is only really suitable when the devices are near to each other so that a special cable can be used. The hardware method is used when a computer communicates with a serial printer. Communication systems which make use of the telephone cable only have a single wire, so hardware handshaking is not possible. Instead software handshaking is used, where special control characters are sent by the receiver to let the sending device know when to send data. One software method used is called XON/XOFF and this uses Ctrl+S to pause sending the data and Ctrl+Q to resume transmission.

Parallel transmission

In parallel transmission groups of bits are transmitted at the same time, making this method faster than serial transmission. However, it is only suitable for transmission over short distances. The number of bits in each group depends on the number of bits used to represent each character and any additional bits needed for control (such as start and stop bits) along with any parity bits used. Parallel communication is the method used between disk drive or printers and the CPU and is usually good provided the length of the cable used does not extend beyond about three metres.

Communication standards

Certain standards are needed to enable networked computers to communicate with each other. In this section we look at what these standards are and their relevance to a networked system.

Protocols

Networking is not just a question of connecting computers with wires and then assuming that they will be able to understand each other. A set of standards is needed to make sure that the computers are communicating with each other in the same way.

When people communicate with each other, a set of rules apply, although they never really think about them. For instance, we wait until the other person has finished talking before we say something and usually acknowledge that we have understood what has been said by nodding occasionally. This represents a protocol between individuals.

A protocol is an agreement as to how computers will exchange information. For example, messages which are sent over a network need to have a certain format. One part of the message represents the data being sent and another part specifies which terminal or devices the message is being sent to.

Protocols need to specify the following to enable two computers to communicate with each other:

- cabling used
- standards for the physical connection
- the mode of transmission
- speed of transmission
- data format
- error detection
- error correction.

Transmission rates

A transmission rate is a measure of the speed at which bits can be transmitted along a communication channel by a modem; it is measured in bits per second (bps). One bit per second is often called a baud so the number of bits per second is the same as the number of bauds.

Transmission rate is an important consideration when buying a modem. Faster modems cost more but their costs may soon be recovered if you consider the shorter time it will take to transfer data. During transmission you may be paying for both the phone call and possibly the on-line connection fee, so the quicker the transmission, the cheaper these will be.

Modems are available in many different speeds, typically 28,800, 33,600 and 56,000 bps. However, these are not necessarily the baud rate since many modems are now able to compress the data before transmitting it. Data compression means that data may be compressed to one quarter or even one sixth of its original size, so such modems have baud rates four or six times higher than their data transmission rates. So, for example, a modem with a transmission rate of 2400 bps and a compression ratio of 4:1 would have a baud rate of $4 \times 2400 = 9600$.

Activity

Look through a couple of recent computer magazines for adverts for different modems. Choose modems that operate at different speeds and have different compression ratios. Produce a comparison of the relative costs of sending different file sizes using the telephone lines for each of the modems you have selected. You will need to calculate the time taken to transmit the various quantities of data and research the cost of using the telephone line (BT, Mercury, Cable, etc.) at different times of the day.

Show evidence of your research and present your findings clearly in a report. Any calculations you use should be shown. The idea is to produce a comparison on which a purchasing decision can be based.

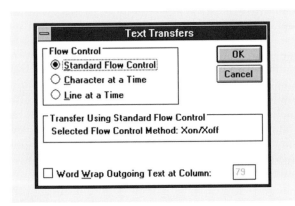

Figure 18.5 *The flow control menu*

Flow control

Flow control is one common method used by the receiving computer to issue start and stop commands to the computer sending the data, thus preventing data from being sent faster than the receiving computer can deal with it. The commands used are sometimes called XON and XOFF commands.

Flow control causes the modem to stop and start data transmission when required.

Figure 18.5 shows the menu used to select the flow control method.

Number of data bits

As mentioned earlier, each character is converted to a certain number of bits (0s and 1s) which is called a byte. A byte may therefore be defined as the number of bits used to represent a single character. Data bit lengths are the number of bits that carry the actual character within a byte. Data bit lengths can be set to five, six, seven or eight but the most popular lengths by far are either seven or eight.

Start and stop bits

In serial communication, where bits are sent one at a time through a single cable, a bit called a start bit is included in the stream of data to tell the receiving computer that a byte of data is to follow. The start bit is added to the start of the data stream.

A stop bit is added to the end of the data stream in serial communication to inform the receiving computer that the transmission of a byte of data is complete.

Asynchronous transmission

If the characters sent along the communication channel can be sent at any time, then there needs to be a method of stopping the flow if either side cannot keep up with the speed of transmission. Start and stop bits mentioned in the previous section overcome this problem. Although the characters can be sent at any time (hence the name asynchronous), the bits for each character are transmitted at a constant rate. Because these extra bits are needed for each character, it means there is more data so this method is slower than the alternative method called synchronous transmission.

Asynchronous transfer mode (ATM) uses high-speed packet switching with fixed length packets of data and operates at speeds of up to 155 Megabits per second (Mbps). ATM was only available on expensive high-speed links between mainframe computers and their terminals, but recently the costs of ATM have come down to such an extent that it is now within the reach of most LAN users. As well as a high transmission speed, ATM is less error-prone than synchronous transmission.

Synchronous transmission

Synchronous means 'happening at the same time'. With synchronous transfer mode, two computers are synchronised so that they keep exact pace with each other as they send and receive binary pulses. This type of communication is suitable for high rates of data transfer.

Figure 18.6 shows how asynchronous and synchronous communications deal with the flow of data.

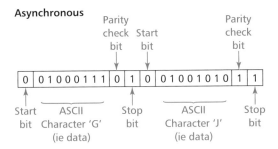

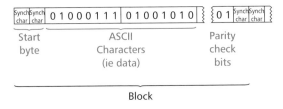

Figure 18.6 *Asynchronous and synchronous data transmission*

The OSI model

OSI stands for open systems interconnection. It is a model created by the International Standards Organisation (ISO) to describe the network communication processes and how any hardware and software should interconnect if they are to be used together in a communication system. The model consists of seven layers with each successive layer getting more detailed. The OSI model is purely conceptual and is used by people involved in networks to gain a better understanding of the interactions that take place when a network operates.

Figure 18.7 shows the seven layers in the OSI model. Each layer can only communicate with the layer directly above or below it (if there are any). Each layer is also dependent on the layer either side and the interface between two layers needs to be as flexible as possible so that those

who design communications systems have the opportunity to experiment on the interface.

The bottom two layers are called hardware layers and these provide the foundations on which all other layers are built.

Figure 18.7 *The seven layers of the OSI model*

The physical layer

This layer is responsible for the sending of bits (i.e. binary digits 0 and 1) from one part of a network to another. It does not concern itself with the meaning of the bits, it deals only with the signals which are used to represent the bits. The physical layer defines the electrical and physical details, such as which signal is used to represent the binary digit 0 and which to represent 1. It also defines what each of the pins does in a network connector and how the data is synchronised.

Data link layer

If you look at the data link layer on the diagram you will see that it is sandwiched between the physical and network layers. The data link layer takes the data from the network layer and packages it into frames which are then presented to the physical layer. In doing this it also adds addressing and error checking.

Network layer

The network layer determines which route data packets will take if they are more than a single link away from the sending and receiving devices. It therefore makes sure that individual messages are switched and routed properly. When data is sent over a network it is divided into chunks of data called packets; the packet also contains information about the type of packet and the network address to which the packet is being sent. When data is sent in packets, one packet can take a different route to another and the destination terminal reassembles the packets in the correct sequence.

The network layer is responsible for communication between logically separate networks, and routers and gateways operate in this layer.

Transport layer

The transport layer makes sure that packets of data arrive at the destination in the right sequence, with none deleted or duplicated and no other errors introduced. Whilst layers 1, 2 and 3 deal with the release of the message onto the network, this layer is more concerned with their arrival. In some ways, this layer does a similar job to the physical layer, except that it deals on a larger scale with, for instance, groups of computers.

Session layer

The session layer's purpose is to allow applications being run on different computers to share a connection, also called a session. The session layer permits programs run on the two computers to locate each other and then establish a communication link. It also provides data synchronisation and a method of detecting what data is being sent when the communication link is lost, so that only part of the data needs be re-sent.

Presentation layer

The presentation layer translates instructions from the form the computer uses to the form the network uses, and vice versa. The presentation layer deals with protocol conversion, translation of data, data compression and encryption, character set conversion and the presentation of graphics on the screen. The network redirector which makes the files on the file server viewable from the client computer, also operates within the presentation layer.

Application layer

The application layer is the highest layer of the OSI seven-layer model and this layer is used to interact with the user and the applications they are running. It is through this layer that all the other layers are eventually accessed. In this layer the user is presented with features which make the actual running of the network invisible, and when network services are being used, they appear as though they are on the user's computer

rather than on a remote server or some other computer. When a programmer is writing a program which uses network services, this is the layer the application program will access.

Activity KEY SKILLS C2.3, C3.2

When two devices A and B are to communicate with each other and A is to send a message to B, device A first has to gain control of the link. Device A then needs to make sure that the data it sends is in a form which can be understood by device B. When device B receives the message it must be able to identify which part of the message is data, since some parts refer to the address of the device to which the message is sent and these parts are also used to control the flow of the data. There must also be a way of detecting any errors in the message and deciding what to do when the communication link is lost.

In other words, the two devices must share the same protocol.

1 Explain what is meant by the phrase 'share the same protocol'.
2 Explain the method or methods by which the system can determine which part of a message is data.
3 Contention control decides which terminal can gain control of the network to send a message. Explain one method by which this is done.
4 There are various ways in which errors are detected. Describe one of them.

CASE STUDY

Improving the communications problems of the emergency services

Picture the following situations.

There is a serious road traffic accident and when the ambulance crew arrive they can relay live pictures direct to doctors in a hospital, who give the paramedics important information about dealing with a very seriously ill patient.

This ultimately means they are able to save the patient's life.

There is an exchange of drugs taking place and a member of the public rings the police who arrive and catch the dealers red-handed. Dealers normally have look-outs who as well as watching for the police, also listen to all police transmissions on the radio so that they can alert the dealer should the police seem to know about their activities. This arrest has only been possible because of a new police radio system which has replaced the analogue radio transmissions with a digital system that makes it hard to tap into, especially as encryption techniques can be used.

A new project is being initiated to update the communications systems used by the emergency services and make use of computers and secure digital radio links. At the moment, if the police want any information from the police national computer about a suspicious vehicle, they must use the radio to contact the station where someone uses a terminal to search for any information held on the vehicle. Clearly this is long-winded, so the new system makes use of terminals in each police vehicle, or alternatively forms part of the radio given to all police officers. If the bandwidth of the transmission is sufficient, it may be possible to send pictures over the network which could be vital for ambulance crews. However, because of the bandwidth problem with the technology at present, it is likely that the emergency services will have to choose between picture transmission or access to the police national computer.

The main features of the proposed system include:

- a much clearer digital transmission
- possible direct access to the police national computer
- the network will be secure since a scrambler using encryption techniques makes it impossible for criminals to monitor messages
- the system can locate an officer anywhere using the signal sent from their radio so

there is no need to send location details (which wastes time) to the control centre

- messages can be exchanged using a small screen and keypad
- if the police, fire brigade and ambulance service all make use of this system there will be a nationwide emergency service network.

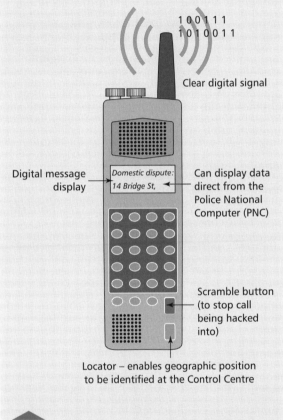

Figure 18.8 *Diagram of the new hand-held terminal to replace the older radio police officers were issued with*

Questions

Answer the following questions based on the above scenario.

1 The new system makes use of digital signals whereas the old system used analogue signals. Draw two diagrams and explain briefly the difference between analogue and digital signals.

2 The case study mentions that there may be a 'bandwidth problem'. Explain what this means.

CASE STUDY

KEY SKILLS IT2.3, IT3.3, C2.1, C3.1, N2.1, N3.1

The costs of security threats

A recent survey by the Security Institute in the USA revealed the extent of hi-tech crime.

Around three-quarters of the 563 organisations who replied to the survey reported that they had suffered financial losses in the last 12 months due to security breaches. These security breaches ranged from a computer virus infecting the system to laptop theft, financial fraud, theft of information and sabotage.

Two hundred and forty-nine organisations worked out how much they lost over the last year.

* 24.9 million dollars were lost due to financial fraud.

* 27.7 million dollars were lost due to telecommunication fraud.

* 21 million dollars were lost due to the theft of information.

* 4.3 million dollars were lost due to the sabotage of data.

* 12.5 million dollars were lost due to computer viruses.

* 6.1 million dollars were lost due to the theft of laptop computers.

Many companies did not take part in the survey or did not file an estimate of the amount lost. Computer crime could therefore be costing much more than these figures suggest.

Forty-nine per cent of the organisations in the survey had suffered an intrusion or other unauthorised use of computer system in the last 12 months but only 17 per cent of the cases were reported to the police because of the adverse publicity that could result. Eighty per cent of respondents believed that disgruntled employees are likely to attack company computer systems and more than 70 per cent see hackers as a threat.

TASKS

You are required to present the information contained in the above passage to your class as a ten-minute presentation called 'Security threats and their costs'. As well as talking about the figures, you are required to show a series of slides to help illustrate the points you are making.

Here are some pointers to start you off:

* Calculate any totals and percentages using the figures in the passage.

* You could convert these figures from dollars into pounds using a suitable conversion rate.

* Produce suitable charts using spreadsheet software to illustrate the figures.

* Produce a set of slides using wordprocessing or presentation graphics software.

* Ensure that you do not put too much material on each slide and check that a suitable font and size has been used for the text and that you can see it when you use it with an overhead projector.

* Use bullet points for impact.

* Outline the security threats as a bulleted list.

* Proof-read, grammar check and spell check your work.

* Keep the style of your slides consistent.

Activity

Definition of terms

A variety of new terms is introduced in this chapter, many of which may be new to you. It is important that you build up vocabulary which can be used when writing essays or answering questions. Write a definition for each of the following terms used in the chapter:

distributed system	PSTN
intranet	backbone
accounting log	UPS
DSVD	analogue
digital	serial transmission
parallel transmission	ISDN
handshaking	baud
asynchronous	synchronous
OSI	

Answering an essay style question

Here is an examination question that requires an answer in essay form. Read the question slowly and then look at the notes on answering the question.

> An international company wants to set up a new computer network. Although many staff currently use stand-alone, desk-top systems, the company has no experience of networking. As an IT consultant you have been asked to prepare a report for the company directors, outlining the issues and the potential benefits to communications and productivity that such a network could bring. Your report should include:
>
> - a description of the various network components which would be involved
> - a description of the relative merits of different types of network which could be considered
> - a description of the security and accounting issues involved

- an explanation of networked applications which could improve communications and productivity within the company.

Quality of language will be assessed in this question.

(NEAB, Module IT05, June 1998, q.10)

Answer pointers

The first thing to do is to read the question a couple of times. Note that the question consists of four bulleted parts. You can use this to help structure the answer. In the first part, there is a short scenario that puts the bulleted points into context. Any answers must refer to and be relevant to this scenario. It is a good idea to highlight those parts of the scenario that are important to you in your answer. You could highlight or underline the following:

> international company
>
> use stand-alone, desk-top systems
>
> no experience of networking
>
> potential benefits to communications and productivity.

Looking at what to include under each of these bulleted points, we have the following:

A description of the various network components that would be involved

Since this is an international company, they will need to use LANs connected to WANs. We can therefore describe any of the components needed such as:

- network interface cards in each workstation/terminal to allow connection to the network
- network cable to link the terminals (coaxial, category 5 UTP, thin ethernet, fibre optic, etc.)
- bridges linking the LANs together so that the signals are kept to the LAN unless needed by another LAN; this reduces congestion on the network
- repeaters to amplify or regenerate signals and compensate for losses in signal strength as the signals travel along a wire; this allows signals to travel much further

- hubs which act like repeaters to increase the strength of a weak signal passing through a cable
- gateways that are used to allow signals to pass from one network to another; in this case LANs in different countries could link to form a WAN.

A description of the relative merits of different types of network which could be considered

Each branch in each country could be connected to a local area network (LAN) where a central store of data can be held on a file server. There are a number of network topologies that could be used:

- Bus is cheap and ideal for small peer-to-peer networks, but probably too small for this organisation. However, bus systems are easy to troubleshoot, which could be ideal for this organisation as it has not used networks before.
- Star is suitable for large LANs and makes it easy to add extra computers as the need arises.
- Ring is ideal if the network needs to be fast, able to cope with heavy demand and if it is unlikely the network will need to be changed.

A description of the security and accounting issues involved

The organisation will need a hierarchical password system and users will need to log on each time they use a terminal. Each user should be assigned access rights to certain folders/files by the network administrator. This will allow some users to only see files and not alter them, while some will be given read/write access and others not allowed access at all. Accounting software will be used to record or track those users who are logged on to the system. It will also record the files they access and what is done with those files whilst on-line. The accounting software will record system resources used by each member of staff while they are logged-on.

So that users of the system do not misuse the data on the network, a code of conduct should be made part of the contract of employment for any employee who will use the network. This should spell out clearly what the user can and cannot do while on the network. It will also set out the penalties for breaches of the code.

The company's LANs could be connected together to form a WAN which would enable data to be sent from one country to another. If this alternative is too expensive, the Internet could be used for the transfer of files on an *ad hoc* basis from one country to another.

An explanation of networked applications which could improve communications and productivity within the company

Electronic mail would increase productivity by allowing memos to be sent to anyone in the company. User groups can function more efficiently as mail is sent to everyone in a certain group, such as all the sales staff.

An organisation intranet would allow access to centrally held data by anyone connected to the network, provided their user rights allowed access. An intranet would allow cheap Internet technology to be used to access the organisation's data.

The Internet could be used to send e-mail to external organisations such as customers and suppliers. They could also develop a website to advertise goods/services. Staff could use the Internet to take customers' orders.

Electronic data interchange could be used to exchange data between customers and suppliers without the need for paperwork, thus cutting down the cost of administration. This should release staff for more customer-focused tasks, such as selling, informing customers of special promotions, etc.

Security is enhanced because the data can be mirrored at more than one site, making use of distributed databases. It is easy to pass data from one site to another so if a problem arises with the equipment on one site processing can continue on one of the other sites.

With a network, the organisation could make use of real-time stock control. This means that as soon as an item is sold, the stock report is adjusted to show the real situation.

Examination Questions

1 With the growth in computer systems being purchased for use on networks, there is a greater need for manufacturers to conform to standard protocols.

(a) What are protocols and why are they required? *(4)*

(b) The application layer is one of seven layers in the OSI model. Name **three** other layers. *(3)*

(c) Briefly describe the role of the application layer in this model. *(3)*

(NEAB, Module IT05, May 97, q6)

2 What is the difference between serial and parallel transmission of data? *(2)*

(NEAB, Module IT05, May 97, q1)

3 A university provides staff and students with access to its computer network.

(a) Activity on the university's networking system is monitored and an accounting log is automatically produced. Suggest what this log might include and explain why it is useful. *(8)*

(b) Appropriate staff have access to personal and financial data. What steps should be taken to preserve the security of the data in such a system? *(4)*

(NEAB, Module IT05, May 97, q4)

4 (a) Describe or draw bus and ring network topologies. *(4)*

(b) Discuss the factors you would take into account in deciding which topology to use for a local area network. *(8)*

(NEAB, Module IT05, May 97, q10)

5 Modems are commonly used for data transmission. Explain why modems might be required.

(NEAB, Module IT05, June 98, q1)

6 A company has a computer network system.

(a) Activity on the network system is monitored and an accounting log is automatically produced.

(i) State **four** items of information that this log might include. *(4)*

(ii) Give **four** reasons why such a log is useful. *(4)*

(b) An IT consultant has suggested that the company changes from a peer-to-peer network to a server-based network. Give **six** features of these network environments which contrast the two different approaches. *(6)*

(NEAB, Module IT05, May 99, q6)

19 Human–Computer Interaction

What is human–computer interaction?

Human–computer interaction is an area concerned with the design, evaluation and implementation of interactive computer systems. Studies of such interaction look at the user interface and at how easy it is for the user to communicate with the computer and vice versa. Improving human–computer interaction is important because it allows the user to work more quickly and hence increases productivity. It can also increase job satisfaction and reduce user stress.

Psychological factors affecting human–computer interaction

Software designers and programmers are constantly developing useful and innovative packages which are commercial failures because they are unusable by those who are inexperienced. They have often been designed from the programmer's perspective and are sometimes simply a means for the programmer to display his or her skills.

Some programs require certain combinations of keystrokes for commands and although the combinations chosen may seem obvious to the programmer, they can be off-putting to a novice user. Sometimes the user may be led down a path in an application only to be left stranded when there is no indication provided as to what to do next. In other applications, when the user presses a key they are not given any indication of whether the key has been accepted or not.

User-friendliness does not just apply to the software itself; it can also apply to the manuals that accompany the software. Many software manuals make too many assumptions as to the user's prior computer knowledge. Software should be designed from the point of view of the novice user.

A book on software development gave the following advice:

> *Software:* You should ask yourself the following question:
> 'What kind of program can I write so that it will meet the needs of 90 per cent of the users rather than the 10 per cent or fewer experienced users who must have enormously varied features and capabilities'?
> *Manuals:* You should ask yourself the following question:
> 'How can I inform a total novice about the most essential elements of any program with just a few pages of text'?

There is often a false assumption that the more complex a program appears, the more features it will have and the more useful it will be. For an application package to be commercially successful, it need not have complex graphics, colour options, windows, toolbars and icons. It needs instead to be user-orientated, so that the minimum number of keystrokes or mouse movements are needed to enable the user to achieve their objective. There must be a coherent logic in the interface which is repeated and reinforced as the user employs its various features.

I bought this computer to help me understand how to use that one!

Figure 19.1

Most user interfaces are now GUIs (graphical user interfaces – see Chapter 10). Explain what is meant by GUI and what it consists of. Describe the features of a GUI that make it easy for an inexperienced user to use.

Technophobia

Many people, when introduced to computing, are afraid to try things out. Some people never seem to grasp the operation of devices such as video recorders, washing machines, etc. Many of these people find it difficult to understand manuals and instruction books. The human/computer interface should therefore be designed for accessibility.

User-friendliness

A user-friendly interface is less frustrating and less stressful to use, and the user can therefore work more quickly.

Documentation accompanying the program should also be user-friendly. The user should not have to wade through a lot of confusing material to learn about basic features of the software, such as how to start the program or print out the results. One of the best methods of ensuring that software interfaces are user-friendly is to pay end users to test the completed version before release. Testers should be picked to include novice users.

Easy access to help

Some help screens can be very off-putting. They frequently use unfamiliar terms in their explanation. Help screens should explain things simply, giving the user examples.

Most users perform a variety of tasks using the software and are expert at some tasks but novice at others. Besides providing help when the user needs it, the software should recognise and anticipate the user's goals and offer assistance to make the task easier. If you have used the integrated package Microsoft Office, you will have come across Wizards that help you through some of the more complex tasks. Figure 19.2 shows the first step of the Chart Wizard in Microsoft Excel.

Software ought to allow novice users to gain confidence in exploring the system. They should know that it is possible to try an action, view the result, and undo the action if the result is not what was wanted.

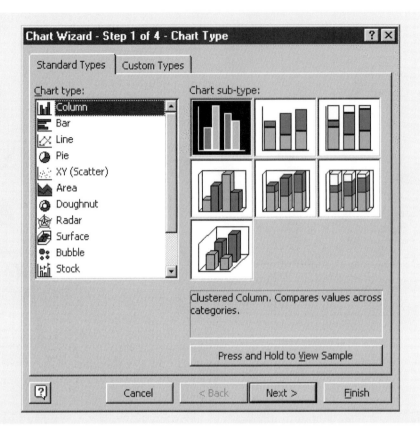

Figure 19.2 *The Wizard in Microsoft Excel guides you through the steps to produce a chart from a set of data*

Providing short-cuts for experts

Expert users, many of whom type quickly, are able to memorise commands composed of combinations of keys and this saves them time compared with using the mouse and clicking on icons and pull-down menus. Novice users are more likely to want to use the mouse, so many packages provide alternative interfaces.

Making use of human long-term memory to maximise efficiency

To develop software which is easy to learn, developers must understand how learning occurs. Human thinking, in many ways, is like a computer with different memory areas. There are three main areas: the **sensory register**, **short-term storage** and **long-term storage**.

The sensory register reacts almost immediately to stimuli to our senses. For example, we quickly move our hand away from a source of heat. Short-term storage is where data is held temporarily. An example of this is when we ask someone for a phone number without writing it down and then remember it for the short period it takes us to dial the number. Long-term storage is for those things we need to remember over a longer period. The more often anything committed to long-term memory is rehearsed, the longer it will usually be remembered for.

The human/computer interface (HCI)

As we saw in Chapter 10, an interface is a point of contact between two systems, and in the human/computer interface, this is the link between the computer and the user.

Human/computer interfaces are as different as their users. Some operators are passive and will only react in accordance with the computer's instructions whilst others will make enquiries, issue commands and get the computer to do things for them.

The response to an error message depends upon the experience of the user. Untrained or inexperienced users will often be scared of error messages and unable to know what to do without help; experienced users are usually able to do something about the problem themselves.

Improving the human/computer interface

We have already looked at what is involved in human–computer interaction. In the following sections we examine the things that can be done when designing an interface to improve it for the eventual user.

Command structures and menus

Command interfaces make use of commands which the user enters via the keyboard to accomplish certain tasks. The main advantage of this approach is that the user can achieve a lot with one simple command. For example, in the command-driven operating system MS-DOS, the user issues commands such as 'FORMAT A:' to format a floppy disk in the A drive. Commands are quick if you are an experienced user but prone to typing errors for the novice user.

When designing a menu system there are a number of things to bear in mind:

- There should be an opening menu, or general menu, from which other menus can be accessed, but you should never go more than three or four levels deep.

- The grouping of items in each menu should be natural and comprehensible.

- There should be either letters or numbers that allow the user to gain quick access to a particular item in the menu.

Menus are ideal if operators are likely to receive very little training or are infrequent users of the system, or are possibly unfamiliar with the terminology of the system.

Screen design

If a source document, such as an application form or an order form, is used to supply the information, then the input screen should mirror the form so that time is not wasted matching an item on the form with its equivalent on the screen. It is much better if a single screen can be used rather than multiple screens, even if it means that the screen is cluttered. It is also important that screen designs are consistent across all the departments in an organisation.

Here are some tips on screen design:

- Put the user in control.

- Do not overwhelm the user's memory. It is a good idea to put a nine-item limit on menus and lists.

- Do not overwhelm the user's senses: use colour and animation wisely.

- Make the design consistent.

- Make sure that help is never more than one click away.

- Layers should be no more than three deep.

- User mistakes should be easily rectifiable. The system should enable users to go forwards and backwards, undo and redo, enter and exit, with ease.

Error messages

Error messages can be infuriating to the user if they just say what is wrong without offering any suggestion as to what to do about it. On the other hand, there is a limit to the help the package can provide since the computer cannot mind-read. If an error message is given and it is impossible for the computer to anticipate what was intended, then the help facility should provide some guide to the likely problems.

Availability of help

All modern software has a help facility but its usefulness varies. A poor help facility can serve to add to the confusion of an inexperienced user. Most help facilities enable the user to search for help on a certain topic; they sometimes look at the context in which the user requires the help. The human/computer interface can do this because it looks at the way the help query is phrased.

User-friendliness

User-friendliness is usually taken to mean the ease with which the software may be learnt and used. User-friendliness is a personal thing – what one person finds user-friendly another person may find off-putting or annoying. When assessing the user-friendliness of software, it is best to get the comments of a range of users with different IT skills.

Ease of learning

There are a number of factors which make software easy to learn, including:

- Make the operation of the package similar to the operation of other packages (this is the factor that makes Windows-based software easy to learn).

- Have an on-line tutorial that takes the user through the basics of the package. This should be interactive and make use of multimedia to add interest and involve the user.

- Provide a user-friendly manual, preferably written with the novice user in mind.

- A solution based on one of the popular packages for which there are many books and training guides facilitates learning.

- The software should be able to anticipate what the user is trying to do and offer appropriate help.

- The user should be able to get out of trouble easily, for example by pressing the ESC key. This will encourage the user to experiment and not worry too much about the consequences.

- Involve lots of users at an early stage so their advice can be obtained if needed.

Figure 19.3 *The on-line help in Microsoft Word*

The features of a sophisticated HCI

The features to consider including when providing a sophisticated human/computer interface are outlined below.

On-line help facility

All software packages should have an on-line help facility, where users can get help from the package rather than having to look through manuals or user guides. On-line help packages increase the size of the package and as a result the size of any backup created. Figure 19.3 shows the on-line help screen in Microsoft Word. Typing in a word or phrase produces information on that topic.

Activity

You have been asked to evaluate the on-line help facility of a popular piece of software.

Write a short outline of the pros and cons of using on-line help.

Graphical user interface (GUI)

GUIs need a lot of main memory to enable them to run at a reasonable speed. The use of Windows-based operating systems and applications software has pushed up the average memory requirements for computers. If you are considering writing a program or developing a system with a GUI, you should always bear in mind the extra resources it requires, which could limit its use for organisations that have older hardware and thus be unable to run your software. One way around the problem is to use only a few pictures, fewer graphics, and to limit the range of colours used.

Increased numbers of ways of performing the same operation

Many user interfaces offer more than one way to achieve the same result, with the choice left to the user. For example, a novice may prefer to use a pull-down menu or click on an icon to print out a file, whereas the experienced user may find it faster to issue a command using a sequence of keys, such as Ctrl+P.

Multi-tasking capabilities

Most modern operating systems support multi-tasking, which makes it easy for the user to switch between applications. Multi-processing, where more than one application is open at any one time, places great demands on the processing power of the chip as well as the main memory requirements. As users demand this facility, faster processors and more main memory are needed.

Faster searching of help files

Chips with a higher clock speed are able to search for on-line help faster and display the results sooner. If help does not appear almost immediately, users may be put off using it.

The resource implications of sophisticated human/computer interfaces (HCIs)

Any sophisticated HCI is going to push the existing technology to the limit as graphical user interfaces need faster processors and more main memory. The easier the interface is to use, the more demands it places on the computer. As we move towards speech recognition systems (where the user can simply speak to the computer) the greater the required level of sophistication of both hardware and software.

Some user interfaces are quite expensive in terms of hardware and software. For example, touch-screen technology enables people who may have never used a computer before to find out about a range of products and services, but this requires an expensive screen. CAD work requires maximum use of the screen uncluttered by toolbars and menus, so these are transferred to an expensive graphics tablet instead.

Resource implications for the processor

The greater the demands placed on the processor by sophisticated operating systems and applications software, the slower they will run. Processors are continually being developed to cope with the demands placed on them by new software. Graphics-hungry applications stretch the capabilities of the chip, and to run such software quickly requires a processor with a high clock speed.

Resource implications for the immediate access store (IAS)

To manipulate large graphics files on the screen the IAS (i.e. the main memory) needs to be large, otherwise the system will be very slow and frustrating to use. Having a large main memory (e.g. 256 MB instead of 128 or 64 MB) means that many windows can be opened at the same time without any appreciable loss of speed.

Resource implications for backing storage

The large files associated with a sophisticated HCI will need a high-capacity hard drive as well as high-capacity removable storage (not floppy disks) such as a Zip or Jaz drive to enable backup copies to be taken (see page 106).

Resources for development

If a company is writing software to do a particular task, a sophisticated HCI will take more time to develop and test which will add to the cost of the project. However, this cost should be balanced against the lower training and support costs incurred as a result of users not getting into difficulty so often. With a good HCI they should be able to solve their own problems more often without ringing the help desk.

Activity

Using the Internet, magazines, software manuals, etc., research the resource implications of making the following upgrades:

1 from either Windows 95 or Windows 98 to Windows 2000

2 from Microsoft Office 97 to Microsoft Office 2000.

The implications for customising software to develop a specialist HCI

Most software packages, for example Microsoft Word, allow users to customise the software to suit their needs. By taking some time initially to look at the customisation options you can often save time in the long run. Such options in Word include:

- You can create new toolbars by adding icons and getting rid of any which you seldom use. In some cases, the software is automatically configured on the basis of what is used most often. In other words, it puts only those items that you use regularly in the toolbars.

- You can customise your documents by altering templates (which come with Word) to suit your preferred document style. These template files give your documents a consistent style.

- It is possible to change the appearance of the Word screen by either hiding or displaying screen items such as the toolbars, rulers, the menu bar, etc.

- You can alter the frequency with which automatic backup copies are made.

- You can alter the directory in which Word stores your data files, and thus avoid having to use the 'save as' function (which wastes time as you must select the directory each time).

Customising is often used to simplify the HCI. For example, you may develop a database using the relational database Microsoft Access. As its developer, you will understand it fully, but will it be as simple to use for a novice? The user's job might be simply to input orders or stock details into the system, and for this task they do not need to understand the intricacies of the package. Instead, they need to be kept away from the interface supplied with the package, since this is really only suitable for experienced users. To do this, you as the developer have to develop menus from which the user can select only what they require for their particular job.

Activity

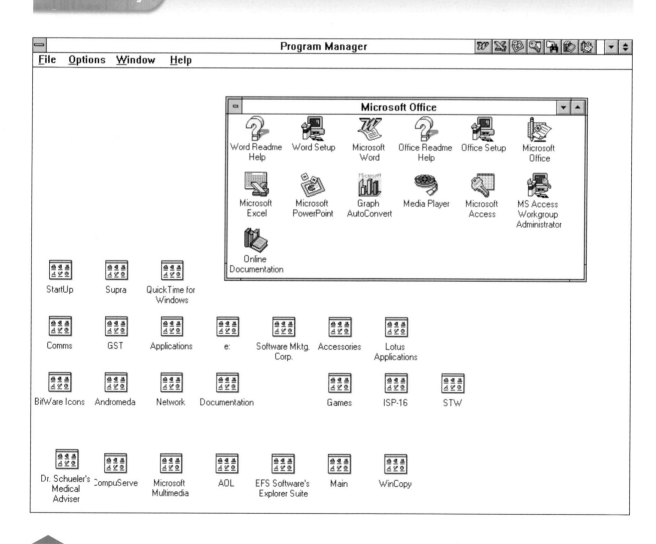

Figure 19.4a *An opening screen from Windows 3.1 operating system*

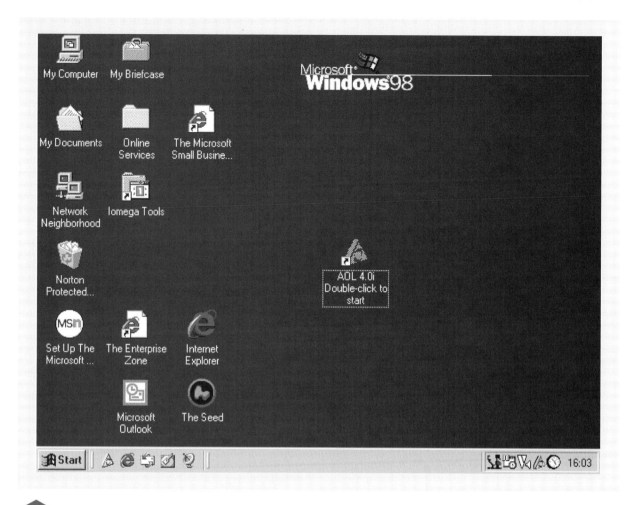

Figure 19.4b *An opening screen from Windows 98 operating system*

On the previous page and above are the opening screens from two operating systems; the older Windows 3.1 and the more recent Windows 98.

By looking at the pictures of these screens, say why you think the interface provided by Windows 98 is an improvement on that of Windows 3.1. (Hint: put yourself in the shoes of an inexperienced user who may have never used a computer before.)

Design of forms for data entry

Forms are used to enter the data into some packages (such as databases) in a user-friendly way. These forms must be designed carefully, since some staff will be using them for several hours a day and entering large amounts of data. Designing this type of human/computer interface

is something anyone who develops databases will need to do.

Suppose you are asked to design a form for entering personal details of sports club members into the computer. As the personal details come from the members themselves, you need to ask them to complete an application form and then use this as the source document for keying the data into the database. There are a number of things that can be done to make it easy for the person who does the keying in. They include:

- The most important fields (i.e. the primary key and keys) should be situated in the most prominent place (usually the top left of the screen).

- The fields on the database form should be in exactly the same positions as the fields on the application form. This means that the person keying knows exactly where to look.

- Help menus that pop up when the cursor is moved to a field can be included; these should give an indication as to the type of data required.

- Suitable fonts and font sizes should be used.

- Colours should be used very carefully.

- An inexperienced user might not understand specialist database terms, so these must not be used on the form.

- There should be a limit to the number of fields on one screen; otherwise the user could be overwhelmed.

- Validation checks should be included, along with useful validation messages that appear if the wrong data is entered.

Questions

Here is a quote:

'To the vast majority of mankind nothing is more agreeable than to escape the need for mental exertion … to most people nothing is more troublesome than the effort of thinking'. (Bryce 1888)

1 Explain how user interfaces can minimise the need for the user to think.

2 Describe three of the features of a sophisticated user interface that makes it easy for a novice to use.

3 Describe three features of a sophisticated user interface that makes it quick for an experienced user.

2 Here are some of the things about a user interface a user might appreciate when working with it.

Explain briefly why each of these features are useful:

(a) easy reversal of actions

(b) the ability to go back to previous screens

(c) using colours/flashing text to give warning messages

(d) offering the user some feedback, such as a sound or a click, or a picture of an egg timer

(e) offering the user a choice in the way that commands are issued.

3 Most modern software can be customised to meet the needs of the user. With reference to a particular piece of software with which you are familiar, explain what 'customised' means.

Activity

Definition of terms

A variety of new terms is introduced in this chapter many of which may be new to you. It is important that you build up vocabulary which can be used when writing essays or answering questions. Write a definition for each of the following terms used in the chapter:

human/computer interface

human–computer interaction

GUI

1 (a) Give **three** psychological factors which govern how people interact with computer systems. *(6)*

(b) Give **three** factors which should be considered when providing a sophisticated human/computer interface, explaining the impact of each one on the system's resources. *(6)*

(NEAB, Module IT05, May 97, q8)

2 (a) What are the factors you would need to take into account when designing a screen layout for a database application? *(6)*

(b) What are the resource implications for providing a sophisticated human/computer interface? *(4)*

(NEAB, Module IT05, Specimen paper, q9)

3 A university uses a complex CAD (computer-aided design) package. The package has a sophisticated human/computer interface which also places considerable demands on the system's resources.

(a) Give **two** examples of the system's resources that would be affected by such a package and explain the demands placed on them. *(4)*

(b) Describe **three** features you would expect to find in the human/computer interface which would merit the description 'sophisticated'. *(6)*

(NEAB, Module IT05, June 98, q6)

4 A supermarket chain has recently implemented a new stock control system in each of its branches. This has affected those staff who have not used computer systems before. Many of the staff have described the system as being 'user friendly'. However, when the package was implemented in one particular store, it was not well received by its staff.

(a) Give **four** features of software packages that would merit the description 'user friendly'. *(4)*

(b) Both physical and psychological factors can influence how people interact with computer systems. Both may have contributed to the poor reception of this system in that store.

(i) Describe **two** such physical factors.

(ii) Describe **two** such psychological factors. *(8)*

(NEAB, Module IT05, May 99, q7)

20 Project work for AS/A2

To understand how project work fits into the advanced subsidiary award (AS for short) and the advanced level award, here are two tables to show you the units you have to complete for each qualification. As you can see from these tables, you spend just one year (usually) taking Units 1, 2 and 3 to obtain the AS qualification. To get the A1 level qualification you take the same units as the AS level in the first year (i.e. Units 1, 2 and 3) and then take the A2 examination units (Units 4, 5 and 6) in the second year.

AS examination		
Unit 1	1¾ hours	30% of the total AS level mark
		15% of the total A level mark
	Short answer and structured questions.	
Unit 2	1¾ hours	30% of the total AS level mark
		15% of the total A level mark
	Short answer and structured questions.	
Unit 3	One project	40% of the total AS level mark
		20% of the total A level mark
	A solution to a task, allowing candidates to demonstrate advanced knowledge of an application package.	

A2 examination		
Unit 4	2 hours	15% of the total A level mark
	Short answer, structured questions and an essay.	
Unit 5	2 hours	15% of the total A level mark
	Short answer, structured questions and an essay.	
Unit 6	One project	20% of the total A level mark
	The project requires candidates to identify and research a realistic problem for a real end user and develop an information system.	

AS level, Unit 3

You must do the project work for this unit whether you are working for the AS level or the A level qualification.

You are required to tackle a task-related problem that has a limited scope and is self-contained. You will usually be able to complete this project using a single piece of generic software but you are not restricted to a single package. Generic software is general purpose software which is not specific to a particular application. Wordprocessors, spreadsheets, databases, project management software and DTP are all classed as generic software.

You can use other software and objects (e.g. clip art put into a wordprocessed file; a spreadsheet placed in a DTP package) to complete the solution. You could use a drawing package for diagrams.

You need not think up your own problem as your teacher/lecturer will be able to give you a problem and act as the end user. However, if possible choose a different person as the end user and develop a solution to a problem identified by them. The end user should be shown the work as the project progresses and their comments sought. Any such comments constitute important feedback and enable the overall quality of the solution to be improved.

If your teacher sets everyone the same task, there has to be a way for him/her to make sure that your solution is your own work and not that of a group.

Before you attempt any project work you need to be able to show you are proficient in using the relevant software and understand its capabilities.

As with all project work, the documentation is very important as it shows that you have approached the problem in the correct way. As part of this documentation you must produce a detailed solution specification with each stage explained carefully.

Process skills required for Unit 3

The following process skills are outlined in the syllabus; they are needed for you to develop coursework.

You will need to be able to:

- navigate packages efficiently and effectively by the appropriate use of menu bars, hot keys, mouse and cursor operations and to fully exploit the human/machine interface

- use appropriate help files and on-line tutorials

- devise and make appropriate and effective use of pre-defined elements, e.g. templates, master pages, styles and glossaries

- use a Wizard to generate the starting point for a solution to a sub-task and tailor-make possible modifications

- devise and make appropriate and effective use of macros, including those in macro libraries and macros attached to global templates

- appreciate the relative merits of embedding an object and of linking to the object in another file (including memory overheads)

- select appropriate types and formats for the presentation of the output.

Package-related skills needed for Unit 3

This list of package-related skills is not exhaustive and should not put you off using other packaged software that may need different advanced skills. The skills mentioned in the syllabus are as follows:

- the use of page or report set-up: margins, headers, footers, columns, tables, footnotes, annotations

- the use of mail-merge header file, data file, standard letter, inserting merge fields, selection criteria to produce conditional merge

- incorporating non-textual material into a text-based document

- the use of constants, absolute and relative replication, functions including conditional and lookup

- selecting the method of recalculation e.g. background mode, automatic or manually on demand

- inserting links between worksheets on sheets grouped as an entity

- selecting appropriate form(s) of chart for the display of spreadsheet data and annotate appropriately

- selecting the appropriate data type and validation technique(s) for each field

- appropriate use of query language facilities for multi-criteria and grouped selection of records

- establishing procedures for recording access and amendments for audit purposes.

What does the project for Unit 3 entail?

This project has the following parts:

- specification

- implementation

- user-testing

- evaluation

- user documentation.

We now look at each of the above in more detail.

Specification

You can start with either your own problem or one supplied by your teacher/lecturer. If your teacher gives you a problem to solve, the outline of the problem will be minimal in order to give you scope for an individual approach. This should ensure your solution is different from those of other members of the class who have been given the same problem.

Try to find and involve an end user (other than yourself or your teacher) since a better project and higher mark will be more likely by this means.

Once you have defined the problem you must refine and develop it, identifying those sub-tasks that make up the whole problem. The IT solution for these sub-tasks should then be identified, bearing in mind that you need to make full use of the advanced features within one package. You will need to contact the end user to make sure that you have identified the sub-tasks correctly.

Next produce a requirements specification for the task to match the end user's needs.

At this stage you are required to determine the evaluation criteria for the overall solution.

You now need to select and apply appropriate design tools and techniques.

Once the problem has been identified and the user's requirements clarified, you can set about the design of the IT solution. Evidence of the following stages must be shown in the project documentation:

1 The input and processing needs are outlined to match the requirements specification. The

requirements specification describes what the user wants (i.e. the output) and in this section you have to say what needs to be input and how it is to be processed to best satisfy the objectives of the specification.

2 Once the input and processing requirements have been decided, the overall task is broken down into a series of smaller, more easily managed sub-tasks and these are then scheduled.

3 The IT component of the solution is outlined to meet the requirements specification of the identified sub-tasks.

4 The fine details of the solution are described, such as the method of data capture, data organisation(s) and relationships, output contents and formats, operational procedures and user interfaces. Examples of this part for the relevant generic package are as follows:

- **Spreadsheet** – plan the layout of the sheets to include blocks of cells dedicated to specific functions such as data entry, calculations and summary reporting.
- **Database** – design a data dictionary, plan data forms and output forms.

5 The proposed solution is related to the capabilities of the available hardware, software and human resources and to the time constraints.

6 The design is documented to provide a detailed solution specification.

7 The last part of the process is to determine the test strategy and a test plan for the solution.

Implementation

This is where you make full and effective use of the hardware and software to produce a working system according to your design. The following parts need to be present in the implementation stage.

- Make full and effective use of the chosen hardware and software facilities to develop and implement a design as an information technology solution.

- Use appropriate data capture and validation procedures, data organisation methods, output contents and formats, operational procedures and user interfaces for the IT solution.

- Relate the solution to the capabilities of the available hardware, software and human resources and to the time constraints.

User-testing

All systems need to be fully tested to ensure that what has been designed and implemented meets the user's requirements and that the solution works as expected.

The following sections need to be present in the testing stage:

- Test the implementation to ensure full compliance with the requirements specification, document the results and annotate any test output.

- Create different scenarios and test with alternative sets of data (for example, for a spreadsheet perform 'what if' projections).

- Follow the test plan in a systematic manner using typical, erroneous and extreme (boundary) data. Annotate each test output and cross-reference to the testing plan.

Evaluation

For the evaluation section, you are required to provide evidence that you have applied the evaluation criteria to assess how effective the solution is and produce an evaluation report.

User documentation

Appropriate user documentation should be produced to show the user how to apply the IT solution. The user guide should be tailored to the IT experience of the user.

Advice on the detail for the documentation for Unit 3

It is important to remember that the moderator will only see your project through the documentation that you supply. It is therefore imperative that everything that you do is shown in comprehensive documentation. To make it easy for both your teacher and the moderator to mark, you should make sure that your documentation follows the structure outlined in the following sections.

Specification

- You need to show evidence that the user's needs have been considered.

- The overall task needs to be broken down into smaller sub-tasks.

- The reason why the problem needs to be solved should be mentioned and, if applicable, why the end-user is dissatisfied with the existing way of doing the task.

- A mention should be made of any constraints or limitations placed on the solution (e.g. human and physical resources).

- The input, output and processing needs that match the requirements specification should be mentioned.

- You could investigate the current IT skills of the people in the organisation who will be using your solution, so that the user interface, user documentation, etc. can be tailored to their skill level.

- The hardware and software platforms need to be considered. The organisation may have existing software it wants to utilise or there may be cost considerations that prevent the purchase of new hardware, software or both.

- You should consider the advanced features of the software that you intend to use and try to match this with the user's skill level.

- A full testing plan should be shown that includes the test data for each element, the reasons why the data has been chosen and the expected outcomes.

- You need to include some evaluation criteria by which the success, or otherwise, of the project can be measured.

Implementation and testing
You need to provide an effective solution to the stated problem which also satisfies the requirements specification.

You need to make sure that you provide a high-quality user interface at the outset, preferably using a graphical interface if the package allows it, and you need to show that you have considered the skills of the end user in your choice of interface.

The interface could use:

- dialogue boxes

- customisation of the package

- drop-down or pop-up menus

- event-driven menus or buttons.

You should make sure that you have chosen sensible and appropriate methods of data capture and validation procedures, data organisation methods, output contents and formats and user interfaces.

It is a good idea for you to implement and then test in a modular fashion. The testing and implementation sections can therefore be presented together. You can also mention improvements, design new test criteria and then implement these and test again once the improvements have been made.

You need to describe fully the implementation by describing what features of the software you have used and why you chose them. A project log should be kept and this should be included as part of the evidence for this section.

The results of any testing should be documented with hard copy evidence and this should be referred back to the original test plan.

Testing must also check that everything the user wanted is actually present. End user testing may identify situations in which the program crashes; you will need to describe these and explain what the user must do to recover from the crash.

Evaluation
Your solution needs to be evaluated. This should be an evaluation of the solution itself and not just an evaluation of the software you have used. It is a good idea to refer back to the end user to find out what they thought of it. You also need to ask yourself if the final solution matched up with what you intended to do. How near did the solution come to matching the initial requirements specification?

Above all, you need to tell the truth, explain any difficulties you encountered and how they were solved or, if they weren't solved, what problems or errors they may cause.

One way of obtaining users' opinions as to your solution is to give them questionnaires to complete. You can submit one of these as an example (not all of them) and produce an analysis of what the results showed. However, this should not be the only method of evaluation used.

As part of the evaluation you can look at the hardware or software limitations, for example not having access rights on a network that would have allowed the use of software facilities you could have utilised. Or it could be that the amount of main memory caused problems.

As part of the documentation, you should discuss the limitations of and possible enhancements to the system. You should also include evidence of successful time management (Gantt charts, timetables, etc.).

User guide

You are required to produce extensive user documentation appropriate to both the solution and the hardware and software used.

The user guide may be provided either on-line or on paper. It should cover anything that is relevant to the solution, including both normal and abnormal operation. Problems that could occur need to be mentioned, along with ways of solving these problems.

Above all, the user guide has to be at a level appropriate to the user.

What is required for Unit 6?

Remember, you only take Unit 6 if you are doing the A level qualification. You are required to have an end-user (i.e. a person other than yourself for whom you are developing the system) for the Unit 6 project and it would be best if you could find a parent, friend, relative, etc. who would be prepared to take on this task. Failing this, your teacher or another member of staff could act as the end user. You should not attempt to act as your own end user. Whatever you do, do **not** fake an end user.

The problem needs to be substantial and in solving it you should draw on the skills and concepts developed during the course. The project should not be isolated from the rest of the course. The problem you try to solve should be open-ended.

The system being developed should be open and cyclic, for instance something that is carried out once a year or once an event. In the solution you should use advanced features and functions of the software, which in most cases could be a suite of generic application software.

To get a high mark in this project you need to show that you have accommodated the system's information flows and data dynamics. This might be done by using data flows between packages, such as by using 'dynamic data exchange'. You will also need to consider the initialisation of the system by clearing the data from the previous use, processing data and transferring data such as logging transactions and archiving data.

There are several parts to the project:

- analysis

- design

- implementation and testing

- user guide

- evaluation

- report.

We now look at each of these in turn.

Analysis

- A real/realistic problem is identified for which an IT solution is appropriate and beneficial. The current system is then analysed and any problems/dissatisfaction with the existing system identified. The current system is analysed in terms of data flows and processing requirements.

- The problem's information flow and data dynamics are described both in time (e.g. from one year to the next) and in processing.

- The problem is subdivided into small, easily defined and accomplishable tasks and these are then integrated into a coherent system.

- A requirements specification is produced for the identified tasks and the system as a whole. You will need to identify the precise needs of the user in relation to the identified tasks and consider human aspects and the physical environment of these tasks.

- The user's current IT skills and further training needs are identified.

- Evaluation criteria for the system are determined.

Design

- The input, processing and output needed to match the requirements specification are identified.

- The overall task is divided into sub-tasks and these are then scheduled.

- Each of the sub-tasks are assigned an IT solution to meet the requirements specification.

- Appropriate data capture and validation procedures are identified along with the data organisation, output contents and formats, operational procedures and user interfaces for the IT system.

- The solutions are related, as far as possible, to the capabilities of the available hardware, software and human resources.

- Any alternative IT strategies for meeting the requirements specification are identified.

- Hardware and software choices need to be justified.

- The financial and human implications of the proposed solution are identified.

- The design is documented to provide a detailed design specification suitable for a third party to implement the solution.

- The various stages of the implementation of the system are scheduled.

- A test strategy is determined, with test data being identified for the system.

Implementation and testing
- Make full use of the chosen hardware and software facilities to implement the design.

- Test the system with typical extreme (boundary) and erroneous data to ensure full compliance with the requirements specification. The results of testing should be fully documented and any output annotated.

- The implementation stage should be documented in a manner that would be suitable for a maintenance developer.

User guide
An appropriate user guide should be produced that includes both the installation and the backup procedures.

Evaluation
An evaluation report should be produced that applies the determined evaluation criteria to the solution to assess its compliance and its degree of effectiveness as a workable system.

The end user should be involved in the evaluation process.

Report
A well written report should be produced that gives an overview of the system and enables the system to be used and maintained unaided.

Project work

The following sections refer to both Unit 3 and Unit 6 project work.

Who will mark my project work?

It is important to note that the project work will be marked by your teacher/lecturer and in turn a moderator will check that the work has been marked to a standard comparable to that of other schools/colleges. The moderator is normally a person with IT expertise (usually another teacher/lecturer) but they may not necessarily have any expertise in the particular software you are using for your project. What this means is that your work will have to be clearly explained and documented so that they can see clearly what you have done; this will enable you to receive the maximum mark possible for your efforts. You may have done a spectacular project, but unless you have supplied proper documentation and evidence you will get only a low mark for it.

What hardware and software can I use?

Any hardware and software can be used but you need to consider the constraints imposed by the hardware on your method of solution, particularly processor speed and memory requirements. Although most people will develop their project using networked or stand-alone PCs you can use Apple or Archimedes computers if you wish.

Any software may be used but the software must be business quality and therefore not too simple. Most integrated packages are suitable, but those containing a non-relational database (i.e. a flat-file database) such as Works, are **not** appropriate.

How much help can my teacher/lecturer give me?

You teacher/lecturer should have given you enough practice at using advanced features of a number of software packages to allow you to identify those features that would be useful in solving your particular problem. Your teacher/lecturer could end up giving you so much help that the project is no longer your own work and this is taken into account when the project is marked. You are still allowed to be given help, but you need to bear in mind that this could be at the expense of some marks. Any help your teacher gives you beyond that given to the group as a whole is recorded on the candidate record form that is sent to the examination board.

Can I do the work at home?

Your teacher must be able to supervise your work so that he/she can be sure that it is your own. You can still do work at home, but enough of the work must be done at your school or college to satisfy the teacher that it is your own work.

No programming please

There is another A level syllabus called Computer Studies, the project work for which can include programming, but programming is **not** appropriate for the IT syllabus and you should not submit any programming projects for assessment.

Presentation of the projects

It goes without saying that all the project documentation should be wordprocessed and diagrams (usually screen dumps) should be incorporated into the documents. Although many of you will be able to produce high quality finished work, if there is very little evidence of analysis, design and testing, you will not obtain high marks. In other words, the examiner will not simply be looking at the presentation of the project.

What software packages can be used?

The best projects are usually implemented using the following types of software:

- document processing (e.g. wordprocessing)
- relational databases (not flat-file databases such as Microsoft Works as these do not have the advanced features required for an A/AS level standard project)
- spreadsheet
- desktop publishing
- project management
- accounting.

You are probably best avoiding the following types of package, mainly because you would find the analysis and design part more difficult:

- garden design software
- room design software
- presentation graphics (e.g. PowerPoint)
- computer-aided design (CAD).

How do I find out about what material to include in my documentation?

Most of what needs to be included in your documentation can be found in the theoretical parts of the syllabus. You should make sure that you examine these sections thoroughly so that you are clear about what is needed before you start documenting your project. Remember that the project should not be done in isolation from the rest of the syllabus.

What general points about documentation should I bear in mind?

All projects should have a signed cover sheet and a project sheet identifying the centre (your school or college), your name and the project title.

Make sure that your documentation includes:

- a contents sheet
- headers (suited to your project)
- footers indicating the page numbers to which the contents refer.

What is the best way to keep the pages of my project together?

Projects must be bound securely in such a way as to reduce bulk and make it easy for the material to be marked.

When binding your project you should **not** use the following methods (see Figure 20.1):

- ring binders or lever arch files, since this makes the material far too bulky and causes storage and transport problems for both your teacher and the moderator
- slide binders which inhibit the reading of the text and diagrams and which also tend to come off in the post or when being read.

Do not put any of your material in plastic covers or plastic presentation folders. Your teacher may need to put marks or comments on your work and removing lots of pages from the plastic wallets is time-consuming and therefore annoying.

It is best to use one of the following methods:

- a thin folder
- punched holes with treasury tags.

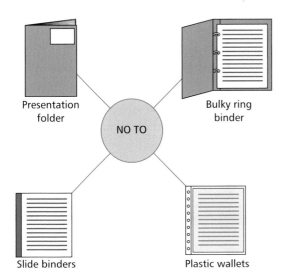

Presentation folder

Bulky ring binder

NO TO

Slide binders

Plastic wallets

Figure 20.1 *Projects must **not** be bound in these ways*

The outside cover sheet should contain the centre number and your name, and each of the projects should have a title and a contents page with all the subsequent pages numbered. Any of the output on continuous sheets should be burst (i.e. separated into single pages) to aid readability.

Project Checklist

Bind correctly? ☐

Cover sheet with name, centre name, signed by you? ☐

Table of contents? ☐

Page numbers? ☐

Padding removed? ☐

Figure 20.2 *Here are a few things to check before handing in your project*

How do I get ideas for projects?

Make use of contacts
Find out what your parents, relatives, neighbours, friends, etc. do in the course of their jobs, since they might be able to suggest an idea for you. If you are able to discuss with them what information you might need, this will be a big help. The best projects are those that have a real end user and which continually refer back to the end user for their reactions and input to the development. The end user will need to be consulted at all stages in the project and should be asked to sign off stages of the project when they have been completed to their satisfaction.

Real projects are often better than artificial ones
There is nothing wrong with creating a new system from scratch rather than improving an existing one. Many people start from scratch, so it could be appropriate for you to design a system to cope with the many tasks they have to perform. However, you will need quite a bit of prior knowledge of the type of business for which the system is designed and there will be no existing system to examine.

Use reference material to help with ideas
A quick look through any magazine or newspaper will give you ideas about businesses, such as mail order companies, that advertise in such places. These all share common problems, so it should not be too difficult to think up a system for them.

Do not choose a system too far outside your own experience
For example, you may choose to create a system to keep records for dentists but unless you know about, or can find out about, how dentists approach their administrative tasks, you could make things difficult for yourself and end up with a very unrealistic system.

Be realistic
It is important to be realistic about what you can achieve in the time. The better projects are usually the ones that comprise fewer tasks. They are usually better designed, documented, fully tested and evaluated and closely focused on the problem to be solved.

Ideas for database projects

If you cannot make use of contacts to find a real system, you could create your own around one of the following ideas:

- a dog boarding kennels or cattery
- a dentist's surgery
- a dating agency
- a job agency for contract workers in computing
- a tutor agency
- a driving school
- a doctor's surgery
- a small, independent travel agency
- a car hire company
- a video hire shop
- a tool and equipment hire company
- a flat rental company
- a wedding dress hire company
- a mail order wine company
- a restaurant
- a mail order bookshop
- a wholesaler
- a school management system
- a coach hire company
- a mail order computer components company
- a membership system for a sports club
- an estate agency
- a stock control system for a builders' merchant.

You need to consult your teacher/lecturer or perhaps make contact with someone who is prepared to help you with the type of business you choose.

Miscellaneous problems

Here is a list of miscellaneous problems that could be used with a variety of different software packages:

- management information system for an organisation
- analysis of examination results for an examination board
- payroll (make sure that you consider the payroll over a period and not just a single week so that cumulative totals will need to be kept)
- stock control
- DTP of magazines and leaflets (remember it will be the advanced features of the package which will be marked and not the content)
- hypertext-linked pages for in-house presentations
- web pages on the Internet
- mail merge using conditional merging
- using the calculation and other features of a wordprocessor to produce an invoice.

How to make a start

Before starting any of the projects, you will need to gain experience in using some of the many pieces of software. You are best advised to use a package which the member of staff who is supervising you is familiar with and which is owned by the school/college. There is a tendency for projects to be developed in isolation, so the only time the teacher sees the results is when the project is handed in at the end. Your teacher/lecturer should be kept up to date with the progress of the project so that if you are going in the wrong direction you can be stopped and put back on course. Too many projects are handed in that are inappropriate to A level requirements and at such a late stage there is no time to do anything about this.

Although you may have a limited knowledge of the features of some generic software you will need to use some of the more advanced features for your project work. You therefore need to develop and practise these skills. Before you start the project work your teacher may have given you booklets to work through with exercises to build up your knowledge of a variety of packages – you should make sure you know about the advanced features of several packages before you embark on your project. One way to learn about such advanced features is to get hold of advanced guides to the software, particularly those guides which concentrate more on the development of applications. But it is important to note that plagiarism is not allowed and is easily detected!

The project for Unit 6

The first thing to note is that the project for Unit 6 should not be regarded as an enlarged project for Unit 3; the projects are marked in a different way. The project for Unit 6 must be a substantial piece of work representing the whole IT system. There needs to be an end-user involved throughout all stages of the project and the end-user must not be you. In most cases the project for Unit 3 is implemented in a single package. The project for Unit 6, however, should be implemented in more than one package and there must be data flows from one package to another, or from one generic function to another.

You need to outline how the computer solution you provide fits in with the rest of the system. For example, if you are using a relational database package, you should have a variety of formal diagrams to show the flows of data within the system being looked at. Such diagrams would typically include data flow diagrams showing the external entities, processes and data stores and the data flows between each of these. For complex systems, the data flow diagram can be shown at different levels, with each level showing progressively greater detail. The layer with the least amount of detail is called the **context diagram**.

A word about user documentation

User documentation must be included and this needs to show how to use the solution that is developed in the application package. The documentation must not be a rewrite of the application package manual and it should enable a novice user to use your system. User documentation should be developed with the user's IT knowledge in mind, it should be well structured and include no computer jargon that is not first explained. To avoid the use of complex descriptions, the user guide should be illustrated with screen dumps from your solution. In addition, there needs to be technical information for the more experienced user, including such things as the minimum configuration needed to

run the solution, along with installation advice, how to load the software, how to cope with errors or system crashes, backup procedures and how to close down the system properly so that no data is lost in the process.

Evidence of end user participation needs to be provided at all stages of the project and in some cases the completion of the various stages of the project can be agreed with and signed off by the end user.

How are projects assessed?

Criteria for the assessment of Unit 3

The project for Unit 3 is marked out of 60 and the breakdown of these marks is shown in the following table.

Specification	13 marks
Implementation	20 marks
User testing	12 marks
Evaluation	6 marks
User documentation	9 marks
Total	60 marks

Criteria for the assessment of Unit 6

The project for Unit 6 is marked out of 90 and the breakdown of these marks is shown in the following table.

Analysis	18 marks
Design	16 marks
Implementation	15 marks
Testing	15 marks
User guide	8 marks
Evaluation	10 marks
Report	8 marks
Total	90 marks

Things you should watch out for

Plagiarism (i.e. copying)

It goes without saying that all project work must be your own work. There is no point in copying parts of examples from text books or specimen project material supplied by the examination board since your teacher will probably have seen it before and the moderator will almost certainly be familiar with the material. In cases where copying is proved, the student can be disqualified from entering the IT examination and possibly any other examinations. Both you and your teacher will have to sign a declaration to confirm that the work you have submitted is your own.

Take regular backups

As an AS/A level IT student, you should be aware of the danger in having only one copy of your work. Regular backups should be taken and the disks not kept together. If you leave your box of disks on the bus, you do not want to lose your backup copy as well as your original. It is also a good idea to print out your work occasionally. If something went seriously wrong with your original and backup, you would still be able to scan your work in using OCR.

Pace yourself

There is a tendency amongst computer students to get on with developing the system and leave all the documentation to the end, when they have a system that works. This should be avoided and you should compile the documentation as you go along. If you need to make changes as you go along, this is fine provided these changes are explained, along with the reasons for the changes.

Try to avoid writing too much on paper before typing it in as this will save you a lot of time. You need to get used to thinking on the screen rather than on paper. Time management is an important skill throughout life and you should manage your time and avoid attending school or college without having some idea as to what you hope to achieve during practical sessions.

Document everything

Although the teachers/lecturers who mark your work will probably be familiar with the software you have used, the moderators may not have used it before. This means that the moderators can only mark your projects on the basis of the documentation you supply. If, for example, you have included a very innovative on-line help system as part of a database project, then the moderator would not know about it unless you have provided evidence in the form of screen designs and screen dumps. If the documentation is missing you will lose marks no matter how clever the IT solution is.

Advice on spreadsheet-based projects

The main thing to remember when you are thinking of developing a spreadsheet-based package is that it must use the advanced features of the spreadsheet. Remember, this is not a GCSE project. Before you think about your spreadsheet application you will need to make sure that you understand enough about the software and its capabilities. If the comments below don't mean a thing to you, then you probably don't know enough about spreadsheets and will need to increase your knowledge. Before embarking on a spreadsheet project make sure that you understand the following:

- logical functions
- financial functions
- statistical functions
- mathematical functions
- database functions.

Here are some useful pieces of advice based on the comments of moderators, who are the people who ultimately decide on the final mark your project should be given.

1 Advanced features must be used. Such advanced features would include:

- solvers
- pivot tables/cross-tab tables
- goal seeking
- multiple scenarios such as best-case and worst-case scenarios.
- dialogue boxes and drop-down lists
- custom menus
- macro code attached to buttons
- circular references for calculations
- the use of complex formulae.

2 It is best to develop an application which makes use of more than one sheet (i.e. use one sheet with links to other sheets).

3 Use cell names rather than cell references, since this aids understanding for future development.

4 Show all the formulae used and make sure that the columns and rows have their references attached to aid readability.

5 Customise the sheets; tailor the solution so that it no longer looks like a spreadsheet.

6 Use a password to increase the security of the system.

7 Testing of a spreadsheet could be carried out by comparing with manual calculations.

Examination marks (a suitable project for Unit 3)

Here a spreadsheet application is developed to convert a mark to a variety of grades at A level (e.g. A to U). The application must count the number of pupils with each grade and will produce a statistical analysis as part of the report provided by the examination board for teachers.

The above system needs to make use of nested IF statements and the COUNT function to calculate the number of candidates at each grade.

Advice on projects based on document processing

Such document-processing packages are usually modern wordprocessing software which possesses a range of advanced features.

Below are notes on some of the advanced features you could think about using.

Make use of fields

A field is a set of codes that instructs the wordprocessing software to insert text, graphics, page numbers or other material into a document automatically. Examples include the DATE field which inserts the current date and the TIME field which inserts the current time. You can also use fields to insert variable data into merged documents such as letters, invoices and memos.

You can use fields for a variety of things, such as:

- placing page numbers into a document where several A4 pages are folded and combined together to form the booklet

- performing calculations on numbers placed in documents, either in table form or in normal text

- using an inserted field to perform a conditional merge (i.e. to send to customers whose credit card balance has exceeded their credit limit).

The quality of the finished document is important

Invoices produced should be professional with such references as customer number, invoice number, etc.

All documents must be dated (use the DATE field) and in appropriate cases, timed (use the TIME field).

The layout of the document should be appropriate for the particular document. It goes without saying that all documents should be proof-read and spell-checked. You can also use the grammar checker (use it with care though).

Mail-merge projects must contain advanced features

Straightforward mail-merge projects are not appropriate at this level, but projects are acceptable that make use of filters, sort criteria or use special instructions so that data is provided conditionally from a data source. You can use either an internal source of data (i.e. where the data source is stored as a data file within the wordprocessing package) or an external source, such as a data file set up in a different package.

You can also use mail merges for the creation of address labels or for printing addresses on envelopes. You could use this technique for sending faxes or e-mail to certain recipients.

For a major project, you could set up a customer database, perform a query to select those customers satisfying certain criteria and then use mail merge to send them letters. For a minor project it is only necessary to use one generic package, so the source of the data could be set up within the wordprocessing package.

Development of a mail-merge application

A mail-merge application could be developed where a menu bar is customised to include macros that open documents and then merge data into the documents. This type of system is ideal where documents need to be sent regularly to clients. Such an application would need thorough testing and would need to look at whether the query being used is case-sensitive or not. The evaluation criteria for such an application could compare the time taken to do the task using the application with that taken to do it without the mail merge.

Advice on database-based projects

If you are going to do a project based around a database package, you need to make sure that you use a relational database. Flat-file databases are not really suited to business use and will not allow you to show your design and analysis skills to their best advantage. Probably the most widely used database is Microsoft Access, which is part of the integrated package Microsoft Office Professional. (Incidentally, at the time of writing, you can buy this package at a special rate if you are a student which considerably reduces its cost. Look at adverts in a magazine such as *Computer Shopper* and you should be able to find this special, discounted price.)

If, when you analyse your system, you find you only have a couple of tables, this could indicate one of several things: it may be that the scope of the project is too narrow. You may need to consider allowing the database to cover more functional areas of the business. Otherwise you may not have normalised your data fully.

Analysis needs to be thorough

The best databases evolve from a period of thorough analysis which is properly documented.

Make sure that you normalise your proposed fields; you should find that you have several tables. Remember that to link tables together to form a fully relational database, common fields are needed in the linked tables. An entity model needs to be constructed to determine whether the links are one-to-one or one-to-many and entity relationship diagrams should be drawn to show these.

End users should be involved as much as possible during database analysis so that all the fields which they need are included.

It must be stressed that for a database to be successful, it is necessary to involve the user and make any alterations to the tables at an early stage, before data is entered and before any other development is performed, such as the testing of data entry forms or the construction of queries and reports.

It is a good idea to print out the graphical display, showing the tables along with the relationships.

Make sure that all relational database projects include the following:

- a customised interface – one with a variety of buttons to enable the user to select options

- data entry screens – databases will produce a data entry screen but you can customise your own to match the input documentation

- methods of controlling the data that is presented to the database; validation checks, data type checks and input masks all help to increase the accuracy of the data input into the system

- the use of action queries to update certain fields (e.g. increase all wages by five per cent)

- produce customised reports (e.g. a list of all employees in the production department in order of surname who are aged 55 or over)

- the use of macros to save time.

Advice on presentation and publishing-based projects

This type of project would cover using such software as PowerPoint, Publisher and HTML editors. Although it is possible to complete successful projects using these packages you must be aware that just because the completed project looks good, you will not necessarily be given a high mark. As with the other types of generic software, advanced features must be used at this level and you must make sure that there is sufficient end user participation.

DTP projects must not be a one-off solution; they must be based around templates and provide repeatability as a system. An example of this might be to produce a letter to parents which needs to be compiled and printed every term.

Index